CHILTON'S
Guide to Consumers'
Auto Repairs & Prices

CHILTON'S
Guide to Consumers' Auto Repairs & Prices

How to save money
on
auto repairs & accessories

Managing Editor KERRY A. FREEMAN, S.A.E.
Senior Editor RICHARD J. RIVELE
Contributing Editor JOHN M. BAXTER

President WILLIAM A. BARBOUR
Executive Vice President RICHARD H. GROVES
Vice President and General Manager JOHN P. KUSHNERICK

Chilton Book Company · Radnor, Pennsylvania

Chilton Book Company gratefully acknowledges the cooperation of the following: George Corsones, Warranty Administration Manager, American Motors Sales Corporation, King of Prussia, PA; Wayne Davison, Sales Manager, Carson-Petit, Inc. (Mercedes-Benz, Peugeot), Devon, PA; and Jack Miller, Jack Miller Auto Repairs, Folsom, PA.

1 2 3 4 5 6 7 8 9 0   9 8 7 6 5 4 3 2 1 0

Contents

PART II PARTS AND LABOR GUIDE

PART

I

Your Car & Your Money

CHAPTER

1

Getting the Most
from Your Car

We all know that the days of inexpensive fuel are gone. But inflation is painfully obvious to the car owner in other ways as well. The result is an increasing awareness of and concern for the costs of operating an automobile.

One thing contributing to the increased overall costs of operating a car are environmental concerns. Federal regulations mandate the construction of smaller cars with more emission controls. These smaller engines operate at higher temperatures and higher rpm's, requiring more frequent maintenance (although on the plus side they are somewhat easier to work on than large engines). Parts that turn faster are under a great deal more stress than they would be in a V8 engine and they tend to wear out faster. Keeping a smaller engine in tune is more of a problem than it would be in a car with a larger engine. The small-car chassis comes in for its share of abuse, too. The lighter weight shocks and front-end components frequently wear out faster than those in a larger car because a larger car is more able to withstand the pounding from a pot-holed road.

Extra maintenance and more frequent adjustments drive up the cost of owning a car. The Automotive Information Council (AIC) pegged the cost of maintenance alone, during 1978, at nearly $400 per year. Of that, one fourth, or almost $100, goes for labor, assuming an average labor rate of $13.50 per hour. The balance goes for parts, gas, oil, tires, and other expendable items. The high cost of maintenance is increasing the consumer's demand for quality service. For the high price paid, consumers want more quality and value.

For some, the apparent answer to rising costs is to hang onto their present large car instead of buying a new one. High prices, social pres-

3

sures, and the genuine need of a larger car are driving up the average age of the national vehicle fleet. The average age of a passenger car in the United States will be about six years by 1980, and the typical car will have travelled almost 60,000 miles. But older cars also require maintenance and repairs, as well as adjustments to meet environmental pressures from city, state, and federal agencies.

Another factor affecting maintenance and operating costs is that the service industry itself is changing. The 1980s will witness the continuing demise of the local full-service station and the continuing growth of the "gas only" or "gas specialty" stations that emerged in the late 1970s. More consumers will become increasingly involved in doing minor maintenance work themselves as the shortage of mechanics, both specialist and general repair, becomes more acute. The cost-conscious consumer will repair and maintain what he or she can and will shop for the most economical services.

Knowing the actual costs of operating and maintaining your car can suggest ways to save money on its operation, maintenance, and repair. That's part of what this book is all about—helping you to decide which repairs you can do economically yourself and which require professional help. Practically, some work should be left to a mechanic, and when you need the help of a professional, this book will help you to know in advance approximately what the job should cost so that you can shop for the most economical and professional repair services.

Other parts of this book help you save money on car expenses by knowing *what* your car requires and *when* it requires it, and where and how to get quality work at fair prices. Knowing what your car needs—and realizing that your mechanic is not trying to take advantage of you every time he has a chance—will remove some of the mystery and confusion about getting your car repaired.

Actually, your local mechanic may be your best friend where your car is concerned. Although, like other businessmen, he must make a profit to stay in business, he depends on your repeat business, and to this end, he must satisfy you that the job he is doing is quality work at fair, competitive prices. The price for a given job may not be as low as you would like, but expecting quality work at cheap prices on something as complicated as a modern automobile is not realistic.

◆ Costs of a Owning a Car

The costs of owning a car are broken down into two categories— variable and fixed. Variable costs include gas, oil, maintenance, tires, and repairs. These are directly related to the number and type of miles driven. Fixed costs include insurance, license and registration, taxes, and depreciation. Though these may vary from car to car or place to place, these costs are established by business conditions beyond the control of the car owner. These costs have little to do with how or when the car is driven.

Variable Costs

MAINTENANCE

Expenses for tune-ups, maintenance, and service items depend largely on the age of the car. The newer it is, the smaller these expenses probably will be. However, even a car under warranty requires regular checkups and service. Money saved by neglecting needed service and repairs will usually be wiped out by increased depreciation. This can be prevented by following a regular maintenance schedule.

The only way to determine accurately the cost of maintenance is to keep a record of all expenditures. It's a good idea to keep a small notebook in the glove compartment for this purpose. If you don't want to bother with this chore, you can use the figures from Table 1-1, "Typical Operating Costs."

Table 1-1
Typical Operating Costs

	Variable Cost (¢ Per Mile)	Total Cost (¢ Per Mile)	Total Annual Cost
Subcompact (4 cyl)			
low-cost area	4.35	12.8	$1,923
high-cost area	5.05	16.4	2,462
Compact (6 cyl)			
low-cost area	5.55	14.6	2,190
high-cost area	6.70	18.7	2,808
Intermediate (8 cyl)			
low-cost area	5.65	16.6	2,486
high-cost area	6.95	21.1	3,170
Standard (8 cyl)			
low-cost area	6.00	17.7	2,659
high-cost area	7.40	22.6	3,391

Note: The 1979 edition of *Your Driving Costs,* published by the American Automobile Association, lists the typical operating costs for a 1979 car in both high- and low-cost areas of the United States. These figures include loan interest, insurance, license, taxes, tags, gas, oil, tires, and maintenance.

GAS AND OIL

The best way to determine your gas and oil operating costs is to develop your own figures. As an example:

Table 1-2
Your Fuel Cost Per Year

Estimated MPG	Price Per Gallon										
	$1.50	$1.40	$1.30	$1.20	$1.10	$1.00	$.95	$.90	$.85	$.80	$.75
50	$ 450	$ 420	$ 390	$ 360	$ 335	$ 300	$ 285	$ 270	$ 255	$ 240	$ 225
48	469	438	406	375	344	313	297	281	266	250	234
46	489	457	424	391	358	326	310	293	277	261	245
44	512	478	444	410	375	341	324	307	290	273	256
42	536	500	464	428	393	358	340	321	304	286	268
40	562	526	488	450	412	375	356	338	319	300	281
38	592	552	514	474	435	395	375	356	336	316	296
36	624	584	542	500	458	416	395	375	354	333	312
34	662	618	574	530	485	441	419	397	375	353	331
32	704	656	610	562	516	469	445	422	399	375	352
30	750	700	650	600	550	500	475	450	425	400	375
28	808	750	696	642	590	536	509	483	456	429	402
26	866	808	750	692	635	578	549	519	491	462	433
24	938	876	812	750	688	625	594	562	531	500	469
22	1022	954	886	818	750	681	647	613	579	545	511
20	1126	1050	976	900	825	750	713	675	638	600	563
18	1250	1166	1084	1000	917	834	792	750	709	667	625
16	1406	1312	1218	1126	1031	938	891	844	797	750	703
14	1608	1500	1392	1286	1178	1071	1018	964	911	857	804
12	1936	1650	1624	1500	1375	1250	1188	1125	1063	1000	938
10	2250	2100	1952	1800	1650	1500	1425	1350	1275	1200	1125
8	2812	2626	2438	2250	2062	1875	1781	1688	1594	1500	1406

Note: This table represents fuel costs per year if you drive 10,000 miles per year. Your fuel cost per year can also be found using the following formula:

$$\frac{\text{Miles driven per year}}{\text{average miles per gallon}} \times \text{fuel cost per gallon} = \text{fuel cost per year}$$

Tank filled   odometer: 8850
Buy gas   9.7 gallons cost $ 9.89   odometer: 9008
Buy gas   9.9 gallons cost $10.10   odometer: 9168
Buy gas   10.7 gallons cost $10.92   odometer: 9343
TOTAL: 30.3 gallons . .cost $30.91

Miles driven: 9343
                          −8850
                          ─────
                           493

Miles per gallon: $\dfrac{493}{30.3} = 16.3$

Cost of gas per mile: $\dfrac{\$30.91}{493} = 6.27$ cents

Oil consumption, though not a major expense, is a variable one and should be figured in the same way as gas consumption. A typical motorist may have the oil changed every 6,000 miles—less often if his car is a recent model and more often if the car is subjected to severe use (continual stop/start driving, extended trailer pulling, and so on). Many owners feel that changing the oil more frequently than recommended is cheap insurance against engine failure. True, changing the oil removes many contaminants and metal particles. And true, old oil, if left inside the engine, will eventually contribute to its demise, or at least to the need for major engine work. These are the reasons for the recommended oil drain interval. But changing the oil more than every 3,000 miles, unless specifically recommended by the manufacturer, is false economy.

In calculating your oil costs, remember to include the cost of every oil change as well as the one or two quarts of oil that may be added between changes. Simply add what you spend on oil during the year, divide the total by the number of miles driven and add this amount to your variable costs. Generally, the cost of oil represents approximately three percent of the cost per mile for gasoline.

While the most accurate figures are obtained by keeping a record each time you buy gas or oil, it may be sufficient to make the test several times during the year.

TIRES

It seems that every time you read something about car care, tires are mentioned. The fact is, they are extremely important. They not only affect operating safety, but they are also one area where you can save substantial amounts of money with proper maintenance. Without going into the technical reasons behind the truths, you can assume that if the car is driven with reasonable care, and the wheels kept properly aligned, tire wear will be kept to a minimum. On the other hand, over- or under-inflation, high speeds, hard cornering, rapid acceleration, and quick stops all contribute to fast tire wear and increased costs of car operation.

Fixed Costs

INSURANCE

There is nothing uniform about insurance premiums. The costs depend on the amount of coverage, where you live, and the intended use of the car. To determine insurance costs, simply add the premiums of all policies you carry that are directly related to car operation, such as property damage and liability, comprehensive and collision.

Many insurance companies are suggesting that policyholders increase their deductible amount for collision and comprehensive. This will usually enable you to save in the area of 15 to 20 percent, if the deductible is increased from $100 to $200, with even greater savings possible if you select higher deductibles. In general, within the limitations of state laws, you should set a higher deductible on physical damage insurance, especially if the vehicle is one with a fairly low value. If the cost of physical damage coverage would be out of proportion to the car's value, consider dropping coverage altogether (see the section on insurance in Chapter 11).

LICENSE, REGISTRATION FEES, AND TAXES

These payments are usually due once a year and vary by car and state. No two states use exactly the same schedules. Determine what you spend for license and registration and add the total to your fixed costs. Taxes, such as property or use taxes, should be treated in the same way. Sales or excise taxes that are paid only when the car is bought should be considered a part of the total purchase price and not be prorated in calculating annual operating costs. If you're paying off a car loan, your annual interest is also part of your operating cost.

DEPRECIATION

Depreciation is the largest single expense in owning a car, and it varies by type of car, condition of the car, and demand. It is the difference between what you paid for it and what you would get in a trade-in or resale. Depreciation also is the most difficult cost to determine. Cars depreciate at different rates, depending on their appearance, mileage on the odometer, and the demand for your particular model at the time you want to dispose of it. During the long gas lines of 1979, demand for large "gas guzzlers" fell to practically zero.

One method the average motorist might use to figure depreciation is

Table 1-3
Typical Depreciation Rates, from List Price

	1977 models	1976 models	1975 models	1974 models	1973 models	1972 models
Standard Cars (mid-sized and larger)						
1977	25%	15%	13%	10%	7%	6%
1978	15%	13%	10%	7%	6%	6%
1979	13%	10%	7%	6%	6%	6%
1980	10%	7%	6%	6%	6%	6%
1981	7%	6%	6%	6%	6%	6%
Compact Cars						
1977	14%	13%	11%	10%	10%	10%
1978	13%	11%	10%	10%	10%	9%
1979	11%	10%	10%	10%	9%	8%
1980	10%	10%	10%	9%	8%	7%
1981	10%	10%	9%	8%	7%	6%
Subcompact Cars						
1977	12%	11%	11%	11%	10%	10%
1978	11%	11%	11%	10%	10%	10%
1979	11%	11%	10%	10%	10%	9%
1980	11%	10%	10%	10%	9%	8%
1981	10%	10%	10%	9%	8%	7%

Source: "Cost of Owning and Operating an Automobile, 1976," U.S. Department of Transportation, Federal Highway Administration.
Note: Due to economic conditions and fuel availability, the depreciation of specific makes and models may vary considerably.

to determine the cash outlay necessary to replace his car with a new one in the same price class and with the same optional equipment. This represents depreciation adjusted for inflation. Check the newspaper ads to find out what your car is currently selling for and subtract this from the replacement cost. The difference is depreciation (com-

Table 1-4
Expected Average Retained Value, 1979 Models

	Standard Cars	Compact Cars	Subcompact Cars
1979	71.9%	83.2%	87.6%
1980	57.2	70.5	76.0
1981	46.0	59.8	64.5
1982	36.0	49.8	53.7
1983	27.5	40.2	43.0
1984	20.5	31.0	33.2
1985	14.2	22.3	24.0
1986	9.0	14.1	15.2
1987	4.0	6.4	7.2
1988	0.0	0.0	0.0

Source: Office of Highway Statistics, U.S. Department of Transportation.

Table 1-5
Figure Your Car Costs

Fixed Costs	Yearly Totals
Depreciation (divide by number of years of ownership)	_____
Insurance	_____
Taxes	_____
Licenses and registration	_____
TOTAL FIXED COSTS	_____

Variable Costs	
Gas and oil per mile	_____
Number of miles driven	_____
Cost per year (multiply miles driven by gas and oil per mile)	_____
Maintenance (use your own figures or average as suggested in text under "Variable Costs," multiplied by miles driven)	_____
Tires (see note for "maintenance")	_____
Other costs (car wash, repairs, accessories, etc.)	_____
TOTAL VARIABLE COSTS	_____

TOTAL DRIVING COSTS PER YEAR	
COST PER MILE (divide yearly total by total miles driven)	_____

bined with inflation). It should be noted that depreciation is higher during the first two years of ownership and tends to level off later.

◆ Maintenance and Repair

Even if your car is under warranty, regular maintenance and repair are your responsibility. You can reduce a lot of your maintenance and repair expenses by doing some of the work yourself, and you can save even more by knowing how and where to buy parts and supplies. This is discussed more thoroughly in Chapters 2 and 3.

If you are already servicing or maintaining your vehicle yourself, you're in the majority. Industry surveys show that more than half of the nation's car owners are into do-it-yourself maintenance or repair work to varying degrees. Many others probably would get into the act if they fully realized how much could be saved.

A regular maintenance program will help you take better care of your car. One such as that described in Tables 1-6 and 1-7 pays dividends in two ways. It will reveal minor problems that can be corrected easily before they add up to a major expense. And, since in any machinery as complicated as an automobile, parts are going to require replacement from time to time, regular maintenance makes sure that you will get maximum use from those parts.

The benefits of regular maintenance include:

- Longer engine life
- Better fuel economy
- Less environmental damage
- Increased safety
- More net value at trade-in time
- Less frequent and less expensive repair bills
- Less annoyance and less inconvenience caused by unanticipated breakdowns

The automobile is a truly amazing machine. Its 15,000 or so parts are expected to function under a wide range of weather conditions and other adverse circumstances, yet it is subjected to careless and hard driving and indifferent maintenance. Recommended service intervals are often ignored by the same car owners who wouldn't let a week go by without vacuuming all the rugs in the house.

Today the automobile is an integral part of our life. We have come to rely on the proper functioning of the family car and seldom if ever make a time allowance in case the car should fail to start. We expect it to start and move out every time, and, fortunately, most of the time it does. But the rare instance when it doesn't causes the owner to forget the thousands of times it started without a problem. The irony is that it failed to start probably because of neglect.

Champion Spark Plug Co. recently completed a two-year test program to discover engine condition and consumer maintenance habits. The tests covered 5,666 cars in twenty-seven cities throughout the United States and Canada and offered some surprising results:

- 79% (8 cars out of 10) had maintenance deficiencies that adversely affected fuel economy, emissions, or performance.
- Cars judged to be in need of a tune-up recorded an 11.36% improvement in fuel economy when tuned to manufacturer's specifications.
- New plugs alone accounted for an average 3.44% improvement in fuel economy.
- A complete tune-up lowered emissions of carbon monoxide at idle by an average 45.37%.
- Engine neglect affects not only safety but starting dependability and general operation as well.
- More than 27% of all cars tested were more than a quart low on oil.
- 34% of all cars had dirty air filters.
- 50% of all cars had substantial deviations from correct timing and idle speed settings.

A periodic maintenance program such as the one shown in these tables can keep the car owner more aware of the condition of his car and save him money.

Table 1-6
Underhood Maintenance Intervals

This chart gives minimum maintenance intervals by miles or time, whichever comes first, based on average of 12,000 miles per year. Obviously, the type of driving you do will also affect your maintenance program.

Diagram Number	Item	Check Every
	Engine ▲	
1	Check oil; add if necessary	Fuel stop
2	Drain oil	6,000 miles/6 months
3	Replace oil filter	6,000 miles/6 months
4	Check valve clearance; adjust if necessary	12,000 miles/12 months
	Ignition System ▲	
5	Replace points and condenser	12,000 miles/12 months
6	Replace spark plugs	
	Point-type ignition	12,000 miles/12 months
	Electronic ignition	18–24,000 miles/18–24 months
6	Check spark plug wires	12,000 miles/12 months
6	Replace spark plug wires	At least every 36,000 miles/3 years
5	Replace distributor cap/rotor	12,000 miles/12 months
7	Check/adjust ignition timing	
	Point-type ignition	12,000 miles/12 months
	Electronic ignition	12,000 miles/12 months (when plugs are replaced)
	Battery	
8	Check electrolyte level/charge	1,000 miles/1 month
9	Check/clean terminals and cables	3,000 miles/3 months
	Starter and Alternator ▲	
9	Check electrical connections	3,000 miles/3 months
10	Check/adjust drive belt	3,000 miles/3 months
10	Replace drive belt*	At least every 24,000 miles/2 years
	Cooling System ▲	
11	Check coolant level	1,000 miles/1 month
12	Check condition of radiator hoses	1,000 miles/1 month

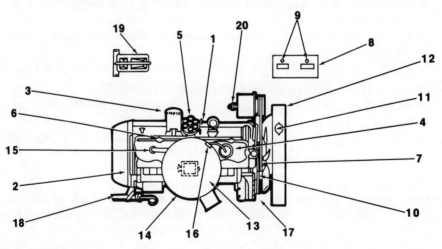

Fig. 1-1 Maintenance points for a typical 4- or 6-cylinder inline type engine. Refer to Table 1-6 for an explanation of the numbered items.

Table 1-6 (continued)

Diagram Number	Item	Check Every
11	Check condition of radiator cap	1,000 miles/1 month
10	Check/adjust drive belt	3,000 miles/3 months
10	Replace drive belt*	At least every 24,000 miles/2 years
12	Clean radiator of debris	3,000 miles/3 months
12	Drain/replace coolant	12,000 miles/12 months (each fall)
	Fuel & Emissions System ▲	
16	Clean crankcase breather	12,000 miles/12 months
13	Replace air filter	12,000 miles/12 months
14	Replace fuel filter	12,000 miles/12 months
15	Check PCV valve	12,000 miles/12 months
10	Check/adjust air pump belt tension	3,000 miles/3 months
10	Replace drive belt*	At least every 24,000 miles/2 years
	Air Conditioning	
12	Clean condenser grille	3,000 miles/3 months
17	Check for leaks at connections	3,000 miles/3 months
17	Check refrigerant level	3,000 miles/3 months
10	Check/adjust compressor belt	1,000 miles/1 month
10	Replace compressor drive belt*	At least every 24,000 miles/2 years
	Automatic transmission ▲	
18	Check fluid level/condition	6,000 miles/6 months
	Brakes	
19	Check master cylinder fluid level	1,000 miles/1 month
	Power Steering	
20	Check pump fluid level	3,000 miles/3 months
10	Replace drive belt*	At least every 24,000 miles/2 years
10	Check drive belt tension	1,000 miles/1 month

▲If the vehicle is used for severe service (trailer pulling, continual stop/start driving, off-road operation), cut the maintenance interval in half.
*New drive belts will stretch with use. Recheck the tension of a newly installed belt after 200 miles.

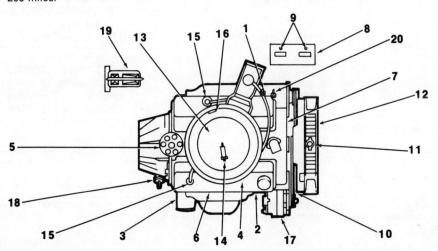

Fig. 1-2 Maintenance points for a typical V6 or V8 engine. Refer to Table 1-6 for an explanation of the numbered items.

Table 1-7
Body and Chassis Maintenance Intervals

This chart gives minimum maintenance intervals in miles or time, whichever comes first, based on an average of 12,000 miles per year. Obviously, the type of driving will also affect your maintenance program.

Diagram Number	Item	Check Every
	Automatic Transmission ▲	
1	Change fluid	24,000 miles/2 years
1	Replace filter or clean screen	24,000 miles/2 years
	Clutch and Manual Transmission ▲	
2	Check lubricant level	3,000 miles/3 months
2	Change lubricant	24,000 miles/2 years
3	Check clutch pedal free-play	6,000 miles/6 months
2	Lubricate shift linkage	6,000 miles/6 months
	Brakes ▲	
4	Check condition of brake pads or brake shoes	6,000 miles/6 months
4	Check wheel cylinders, return springs, calipers, hoses, drums, and/or rotors	6,000 miles/6 months
5	Adjust parking brake	As necessary
	Suspension ▲	
6	Check shock absorbers	12,000 miles/12 months
7	Check tires for abnormal wear	1,000 miles/1 month
8	Lubricate front end	3,000 miles/3 months
	Driveshaft ▲	
9	Lubricate U-joints	6,000 miles/6 months
	Rear Axle ▲	
10	Check level of rear axle fluid	6,000 miles/6 months
10	Replace rear axle fluid	24,000 miles/2 years
	Tires ▲	
11	Clean tread of debris	As necessary
12	Check tire pressure	Each fuel stop/2 weeks
11	Rotate tires	6,000 miles/6 months
11	Check tread depth	6,000 miles/6 months
	Wheels	
12	Clean wheels	As necessary
12	Check wheel weights	Each fuel stop/2 weeks (when you check tire pressure)
11	Rotate wheels/tires	6,000 miles/6 months
	Windshield wipers	
	Check wiper blades	3,000 miles/3 months
	Replace wiper blades	12,000 miles/12 months
	Lubricate linkage and pivots	6,000 miles/6 months
	Check hoses and clean nozzles	3,000 miles/3 months
	Windshield	
	Clean glass	Each fuel stop
	Air Conditioner	
13	Operate air conditioner for a few minutes	Once a week

▲If the vehicle is used for severe service (trailer pulling, continual stop/start driving, off-road operation) cut the maintenance interval in half.

14

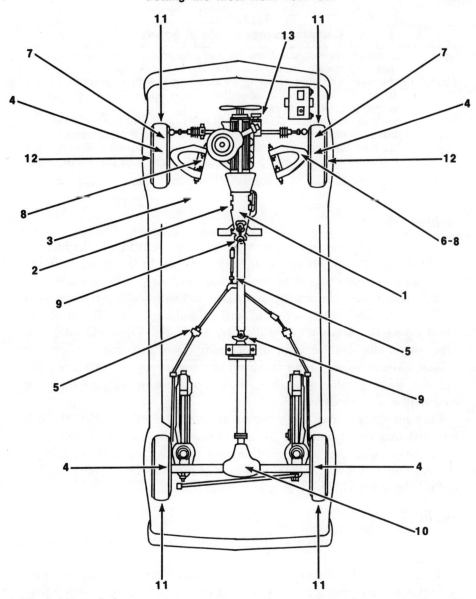

Fig. 1-3 Typical chassis maintenance points. Refer to Table 1-7 for an explanation of the numbered items.

◆ Safety on the Road

One of the most important benefits of proper maintenance is a safe vehicle. While you're on the road, pay attention to your car—it may be trying to tell you something. Look, listen, smell, and feel for possible problems. Warning signals come in many forms—noises, different handling, and vibrations.

Table 1-8
Common Sense Guide to Safety

Sight	Be alert to appearance. Look for sagging on either end or side, puddles underneath, or anything that doesn't look right.
Sound	If you hear a strange noise, try to associate it with a particular action, such as braking or accelerating. Then you'll have a good idea where to look for its cause.
Smell	Smells are deceptive. Does it smell like burned rubber, oil, or insulation? Gas or exhaust fumes point out leaks in their systems.
Feel	If car handles strangely, is it a constant feel, or does it pull only while braking? Learn to associate behavior of car with particular action to help determine the cause of any problem.

Sights

Part of any walk-around inspection of your vehicle should include checking underneath for spots and drips. Get into the habit of doing this regularly, especially after the car has been driven for a while.

Red spots under the transmission area indicate leaking transmission fluid. Try to find out where the leak is coming from. The problem could be as simple as an overfilled transmission. The fluid could be foaming out the dipstick tube and running down the case.

Rust spots or water under the front of the car may indicate a leaking radiator, leaking radiator hoses, or simply overflow from the radiator or air-conditioning condenser.

Dark oil spots under the differential probably indicate that the differential rear cover bolts are loose and should be tightened. Oil spots under the engine can mean anything from leaking valve cover gaskets (the oil runs down the engine) to a host of more serious problems. Try to find the source of the leak and correct it.

Smells

Strange odors are often a clue to something gone (or about to go) wrong.

An overheated radiator gives off a steamy vapor and a mild odor something like burning paint. It should warn you to check the temperature gauge or to stop and check the coolant level.

Burning oil or grease is a strong, pungent odor, usually more noticeable when the car is not moving. Occasionally, wisps of smoke will come from under the hood. It could be a simple problem of oil leaking from valve cover gaskets onto hot exhaust manifolds, or it could be just accumulated grease from a delayed engine cleaning.

Frequently associated with newer cars equipped with catalytic converters is the rotten egg smell, which is unmistakable for anything else. One of the by-products of the reaction in the catalytic converter is sulphur dioxide, which is responsible for the odor. It does not indicate a malfunction, but is extremely unpleasant.

Feel

All good drivers learn to recognize when the car is behaving differently from normal. Vibrations often warn of a great many mechanical problems that can be located and corrected before they become serious. Be suspicious of any vibrations that are out of the ordinary—be alert and train yourself to recognize the warning signs.

◆ Walk-Around Safety Check

Get into the habit of taking a few minutes to walk around your car or truck every now and then, especially during a long trip. Checking out all of the things that affect your driving safety won't take more than five minutes and could uncover a small problem that can be repaired easily or inexpensively before it gets dangerous or expensive.

Tires and Wheels

Check for uneven wear patterns, excessive wear, nails, cuts, or other damage. Uneven wear may indicate alignment problems in the front end or uneven inflation pressure. Check the inflation pressure with a gauge.

Lighting System

Check the headlights, turn signals, and taillights for proper operation. Take a look at the operation of all exterior lights while someone else operates them.

Clean the headlights with a rag. You'll be amazed at the difference it makes at night.

Mirrors

Be sure that the mirrors are clean and adjusted properly for the best view of what's behind you.

Windshield and Wipers

Clean the windshield for maximum visibility. While you're about it, take a quick look at the wiper blades. They should be in good condition for when they're needed. The rubber wiping element should be soft and pliable. Replace any refills that are torn, cracked or streak the windshield as they wipe. Blades that "chatter" across the windshield in a jerking motion show that the rubber element is getting hard and should be replaced.

Tailpipe

Checking the color of the tailpipe is a good habit to develop. It can provide a quick check on how your engine is operating.

On a long trip, or when the car has been run at highway speeds for a while, the inside of the tailpipe should be a light gray or white. This indicates that the engine is running properly.

A blackish or sooty tailpipe indicates that the carburetor is set too rich and probably needs adjusting. A carburetor that is too rich means that the mixture contains too much fuel which is not being burned completely.

Fluid Leaks

Look for fuel, oil, or water leaks. The color and location of the spots under the car can give a clue to the source of the leak. Remember that there are no normal fluid leaks, other than clear water from the air-conditioning condenser on a hot day.

Red is probably automatic transmission fluid. *Black or brown* is most likely engine oil or rear axle lube. *Clear water* under the front of the car will usually come from the air-conditioning condenser. This is normal on a hot day. *Greenish water* is usually antifreeze, and it indicates a leak in the cooling system that should be located and repaired as soon as possible. Otherwise the cooling system will gradually lose coolant, and the engine will overheat.

Fuel Cap

If you just stopped for fuel, be sure that the fuel cap was put back.

Underhood Check

Your walk-around safety check should include a routine check under the hood. Here's a list of things to check:

- Engine oil level
- Radiator coolant level
- Battery electrolyte level
- Automatic transmission fluid level
- Master cylinder fluid level
- Windshield washer fluid level
- All belt and hoses for wear

CHAPTER

2

When to Do It Yourself

Knowing when to do a job yourself and when to seek professional help could be the most valuable skill you can acquire as a car owner/mechanic. One of the best ways to find out what's involved in a repair is to purchase a good repair manual and read all about the repair you're considering. In deciding where to draw the line on do-it-yourself repairs, you must answer some basic questions that will put the whole job in perspective:

1. How difficult is the job?
2. Do you have the necessary skill to complete the job properly?
3. Do you have the necessary tools and equipment?
4. How much can you save in terms of labor costs and parts prices?
5. How valuable is the warranty on professional repairs? (See "Two Views of Warranty" later in this chapter.)

The answers to these questions will allow you to make an informed decision as to whether or not you want to undertake the work yourself. There will be some borderline cases, but most of the time you will have a clear-cut choice.

The simple mathematics of dollars saved versus investment in time, parts, and tools may often be the determining factor in deciding whether to repair the car yourself. But some things do not lend themselves easily to assignment of a dollar value. Considerations such as personal inconvenience or uncertainty about your ability to handle a given repair may weigh heavily in the decision. You may want to work on your own car for the pleasure you derive. The job may be one that you are sure of handling adequately, but it will involve getting very dirty, crawling around on the cold ground, or any number of other unpleasantries that could make an economical shop repair more convenient. You'll have to compare these considerations and the time involved to do a job with the actual reduction in cost to give you some idea of the advantages and disadvantageous.

◆ Is It Worthwhile?

In weighing whether to do the job yourself, it is often helpful to think in terms of a formula. You will have to place a value on each element of the formula, but when you add up each side, your decision should then be clear. The formula is:

Labor charged by a professional mechanic	$ value of your time to do the job
+ Cost of parts charged by a professional mechanic	+ Cost of parts if *you* buy them
+ $ value of any personal inconvenience	+ Cost of special tools
	+ $ value of any personal inconvenience
	+ Value you place on any uncertainty about your ability
Total	≠ Total

(does *not* equal)

Yes, one side of the "formula" does not equal the other. If it did you'd be hard pressed to make a choice between getting professional service or doing it yourself. The formula is a means of comparing one set of values with another. In most cases, one side will have more value than the other, giving you a clear choice. The value you place on any personal inconvenience can appear on either or both sides of the comparison, depending on whether you will be inconvenienced by having the car repaired by someone else or by doing the job yourself. It frequently happens with minor repair jobs that you could easily do the work yourself before a busy mechanic could fit the work into his schedule.

The uncertainty factor really deserves emphasis. Frequently, simple arithmetic will make you decide either to do the work yourself or have someone do it for you, but many other times a sense of uncertainty about your abilities may be the biggest factor in your decision. If you are strongly apprehensive about your ability to handle the job, you may rightfully decide to skip doing it yourself without even stopping to figure out how much you could save.

◆ Can You Handle the Job?

Knowing what is involved in doing any work on your vehicle will help you decide whether or not the given job is for you. In the sections below, several categories of maintenance and repair work are described briefly to give you an idea of the amount of difficulty the job entails. Naturally not all repair situations are covered; the ones listed represent typical work that vehicle owners might consider doing themselves.

Oil and Lube

An oil and lube job gets a green light for almost anyone. Probably the toughest thing you will have to do is get under the car and manage to reinstall a drain plug. If you can point a bolt in the proper direction and turn it gently to start it in a nut, you've practically got the job licked.

Tune-Up

Performing a general tune-up requires a lot more understanding of what you are doing than does oil and lube work, but it is easy in terms of working with your hands. Usually about the toughest thing is installing little mounting screws in the distributor, but a magnetic screwdriver, which holds the screw while you hold the screwdriver handle, will make even that easy. If you have patience, all the required information (such as found in a repair guide or service manual), and the special tools you need, go ahead and give it a try.

Cooling System Repairs

Belt and hose replacement, thermostat replacement, and system flushing are easy jobs. If your radiator springs a leak, it's pretty easy to remove it yourself and take it to a radiator repair shop for soldering.

Water pump replacement may require removing accessories or mounting brackets to gain access to the water pump itself. Leaks can be troublesome, and they are about the only problem you will encounter with the pump, but using a new gasket and plenty of sealer minimize the chances of a leak. Water pump replacement is an excellent job to start with if you want to get involved in servicing your car but don't want to begin with a job that is too difficult. It also offers the opportunity for considerable savings.

Torquing the Cylinder Head Bolts

On some engines, torquing (tightening) the cylinder head bolts is considered part of a tune-up. It is an easy job, provided (1) you use a torque wrench, (2) you know the specifications and tighten the bolts in the proper sequence, and (3) you can get to the cylinder head bolts with a minimum of difficulty. On some engines, you have to remove the exhaust manifolds or the air conditioning compressor or do something else that increases the difficulty of this job. However, if you can get to the bolts easily and have the tools and specifications, don't be afraid to try it.

Valve Adjustment

On some engines, adjusting the valves is part of a tune-up. To adjust them you must be able to do several things at once. You have to rotate the engine to a specified point as indicated by certain movements of the valves; you have to know a little about how the engine works; and you have to be able to judge thickness with a feeler gauge and tighten a locknut while holding the adjustment. Before trying this particular operation, it would be wise to get a little mechanical experience with the simpler parts of a tune-up, like replacing spark plugs or breaker points.

Rebuilding a Carburetor

Complete instructions and patience with small parts are absolute necessities for rebuilding a carburetor. All the parts are small and light, and you can take the whole thing inside and rebuild it at your desk or table. You also may need a few little special screwdrivers and, in some cases, measuring gauges, but usually these items are included in an overhaul kit.

A knack for remembering how things go together or visualizing how they work will ease reassembly. You'll also have to have a feel for how to tighten down the screws which hold a light aluminum casting so it gets pulled down evenly and you don't strip any threads. And you'll have to be able to keep everything absolutely free of dust and dirt. This job is not for a beginner, but it is perfectly okay (and very satisfying) for anyone who has a little bit of mechanical experience and has performed routine maintenance or tune-ups successfully a number of times.

Automatic Transmission Pan Gasket and Filter Replacement

Replacing the pan gasket and filter is not difficult at all if you can start bolts into aluminum without stripping the threads and have a feel for tightening things gently.

Automatic Transmission Band Adjustment

This job has the same qualifications as replacing the pan gasket and filter except that a torque wrench is required, not optional. Look up the torque figures involved in a reliable manual. If the figure is in inch-pounds, you'll have to buy a special tool (an "inch-pound torque wrench") to do the job.

Brakes

The problem here is the consequence of failure. You have to have done enough mechanical work to be sure you can put everything back the way it came off. The uncertainty can often be eased by doing one side at a time and using the other side as an example. As long as you put everything back where it belongs, there really isn't anything unduly complex about the job. To replace the shoes on front drum brakes or to the pads on disc brakes you'll need good instructions that apply to your car. Don't be put off by the need for a few special tools. They're inexpensive and well worth the investment.

Front End Parts Replacement

If you're working on the suspension, you're just starting to get into heavy-duty work. Actually, if you have a good repair manual and follow it's instructions right down to using new cotter pins instead of reusing old ones, look up the proper torque figures, and rely on a torque wrench, you'll be pretty safe. Most automotive suspension components are designed to be installed only one way. The problem with suspension work is that some of it requires using heavy duty special tools, such as prying devices and pullers, to complete the job.

This work is not for a beginner and you ought to consider the price of failure. If you can't finish the repair, the car will usually have to be towed to a shop. It would also be easy for a car to lose control almost completely due to a failed front end part. On the other hand, you do have one assembled side to use as an example of proper assembly. But if you've gained enough confidence and ability, if you follow instructions to the letter, and you have the right tools, give yourself the green light on this one.

Underdash and Electrical Work

You can easily replace or lubricate a speedometer cable. Pulling a dashboard out to replace a bad instrument is very time consuming, but low on risk. If you have plenty of time, lots of patience, and have learned to use your fingers in cramped quarters, go right ahead.

As far as general electrical work goes, if you disconnect the battery, you won't damage anything. However, when it comes to electrical fault finding, you'll need the right instruments (a volt-meter and perhaps an ammeter) and you'll have to understand how electricity works. In many cases you'll absolutely have to get an automotive manual that has the right wiring diagrams. Many auto manuals feature a section on basic electricity and fault finding that will help you learn how the electrical system works. It's okay to start on something simple (repairing broken wires or rewiring a bulb), but leave the really tough wiring problems to a pro unless you've had a little experience.

Major Component Removal

Removing major components, such as the transmission or cylinder heads, is absolutely not for the amateur, on safety grounds alone. The car must be safely supported at least four feet off the ground, and a floor jack is required in many cases. Even experienced amateurs stay away from transmission work, the only possible exception being removing manual gearboxes to bring them in to a shop for repair. They aren't terribly heavy, especially on small cars, and may not even require too much unbolting. Just don't try such a job until you're accustomed to working on cars and have all the proper equipment.

About the most common job of this sort for do-it-yourselfers is replacing the clutch. On small cars it's not too bad, although you must be equipped to check out the flatness of the pressure plate with a good straightedge, and have an old transmission shaft or special tool to center the clutch plate. Also, make sure you have good instructions and follow them, or you could injure yourself or damage the car.

Cylinder head removal is another job in the area of major component removal. It's nowhere as dangerous as working under the car, but the cylinder heads are heavy (sometimes over 100 lbs), so you'll need a strong and willing friend, lots of patience, and that ability to coax large hunks of metal to do your bidding which comes with experience. Following all the directions, tightening sequences, and torque specifications to the letter virtually guarantees success. However, on overhead cam engines, you'll have to disconnect the timing chain and then, upon replacement, check or reset the valve timing, which is very critical to the success of the job. Depending on the design of the engine, this can be fairly straightforward or a little tricky. Carefully check the instructions in a good car manual to get a feel for just how much work is involved to remove the cylinder head on your car.

Air Conditioning Repair

Replacing blowers, resistors, switches, and other small parts is fairly easy if you can gain access to the parts. However, the refrigerant used in the air conditioning system is a deadly poison. Never attempt to repair or remove any component that requires disconnecting any of the refrigerant lines. Even with the proper tools and instructions you shouldn't work on the refrigerant system itself without special training.

Exhaust System

There's just one thing that makes exhaust system work extremely difficult—corrosion. Rust forms an incredibly tight bond between exhaust pipes and the pros who do this type of work regularly, or even specialize in it, have a great many tools to handle tough rust problems. An air chisel or cutting torch to get rusted, tight-fitting pipes apart is the best example. Another problem is cutting original equipment exhaust systems apart to install a new section. Original equipment systems are almost completely welded, and cutting a pipe with a hacksaw is very slow going. If you look at your system and the part which must be replaced looks fairly clean at the connections, if any, doing your own work might be worth a try. But most of the time it is dirty, aggravating work that is not worth the effort. Even doing the work yourself, it's difficult to compete with the price and guarantee of a muffler specialty shop.

◆ Special Tools

Some tools will be necessary for virtually any work you do on your car. The number of tools and the need for special tools will be determined by the job itself and by your particular car. If you're talking about a really oddball special tool that has only one function related to a very unusual repair for your car (such as a transmission rebuild or major part replacement), add the cost of the tool into the price of the job. Of course, in these circumstances, it would certainly pay to shop wisely and buy the least expensive one you can find.

Most special tools (pullers, brake spoons, etc) are usable for similar jobs on any car, or can and will be used repeatedly on your present car. You may even be able to rent them from an establishment just for auto do-it-youselfers. A good example would be the special valve adjusting tool made for the Datsun 240-260-280Z and 280ZX engine. It's an expensive item, but will be used at least seven times during the full life expectancy of the car. If you plan to do all your own tune-ups and keep the car as long as possible, you could confidently divide the tool's cost by seven.

The same kind of thinking applies to other kinds of jobs, even when they don't involve regularly scheduled maintenance, such as brake replacement. A tool designed to help you remove drum brake return springs from the backing plates could be used four times or more on one car and the cost amortized accordingly.

◆ How Much Can You Save?

There are two areas in which you can save money by repairing your car yourself. You can save the amount a professional would charge for his labor and you can save the difference between what a professional mechanic charges for parts and what you will pay for those same parts over the counter.

Consider the cost of a tune-up on a typical American sedan equipped with a 350V8 engine, but with no air conditioning. According to the *1980 Chilton's Professional Labor Guide and Parts Manual*, a major tune-up includes the following:

- Check compression
- Clean or renew spark plugs
- Test battery; clean terminals
- Renew and adjust distributor points
- Renew condenser
- Check distributor cap and rotor
- Set ignition timing
- Test coil
- Free up manifold heat control valve
- Tighten intake manifold and carburetor mounting bolts
- Adjust idle speed
- Inspect and tighten hose connections
- Adjust fan belt
- Renew PCV valve
- Service carburetor air cleaner
- Renew carburetor fuel filter

We compared the parts prices and the time required for a major tune-up as listed in the *Chilton's Professional Labor Guide and Parts Manual* with the costs to do the same job yourself. This comparison assumes you already own the tools, and that their cost is being amortized over a number of years. Prices for some fast-moving parts such as spark plugs are not listed in the *Labor Guide* because of wide variances in retail prices of these items. The average costs of these items are estimated in the following comparison. We assumed an average labor rate of $13.50/hour.

Job: Major tune-up of 1974 Malibu 350V8
Tools: Timing light, dwell/tachometer, compression gauge, assorted wrenches and screwdrivers

		Independent Mechanic		Do-It-Yourself
Parts:	Spark plugs (8)	$10.00		$6.00
	Points*	5.00		1.50
	Condenser*	2.50		1.00
	PCV valve	2.75		1.50
	Air filter	3.00		2.00
	Fuel filter	1.00		.75
	Distributor cap*	7.50		3.00
	Distributor rotor*	3.00		2.00
Time:	3.1 hours	$41.85	4.5 hours**	$ 0.00
Total cost:		$76.60		$17.75
Savings:		—		$58.85

*These parts can also be purchased over the counter as part of a tune-up kit.
**Assuming you are doing the job for the first time.

Even throwing in the cost of a Chilton Repair & Tune-Up Guide ($7.95) for the car in question, the savings are considerable.

◆ Saving Labor Costs

As a do-it-yourselfer, you'll be saving a substantial amount of money for every hour's worth of repairs your car undergoes in your own hands rather than in the shop. This is because the labor rate charged by the shop must pay for many types of shop expenses, as well as the labor itself.

Most shops work on a system commonly known as "flat rate," a system sometimes criticized because it is not well understood. The "flat rate" reflects the amount of time it should take a mechanic to perform a particular job. The "flat rate" is a kind of incentive program that encourages the mechanic to be productive. In most shops, the mechanic gets paid by the job. The actual number of hours he works on your car may be more or less than the "flat rate," but a mechanic who is faster than average is probably worth more than the average hourly labor rate, so things tend to average out. Labor times for many common repairs are given in Part II; the beginning of that chapter has more information on understanding flat rate and estimating your repair bill.

The amount you are charged on your repair bill must pay for far more than the mechanic's salary. It must also pay for the shop overhead (expenses such as rent and electricity), health insurance, unemployment insurance, Social Security, and probably some sort of retirement program. A large shop will also employ service advisors, cashiers and clerks to help the business run smoothly, and your repair bill helps pay their wages. On top of the personnel expenses, there is a tremendous investment in tools, equipment, and parts. Sophisticated diagnostic equipment necessary for today's cars can run into the thousands of dollars, but all these tools and equipment make it easier for the mechanic to do a better job.

In evaluating the labor charged by a professional, remember also that very often even a large shop will sublet work that requires specialized skills or equipment. Few general repair shops will overhaul a cylinder head, for example. Because of the precision machining involved, almost all work of this type is sent to a specialty machine shop. The general repair shop passes this labor charge on to the customer and may even add a mark-up to cover the costs of transporting the parts to a specialty shop.

Obviously you could save the labor and mark-up by removing the part and transporting it to the specialty repair shop yourself. But don't assume you'll save a great amount by dealing directly with a specialty shop. The mechanic at the general repair shop may deal with the specialty shop at wholesale prices. You may have to deal with a specialty shop at retail prices. Furthermore, since *you* are removing and installing the part, the specialty shop may abbreviate their normal warranty on the work they perform.

In figuring the cost of major work, get several estimates, both from general repair shops and the specialty shop, if need be. Make sure you provide the mechanic with all the information he'll need so that he can give you an accurate estimate. Don't forget to include tax and miscellaneous charges in your figuring. If getting the car to the repair shop will be particularly expensive (it may have to be towed), add that in, too, unless that charge appears as sublet repairs on the shop's estimate or work order. It may also be necessary to value the cost and inconvenience of alternate transportation (public transportation, borrowed car, loaner, rental car, etc.) if your car will be in the shop for much longer than it would take you to do the repair yourself.

The tough part for the do-it-yourself mechanic is estimating how long it will take to do the job. The estimates you have from professionals are a starting point, and the Labor Guide in Part II will help with common repair work. But you must realize that you may not be able to work as fast as a pro, for a number of reasons:

1. A pro uses a lift, and if you have to crawl under a car supported only a couple of feet above the ground, it's going to take time to crawl in and out, go in and out for tools, and to situate yourself so you can reach each part. It's also much easier to support and mount something bulky (like a starter) from under the car with a lift.

2. A pro uses an air wrench for most bolts to speed his work. You're going to spend much more time just turning wrenches than he will.

3. A pro can handle precise adjustments more quickly because of his considerable experience. If, for example, you are setting the dwell angle or valves of your car, it's going to take you some time the first few tries. So where precise adjustments are necessary allow yourself plenty of time.

You'll get a feel for how long it will take you to do a job by consulting a Chilton repair guide, which will describe the steps that have to be done for each job. As a rule of thumb, on a very simple job you won't need much more time than the pro, but multiply by about 1.5 if the job involves difficult access or if you're doing the job the first time. The harder the job, the more time it will take you. Remember, too, that old parts which may be rusted in place will give any mechanic fits—and be very time consuming to replace.

◆ Saving on Parts

Parts are often expensive, and the shop's overhead and profit requirements make them more so. Doing the job yourself will allow you to save on the parts portion of the repair bill by purchasing the parts yourself. The same or equivalent parts that repair shops sell can usually be purchased at substantial savings at any of the auto outlets discussed in Chapter 3.

It's fairly easy for you or a mechanic to figure parts cost if the job is a simple one. But if it's a major job or if there are many small parts involved, it will help you to have a repair manual. The manual will tell you which minor parts, such as gaskets and fasteners, have to be renewed and what you'll need in the way of associated parts, such as sealants or adhesives. It will also have an exploded view of major components, showing all the small parts, the cost of which can't be ignored. In some cases, several small parts could make a big difference in the final bill. (But don't expect a mechanic to price out every little 10¢ item.)

The repair shop's parts bill also includes the cost of assorted sealants, penetrants, lubricants, and other chemicals necessary to get the job done right. These are not listed on the bill, since the repair shop buys them in quantity and covers the cost through the mark-up on hard parts or service. But you'll need those items to do the job yourself, so you can't ignore the cost. It's probably wisest to buy what you need in the smallest quantity, particularly if it's something you will use infrequently. A small can of gasket sealer, for example, will be expensive by the ounce, but even a small can will take you through several water pump replacements, a half dozen new thermostats, or several valve cover removals.

◆ Two Views of Warranty

Warranty on labor is one thing do-it-yourself auto repair simply cannot offer. If you fix it yourself and the repair fails in some way, you have no recourse. On many types of repairs, however, the part itself will be guaranteed. As an example, look at the job of replacing an alternator. The mechanics of replacing it really aren't difficult. The alternator itself, however, is an expensive part. A completely rebuilt unit will usually cost between $50 and $100, even with your old alternator in exchange. If you simply have your unit repaired to cure an isolated problem like worn brushes or a worn bearing, the bill will be well over $20. However, the repair job or the overhauled unit will frequently be fully guaranteed so that within a period of, for example, 4,000 miles or three months, the repair will be redone or the unit replaced free of charge. Even though you would have to get your hands dirty again, the warranty on the part ensures that it will be replaced if defective.

On other items, however, the picture may be a bit darker. Suppose, for example, that you install an electrical component which fails immediately. Many parts houses will not guarantee such an item because there are any number of ways almost any electrical part can be short-circuited and burned out through no fault of the manufacturer. Or consider what might happen if you removed your car's cylinder head and took it to a dealer for a valve job. If the dealership mechanic does the whole job, he can do a number of things to ensure that the valves in your engine will not overheat. These things include setting the valve clearances carefully, torquing the cylinder head properly, and setting the ignition timing. If you remove the head yourself, he will not be able to perform many of these installation procedures and adjustments that, properly done, ensure a quality job, but if improperly done, could doom the job to failure. Often he will do the job under these conditions only if there is no warranty or if the warranty is sharply abbreviated.

The most important point about a warranty if you're doing part of the work yourself is: *find out what the warranty will be and get a copy in writing*. Then compare what you'll be getting with the standard 3,000-mile/4-month warranty on full repairs. Don't just assume you will get a warranty or that it will last X number of miles. After you know the exact terms of the warranty, judge for yourself how much you need it. There is no completely adequate way to do this, but you can come up with a reasonable evaluation.

Consider the valve job situation we've been discussing. If your car has little valve trouble, you are satisfied with the reputation of the machine shop who will do the machine work and you have faith in your own ability to complete the installation of the cylinder head with precision, the risks are minimal. But if you're considering an expensive job dealing with a part of your car that commonly gives trouble, or you're not satisfied with your ability to do the work, you probably should consider the warranty offered by a reputable mechanic a valuable part of the job.

Other factors to consider include the time and money it might take to further repair the car if your job does not turn out perfectly. If you're driving a mechanically sophisticated $25,000 car and you are not completely confident about your abilities as a mechanic, you would be foolish to do major work without full warranty protection, regardless of cost. But if the car is not needed for commuting, if you can afford to re-do part of the job, and if you don't mind the inconvenience of going over part of the job again, it might be worth it financially to take the chance on doing the work yourself.

◆ Making the Final Decision

In most cases, your final decision will be based on your own arithmetic and judgment. If you can't decide almost immediately on the basis of what's already been presented, there's one factor that might break the tie. That's whether or not you really enjoy working on cars, or are at least convinced that it's your type of thing. If you're very uncertain about a job, doing it only to save money is going to make things pretty tough if you run into trouble. On the other hand, if you like this sort of challenge, running into a little trouble may not bother you at all and may even increase the fun you get out of the whole thing.

One final point: if you decide to do it yourself, especially if you're a bit uncertain about it, do yourself three favors:

1. Work on a weekday or Saturday during hours when local parts shops are open. Then if you need parts or supplies unexpectedly you can get them and finish the job. Also, make sure you have a way to get to the parts store.

2. Make sure you are prepared for bad weather by having a place to work.

3. In case the car is unexpectedly out of commission for a few days while awaiting something you did not anticipate needing, make sure you have an alternate way to get to work, buy groceries, and so forth.

If you avoid getting yourself into a situation in which you're under too much pressure, your chances of getting through the job successfully are much greater.

3

Shopping for Parts
and Tools

Do-it-yourself has become an economic necessity for many of us today. It's an opportunity to save some money and have some measure of fun working on the old buggy at the same time.

You'll find, if you haven't already, that it's easy to change the oil and filters and handle minor repairs. Once you've started raising the hood with confidence, you may be tempted to get involved with replacing hard parts.

You could tackle a minor tune-up, install your own brake linings, a set of shock absorbers, or replace an old muffler. This is where your savings really start to show. You can cut 20% to 50% off regular repair bills since you do it yourself and thereby eliminate labor costs.

At a local service outlet, for instance, you'll pay anywhere from about $35 to $100 for a tune-up, depending on the make and model of your car and what work is performed. Usually, it takes about one to two hours for the mechanic to perform this service. Besides parts replacement (plugs, points, rotor, and condenser), he checks and adjusts dwell, timing, idle speed and mixture, and services the carburetor/air cleaner.

With the right tools and equipment (dwell/tachometer and timing light), you can do the job yourself and save the $15 to $50 labor charge. If you shop smart, you'll probably be able to buy the parts at lower prices, too. The money you save just about pays for the equipment after a few tune-ups.

Today, manufacturers and retailers know you're interested in trying these repairs to save money. That's why you'll find parts packaged with complete installation instructions and displays with application charts to help you select the right parts for your car.

Auto supply stores, discount and department stores, automotive job-bers, and other sources sell complete lines of quality parts for auto repair enthusiasts like yourself. You may want to comparison shop these outlets to see where you can get the most for your money. It's wise to compare price tags and quality all year, instead of expecting to find bargains on infrequent shopping tours. Sales on replacement parts are common. Weekly specials, holiday, and seasonal promotions all offer a chance to save on your automotive needs.

It doesn't really matter whether you buy name-brand or store-brand tune-up parts. You can save a little money on the store-brand items as opposed to OEM (Original Equipment Manufactured) parts, but you may end up replacing them a little sooner if you buy too far down on the price scale.

The main thing is to be sure to get the correct part for your car. An incorrect tune-up part can adversely affect the engine performance, fuel economy, and emissions, and will cost you more money and aggra-vation in the end. To avoid buying the parts piecemeal, many manu-facturers have taken to offering do-it-yourself tune-up packages, con-taining points, condenser, plugs, rotor, and sometimes distributor cap. Spark plug wires can be purchased already cut to length and ready to install, or as a kit, in which case you cut the necessary lengths yourself.

To get the proper parts for your car, you will probably need to know the following information:

Make: Chevrolet, Datsun, etc.

Model: Impala, 710 Station wagon, etc.

Year: 1976 (example)

Engine size: The engine size is usually designated in cubic inches (350, 260, etc.) or in cubic centimeters (cc) on imports (1600, 2000, etc.). Occasionally, it will be given in liters (1.6, 2.0, etc.). If you are not sure, there is usually a sticker on the air cleaner or under the hood that tells you the engine size. There may be a letter with the number which you should copy down, too.

Number of cylinders: 4, 5, 6, 8, etc.

Carburetor (or fuel injection): If the engine is carbureted, you'll need to know if the carburetor is a 1, 2, 3, or 4 barrel (abbreviated bbl) model. You may also find the word venturi (abbreviated V) used in-terchangeably with the word barrel when describing carburetors.

Air conditioner: Yes or No

Quantity of oil: How many quarts

Engine code: Since 1976, this code has been important to domestic cars. The engine code is part of the VIN (Vehicle Identification Number), which is visible through the front windshield on the dri-ver's side. On AMC cars, the engine code is the 7th digit of the

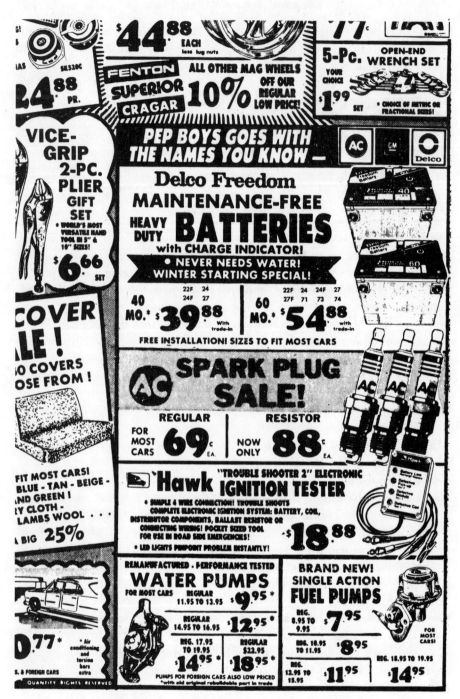

Fig. 3-1 Watch the newspapers for sales of replacement parts.

VIN; on GM, Ford and Chrysler cars, the engine code is the 5th digit.

Electronic ignition: Yes or No

On imports, in addition to the above, you may need to know the distributor number (located on a metal tag on the distributor), the chassis serial number (located on a plate on the body), and the engine serial number (located on a pad on the engine).

◆ Sources for Parts

There are many sources for the parts you will need. Where you shop for parts will be determined by what kind of parts you need, how much you want to pay for the parts, and the types of stores in your neighborhood.

New Car Dealers

New car dealers almost always have parts for your car, but the prices are almost always higher than other sources. The dealer carries what are known in the auto trade as OEM (Original Equipment Manufactured) parts. OEM parts are those supplied by the car manufacturer and are the same parts installed on the car when it was built. Because of the higher overhead expenses, these parts are generally a little more expensive than the same item available through other outlets.

The higher cost of OEM parts does not necessarily indicate a better value, or higher quality. Automotive jobbers and auto discount stores regularly stock high quality replacement parts in addition to OEM parts. Even though the car manufacturer will recommend that you use OEM parts for replacement or service work, he will also specify that you can use an equivalent replacement part. Many replacement parts are made by or sold by reputable companies and are built to the same specifications as OEM parts. In many cases, replacement parts may even be identical to OEM parts, since many parts manufacturers sell parts to car makers as OEM parts and also sell the same part to other companies, who market the part under a different brand name. The parts you have to be careful of are "gypsy" parts, which are discussed later in this chapter. Fortunately there are very few of them.

There are some parts for your vehicle—cylinder heads, crankshafts, body parts, and other slow movers—that you will be unlikely to obtain anywhere but at your dealer. These parts are not sold in sufficient quantity to make it attractive for any other outlet to stock them.

Service Stations

Your local service station can supply you with many of the common parts you require, though they stock these parts mainly for their own use in the repair end of the business. The problem, from the consumer's standpoint, is the cost—it will be high. The reason is that the service station operator buys the same part from a jobber that you can buy over the counter. Although he buys at a discount, he must make a profit on the resale of the item, whether through direct sale of the item or as part of repair charges. Really, when your service station sells parts to you over the counter, they are competing with the local parts stores and discount merchandisers, and most service stations do not buy or sell parts in sufficient volume to offer a competitive price. They are in business to sell "service," not to sell parts.

Parts Jobber

The local parts jobber, who is usually listed in the yellow pages or whose name can be obtained from the local gas station, supplies most of the parts that are purchased by service stations and repair shops. He also does a sizeable business in over-the-counter parts sales for the do-it-yourselfer, and this may constitute as much as 30 to 50% of his business. Lately, jobbers have been offering more do-it-yourself items as the number of backyard mechanics increases.

The jobber usually has at least two prices—one for the local mechanic or service station and an over-the-counter retail price. The local mechanic, like the service station, does not pay the retail price for a given part, and he marks up the price of the part to his customer, making a profit on the resale. Most jobbers will offer you a 10 to 15% discount off the retail prices on over-the-counter sales. But don't automatically buy from a jobber just because he offers a discount. Many jobbers will have automatically raised the retail price 10% so that giving a 10% discount to all retail customers will, in effect, be no discount at all. However, if you do a fair amount of business with the jobber, or if you are known to him, you may rate a break on the retail price.

The prices charged by jobbers are usually lower than the new car dealers and service stations but slightly higher than discount or mass merchandisers. The reason is that the jobber is used to dealing with professional mechanics and usually sells name-brand or OEM parts. His volume is such that he sells more than a service station, but less than a discount merchandiser, and thus his prices fall somewhere between the two.

The people who work the counters in the jobber stores know a great deal about cars—far more than the clerk in a discount store or the salesperson in the auto section of a department store. Unless they are extremely busy or very rushed, they can usually offer valuable advice on quality parts or tools needed to do the job right.

In addition to selling parts, many jobbers are also associated with machine shops. They handle the machine work that the smaller repair

Fig. 3-2 The automotive jobber carries a full line of parts and supplies, and many jobbers do a sizeable do-it-yourself business. Most jobbers carry parts behind the counter, in contrast to the auto discount stores.

shops farm out. They are usually equipped to do specialized work— assemble press-fit parts, rebuild a cylinder head, boil out a cylinder block—virtually any job requiring machine shop services. This is valuable to know, because sometimes you can save a good deal of money dealing directly with the jobber or his associated machine shop, rather than paying a mechanic or service station the fee they would normally charge as part of their repair fee.

If you require specialized work, the jobber can usually suggest a competent source to handle the work, or they may even handle the whole thing on a commission basis. But, in any case, the jobber can save you a lot of time searching out someone to do the work for you.

Automotive Chain Stores

Almost every community has one or more convenient automotive chain stores, the equivalent of a Pep Boys or Penn Jersey. These stores often offer the best retail prices and the convenience of one-stop shopping for all your automotive needs. Since they cater to the automotive do-it-yourselfer, these stores are almost always open weekday

Fig. 3-3 The auto chain stores carry name brand as well as store brand replacement parts. Most parts are on display in the aisles, allowing inspection.

nights, Saturdays, and Sundays, when the automotive jobbers are usually closed.

Chain stores are the automotive "supermarkets." Hardly a week goes by that they are not running advertised specials or a seasonal promotion of some type. The ads normally appear in the local newspapers and offer substantial savings on both name and store-brand items. In contrast to the traditional jobber stores, where most merchandise is located behind the counter, you can walk through the auto chain stores and browse among most products, picking and choosing from a large stock of brand names.

Prices in the auto chain stores will normally be competitive with the discount stores and mass merchandisers, and they will usually be slightly lower than the jobber. Counter personnel working in the chain stores are slighly less experienced than those working for the jobber, but they are usually familiar with their products and common automotive problems and can offer good advice.

Discount Stores

The lowest prices for parts are most often found in discount stores or the auto department of mass merchandisers, such as K-Mart, Sears, and Woolco. Parts sold here are name and private brand parts bought in huge quantities, so they can offer a competitive price. Private brand parts are made by major manufacturers and sold to large chains under a store label.

You have to have a good idea of what you're looking for when you buy from these outlets. Many are self-serve, in direct contrast to the older, traditional jobbers where they still look up the part number and get the part for you.

Auto Junkyards

Wrecking yards, junkyards, salvage yards, previously owned parts yards—call them what you will—are good sources of parts, particularly

Fig. 3-4 The automotive sections of discount stores take a "supermarket" approach to replacement parts.

for older cars or limited budgets. Auto wrecking yards run from the incredibly sophisticated computer run inventories to stumblebum one-man operations where nobody knows exactly what they have except the inevitable snarling dog.

In most cases, don't expect the wrecking yards to supply the smaller parts. They prefer to deal in complete assemblies. Among the better deals in wrecking yards are engines, transmissions, rear axles, body parts, and wheels. The cost of these parts from a yard is generally about one-half the cost of new parts. Most junkyards are not interested in selling carburetors, voltage regulators, and other small parts, but if they do, their cost will be negligibly less than the cost of rebuilt parts, and rebuilt parts are a far better deal.

Some wrecking yards may have two prices—one if they remove the parts and one if you do it. Most yards will prefer to remove parts themselves, but be careful. Time is money when removing parts, so a lot of yards, particularly the less organized, will remove an engine or rear axle with a cutting torch instead of unbolting it. This makes it necessary for you to buy small parts, such as motor mounts, brake lines, spring hangers, and other hardware, that were destroyed by the cutting torch.

◆ New or Rebuilt Parts

Many times you will be required to return your old starter, clutch, alternator, fuel pump, or carburetor when you buy a new one. These old parts are returned to a professional parts rebuilding service and are reconditioned to be sold over the counter as remanufactured or rebuilt parts.

Most parts stores will carry both new and rebuilt parts. There is nothing wrong with buying remanufactured parts. Many are just as good as the new ones but can be bought at a considerable savings. Compare the price and warranty on a remanufactured part with that of a new part. In general, the higher the quality of a remanufactured part, the closer the price will be to a new part and the better the warranty. See "Two Views of Warranty" in Chapter 2, and Chapter 8.

Inordinately low prices for remanufactured parts usually mean shorter parts life and earlier failures. In this case, it will be worthwhile to spend a little extra money for higher quality.

◆ Gypsy Parts

The packaging of many name brand auto parts is familiar to most do-it-yourselfer's, but those who buy parts on the basis of familiar pack-

Fig. 3-5 These are high quality, legitimately repackaged parts, with no attempt at deception. But, beware of "gypsy" parts (see text).

aging should beware. You may be buying bogus or "gypsy" parts, which are generally inferior to the name brand item and slyly packaged to resemble the name brand packaging. Some independent suppliers and manufacturers are packaging fast-moving auto parts to closely resemble the name brand items such as GM, Ford, Delco, Mopar, or Champion. Above the name brand in very small type is the word "Replaces." The part inside the box is probably inferior in quality or performance compared to the name brand item.

To be sure you're getting your money's worth, if you're buying a name brand, examine the package for trademarks and manufacturer's name and address. If someone other than yourself or a person you trust is installing the part, ask to see the package it came in. Even mechanics are not immune to assuming mistakenly they are buying name brand parts.

◆ Using Automotive Catalogs

For the person looking for a part for his or her car, the catalog is the most important tool to know how to use. Automotive parts catalogs are what you make them—a confusing foreign language or an easy-to-understand reference to get the correct part number and price the first time.

Almost all manufacturers of hard parts make a catalog listing the part number, application, and sometimes the price of the item. The catalog may take the form of a large book with thousands of entries if the manufacturer makes many parts for a lot of applications, or it may be as simple as a single card if the manufacturer has relatively few variations. If you are purchasing oil filters, air filters, PCV valves, belts, hoses, and similar common parts, you will usually find the catalog near the merchandise in the parts store, though from time to time they will disappear. Wherever they are located and whatever form they take,

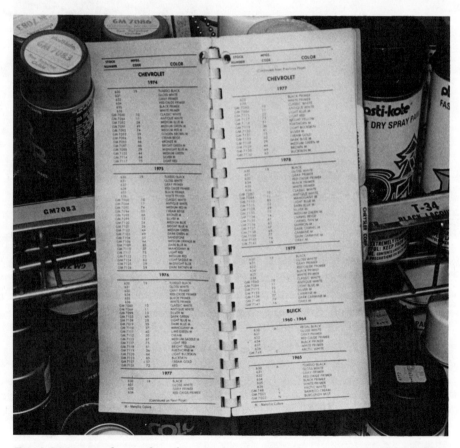

Fig. 3-6 Many catalogs and application charts are found on the store's parts shelves along with the merchandise. This one is the application chart for automotive paints.

Fig. 3-7 Parts catalogs, giving part number and application, are provided by manufacturers for most replacement parts.

learning to use them will assure that you get the correct part the first time, saving a lot of time and energy to return parts that don't fit.

General Layout

Catalogs normally contain a descriptive and dated (sometimes coded) cover, a table of contents, index, illustrations, and then the meat of the catalog, the applications. The applications are normally arranged two ways—(1) alphabetically by car name, and (2) numerically by part number. Jobbers may store their catalogs using the Weatherly filing system, a three-digit number on the front of the catalog, but this is of little interest to the do-it-yourselfer. What does interest you is the alphabetical listing of vehicles by make and model.

Many manufacturers print their parts catalogs every year, but some only print every two years and supply a supplement during the off year. It is essential to check the date of the catalog to be sure it has the latest information. Working with an outdated catalog is sometimes worse than working with no catalog at all.

Locating Applications

Let's say you want to look up the spark plug for your 1973 Oldsmobile 350 V8 engine. The first thing you do is find a spark plug catalog and check the date to make sure it is current. Then you look in the index for "Oldsmobile." In this particular catalog there is no listing by make and model in the index. The spark plug applications are broken down by American Passenger Cars, Import Passenger Cars, and several other listings. Turn to the page starting American Passenger Cars.

Under American Passenger Cars, you'll find they are broken down into individual makes starting with American Motors and working back to Willys. Scan the pages until you find the heading Oldsmobile. Under Oldsmobile you'll find the applications further broken by 6-cylinder and V8 engines. Your Oldsmobile has a V8, so look under the appropriate heading. V8 engines are further categorized by year, beginning with the most recent, and by engine size (260, 305, 350, 455, etc). Running down the entries under V8 engines shows three possible listings:

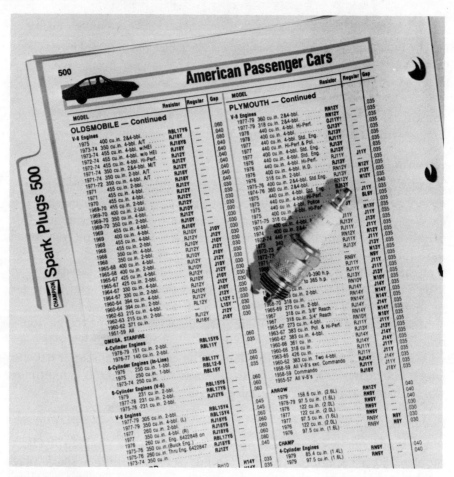

Fig 3-8 A good way to check your ability to read the catalog is to first look up the part number and then check the actual number on the part.

1973–74 350 cu.in. 4-bbl. A/T
1971–74 350 cu.in. 2- and 4-bbl. M/T
1971–74 350 cu.in. 2-bbl. A/T

There are a number of variables that could affect the part number, such as whether the engine has high energy (electronic) ignition or whether it is a California or Federal car, but since your engine is a 350-cubic-inch V8 with a 4-barrel carburetor (you can find out by consulting the tune-up decal under the hood) and automatic transmission, read across the column from the first entry and find the number of the spark plug.

Abbreviations and Footnotes

If you have trouble deciphering the abbreviations used in the parts catalog, they are usually identified in the front of the catalog.

The biggest distraction in all automotive catalogs is the footnotes. Asterisks, daggers, numerals, and letters that appear after a part number or listing indicate that you are up against a footnote. If such a notation is present, you must look further for more information. Most likely you will go to the bottom of the page for an explanation of why the notation was used. And the explanation could be almost anything. Special kits, superceded parts, special applications, and a myriad other pieces of information all are deserving of footnotes. To get the right part for your car you cannot afford to skip over the footnotes.

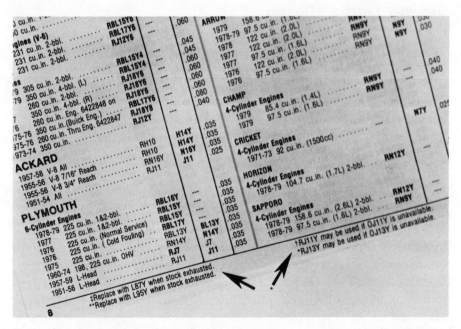

Fig. 3-9 Catalog footnotes are important to getting the proper application. They frequently contain replacement part numbers or other pertinent information.

Cross Reference

Many catalogs include a cross reference so you can double check information. A cross-reference could be original equipment-to-independent supplier part numbers, or application by part number. Let's assume we are looking for a standard equipment alternator belt for a 1972 Ford F100 truck with a 351V8 engine. We get the belt catalog and turn to the table of contents. Belts are listed by part number under vehicle and application. Since we don't know the part number, we turn to Application by Vehicle. The top listing is American Motors, so you know you are working with an alphabetical listing, but you have to be careful because sometimes American Motors vehicles are listed under "Rambler."

Scanning from American Motors through Willys (Kaiser-Jeep) does not locate the vehicle you have, so turn the page. Imported cars are next, listed alphabetically from Alpha-Romeo to Volvo. The next page is headlined Trucks, so you have found the right spot. The first listing on this page is probably Chevrolet and the last is Studebaker.

It is an alphabetical listing by make and model, so go down the line to Ford. This listing starts with 1959–69 model, so proceed until you come to 1972. A 1972 listing of the F100 shows "351V8 except air conditioning." Continuing down the column you come across "F100, 351V8 with air conditioning. Read across the page and you will find the replacement belt number.

Common Catalog Mistakes

Catalogs are designed for using, not confusing, but it is not unusual for catalog users to make mistakes in tracking down part numbers. Simple goofs are the most common and costly. For instance, often the user will find the correct listing, but then he or she reads across the wrong line. Or everything is done correctly, but a mistake is made in copying or trying to remember the part number. Or you can get mixed up in using a cross-reference, or working with an outdated catalog, or overlooking a footnote. Such mistakes happen every day to even the most experienced. All you can do is try your best to avoid them.

◆ Maintenance and Tune-Up Tools

Naturally, without the proper tools and equipment it is impossible to properly service or maintain your vehicle. It would be impossible to catalog each tool that you would need to perform any repair operation. It would also be unwise for the amateur to rush out and buy an expensive set of tools on the theory that he may need one or more of them at some time.

The best approach is to proceed slowly gathering together a good

American Passenger Cars

OLDSMOBILE — Continued

V-8 Engines

MODEL	Resistor	Regular	Gap
1975 400 cu.in. 2&4-bbl.	RBL17Y6	---	.060
1973-74 350 cu.in. 4-bbl. A/T	RJ18Y	---	.040
1973-74 455 cu.in. 4-bbl. w/HEI	RJ18Y8	---	.080
1972-74 455 cu.in. 4-bbl. w/o HEI	RJ18Y	---	.040
1972-74 455 cu.in. 4-bbl. Hi-Perf.	RJ12Y	---	.040
1971-74 350 cu.in. 2&4-bbl. M/T	RJ12Y	---	.040
1971-74 350 cu.in. 2-bbl. A/T	RJ12Y	---	.040
~~1971-72 350 cu.in. 4-bbl. A/T~~	~~RJ18Y~~	~~---~~	~~.040~~
1971 455 cu.in. 2-bbl.	RJ18Y	---	.040
1971 455 cu.in. 4-bbl.	RJ12Y	---	.040
1970 455 cu.in. 4-bbl.	RJ12Y	---	.030
1969-70 455 cu.in. 2-bbl.	RJ12Y	---	.030
1969-70 400 cu.in. 4-bbl.	RJ10Y	---	.030
1969-70 350 cu.in. 4-bbl.	RJ10Y	---	.030
1969-70 350 cu.in. 2-bbl.	RJ12Y	---	.030
1969 455 cu.in. 4-bbl.	RJ10Y	---	.030
1969 400 cu.in. 4-bbl.	RJ10Y	---	.030
1968 455 cu.in. 4-bbl.	RJ10Y	J10Y	.030
1968 455 cu.in. 2-bbl.	RJ12Y	J12Y	.030
1968 350 cu.in. 4-bbl.	RJ10Y	J10Y	.030
1968 350 cu.in. 2-bbl.	RJ12Y	J12Y	.030
1965-68 400 cu.in. 4-bbl.	RJ10Y	J10Y	.030
1965-68 400 cu.in. 2-bbl.	RJ12Y	J12Y	.030
1965-67 425 cu.in. 4-bbl.	RJ10Y	J10Y	.030
1965-67 425 cu.in. 2-bbl.	RJ12Y	J12Y	.030
1964-67 330 cu.in. 4-bbl.	RJ10Y	J10Y	.030
1964-67 330 cu.in. 2-bbl.	RJ12Y	J12Y	.030
1960-64 394 cu.in. 4-bbl.	RJ10Y	J10Y	.030
1960-64 394 cu.in. 2-bbl.	RJ12Y	J12Y	.030
1962-63 215 cu.in. 4-bbl.	RL12Y	L12Y ‡	.030
1962-63 215 cu.in. 2-bbl.	---	L15Y **	.030
1960-62 371 cu.in.	RJ12Y	J12Y	.030
1951-59 All	RJ18Y	J18Y	.030

OMEGA, STARFIRE

4-Cylinder Engines

MODEL	Resistor	Regular	Gap
1978-79 151 cu.in. 2-bbl.	RBL15Y6	---	.060
1976-77 140 cu.in. 2-bbl.	RBL11Y	---	.035

6-Cylinder Engines (In-Line)

1976 250 cu.in. 1-bbl.	RBL17Y	---	.035
1975 250 cu.in. 1-bbl.	RBL12-6	---	.060
1973-74 250 cu.in.	RBL15Y	---	.035

6-Cylinder Engines (V-6)

1979 231 cu.in. 2-bbl.	RBL15Y6	---	.060
1977-78 231 cu.in. 2-bbl.	RBL17Y6	---	.060
1975-76 231 cu.in. 2-bbl.	RJ12Y6	---	.060

V-8 Engines

1977-79 305 cu.in. 2-bbl.	RBL15Y4	---	.045
1977-79 350 cu.in. 4-bbl. (L)	RBL15Y4	---	.045
1977 260 cu.in. 2-bbl.	RJ18Y6	---	.060
1977 350 cu.in. 4-bbl. (R)	RJ18Y6	---	.060
1976 260 cu.in. Eng. 6422848 on	RJ18Y6	---	.060
1975-76 350 cu.in.(Buick Eng.)	RBL17Y6	---	.060
1975-76 260 cu.in. Thru Eng. 6422847	RJ18Y8	---	.080
1973-74 350 cu.in.	RJ12Y	---	.040

PACKARD

1957-58 V-8 All	RH10	H14Y	.035
1955-56 V-8 7/16" Reach	RH10	H14Y	.035
1955-56 V-8 3/4" Reach	RN16Y	N16Y	.035
1951-54 All	RJ11	J11	.025

PLYMOUTH

6-Cylinder Engines

1978-79 225 cu.in. 1&2-bbl.	RBL16Y	---	.035
1977 225 cu.in. 1&2-bbl.	RBL15Y	---	.035
1976 225 cu.in. (Normal Service)	RBL15Y	---	.035
1976 225 cu.in. (Cold Fouling)	RBL17Y	---	.035
1975 225 cu.in.	RBL13Y	BL13Y	.035
1960-74 198, 225 cu.in. OHV	RN14Y	N14Y	.035
1957-59 L-Head	RJ7	J7	.035
1951-56 L-Head	RJ11	J11	.035

PLYMOUTH — Continued

V-8 Engines

MODEL	Resistor	Regular	Gap
1977-79 360 cu.in. 2&4-bbl.	RN12Y	---	.035
1977-79 318 cu.in. 2&4-bbl.	RN12Y	---	.035
1978 440 cu.in. 4-bbl. Hi-Perf.	OJ11Y†	---	.035
1978 400 cu.in. 4-bbl.	OJ13Y*	---	.035
1977 440 cu.in. 4-bbl. Std. Eng.	RJ13Y	---	.035
1977 440 cu.in. Hi-Perf.& Pol.	RJ11Y	---	.035
1977 400 cu.in. 4-bbl. Std. Eng.	RJ13Y	---	.035
1976 440 cu.in. 4-bbl. Std. Eng.	RJ13Y	---	.035
1976 440 cu.in. 4-bbl. Hi-Perf.	RJ11Y	J11Y	.035
1970 400 cu.in. 1 bbl. H.D.	RJ13Y	---	.035
1976 318 cu.in. 2-bbl.	RN12Y	N12Y	.035
1975-76 400 cu.in. 2&4-bbl. Std.Eng.	RJ13Y	J13Y	.035
1974-76 360 cu.in. 2&4-bbl.	RN12Y	N12Y	.035
1975 440 cu.in. 4-bbl. Std. Eng.	RJ13Y	---	.040
1975 440 cu.in. 4-bbl. Hi-Perf.	RJ11Y	J11Y	.035
1975 440 cu.in. 4-bbl. Police	RBL9Y	BL9Y	.035
1975 400 cu.in. 4-bbl. Hi-Perf.	RJ13Y	---	.035
1971-75 318 cu.in.	---	N13Y	.035
1974 400 cu.in. 4-bbl. Hi-Perf.	RJ11Y	J11Y	.035
1974 440 cu.in. 2&4-bbl. Std.Eng.	RJ13Y	J13Y	.035
1972-74 440 cu.in.	RJ11Y	J11Y	.035
1973 340 cu.in.	RN12Y	N12Y	.035
1972-73 400 cu.in. 4-bbl.	RJ11Y	J11Y	.035
1972-73 400 cu.in. 2-bbl.	RJ13Y	J13Y	.035
1971-73 360 cu.in.	---	N13Y	.035
1968-72 340 cu.in.	RN9Y	N9Y	.035
1968-71 383 cu.in. 4-bbl.	RJ11Y	J11Y	.035
1966-71 440 cu.in. 370-390 h.p.	RJ11Y	J11Y	.035
1966-71 440 cu.in. to 365 h.p.	RJ13Y	J13Y	.035
1966-71 426 cu.in.	RN10Y	N10Y	.035
1960-71 383 cu.in. 2-bbl.	RJ14Y	J14Y	.035
1968-70 318 cu.in.	RN14Y	N14Y	.035
1965-69 273 cu.in. 2-bbl.	RN14Y	N14Y	.035
1967 318 cu.in. 3/8" Reach	RJ14Y	J14Y	.035
1967 318 cu.in. 3/4" Reach	RN14Y	N14Y	.035
1965-67 273 cu.in. 4-bbl.	RN10Y	N10Y	.035
1963-67 383 cu.in. Pol. & Hi-Perf.	RJ11Y	J11Y	.035
1960-67 383 cu.in. 4-bbl.	RJ13Y	J13Y	.035
1960-66 361 cu. in.	RJ14Y	J14Y	.035
1960-66 318 cu. in.	RJ14Y	J14Y	.035
1963-65 426 cu.in.	RJ11Y	J11Y	.035
1960-62 383 cu.in. Two 4-bbl.	RJ11Y	J11Y	.035
1958-59 All V-8's exc. Commando	RJ14Y	J14Y	.035
1958-59 Commando	RJ11Y	J11Y	.035
1955-57 All V-8's	RJ18Y	J18Y	.035

ARROW

1979 158.6 cu.in. (2.6L)	RN12Y	---	.040
1978-79 97.5 cu.in. (1.6L)	RN9Y	---	.040
1978 122 cu.in. (2.0L)	RN9Y	---	.040
1977 122 cu.in. (2.0L)	RN9Y	---	.030
1977 97.5 cu.in. (1.6L)	RN9Y	---	.030
1976 122 cu.in. (2.0L)	RN9Y	N9Y	.030
1976 97.5 cu.in. (1.6L)	RN9Y	N9Y	.030

CHAMP

4-Cylinder Engines

1979 85.4 cu.in. (1.4L)	RN9Y	---	.040
1979 97.5 cu.in. (1.6L)	RN9Y	---	.040

CRICKET

4-Cylinder Engines

1971-73 92 cu.in. (1500cc)	---	N7Y	.025

HORIZON

4-Cylinder Engines

1978-79 104.7 cu.in. (1.7L) 2-bbl.	RN12Y	---	.035

SAPPORO

4-Cylinder Engines

1978-79 158.6 cu.in. (2.6L) 2-bbl.	RN12Y	---	.040
1978-79 97.5 cu.in. (1.6L) 2-bbl.	RN9Y	---	.040

‡Replace with L87Y when stock exhausted.
**Replace with L95Y when stock exhausted.

†RJ11Y may be used if 0J11Y is unavailable.
*RJ13Y may be used if 0J13Y is unavailable.

Fig. 3-10 One of the most common catalog mistakes is failing to read straight across the page.

quality set of those tools that are used most frequently. Don't be misled by the low cost of bargain tools. It is far better to spend a little more for better quality. Forged wrenches, 10 or 12 point sockets, and fine tooth ratchets are by far preferable to their less expensive counterparts, and most are sold with a "no-questions" guarantee. If you break it, take it back and it will be replaced, no questions asked. It will cost a little more, but, as any good mechanic can tell you, there are few experiences worse than trying to work on a car or truck with bad tools. Your monetary savings will be far outweighed by frustration and mangled knuckles.

Metric or SAE?

Deciding whether you needed metric or SAE tools wasn't a problem until recently. All American cars used SAE fasteners, and foreign cars weren't all that popular. SAE fasteners are measured in inches, and standards for these are developed by the Society of Automotive Engineers. SAE sizes and standards are different from those established by the International Standards Organization (ISO) for metric fasteners.

Now the picture has changed. Not only do foreign cars represent a sizable portion of the market, but a number of American auto makers are using some metric sizes. The Chevette, for instance, uses more metric fasteners than SAE fasteners. So if you own a foreign car, more than likely you'll need metric tools. Likewise, if you have a late-model American car, you *might* need some metric tools.

Before you buy any tools, check with your dealer to determine just what kind of fasteners your car is put together with. Some American cars (such as the Vega) are entirely metric, while some are part metric and part SAE. Most American cars are still entirely SAE, however. Also keep in mind that some foreign cars (such as Volvo) utilize some SAE fasteners.

While there are some points of interchange between the metric and inch sizes, it's not a good idea to use metric wrenches on SAE fasteners and vice versa. In an emergency, you can use anything that will fit, but prolonged use will only ruin the fastener.

Begin by accumulating those tools that are used most frequently; namely those associated with routine maintenance and tune-up. In addition to the normal assortment of screwdrivers and pliers, you should have the following tools for routine maintenance jobs:

1. SAE (or Metric) or SAE/Metric wrenches. Buy sockets and combination open-end/box-end wrenches in sizes from ⅛ inch (3 mm) to ¾ inch (19 mm); and a spark plug socket (13/16 or ⅝ inch depending on plug type). If possible, buy various length socket drive extensions. Metric sockets available in the U.S. will all fit the ratchet handles and extensions you may already have (¼, ⅜, and ½ in drive).

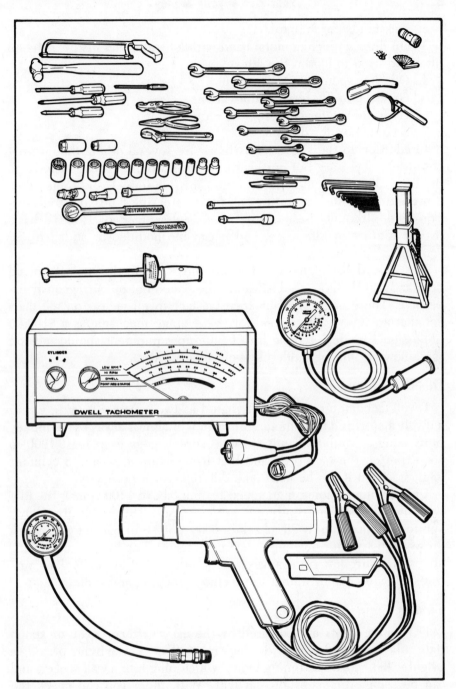

Fig. 3-11 These common hand tools will handle most basic service and maintenance jobs. You can add to this collection as the need arises. The instruments in the lower half of the picture, clockwise from the dwell tachometer, are: dwell tachometer, vacuum gauge, timing light, compression gauge.

49

2. Jackstands (for support).

3. Oil filter wrench (a metal band with a handle that fits over the oil filter and used to loosen the filter).

4. Oil filler spout (for pouring oil).

5. Grease gun (for chassis lubrication).

6. Hydrometer (for checking the battery).

7. A container (for draining oil).

In addition to the above items there are several others that are not absolutely necessary but are handy to have around. These include oil dry for soaking up spilled fluids, a transmission funnel, and some lubricants and fluids such as antifreeze, power steering fluid, and transmission fluid, although these can be purchased as needed. This is a basic list for routine maintenance, and it can be modified or added to according to your personal needs.

The second list of tools is for tune-ups. While the tools involved here are slightly more sophisticated, they need not be outrageously expensive. There are several inexpensive tach/dwell meters on the market that are every bit as good for the average mechanic as a $100.00 professional model. A basic list of tune-up equipment should include the following, but be guided by your own needs.

Dwell/Tachometer

Dwell/tachometers can be purchased as two separate gauges, either a dwell meter or a tachometer. But you will almost always save money purchasing a combined unit. Just be sure it goes to at least 1200 to 1500 rpm on the tach scale and that it works on 4, 6, and 8 cylinder engines. Then it can be used on a different car if necessary.

Unless you are doing high speed testing (above 1100 rpms), the idle type should serve your purposes in most cases. This meter also allows you to measure cam dwell; check breaker points for correct gap; check for worn distributor bushings, shaft or breaker plate by cam angle variations; measure low rpm ranges; and it aids in carburetor fuel/air mixtures adjustments for idling, to preclude creeping and stalling.

Timing Light

DC timing lights are powered by the car's battery. Neon or xenon light tubes are used to provide the strobe effect. These lights provide a brighter light than AC timing lights, which plug into a wall socket, and can be seen even in bright daylight. With them you can check the spark advance, distributor shaft wear, wear and wobble in external pulleys and shafts, plus diagnose other problems.

Compression Tester

The name tells you exactly what this piece of equipment does. Using a remote starter switch, with the coil-distributor wire disconnected, you check each cylinder for compression. This unit checks for valve problems, worn or broken piston rings, and piston damage.

In many engines, particularly large V8s, the spark plugs are hard to reach. A flexible extension tube makes it easier to lock the unit in the spark plug hole in tight places. The small extra cost is worth it.

Vacuum and Fuel Pump Tester

Again, the name indicates most uses for this unit, and it doesn't need electricity to make it work. Any and all parts or systems that operate by means of vacuum can be checked for operating condition. This gauge will help diagnose sticking valves, leaking intake manifold, late timing, vacuum fuel pump pressure, and worn rings or cylinder walls.

Volt/Ohm/Amp Tester

If you go for a more expensive form of a test light, a volt/amp tester is what you're looking for. It can test and troubleshoot almost any electric component including the electronic ignition. These testers draw power from the car's battery and are available as a combination meter measuring all three functions in a single housing.

Test Light

This is a simple device using a light bulb to indicate if current is available at any check point. It is inexpensive to buy or easy to make with a 12-volt light bulb, wire, and a soldering gun. The homemade version works best with small foreign cars.

Other Useful Tools

When you work on your car, you'll soon discover that there are some tools that, while not absolutely necessary, make servicing your car easier, quicker, and more enjoyable. Items that fall into the nice-to-have category include such tools as remote starter switches, jumper leads, brake spring pliers, and magnetic screwdrivers.

Remote starter switches allow you to crank, start, and run the engine from outside the car. They save you running around the car, getting in, and starting the engine every time the need arises. They are well worth the $5 or so they cost.

A set of jumper wires can be made at home from 16- or 18-gauge primary wire and alligator clips. They are extremely useful for making temporary electrical connections when performing tests. They also help check for broken and loose wires, faulty dash instruments, and circuit continuity.

Brake spring pliers are invaluable in safely and easily removing the common brake shoe hold-down springs on drum brakes. Without these special pliers, you will have to coax and coerce the springs into place when relining the brakes. Magnetic screwdrivers allow you to make sure that small screws, nuts, and washers do not fall into the engine or other places where they don't belong but for which they seem to have a particular affinity.

As a final note, you will probably find a torque wrench necessary for all but the most basic work. The beam-type models are perfectly adequate, although the newer click type are more precise and more expensive.

Table 3-1
Your Pricing Guide for Test & Tune
Equipment

Item	Price Range
Timing light (DC powered)	$10–45
Timing light	$ 4–10
Neon tube replacements	$ 4
Xenon tube replacements	$11–15
Dwell tachometer	$15–30
Dwell tachometer (DC powered)	$29–60
Compression tester	$ 8–30
Vacuum/fuel pump tester	$ 8–35
Volt/amp tester	$18–35
Test light	$ 1–3
Remote starter switch	$ 5–15
Jumper leads	$ 2–5
Spark plug gap gauge	$ 1–3
Points feeler gauge (Be certain it's nonmagnetic for electronic ignitions)	$ 1–10
Tune-up guides	$ 7–15

Note: Automotive supply stores often run specials, with discounts from 15–25 percent. Also, purchasing more than one piece at a time can put you in a bargaining position for a price deal. Packaged assortments bring the unit cost down, too. Avoid duplication.

◆ Repair Guides and Manuals

Even though your labor is "free," you can't save much money repairing your car if you have to guess how to do it. A repair guide or manual for your car is one of the most valuable tools the do-it-yourself mechanic can own. Not only will it tell you exactly how to repair almost every major part on your car, it will also tell you when you are getting in over your head, or allow you to make the decision yourself, based on a knowledge of what must be done and what tools or special equipment are needed.

Even professional mechanics who work with cars every day cannot keep every fact and specification for every car catalogued in their heads. In any good mechanic's work area, you will find a virtual library of professional automotive service manuals to aid in diagnosing and correcting problems. So valuable are these manuals that the annual Chilton Auto Repair Manual, for instance, is considered the "bible" of the automotive repair industry.

Chilton and other publishers offer the do-it-yourself mechanic the same kind of accurate, up-to-date service information in manuals and repair and tune-up guides for individual makes of cars. These books are written for the do-it-yourself mechanic, and contain detailed, step-by-step instructions the backyard mechanic can use. They are comprehensive enough to rebuild an engine, yet basic enough for the beginning weekend tinkerer to use easily and successfully.

Fig. 3-12 Chilton offers the do-it-yourselfer an entire line of Repair & Tune-Up Guides, repair manuals and other specialty products for virtually all popular cars, light trucks, vans, RV's and motorcycles.

4

Fuels, Fluids, and Filters

◆ Gasoline

There are three basic grades of gasoline to choose from: unleaded regular, leaded regular, and leaded premium. The most important factor governing your choice is your car. With few exceptions, 1975 and later models must use unleaded fuel because they are equipped with catalytic converters and lead will poison the catalytic elements. Various decals and a specially designed filler neck all warn you against the use of leaded fuel in these cars. Most 1971–74 cars were designed to use regular fuel with or without lead, and most cars earlier than 1970 must use leaded gasoline.

Octane Rating

Simply put, the octane rating of a gasoline is its ability to resist knock, a sharp metallic noise resulting from detonation or uncontrolled combustion in the cylinder. Knock can occur for a variety of reasons, one of which is using gasoline with the incorrect octane rating for the engine in your car.

Engine knock (indicated by a sharp, rapping sound) is very damaging to the engine, and it is controlled by using a gas with the proper octane rating. Octane measurements made under laboratory conditions have led to "Research" and "Motor" octane ratings. In general, the research octane number tends to be about 6 to 10 points higher than the motor octane rating (for what is essentially the same gasoline). Since the early seventies, most octane ratings on gas pumps represent the average of the research and motor octane numbers. For instance, if the gasoline formerly had a research octane rating of 100, and a motor octane rating of 90, the octane rating found on the pump now would be 95. Most regular gasolines today are near 87 octane.

Your owner's manual will probably indicate the type and octane of gasoline recommended for use in your car. However, octane requirements can vary according to the vehicle and the conditions under which it is operating. As a new car is driven, combustion deposits build up and the octane requirement increases until an equilibrium level, normally between 4 and 6 octane numbers higher than the new-car requirement, is reached. Other factors which can increase the octane an engine requires are higher air or engine temperatures, lower altitudes, lower humidity, a more advanced ignition spark timing, a leaner carburetor setting, sudden acceleration, and frequent stop-and-go driving which increases the build-up of combustion chamber deposits.

If you encounter sustained engine knock, wait until your tank is nearly empty, then try a gasoline with a higher octane rating. Don't overbuy—it's a waste of money to buy gasoline of a higher octane than your engine requires in order to satisfy its anti-knock need.

Lead Content

The most efficient way of increasing the octane rating of a gasoline is to add a compound called tetraethyl lead. Therefore, if your owner's manual specifies the use of premium gasoline, you may have to use leaded fuels in order to avoid engine knock. However, if circumstances force you to use a low-lead or no-lead gasoline with lower octane than the car manufacturer specifies, you should temporarily retard the ignition timing very slightly in order to lessen the possibility of knocking.

Some cars, though designed to operate on leaded gasoline, may be able to use the new low-lead and no-lead fuels. Don't automatically rule out a low-lead gasoline. Again, experimentation is helpful in determining the gasoline octane which your car and your driving require. If your car has a catalytic converter, it *requires* unleaded fuel. The use of leaded gas will not harm the engine, but will destroy the effectivness of the converter and void your warranty.

Additives

Gasolines normally contain several additives put there by the refiners to improve engine performance. Carburetor detergent additives help clean the tiny passages in the carburetor, ensuring consistent fuel-air mixtures necessary for smooth running and good gas mileage. Winter additives include fuel line de-icers to reduce carburetor icing at the throttle plate. Other additives help control combustion chamber deposits, gum formation, rust, and wear.

One additive you may have noticed in your late-model car is manganese. Since the advent of the catalytic converter and the resultant widespread use of unleaded gas, manganese has been used by an increasing number of refiners as an anti-knock additive in unleaded gasoline. Manganese works, but it leaves reddish deposits on spark plugs. So if you pull your spark plugs and notice that they are covered with what looks like rust, don't panic. It's only manganese and it's as harmless as the lead deposits it replaces.

◆ Diesel Fuel

Because of their unique compression-ignition principle, diesel engines run on fuel oil instead of gasoline. The fuel is injected into the cylinder at the end of the compression stroke and the heat of compression ignites the mixture. Diesel fuel used in automotive applications comes in two grades, No. 1 diesel fuel and No. 2 diesel fuel. No. 1 diesel is the more volatile of the two and is designed for engines which will operate under varying load and speed conditions. No. 2 diesel is designed for a relatively uniform speed and high loads. The two grades of fuel will mix and burn with no ill effects, although the engine manufacturer will undoubtedly recommend one or the other.

Two important characteristics of diesel fuel are its cetane number and its viscosity. These are discussed below.

Cetane Number

The cetane number of a diesel fuel refers to the ease with which a diesel fuel ignites. Don't confuse cetane ratings with octane ratings. Octane ratings refer to the slowing or controlling of the burning of gasoline. Cetane ratings refer only to the ease or speed of the ignition of diesel fuel. High cetane numbers mean that the fuel will ignite with relative ease or that it ignites well at low temperatures. Naturally, the lower the cetane number, the higher the temperature must be to ignite the fuel. Most commercial fuels have cetane numbers that range from 35 to 65. Manufacturers of cars or light trucks that use diesel engines recommend diesel fuel with a minimum cetane rating of 40, regardless of whether the fuel is No. 1 or No. 2.

Viscosity

Viscosity refers to the ability of a liquid to flow. Water has a low viscosity since it flows so easily. The viscosity of diesel fuel is important since it must be low enough that it flows easily through the injection system, but high enough to lubricate the moving parts in the injection system. No. 2 diesel fuel has a higher viscosity than No. 1, which means it lubricates better but does not flow as well. Because of this and its lower cetane rating, No. 2 diesel is not as satisfactory as No. 1 in extremely cold weather.

◆ Engine Oil

What does oil do in your car's engine? If you answered "lubricate," you're only partially right. While oil is primarily a lubricant, it also performs a number of other functions which are vital to the life and performance of your engine.

In addition to being a lubricant, oil also dissipates heat and makes parts run cooler; it helps reduce engine noise; it combats rust and corrosion of metal surfaces; it acts as a seal for pistons, rings, and cylinder walls; it combines with the oil filter to remove foreign substances from the engine.

Oil must be thin enough to get between the close-tolerance moving parts it must lubricate. Once there, it must be thick enough to separate them with a slippery oil film. If the oil is too thin, it won't separate the parts; if it's too thick, it can't squeeze between them in the first place—either way, excess friction and wear takes place. To complicate matters, cold-morning starts require a thin oil to reduce engine

Fig. 4-1 The top of the oil can tells you all you need to know about the oil you're buying.

A. This is the oil's SAE viscosity grade. The numbers followed by a 'W' indicate an oil with low temperature performance characteristics and the 'non-W' numbers describe an oil with high temperature characteristics. If there is one number, it is a single grade. Two or more numbers indicate a 'multi-viscosity' oil which has both low and high temperature characteristics.

B. This means that the oil will protect expensive engine components. Even if your car is no longer under warranty, it indicates that the oil is of good quality.

C. This is the manufacturer's brand name.

D. These letters generally mean that the oil meets or exceeds established standards for use in gasoline (indicated by 'S' and a following letter) and diesel and commercial engines (indicated by 'C' and a following letter). These designations replace the older classifications which may be called for in some owners' manuals. The SE rating is the highest standard for gasoline automobiles.

resistance, while high-speed driving requires a thick oil which can lubricate vital engine parts at temperatures up to 250° F.

According to the Society of Automotive Engineers' viscosity classification system, an oil with a high viscosity number (e.g., 40) will be thicker than one with a lower number (e.g., 10W). The "W" in 10W indicates that the oil is desirable for use in winter driving. Through the use of special additives, multiple-viscosity oils are available to combine easy starting at cold temperatures with engine protection at turnpike speeds. For example, a 10W-40 oil will have the viscosity of a 10W oil when the engine is cold and that of a 40 oil when the engine is warm. The use of such an oil will decrease engine resistance and improve your miles per gallon during short trips in which the oil doesn't have a chance to warm up.

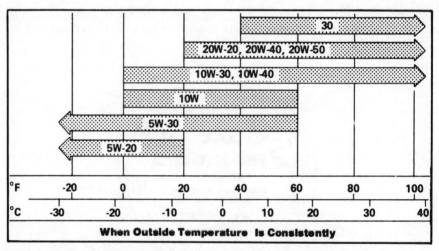

Fig. 4-2 Use this chart to select the viscosity of the oil you need. Choose an oil compatible with the lowest anticipated temperature before the next oil change.

Since oils all conform to the same rating standards and are all classified according to intended use (see the Motor Oil Guide in Table 4-1), price will not be a large factor in your choice. But the same product may be less expensive in a discount store than in a gas station, for example.

Some of the more popular multiple-viscosity oils are 5W-20, 5W-30, 10W-30, 10W-40, 20W-40, 20W-50, and 10W-50. In general, a 5W-20 or 50W-30 oil is suitable for temperatures below 0° F, 10W-30 or 10W-40 whenever the lowest temperature expected is 0° F, and 20W-40 whenever the lowest temperature expected is 32° F. However, consult your owner's manual or a reputable oil dealer for the recommended viscosity range for your car and the outside temperature in which it operates.

Table 4-1
Motor Oil Guide

The American Petroleum Institute (API) has classified and identified oil according to its use. The API service recommendations are listed on the top of the oil can and all car manufacturers use API letters to indicate recommended oils. Almost all oils meet or exceed the highest service rating (SE), but viscosity should be selected to match the highest anticipated temperature before the next oil change.
S = Gasoline   C = Diesel

API Symbol	Use & Definition
SE	SE represents the most severe service. It is recommended for use in all 4-cycle gasoline engines, and cars used for stop and start or high speed, long distance driving. It has increased detergency and can withstand higher temperatures, while providing maximum protection against corrosion, rust and oxidation. Meets all service requirements for classifications SD, SC, SB and SA.
SD (formerly MS 1968)	These oils provide more protection against rust, corrosion and oxidation than oils classified SC. Meet minimum gasoline engine warranties in effect from 1968–70.
SC (formerly MS 1964)	These oils control rust and corrosion and retard the formation of high and low temperature deposits and meet minimum warranty requirements in effect for 1964–67 gasoline engines.
SB (formerly MM)	These oils have anti-scuff properties and will slow down oxidation and corrosion. Oils designed for this service afford minimum protection under moderate operating conditions.
SA (formerly ML)	These oils have no protective properties and have no performance requirements.
CD (formerly DS)	These oils provide protection from high temperature deposits and bearing corrosion in diesel engines used in severe service.
CC (formerly DM)	These oils provide protection from rust, corrosion and high temperature deposits in diesel engines used in moderate to severe service.
CB (formerly DM)	These oils are designed to provide protection from bearing corrosion and deposits from diesel engines using high sulphur fuel. Service is meant for engines used in mild to moderate service with lower quality fuels.
CA (formerly DG)	This is a general diesel service classification. These oils should not be used when sulphur content of fuel exceeds 0.4%. Oils will provide protection from bearing corrosion when high quality fuels are used.

◆ Synthetic Oils

Recently, a number of major oil companies have introduced synthetic oils which are composed of man-made hydrocarbons instead of petroleum-based hydrocarbons. There are quite a few claims being made for synthetic oils, including increased gas mileage, extended oil drain intervals, improved hot and cold weather engine performance, and less wear and tear on engines. Whether or not these claims are true has yet to be decided. One thing is certain, however. Synthetic oil is expensive. At prices that range up to three dollars a quart, synthetic oils will have to live up to every one of their claims to be cost-effective.

◆ Other Lubricants

Automatic Transmission Fluid

Automatic transmission fluids (ATF) are specific to the car using them and you should refer to your owner's manual or repair guide for the kind your vehicle takes.

There are basically three types of fluids, and the tops of all cans are clearly marked to indicate the type.

Type A, Suffix A, was recommended by GM, Chrysler, and AMC between 1956 and 1967. Type A was superseded by Dexron®.

Dexron® was recommended by GM, Chrysler, and AMC from 1967–75, and in any transmission that had previously specified Type A. In 1975 Dexron II® superseded Dexron®.

Type F fluid is recommended by Ford Motor Co. and a few imported manufacturers, and contains certain frictional compounds required for proper operation in these transmissions. Containers marked with a qualification number 1P-XXXXXX are suitable for Ford transmissions prior to 1967, while a qualification number of 2P-XXXXXX is suitable in all Ford transmissions.

1977 and later Ford cars with a C6 automatic transmission use a new Type F fluid known as a CJ fluid. The dipstick of these transmissions is marked "Use ESP-M2C138-CJ Fluid Only."

Manual Transmission Lubricant

Generally speaking, manual transmissions use a gear oil of about SAE 80 or 90 viscosity. Gear oil viscosity has nothing to do with motor oil viscosity. For instance, an SAE 80W gear oil can have the same viscosity characteristics as an SAE 40 or 50 motor oil.

Not all manual transmissions use gear oil. For years, Chrysler Corporation specified the use of automatic transmission fluid in their manual transmission cars. Some transaxles, both foreign and domestic, use either ATF or engine oil to lubricate the transmission. For this reason, it is always best to consult your owner's manual or your dealer if you are unsure about what sort of lubricant to use in your manual transmission.

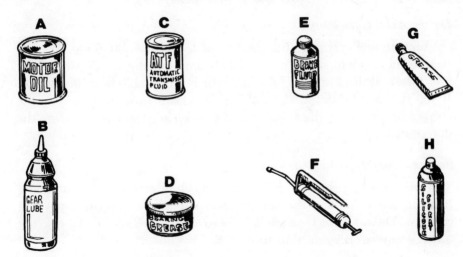

Fig. 4-3 Common automotive lubricants and fluids.

Every manufacturer has specific recommendations for fluids and lubricants used in their vehicles. These are generally listed in the owner's manual. In the absence of specific recommendations, use the following as a general guide.

Part	Symbol	Lubricant
Engine	A	Engine oil SE viscosity determined by anticipated temperatures before next oil change
Manual transmission	B	SAE 80W-90 gear lubricant (API-GL4)
Manual transmission (with overdrive)	B	SAE 80W-140 gear lubricant (API-GL4)
Automatic transmission	C	Automatic transmission fluid Dexron® Dexron II® Type F
Power steering pump	C	Automatic transmission fluid
Conventional rear axle	B	SAE 80W-90 gear lubricant (API-GL5)
Limited slip rear axle	B	SAE 80W-90 limited slip gear lubricant (API-GL5). *Note:* Special limited slip additive may be required
Front wheel bearing	D	High melting point, long fiber wheel bearing grease
Brake master cylinder (drum or disc brakes)	E	Heavy duty brake fluid meeting DOT-3 minimum
Clutch master cylinder	E	Heavy duty brake fluid meeting DOT-3 minimum
Manual steering gear, suspension, ball joints, U-joints, clutch and gear shift linkage, steering linkage and other chassis lubrication points	F	Lithium base, multi-purpose chassis lubricant
Doors, hood, trunk and tailgate locks, seat tracks, parking brake	G	White grease
Accelerator linkage, door hinges, trunk and hood hinges	A	SAE 30 motor oil
Lock cylinders	H	Silicone spray lubricant or thin oil applied to key and inserted in lock
Weather stripping	H	Silicone spray lubricant

Drive Axle Lubricants

Conventional rear axles use gear oil of about 80 or 90 grade. Consult your owner's manual for more detail. Limited-slip or Posi-traction® rear axles require a special lubricant which is available from the dealer. If you do have a limited-slip differential, make sure you use only the correct lubricant, as the use of the incorrect lubricant can destroy the differential.

Power Steering Fluid

Power steering pumps are ordinarily lubricated with automatic transmission fluid. Use the correct fluid for the car. For instance GM cars use Dexron® or Dexron II®. Ford cars use Type F. Check the owner's manual if you are unsure.

Chassis Greases

Quite a few late-model cars, especially American ones, no longer require chassis lubrication, but for those that do, the correct grease is generally an EP (extreme pressure) chassis lube. If you lube your own car, there's not really much problem, since it's about the only thing you can get that will fit in your hand-operated grease gun.

Wheel Bearing Lubricant

There are two types of wheel bearing lubricant: low temperature (short fiber grease) and high temperature (long fiber grease). The high temperature wheel bearing lubricant is the only one suitable for modern cars.

Master Cylinder Fluid

Brake fluid is used for both the brake master cylinder and the clutch master cylinder (if your car is equipped with a hydraulic clutch). Use only brake fluid rated DOT 3 or 4 or conforming to SAE Standard J1709. The rating can be found on the can.

◆ Automotive Chemicals

Even if you don't know one end of a screwdriver from another, you can still solve some of your car's ailments with the twist of a cap. Chemical additives hold the answer to many automotive ills and, more importantly, can prevent them from occurring in the first place.

Automotive chemical additives do work when used properly. Just remember they don't perform miracles. If a part on your car is broken or badly worn, no amount of "Acme Snake Oil" is going to cure it.

Chemical-related jobs are one of the easier do-it-yourself functions to perform. Packages contain all necessary information and directions you'll need to add or replace chemicals. Most automotive chemicals are priced under $2, and they may be bought for less during sales and promotions. You can save on your car's chemical needs by checking newspapers, mailers, and circulars for special prices.

Most automotive outlets offer a selection of their own store brand chemicals along with those from name brand manufacturers. You're probably better acquainted with the latter because of their advertising but don't be afraid to try the store-brand chemicals.

Oil Additives

All engine oils have additives for specific purposes. If you are using an SE rated motor oil, you should have no need of other additives, and car manufacturers do not recommend their use, especially while the car is under warranty. However, engines with a lot of wear from heavy use may benefit from an oil additive.

There are two types of crankcase additives. First is the "honey" or oil improver. This type of additive helps your engine oil flow and lubricate better. When added to older engines, the honey types help the engine oil lubricate within the relatively open wear spaces between the parts. This action also cushions the parts and thus reduces engine noise.

The other type of crankcase additive is the friction reducer. This additive is a chemical compound that bonds to the metal of moving parts, combining with the oil to provide a tough film of lubricant between the metal surfaces.

Another internal engine additive is top oil or upper cylinder lubricant. This additive also cuts friction by providing extra lubrication to valves and piston rings.

Cooling System

Antifreeze heads the list of chemicals for the cooling system. Today's quality antifreeze is recommended for year-round use by all leading car makers. A mixture of 50% water and 50% antifreeze will not only drop your coolant's freezing point to $-35°$ F, but it will also raise its boiling point 15° higher than plain water.

Before adding new antifreeze to your car's cooling system (see Chapter 1 for recommended intervals), you would be wise to flush out the system with a radiator cleaning solution. Cooling system flushing kits are available for less than $4.00 and can be installed in 10 to 15 minutes on virtually any car. The kit uses a garden hose to flush the cooling system of rust and scale that, if not flushed out, will clog the fluid passages and cause the engine to overheat.

Other cooling system chemicals to consider include stop-leaks, rust and corrosion inhibitors, belt dressings, and water pump lubes.

Fuel System

Carburetor cleaning chemicals may be just the answer for a rough-running engine. These chemicals contain compounds that strip away gum and varnish in the fuel system and reduce the buildup of sludge and corrosion.

Once the fuel system is clean, periodic use of a gas treatment additive prevents dirt problems from recurring. Anyone living in a particularly cold region should consider using a gas treatment which prevents fuel line freeze-ups.

Electrical System

Automotive chemicals for your car's electrical system are basically designed to combat the bad effects of wet weather. From the day they roll off the assembly line, some cars are just more susceptible to moisture problems than others, and an engine soaked by a car wash or rainstorm sometimes just won't start. If your electrical system does get wet, there are sprays that coat the distributor and ignition wires, dry them out, and can get you on your way.

Battery terminals can corrode, fail to transmit power, and leave you suddenly stranded. To prevent this, clean the terminals and spray them with a protective terminal coating.

Visibility

One of the most often overlooked yet necessary group of automotive chemicals are those that help you see where you're going. Washer fluid does more than just clean the windshield. It also conditions the rubber of the wiper blade and keeps it flexible. In addition, washer fluid cleans film off the glass that traps dirt and grit which wear the blade edge away.

De-icers, available in spray cans, quickly melt ice off windshields and get you going while your neighbor is still scraping. Many washer fluids also include the "de-icer" compound in their formula.

On the inside, "de-misters" will prevent your windows from fogging up. De-misters either spray on or wipe on with a chemical impregnated cloth.

Body Care

Automotive chemicals in the form of cleaners and waxes are also necessary to protect your car through the winter months. Besides making your car look good, regular cleaning will protect it from the effects of the harsh ice-melting chemicals most highway departments now use.

◆ Filters

As an engine runs, it gradually picks up dirt and deposits from within and outside the engine. If the engine's oil, air, and fuel systems weren't filtered, all the moving parts would wear out quickly because of abrasion from tiny dirt and metal particles circulating throughout the system. The interior surfaces of the moving parts would eventually be eaten away by acids and abrasion formed from the burning of additives in the gasoline and oils. And vital parts like the carburetor would become clogged with dirt and chips of hardened fuel residue.

Filters trap and hold dust, dirt, and residue. Yet, with enough time and miles, they also become clogged. And that's why they must be changed.

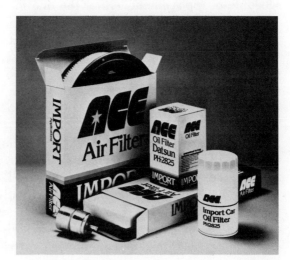

Fig. 4-4 Filters are manufactured and sold under many brand names. Many discount stores sell parts under a store-brand label at attractive prices. Be sure to check the application on the package or in the application catalog.

Oil Filters

Oil filters are rather simple devices. Basically, they're composed of an outside housing, a filtering element, and a one-way valve that keeps oil from draining back into the oil pan. Modern full-flow filters also have a relief valve. Should the filter become clogged, the valve opens and allows a full flow of unfiltered oil to return to the engine. Naturally, unfiltered oil is better than no oil at all.

Unfortunately, oil filters give no warning when they need changing. After initial oil and filter maintenance, car manufacturers usually recommend changing the filter at every other oil change. But the oil filter usually contains about one quart of oil at any given time, so you're leaving a quart of dirty oil in the engine to be recirculated. The best way to eliminate this problem is to change the oil filter at every oil change. It costs a little more, but the small additional expense will more than pay for itself in longer engine life.

Air Filters

The air filter is seldom very difficult to find. It is almost always located inside a large, round, can-type housing on top of the engine. Routine maintenance includes checking the air filter for dirt and replacing it if necessary. Usually all you have to do is remove a wing-nut from the top of the air cleaner housing to remove the cover and pull the air cleaner out of the housing. Tap it on a flat, hard surface to dislodge the dirt and check to see if you can shine a light through the filter element. If it doesn't shine through, it's time for a replacement. If you're in doubt, replace it. In any case, follow the recommended schedule of replacement, either the one in your owner's manual or in Chapter 1.

Before dropping in the new filter element, wipe out any dust or dirt that remains in the filter housing. Otherwise, whatever is in the housing will be sucked into the carburetor (and then into the engine) as soon as the engine is started.

Fuel Filters

Fuel filters, like air filters, send out warning signals when they need replacing. Typical signals include lack of power and engine sputtering and missing, especially when climbing a hill.

Many fuel filters can be inspected visually. They may be made of glass or plastic. And you can tell at a glance whether or not they need changing. Some see-through in-line models are made from pleated paper, ceramic stone, or composition cartridges in a glass sediment bowl.

Metallic types, usually found either at the fuel pump or just inside the carburetor inlet, should be replaced at the specified interval.

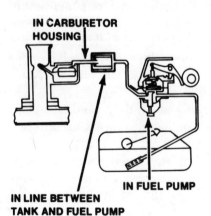

IN CARBURETOR HOUSING

IN FUEL PUMP

IN LINE BETWEEN TANK AND FUEL PUMP

Fig. 4-5 On virtually all cars, the fuel filter will be found in one of these locations.

In practically all cases you'll find the fuel filter somewhere in the line between the fuel pump and the carburetor. With the visual type, simply replace the entire unit. With most carb-mounted filters, just replace the element. Fuel-pump mounted filters usually just screw in place. Most filters have an inlet side and an outlet side. The outlet side should always face the carburetor. After installing, check for leaks with the engine running.

PCV Valves

While you're checking and replacing all these filters, don't forget the PCV valve. It's typical locations are shown in Figure 4-6. PCV stands for "Positive Crankcase Ventilation." This small unit, not much larger than your thumb, controls the flow of burnt and partially unburnt gases back into the combustion chambers.

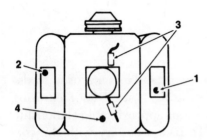

Fig. 4-6 The PCV valve will usually be found in one of these locations: (1 and 2) in either valve cover, (3) at the carburetor, or (4) in the intake manifold.

These gases contain resins and varnishes. Hence, the valve is likely to become clogged. When the PCV valve fails, these gases just turn around and flow back into the crankcase where they can blow out your seals and gaskets and form corrosive acids and sludges that can seriously damage the engine.

Typical indications of the need to replace the valve are rough idling, hard starting, and poor gas mileage. See chapter 1 or your owner's manual for replacement interval.

5

Buying a Battery and Tires

◆ Battery

Under the new battery rating system, two standards are used to determine battery power. The *cold power rating* is used for measuring battery starting performance and provides an approximate relationship between battery size and engine size. To pick a battery with the correct cold power rating for your car, simply match the cold power rating to the engine size in cubic inches. For instance, if your car has a 350 cubic inch engine, select a battery with a cold power rating of 350 or greater. In no event should the rating be less than 250.

The *reserve capacity rating* is used for measuring electrical capacity. It shows how long (in minutes) the battery will operate the car's electrical system in the event of a charging system failure. For example, if your battery has a reserve capacity rating of 135, this means you have approximately 2 hours and 15 minutes before the battery goes completely dead if you forget to turn the lights off when you park.

By anticipating battery replacement, you can plan the purchase of a battery, and shop around for a money-saving buy. Comparison shop at several automotive outlets for the best price. Take advantage of frequent special sales on batteries. Some stores will allow a trade-in on your old battery when buying a new one. Considering trade-in possibilities and the price differences of batteries at various outlets (see Table 5-1), you can realize considerable savings.

Just as important as shopping for the right price is looking for the proper battery to suit the performance needs of your car. Today's cars make heavy demands on the battery. Therefore, match the correct type and grade of battery with your car. Most auto stores have application charts along with their battery displays. These charts pinpoint your specific needs.

Guarantees should play a major role in your battery selection. Lower-priced batteries usually carry a 24-month guarantee, while better-quality ones come with 48, 60, or lifetime guarantee. Which is best for you depends on how long you expect to keep your car and how well it is equipped. If you're going to keep it for only a year or two, the less expensive, promotional-priced battery may be your best bet. But if you are planning to hold onto your car for years (as many people are doing today), you should consider buying the higher-quality, higher-priced battery. But keep in mind that most warranties will require that you return the battery to one of the chain's stores for a replacement, so don't let price or length of warranty be the only determining factor. Convenience has something to do with it, too. Either way you want to hold onto the guarantee and sales receipt. They probably will be needed if the battery fails.

Table 5-1
A Look at Battery Prices and Guarantees

	Good	*Better*	*Best*
Major retail chain	$29.95/36 mos.	$39.95/48 mos.	$45.95/60 mos.
Discount store	$27.99/36 mos.	$33.99/48 mos.	$39.99/life
Tire store	$22.95/12 mos.	$30.99/36 mos.	$39.99/60 mos.
Automotive Jobber	$34.95/36 mos.	$48.70/48 mos.	$64.35/60 mos.
Gasoline Station	$28.44/24 mos.	$42.68/42 mos.	$56.98/life
Car Dealer	$31.50/48 mos.	$48.70/48 mos.	$55.30/60 mos.
Auto Supply store	$31.95/36 mos.	$35.95/50 mos.	$42.95/life

Note: Above prices and guarantees are guidelines for buying a battery. Good, better and best reflect the difference in battery quality, cranking power, price, and guarantee.

◆ Types of Tires

Tires are among the most important and least understood parts of the car. Everything concerned with driving—starting, moving, and stopping—involves the tires. Because of their importance to driving ease and safety, learning the basics of tires will pay off in dollar savings and safe driving.

It may be that for your type of driving, you don't need expensive radial tires that will crack from age before you wear them out. The section on Tire Selection should help you decide which tires are best for you.

Tires use a combination of materials to contain pressurized air. The foundation of the tire is the plies (layers of nylon, polyester, or steel) just beneath the tread that provide flexibility and strength. Regardless

BIAS PLY   RADIAL   BELTED BIAS

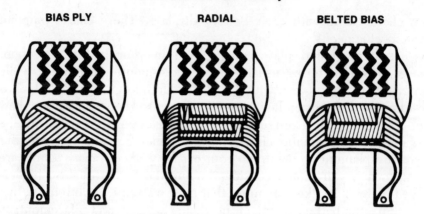

Fig. 5-1 There are basically three types of tires: bias ply, radial, and belted bias.

of size, cost or brand, there are basically only three types of tires—
bias, bias belted, and radial.

Bias tires, the old stand-by, are constructed with cords running
across the tread (from bead to bead) at an angle about 35° to the tread
centerline; alternate plies reverse direction. Crisscrossing adds
strength to the tire sidewalls and tread. When properly inflated, these
tires gave a relatively soft, comfortable ride.

Bias belted tires are similar, but additional belts of fiberglass or
rayon encircle the tire under the tread. The belts stabilize the tread,
holding it flatter against the road with less squirm (side movement).
Belted tires offer a firmer ride, better traction, improved puncture
resistance, and longer life than bias ply tires.

Radials are constructed with steel or fabric carcass plies crossing the
tread at approximately a 90° angle. Two or more belts circle the tire
under the tread. The sidewalls flex while the tread remains rigid, ac-
counting for the characteristic sidewall bulge of a radial. The tread
runs flatter on the road with a better grip and the inherently harsher
ride is offset by superior handling and mileage.

A recent variation of the radial tire is the elliptic tire—a polyester
cord body within steel belts. It resembles a conventional radial except
that it is a little more squatty. The elliptically shaped sidewall forms a
curve to the point where the tire meets the wheel rim, allowing up to
50° higher inflation pressures, without causing an uncomfortable ride.
The higher inflation pressures reduce rolling resistance and can increase fuel economy up to 3–4% at highway speeds.

◆ Tire Labeling

The tire sidewall contains just about anything you would want to
know about your tires, including size, maximum pressure and load,
and type of cord and number of plies. Figure 5-2 shows the labeling
that appeared on tires up until 1978. Figure 5-3 shows the kind of

Fig. 5-2 The alpha-numeric system
of labeling tires was used until 1978.

P	215/	75	R	15
Tire Use	Tire	Tire Series	Tire Type	Wheel
P = Passenger	Width	Ratio of	R = Radial	Diameter
T = Temporary	Sidewall-to	height to	B = Bias Belt	in
	sidewall in	width	D = Bias	inches
	millimeters		E = Elliptic	

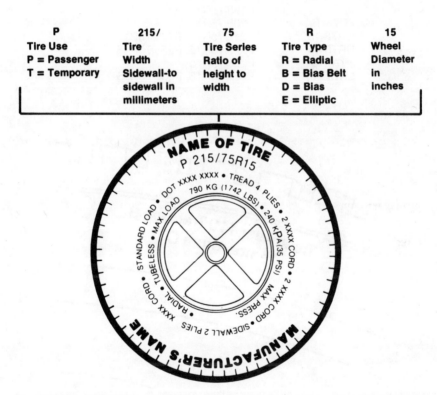

Fig. 5-3 The sidewall of a 1978 or later tire looks like this. It's part of a program to
standardize tire labeling. Although the designations are metric, wheel diameter is
still given in inches, and load and pressure in both metric (kg/KPA) and English (lb/psi).

Table 5-2
Substitutes for Alpha-Numeric Tire Sizes

All sizes are Load Range B or Standard Load. *Important:* Add 3 psi above the pressure specified on tire sidewall to assure adequate load capacity.

Alpha-Numeric Size (78 & 70 Series)	Acceptable Substitute Size
AR78-13	P165/80R13, P175/75R13, P185/70R13
BR78-13	P175/80R13, P185/75R13, P195/70R13
CR78-13	P185/80R13, P205/70R13
BR78-14	P175/75R14
CR78-14	P185/75R14
DR78-14	P195/75R14, P205/70R14
ER78-14	P195/75R14, P215/70R14
FR78-14	P205/75R14, P225/70R14
GR78-14	P215/75R14, P235/70R14
HR78-14	P225/75R14, P245/70R14
BR78-15	P165/80R15
ER78-15	P195/75R15
FR78-15	P205/75R15
GR78-15	P215/75R15, P225/70R15
HR78-15	P225/75R15, P235/70R15
JR78-15	P225/75R15
LR78-15	P235/75R15, P255/70R15

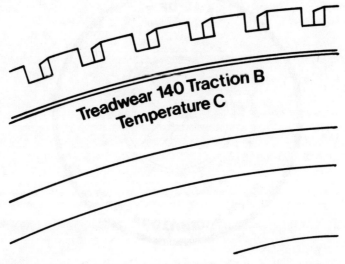

Fig. 5-4 The sidewall of new tires will also contain a tire grading system.

Table 5-3
Substitutes for P-Metric Tire Sizes

All sizes are Load Range B or Standard Load, unless noted. Do not exceed maximum pressure marked on tire sidewall.

P-Metric Size	Acceptable Substitute Size
P155/80R13	P165/75R13, P175/70R13
P165/80R13	P175/75R13, P185/70R13, AR78-13, AR70-13
P175/80R13	P185/75R13, P195/70R13, CR78-13, CR70-13
P185/80R13	
P165/75R13	P165/80R13, P185/70R13, AR78-13, AR70-13
P175/75R13	P175/80R13, P195/70R13, BR78-13, BR70-13
P185/75R13	P185/80R13, P205/70R13, CR78-13, CR70-13
P185/70R13	P175/80R13, P185/75R13, BR78-13, BR70-13
P195/70R13	P185/80R13, CR78-13, CR70-13
P205/70R13	
P165/80R14	P175/75R14, BR78-14
P175/75R14	BR78-14
P185/75R14	P205/70R14, DR78-14, DR70-14
P195/75R14	P215/70R14, ER78-14, ER70-14
P205/75R14	P225/70R14, FR78-14, FR70-14
P205/75R14 (Extra Load)	FR78-14 (Load Range D), FR70-14 (Load Range D)
P215/75R14	P235/70R14, GR78-14, GR70-14
P225/75R14	P245/70R14, HR78-14, HR70-14
P205/70R14	P205/75R14, FR78-14, FR70-14
P215/70R14	P215/75R14, GR78-14, GR70-14
P225/70R14	P225/75R14, HR78-14, HR70-14
P235/70R14	JR78-14
P245/70R14	
P155/80R15	P165/75R15
P165/80R15	CR78-15
P165/75R15	P165/80R15, BR78-15
P195/75R15	FR78-15, FR70-15
P205/75R15	P225/70R15, GR78-15, GR70-15
P215/75R15	P235/70R15, HR78-15, HR70-15
P225/75R15	JR78-15
P235/75R15	P255/70R15
P225/70R15	P225/75R15, HR78-15, HR70-15
P235/70R15	P235/75R15, LR78-15
P255/70R15	

labeling that is in use since 1978. The new system is basically metric, but wheel diameter is still given in inches, and load and pressure will be given in both metric (kg/kPA) and English units (lb/psi). Since the new metric labeling may not exactly correspond with the old alpha-numeric system, you'll have to be careful when changing to new tires. Tables 5-2, 5-3, and 5-4 give acceptable substitutes for tires.

On new tires, the sidewall will also contain a tire grading system code, which is explained in the next section.

Table 5-4
Substitutes for European Metric Tire Sizes

All sizes are Load Range B or Standard Load.
Important: Add 3 psi above the pressure specified on
the tire sidewall to assure adequate load capacity.

European Metric Size	Acceptable Substitute Size
155R13	P155/80R13, P165/75R13, P175/70R13
165R13	P165/80R13, P175/75R13, P185/70R13
175R13	P175/80R13, P185/75R13, P195/70R13
185R13	P185/80R13, P205/70R13
175/70R13	P165/80R13, P175/75R13, P185/70R13
185/70R13	P175/80R13, P185/75R13, P195/70R13
165R14	P165/80R14, P175/75R14
175R14	P185/75R14
185R14	P195/75R14, P205/70R14
185/70R14	P185/75R14
195/70R14	P195/75R14, P205/70R14
155R15	P155/80R15, P165/75R15
165R15	P165/80R15
175R15	P175/75R15

◆ Tire Grading

In April 1979, the Uniform Tire Quality Grading System took effect.
This system provides for a gradual phasing-in (bias tires first, followed
by bias belted) of a uniform grading system to compare tires in three
areas: traction, treadwear and resistance to heat.

The treadwear grade is expressed by a number in multiples of
10—a higher number indicating a comparatively longer tread life. The
number 100 is assigned as the standard of 30,000 mile tread life on a
test track under controlled conditions. Other numbers represent a percentage up or down from 100. For example, a grade of 150 represents
a tread life 50% greater than 30,000 miles, or 45,000 miles.

The test for traction involves towing a trailer mounted with the test
tires over a concrete and an asphalt course wetted with a controlled
amount of water. As the brakes are slammed on, the tires' coefficient of
friction is measured. An "A" grade means that its traction exceeds a
predetermined standard on both courses. A "B" grade indicates that it
exceeds a lower predetermined standard on both courses. If the tire
can't make the "B" grade on either concrete or asphalt, it receives a
"C" grade.

The test for temperature resistance consists of rolling the tire against
a large steel wheel at increasing speeds until the tire is destroyed or
achieves a grade of "A," indicating that it can survive a sustained run of
115 mph at 95° F. A grade of "B" indicates endurance at 100 mph.

Anything less than "B," but still above the federal minimum tire safety standard, receives a grade of "C."

◆ Tire Selection

Your choice of tires depends on your driving habits. Bias tires cost the least and give the poorest wear, but they are fine for short trips around town. Radials are relatively expensive, but they give superior performance and wear in addition to better fuel economy. Bias belted tires strike a middle ground between bias and radials in almost all areas, including cost.

One of the better buys for areas where there are extremes of weather conditions but not a great deal of snow at any one time, is the all-weather tire. These are usually radial tires that provide good traction and wear, combined with a tread pattern that gives good performance on snowy, rainy, or dry roads with little of the noise or loss of handling associated with deep-lugged snow tires. They are essentially a compromise tire, but perform well under all conditions, saving you the expense of a set of snow tires.

Retreaded tires can save as much as half over the cost of comparable new tires. Retreads are made by replacing the tread on salvageable, but closely inspected, tire casings. Forget the reputation of older recaps—today's retreaded tires are difficult to distinguish from new tires. They are so reliable that 98% of the world's airlines use retreads, as do many heavy equipment and trucking firms.

When shopping for retreads, look for a written guarantee with no unusual conditions, such as having to use a tube within tubeless tire. If you frequently travel out of your locality, look for a national guarantee.

When replacing tires, it's best to buy the same size and type that's on the car. Because of different handling and traction characteristics, it is also best not to mix types or sizes of tires on any one car or axle. In particular, radials should not be mixed with other types. Ideally, radials should be used in sets of five, but, if absolutely unavoidable, radials can be used in pairs, on the rear axle only—never on the front axle only.

Snow tires can be purchased like any other tire. They are constructed as bias, belted bias, and radial snow tires and the same cautions regarding mixing tire types discussed in the previous section apply to these. Studs are helpful on all types of snow tires, but you'd be wise to check the state laws before having them installed. In many states, they're illegal.

◆ Tire Balancing

When you purchase new tires, have them balanced. Balancing involves installing small lead weights on the edge of the wheel to correct any out-of-balance condition caused by small imperfections in the tire and wheel combination.

Most tire pros feel that computer balancing (off-car, two-plane spin balancing) is the best method. This is done by a computerized balancer, and it balances the tire in both vertical and horizontal planes. How does the computer balancer work? Its sensors measure the unbalanced forces acting upon the shaft on which the spinning wheel is mounted. This input is fed into a preprogrammed minicomputer, which indiates how much weight should be applied to each side of the wheel-tire assembly, and where.

Static balancing with a bubble balancer, perhaps the most common form of balancing done today, balances the tire in only the vertical plane. Although this type of balancing, if done properly, will adequately balance most wheel-tire assemblies, it will not do the job if there is a significant imbalance in the horizontal plane (dynamic imbalance).

Here are two things to look for if you're watching your tires being statically balanced: (1) An equal number of wheel weights should be placed on each side of the rim, directly opposite each other; (2) after the weights are applied, the conscientious balancer should rotate the tire 180° to double-check his reading of the bubble.

What about on-car balancing, where the entire wheel-tire brake-drum/rotor assembly is balanced? According to most pros, this is recommended only when a standard off-car static or off-car two-plane spin balance cannot solve the vibration problem. This type of problem is usually found only on older cars. One of the drawbacks to on-car balancing is that when the tires are rotated from wheel to wheel to equalize wear, the balance is lost because the tire wheel assembly has been balanced to only one hub.

6

Selecting a Repair Facility

Understanding the structure of the auto repair industry is important in helping you select the right repair facility and deal with it effectively. And in dealing with large repair shops, such as car dealers, it is important to understand the internal structure of the service establishment. This can be the key to getting work done properly at a fair price, and to avoiding the headaches and frustration that occasionally accompany auto repair.

Selecting a repair shop involves two decisions. First, you have to decide what type of shop can best handle your work at the best price. You will not necessarily go to the same shop for all jobs. After selecting the *type* of shop that best suits your needs, you'll need to pick the individual shop that offers the best quality service at a fair price.

There are many different types of repair facilities, each offering their own unique services. We'll identify them as follows:

- Service stations (as opposed to those offering only gas and no service)
- Independent repair shops
- Specialty repair shops (franchised or independent)
- Mass merchandisers who also offer service
- Dealerships (new or used cars)

The type of shop you pick depends on the work that you need done. The following sections will summarize the advantages and disadvantages of of each type.

◆ Service Stations

For many years, service stations were the backbone of the auto repair business. But recently the trend has been reversed as many service stations have gone out of business or switched to a "gas only" business. Many service station operators found that they were having trouble competing with the proliferation of specialty repair shops and mass merchandisers who were offering attractive prices on the kind of high volume work that was the forte of service stations.

The service station, especially in the last several years, is almost always a franchise, owned by a major oil company and operated by an independent businessman. Some service stations are independently owned and operated, but these are in the minority ever since the gasoline "shortage" of 1973–74.

The biggest advantages offered by service stations are convenient location and long hours of operation, though the operating hours are not as long as they used to be. Such stations can usually provide quality repairs, even though they don't have the facilities and large staffs of other shops. They would not be able to survive if they could not fix cars, and the owners of many service stations go through courses in auto repairs required and sponsored by the oil companies.

The thing you want to check out thoroughly is reputation. Since a service station operates on a low overhead, in some cases you may find relatively unskilled mechanics. On the other hand, many larger shops employ certified mechanics. If you find a service station with a high percentage of satisfied customers, you've probably found a good deal.

You won't be able to go to a service station for all your repair needs, but for those that the station specializes in, it can be a good choice. The internal structure of the service station is virtually identical to that of the independent repair shop.

◆ Independent Repair Shops

The structure of the independent repair shop depends mainly on the size of the shop. The smallest shops will combine the functions of owner, service writer, service manager, and mechanic all in one person. Larger shops may have a manager who takes care of dealing with customers and serves as shop foreman. In many cases, this person will also be the owner.

The smaller shops are definitely more common. The owner may either rent or own the property, but he runs the business as his own. He is often a mechanic himself and will probably employ one or two other mechanics, depending on the size of his business. The person who writes the estimate and decides who does the work will most often be the owner, and he is the one with whom people come in contact.

The independent repair shops have survived the competition from the dealership service department primarily because they offer quality repairs at lower prices. They keep their overhead down by engaging in general repair and not hiring extra people with narrow specialties. In most cases, they keep advertising to a minimum, depending instead on word of mouth from satisfied customers. The owners know most of their customers and their business is based on reputation and personal trust.

The small size of the independent operation can pay off in other ways. The same person is likely to work on your car each time, and he will get to know not only the service history of the car but your driving habits as well. This can help when it comes to diagnosing complaints or deciding to go ahead with a certain type of repair. Since he views you as a long-term customer, the trust that is built up may reduce some of the inconvenience of car repair. You might allow him to make certain repairs without consulting you for approval.

The independent may not be able to offer the the full line of services furnished by a dealership, or there may be certain types of work that don't interest him. He might, for example, sublet an automatic transmission overhaul to a shop known to him who will offer a warranty on sublet work.

The prices charged by the independent repair shop will be competitive with service stations and most specialty shop work, and a little lower than dealerships.

◆ Specialty Repair Shops

Specialty repair shops specialize in one or two types of repair (for example, mufflers, brakes, tune-up and diagnostic work, transmissions, tires or front-end work). These shops can be either independent or franchised operations, which are licensed to use a national name or certain techniques in the conduct of their business. Major automotive specialty chains include familiar names such as Midas (muffler), AAMCO (auto transmission), Goodyear (tires), and a host of others that advertise heavily to promote their particular expertise.

Most specialty shops, whether franchised or independently run, offer good values. They have found their particular niche in the automotive service world and exist because they can do something better or less expensively, or because they perform services that others do not want to perform. Muffler shops are a good example. Hardly anyone can compete with the major national muffler and exhaust system chains. They offer convenience, price and a lifetime guarantee. Exhaust system work is time consuming for an independent mechanic, and the independent cannot charge enough for the job relative to the time invested. Specialty muffler shops usually operate on a no-appointment, first-come, first-served, high-volume basis and do only exhaust system work, which they have reduced to a near science. You will generally be in and out of a muffler shop inside of 30 minutes, and have a new muffler with a full lifetime warranty at a low price.

In most specialty shops, if of moderate size, you will deal with a manager/service writer/shop foreman. Many times, this person is a businessman who simply operates the business, so don't be surprised if he has a minimum of actual mechanical experience. The larger specialty shops, such as the tire and brake shops, may also have a sales department run by a combination shop foreman/store manager or by a parts/store manager. In any event, unless the operation is a small, independent one, the owner is not likely to be found on the premises, preferring instead to leave the day-to-day operations to others.

Shops that specialize in one or a few areas of repair offer a competitive edge in their specialty and are more familiar with the type of work they perform. While a general mechanic does the same repair maybe three or four times a week, specialty shop mechanics do the same job day in and day out. They are familiar with all the subtle tricks that come from long experience with the same job. The other advantage to these shops is their association (in most cases) with a national organization. As a result, the specialty shop may offer a warranty package—2 years on front-end alignment, lifetime "as long as you own your car" on mufflers, 12 months on automatic transmission overhaul—that is hard to beat.

The one thing the specialty repair shops can't offer is a wide range of repair services, but if you're really shopping for the best deal and can take advantage of the services a specialty shop offers, you'll find they're often the lowest priced.

Two other specialty shops are worth mentioning separately because of the services they perform—the body shop and the diagnostic specialty shop. Like anything else, it's possible to pay a high price for body work and end up with a poor job. The franchised body shops usually do quality work at reasonable prices. Frequently you'll find that many body shops send their work to the franchised operations, rather than paint an entire car themselves. For the names of independent body shops, look in the yellow pages of your phone book. Many of the independent shops are low volume shops that concentrate on bodywork and spot painting or panel refinishing. Talk to your friends or people at a local body shop. Frequently there is someone locally who "moonlights" out of his garage and works for a local body shop during the day. You can get very satisfactory results, this way, but the job is almost always a cash deal.

If you've got one of those mysterious auto problems that seems to puzzle everyone, your best bet may be an automotive diagnostic center. The people there usually only deal in diagnostic and tune-up work. Although they are more expensive than other shops, they have the latest equipment and information to find obscure problems. You shouldn't be put off by the fact that you're paying to have your car checked out, because if it's a really tough problem, the money you save in parts replacement will usually be more than enough to pay the diagnostic bill. (The fact is, that not all mechanics are equipped with expensive tools to properly diagnose complex problems and pinpoint their cause. The result is a "trial-and-error" approach of replacing parts until the problem is cured.)

◆ Mass Merchandisers

A fairly recent development has been the emergence of the repair shop as a part of the mass merchandisers automotive operation. These are really a variation of the specialty repair shops, except that the mass merchandisers (K-Mart, Sears, J.C. Penney, etc.) cover a slightly wider variety of repairs, including brakes, tune-ups, shocks, mufflers, and some general repairs except major mechanical work. They concentrate on high-volume, fast-moving parts and repairs that are high profit jobs. Because they deal in high volume parts, they can often offer a competitive price on some jobs, compared to independent and specialty shops. The work done in the mass merchandisers shop is generally good. If your car requires work where most of the expense will be parts and very little labor, the mass merchandisers are well worth considering.

The mass merchandiser offers the advantages of convenient location and speed. They are usually located in large shopping complexes where you can leave your car, do your shopping, and pick up your car on the way home. The internal set-up is close to that of a specialty shop with a sales room. The service writer or manager will usually write the estimate and assign the work to a mechanic. The service manager is usually in the employ of the store or may even be a regional service manager for several of the chain's stores.

◆ Car Dealerships

The service department of a new or used car dealership is organized quite differently from the sales department. Failure to realize this is frequently responsible for customer dissatisfaction and suspicion concerning the motives of dealership management.

The dealership's first job is to sell the car. To do this the salesman must convince you of the virtues of the car he is selling. He points out its superior qualities, its advantages over comparable models, in short, all its good points. Many customers feel they are told an entirely different story—later—by the service department. The service writer, mechanics, and service manager deal only with problems. The customer conceives of his new car as trouble-free, but then is told by the service department that the work will take longer than expected, the parts weren't in stock, or any number of other perfectly reasonable explanations of why the car isn't going to be fixed immediately.

Sales and service departments in dealerships are largely independent of each other. Involving the sales department in a dispute with the service department is not a constructive policy. The salesman is not in a position to assist you and you should not assume that he can.

So when you're ready to buy your car, don't stop at the showroom. Visit the service department. If you can't get there when the service department is open, at least check with other customers who regularly use the dealer's service facilities. You can also ask to be introduced to the customer service manager or the service manager, although many salesmen will do this as part of the new car sales pitch. Talk with these people. Ask if they can suggest the best time for service, what information to bring with you, or things you can do to facilitate the handling of problems that may arise. Chances are they will have very specific advice, will appreciate the fact that you are taking the trouble to find out, and will remember that when your car needs work. Try to build a rapport with the service personnel, because these are the people you will have to deal with after you've purchased your car.

The Dealership Staff

Regardless of whether you are using the dealership service department for warranty repairs or for normal service work, the first person you will encounter when you bring the car in is the service writer, or "service advisor" as he is sometimes called. This is the person in charge of translating the problems described by the customer into a work order for the mechanic. He does not just copy down what you say. He can't put on the work order "Find out why the car won't start." He must attempt to find out more about the problem so that his final work order gives the mechanic a reasonable idea of the problem. This is why it's so important that you learn to communicate as much of the problem as possible to the mechanic or service writer. If he cannot determine the problem by talking with you, then he will probably ask that you take a road-test drive with him. The final work order should be fairly specific in terms of what is going to be done and what the problem is.

Eventually, the work order and your car will be passed to the mechanic who is going to do the work. The mechanic has a rather special relationship with the shop. He is an independent businessman, even though he is on the dealership payroll. He gets paid a percentage, usually one half, of the hourly fee you are charged for labor. Since there is usually a flat charge per job (except on small jobs such as oil changes or transmission filter replacement), he will make more money if he does more jobs. If the service writer brings him a problem that is long on diagnosis and short on actual labor for repairs, it will be unprofitable unless you are also charged for diagnosis time. You can help here by providing all the information possible about the problem. The small bit of information that you considered irrelevant might be the clue that would save the mechanic an hour diagnosing the problem.

Somebody in the shop has the thankless job of doling out the work so that each mechanic gets his share of good and poor jobs (in terms of money making potential). Usually this person is the shop foreman; sometimes it is the service writer. Find out who it is and cultivate that person's friendship. Your car is going to sit until he assigns a mechanic to work on it. And after that, it may need to be assigned to a specialist. The way you treat the foreman or service writer can have a positive or negative effect on the speed and quality of the service your car receives.

The service manager is responsible for the performance of the entire service department, interpreting service policy, and handling communications with the factory or zone service representatives. People above him make policy, and people below him mostly carry out instructions. The service manager, however, must constantly digest facts, analyze situations, and make judgments about the best means of handling a car or a customer that reflects both those facts and the service policy of the dealership. He is also the final arbiter of service disputes with the dealership before the zone representative becomes involved.

The next man up the ladder is the dealership's general manager. Theoretically, he is in charge of both the service and sales departments, but very often his primary energies are devoted to being a sales manager. Even if he can hire and fire the service manager, he very likely sells cars but does not sell any service. Handling a service complaint is, to him, just time away from selling. This is important to remember when communicating a problem to dealership management.

In some dealerships, there may be an executive or two above the general manager, for example, a president, or a president and vice president. In most cases, if you have a complaint and you're taking it all the way to the top, the man above the general manager that you'll have to talk to is the owner. Most owners, if you can get to see them, are quite different in their attitude about what can be done to solve a problem and maintain goodwill. They'll hardly get fired for going outside policy. This is the big advantage to seeing the owner—his hands are not tied.

Pros and Cons of the Dealership

There are several advantages in using your dealership's service shop. For one thing, the service shop is a necessary adjunct to selling cars successfully, and getting and keeping your goodwill can be very important to the dealer. In spite of the high overhead involved, you might get a lot for your money. A good dealership divides the work among several specialists, a luxury many other shops cannot afford. This increases the chances of good repairs on tough problems. The service writer is also instrumental in providing good service by analyzing your description of the car's problem and conveying the information clearly to the mechanic in a well-written work order.

Dealerships can also be quite expert when it comes to diagnosing obscure complaints. They know their brand of car best, and have a maximum of detailed information available. Their strong point is finding and solving unusual trouble.

Still another advantage is the ready availability of parts. If you are in a hurry, and your car needs something a bit unusual, it could save time getting it repaired at a dealership. Where the dealership uses only OEM parts, it is more likely that they'll have the parts on hand.

If you're most interested in "one stop shopping," it should be pointed out that a dealership offers the maximum range of repairs. If you want to avoid the inconvenience of taking your car several different places, and prefer familiarity, the dealership will probably be able to offer just about everything your car will ever need from maintenance and tune-up to automatic transmission repair and body work.

On the negative side, it must be pointed out that running a sophisticated dealership service department is expensive. In general, dealerships tend to charge more than their independent counterparts, though this may not always hold true. For example, an independent may be forced to buy his parts at a dealership and *then* mark them up. So shop a little before you draw your final conclusions. Also, if the dealership is a large one, you can end up in a very impersonal atmosphere, dealing with a different person almost every time you come in. If you like a strong personal relationship with whoever handles your car, you may have to shop for it among the dealerships.

◆ Finding a Good Mechanic

How do you know if you've chosen a good shop that does quality work at fair prices? What do you look for in a good mechanic or shop? A good mechanic:

- Knows his work and cares about its quality
- Cares about the satisfaction of his customers
- Diagnoses problems accurately and quickly
- Has good equipment and tools
- Performs work promptly
- Charges a reasonable price
- Is trustworthy.

Word of Mouth

Word of mouth advertising is one of the best recommendations, so ask friends where they get their cars repaired. Chances are they will have something to say about their satisfaction or lack of it. Check with sources such as the Better Business Bureau and the American Automobile Association (AAA) if you are a member. For what it's worth, the AAA has attempted to identify shops which provide quality repair, under a pilot program operating in certain regions of the country. Under the program, the AAA rates participating repair shops in five categories. Shops meeting with the standards of the Approved Auto Repair Program agree to provide AAA members with a written estimate, make replaced parts available for inspection (except those parts that must be returned to the manufacturer for warranty reasons), guarantee their work, and abide by AAA arbitration in cases of dispute.

Personal Inspection

In addition to relying on the opinions of others, you should personally try to judge the quality of the service your car will receive. Visit the shop and talk to the owner. Check their policies regarding certified mechanics, estimates, guarantees, and return of parts. The latter varies from state to state. (Check the Appendix for a summary of state auto repair legislation.)

When choosing a repair facility, consider:
- Reputation
    Consult with your friends and neighbors.
    Check with your local consumer office, Better Business Bureau and voluntary consumer groups.
- Qualifications
    Are the mechanics certified or licensed?
- Facilities
    How long has the shop been at its present location?
    Does the shop appear to be well equipped?
    Is it clean and organized?
- Repair Practices
    Will the shop give you a written estimate?
    Will it advise you on additional costs?
    How does it handle complaints?
    Does it guarantee its work in writing?
- Cost
    Do the shop's prices seem competitive?
- Convenience
    Is it close to where you live or work?

A good, efficient shop will almost always be busy, since a good reputation tends to spread quickly. Space will be at a premium, so there won't be many junkers lying around taking up room that could be used for paying customers. Good mechanics tend to prefer a neat work area, so they will sweep up at the end of the day and keep their toolboxes and tools clean and orderly.

Fig. 6-1 A well-equipped shop with the proper equipment is necessary to properly service modern automobiles.

Modern Diagnostic Equipment

Good mechanics find that "come-backs" are expensive and do not promote a good reputation. Doing the job right the first time requires modern test and diagnostic equipment. A complete list of equipment that mechanics use won't help the consumer much, since few consumers would recognize most of the pieces. But there are certain pieces of equipment that are considered standard in almost any shop. Dwell/tachometers, timing lights, electronic ignition testers, vacuum gauges, compression testers, exhaust gas analyzers, oscilloscopes, and engine analyzers all help take the guesswork out of auto repair. Look for shops that have up-to-date service information and current repair manuals. The day of the mechanic who relies solely on experience and the shot-gun approach of replacing parts until you find the defective one is rapidly disappearing.

Certified Mechanics

The National Institute for Automotive Service Excellence (NIASE) operates a voluntary mechanic certification program. Tests of a mechanic's competency in any or all of the following areas are given twice a year:

- Engine repair
- Automatic transmission
- Manual transmission and rear axle
- Front end
- Brakes
- Electrical systems
- Heating and air conditioning
- Engine tune-up
- Body repair

The tests are developed by the highly respected Educational Testing Service of Princeton, New Jersey, and a passing grade on the tests allows the mechanic to wear the orange, blue, and white shoulder patch and to display a sign that he is a NIASE-certified mechanic. Wherever you see these symbols you can be sure that the mechanics working there are qualified and keep up with changes in their trade.

NIASE publishes a national directory of employers of certified automobile mechanics. It is available for purchase from NIASE, 1825 K Street NW, Washington, D.C. 20006. Ask for the booklet "Where to Find Certified Mechanics for Your Car." From the same address you can also order free a list of employers of NIASE certified mechanics in your state.

Another organization called the Certified Automotive Repairmen's Society (CARS) issued certification credentials until the late 1970s when it merged with NIASE. You may still find some of the CARS credentials on display, either as uniform patches or wall certificates.

Estimates, Guarantees, and Returned Parts

Only deal with those shops that are willing to treat you fairly. There are certain criteria to go by:

1. A reputable shop will agree to a written estimate and will agree not to exceed that estimate without checking with you first.

Fig. 6-2 The role of the automotive mechanic is a vital one and this sign assures the customer that the mechanic has successfully passed the NIASE tests and has a high degree of competency. This certification is also displayed as a shoulder patch and wall hanging.

2. Don't let someone talk you out of an estimate because "they can't say what's wrong until it's taken apart." These situations happen, but most shops will give you an estimate for the work necessary to make a diagnosis and then get an authorization from you to actually make the repair. (However, if you refuse to authorize the repair, you may have to pay to put the whole job back together, if it was disassembled.)

3. Ask for a written guarantee. Major parts are usually guaranteed by the manufacturer for 90 days or 4,000 miles, whichever comes first. If the work is major, such as a transmission overhaul or engine rebuild, the guarantee may be longer.

4. Most reputable shops will agree to show you the old, replaced parts or to furnish these parts unless they had to be returned to the manufacturer for warranty reasons. In some states they *have* to; see Appendix.

Once you've found a good mechanic, don't change without good reason. If he switches to another shop, take your business where he goes. And, make sure that you treat him fairly, if you expect to be treated fairly in return.

7

Dealing with Your Mechanic

Getting your car repaired can be a tricky business, especially for the car owner who has little knowledge of how to go about it. But there are certain steps that you can take to make things go easier.

Begin by realizing that the car owner who casually enters a shop and demands immediate attention has already started off on the wrong foot. Repair shops, whether dealerships or independent one-man operations, are in business to make money—and time is money to a mechanic. Except in emergencies, it's always best to make an appointment, either over the phone or in person. Plan on discussing the problem and making a date for service. This will allow the shop to make sure they have the parts on hand and that someone will be available to work on the car. If you find that you cannot keep the appointment, be sure to call and tell someone as soon as possible. The shop owner or mechanic will appreciate your awareness of his workload, which will be heavy if he does good work.

Once you get to the shop, don't try to do the mechanic's job. Mechanics are professionals and take a great deal of pride in their abilities, especially when they are specialists. It is your responsibility as the car owner to completely and accurately describe the car's symptoms to the mechanic or service manager. Don't try to diagnose the problem, but give all the clues you can. This will save their time and your money, and avoid unnecessary parts replacement.

◆ Describe the Problem

Descriptions of the symptoms are much more useful to the mechanic or service writer than just saying the car won't start. Tell the service man how the car sounds and how it feels when you drive it. Point out any unusual odor or any drips under the car. Don't leave anything out. Such clues as when the problem occurs (for example, when the engine is hot or cold) can give the mechanic an indication of the problem's cause. Let him know how long the trouble has been occurring. Don't be bashful if the repair has been neglected; tell him anyway.

Also be prepared to tell him what maintenance was performed and when it was done. It is valuable to keep a maintenance log to avoid lapses of memory. Of course, if you deal with the same shop, they will be familiar with your car and its service history.

Back up your verbal description of the symptoms with a written list. This will be especially helpful if you're dealing with a large shop where the work will be passed from the service writer to the mechanic. Include a phone number where you can be reached during the day in case any questions need to be answered. (If you don't feel you can adequately put the problem into words, ask the service man to go with you for a test drive.)

The rest is up to the service expert. Let him put his equipment and expertise to work to arrive at the proper solution.

Tell him he can have the car as long as necessary to do the job properly. If you don't demand the car back the same day, chances are the shop will do the job as soon as possible. In some cases, the only way the shop can even find the problem is to keep the car overnight or long enough to duplicate the conditions which make it malfunction.

◆ The Work Order and Estimate

The service manager at a large shop, or the mechanic at a smaller one, will list the items to be done on a form, sometimes called a work order. He will almost always ask you to sign it. This is your promise to pay for the work done. Read it very carefully to be sure you understand everything and that everything is listed correctly. If you can't make sense out of the comments on the work order, ask for clarification. Be wary of blanket statements such as "Check and correct transmission noise" or "Repair engine." You could wind up with a new transmission or engine. Never sign a blank order, and never tell the shop personnel to "do what is necessary," unless you have a lot of money to burn or the problem will clearly be covered by warranty. Instead, ask what exactly is being done and how much it will cost you. Before signing the order, read any fine print in the corners or on the back.

Request a copy of the written estimate and insist on a notation that you be called if the work will exceed the estimate or if they are not sure how much work will be necessary. Tell him you would like to see any replaced parts when you return to pick up the car. Most good shops will comply unless the parts must be returned to the maker for warranty reasons or sent to a specialist for rebuilding. However, you still have a right to see them before they're sent away.

If you just want something checked, expect to pay a diagnosis fee. Some shops will charge to check components which must be taken apart to determine the trouble. Considerable labor and time charges can be involved in this type of work.

Dealing with the Repair Shop

- Call ahead for an appointment.
- If only a few of the shop's mechanics are certified, ask that a certified mechanic do the repair work on your car.
- Describe the problem as specifically as possible to the mechanic who will work on your car or to the service manager.
- Don't tell the shop what repairs to do unless you are absolutely sure that the repairs are needed.
- Ask for a written estimate and tell the shop to get your OK for any additional repair work.
- If you are asking for a diagnosis of the problem, ask the shop how much the diagnosis will cost if you don't have the repair work done.
- Ask for the return of replaced parts.
- Make sure to get any guarantees in writing and ask the shop to explain time limitations or other restrictions on guarantees.

◆ Checking the Repair Bill

Before you go to pick up the car, call to ask if it is ready. Something could have delayed the work, so don't make a trip in vain.

When you pick up the car, check the receipt. If there is anything you don't understand, ask about it. Make sure you save your copy. If you find out later the repair work didn't solve your car's problem, you will need the receipt to confirm what work was done on the car. These receipts provide a good record of all repair and maintenance work done on the car.

Make sure you get a copy of the shop's warranty. It usually is printed on the bill. Otherwise, ask for it in writing.

Feel free to ask for a test drive. After all, if the car is still not running right, it is best not to take it home. If you discover the problem is not solved after you leave the garage, return as soon as possible and request satisfaction.

A repair bill is actually a contract for automotive service performed on your car. In many cases, you're talking about a major investment, so give it the same attention you give other large expenditures. You are entitled to—and should request—an itemized bill for any extensive repair job. The bill should be completely and properly filled out, in-

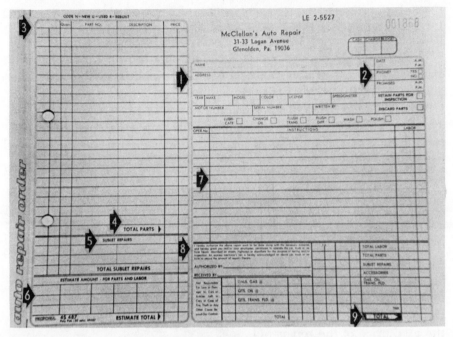

Fig. 7-1 Parts of a typical repair bill.

1. All of this information (name, address, make/model of car, etc.) should be recorded on the bill. In particular, the odometer reading and the name of the person giving the estimate should be recorded.

2. Be sure to leave a phone number where you can be reached in case a problem develops, or if you have to be contacted for some other reason.

3. This is the space where the parts used in the repair are listed. The quantity, part number, description of the part, and the price should all appear.

4. The total cost of the parts used.

5. This portion of the bill is for sublet repairs. Sublet repairs are those not actually performed by the shop, such as towing or machine shop operations.

6. This is the estimated amount for parts and labor to do the work stated in #7.

7. This is the area of the bill that states exactly what is to be done. Be sure that you have provided explicit instructions or have given as much pertinent information as possible.

8. Your signature is required here. Although the wording varies according to the individual form, it basically states that you authorize the repair and give your permission for the car to be operated in the course of the repair and in testing the results of the repair. Be sure to read this section carefully.

9. This is the total amount you will be expected to pay and is the total cost for labor, parts, sublet repairs, accessories, and fluids. Some states specify that the total may not be more than a stated percentage of the estimate, unless your permission has been obtained.

cluding things such as your name, car description, and mileage (so you can remember when it was last serviced).

The following charges should be itemized on your repair bill:

- Parts—prices and description
- Service charges and description

- Subcontracting (this is for specialized services that may be sent out, such as rebuilding of parts, turning brake drums, etc.)

The first thing you want to do is to compare the final total with the original estimated price given you when you discussed the work and left the car at the shop.

Next, compare the list and charges for parts against the work you asked to be done. For instance, a minor-tune-up could include points, condensor, and spark plugs—6 for a 6-cylinder engine, 8 for a V-8. It could also include a carburetor air filter, a PCV valve, and maybe even a PCV filter.

Other things that may sometimes be part of a tune-up are an oil change, a new oil filter, and maybe a new fuel filter. If you have a 6-cylinder car and you're paying for 8 plugs, then it's time to say something to your mechanic.

Once the parts list matches reasonably with the work your car needed, the next item to check is the shop labor charge. The time it took to do the job multiplied by the shop's hourly rate will give you the total labor cost. The labor cost plus the parts cost and tax will be the total price of the repair bill.

If you think you have been overcharged, ask the shop owner to show you the basis for his labor charges. If he doesn't use a professional automotive labor guide which reveals the average times to do given automotive service work, he may be running his business and calculating his charges by the seat of his pants; and you're the one paying for this poor management.

You'll want to be extra careful about repair work performed on a car covered by warranty. Most warranties do not cover normal maintenance. However, where defects and the correction of failures are involved, you shouldn't have to pay for normal parts and labor involved in this type of warranty work. So be sure you know what is covered and then keep a watchful eye on your repair bill.

Not everyone is out to rip you off. Your bill could be higher than you expected for any one of a number of legitimate reasons. Your mechanic might even have installed a part now that he knows you'll need within a month or so. You've shopped carefully for your mechanic and you can be fairly certain of reliable service. But it's still wise to check the repair bill before you pull out your checkbook.

◆ If You Have a Complaint

Most complaints involving car repairs are a result of misunderstanding or a lack of communication and can be straightened out to everyone's satisfaction before it becomes a major issue.

Here are some general points to remember before registering a complaint:

1. Make sure that the first person you contact is the person closest to the problem. By starting with this person, usually the mechanic or service writer, you will hear the arguments on the other side, and they may be quite valid. If it turns out you were wrong, you may be glad you started out this way.

2. In the case of product complaints, if you purchased or installed the part yourself, try settling the matter with the store where you purchased the part. If a mechanic installed the parts, check with him. Most parts carry a warranty or the mechanic should be willing to correct the problem to keep your business and goodwill. If either of the above fail, contact the manufacturer or his representative. (See also the chapter on warranties.)

3. Know what your warranty covers and does not cover. And be sure you know what your responsibilities are to keep the warranty in effect.

4. Don't put off doing something about problems. The quicker you complain, the better off you're going to be.

5. The keeping of records is essential to any complaint. Insist on itemized receipts for service work, even if there is no charge. Many times in the course of a dispute an owner will complain about repeated attempts to have work performed, only to find that they have no records of when work was supposed to have been performed and by whom. Make sure the receipt or your copy of the work order mentions everything that was done and lists the part numbers of parts that were installed.

6. Be persistent, but polite. If they know you'll keep coming back until it's fixed, it will probably be done properly.

7. Disputes between car owners and repair shops cannot always be settled by discussion, but do not resort to refusing to pay the bill. In most states, the shop can levy a "mechanic's lien" against your car for unpaid repairs or storage (see Appendix). This is a rare occurrence.

Occasionally, problems arise that cannot be settled without involving other parties. If the service manager in a dealership has not taken sufficient action, there is a definite procedure to follow in complaining to a dealership. The procedure must be followed to the letter.

Service problems with independent repair shops, specialty repair shops, franchised operations, and other shops that are not dealerships should be handled by first contacting the shop manager or owner. If the problem cannot be satisfactorily resolved at this level, follow steps 3 through 7 below.

1. Take your complaint to the general manager or owner.

2. Write to the manufacturer's zone office. The addresses will be listed in the owner's manual or in the phone book. Your complaint to the zone office should include the following:

Your name, address, and telephone number
Vehicle Identification Number (from the registration or the plate attached to the dashboard visible through the windshield)
Dealer's name and address
Vehicle delivery date and mileage
Nature of problem

3. Write to the Consumer Relations Representative at the manufacturer's or franchise operator's address, which is listed in the owner's manual. This representative will review the facts and instruct the zone office on what action to take. In any case, your correspondence will be acknowledged. Keep in mind that the problem will likely be resolved at the local dealership, using the dealer's tools and personnel, so be firm, but polite and courteous.

4. In the unlikely event that none of these steps brings about a resolution of the problem, send a brief, typewritten, registered letter to the manufacturer's or franchise operator's service manager or vice-president in charge of sales, with copies to the dealer, zone representative, local Better Business Bureau, and state consumer protection agency.

5. You can also complain to a mediator. The city, county or state consumer protection agencies can recommend mediation services that may or may not be binding on the parties involved. One of the mediation services that has obtained good results is AUTOCAP (Automotive Consumer Action Panel). It was formed in 1973, and now exists in eighteen states. They usually meet monthly and can be reached through the phone book, by contacting the Better Business Bureau or by writing AUTOCAP, National Automobile Dealer Association, 1640 West Park Drive, McClean, VA 22101.

AUTOCAP reviews your records (you must have them) and puts you in touch with the right person at the dealership or the manufacturer. If the two parties cannot reach a settlement, the case is brought before an AUTOCAP panel, which usually consists of six representatives—three volunteer consumers and three volunteer dealers. The decision of AUTOCAP is not binding on either party, but the organization has a great deal of leverage with dealers. They also mediate in disputes with insurance companies and finance companies, but they cannot become involved with independent service establishments because they have no leverage with them.

6. The next step is to register your complaint directly with a formal

city, county or state consumer protection agency, the state attorney-general's office, or the U.S. Office of Consumer Affairs. It should be noted that these organizations are different from the organizations mentioned in the preceding paragraph. These organizations are funded government agencies as opposed to agencies independent of the city, county, or state governments. There are other agencies and consumer groups that handle consumer complaints depending on whom your gripe is directed at. An incomplete list follows; you should also see the Appendix on automobile repair laws.

American Automobile Association (AAA)
  8111 Gatehouse Road
  Falls Church, Virginia 22042
Canada Safety Council
  1765 St. Laurent Boulevard
  Ottawa, Ontario K1G 3V4
Car and Truck Renting and Leasing Association
  1725 K Street, N.W.
  Washington, D.C. 20006
Consumer Services Branch
  Department of Consumer and Corporate Affairs
  1 Place du Portage
  Ottawa/Hull, Ontario K1A 0C9
Council of Better Business Bureaus, Inc.
  1150 17th Street, N.W.
  Washington, D.C. 20036
Department of Health, Education and Welfare
  Office of Consumer Affairs
  621 Reporters Building
  Washington, D.C. 20201
Federation of Automobile Dealer Associations of Canada
  2221 Yonge Street, Suite 606
  Toronto, Ontario M4S 1B6
Federal Trade Commission
  Bureau of Consumer Protection,
  Pennsylvania Avenue at 6th Street, N.W.
  Washington, D.C., 20580 (or its regional offices)
Independent Garage Owners of America
  624 South Michigan Avenue
  Chicago, Illinois 60605
Insurance Bureau of Canada
  181 University Avenue
  Toronto, Ontario M5H 3M7

National Automobile Dealers Association
  8400 Westpark Drive
  McLean, Virginia 22101
National Highway Traffic Safety Administration
  Office of Public Affairs and Consumer Services
  400 7th Street, S.W.
  Washington, D.C. 20590
National Institute for Automotive Service Excellence
  1825 K Street, N.W.
  Washington, D.C. 20006
United States Department of Transportation
  400 7th Street, S.W.
  Washington, D.C. 20590
White House Office of Consumer Affairs
  New Executive Office Building
  Washington, D.C. 20506
The State Attorney General, in your state capital

7. As a last resort, you can take the case to court. A case involving a relatively small amount of money will often be heard in small claims court where you can file without the aid of a lawyer. If a substantial amount of money is involved, you'll probably need the services of a lawyer.

◆ Ten Commandments of Auto Repair

If you know someone who leads a charmed life when it comes to automobiles—no service problems, no gripes when their car or truck goes to a dealer for service—that someone is not just lucky. He or she simply knows how to make the vehicle servicing system work for, instead of against, them. These ten commandments of auto repair can make life easier for you and your mechanic.

1. *Practice preventive maintenance.* All manufacturers establish a schedule of routine servicing procedures for every model they make. This maintenance is designed to prevent expensive mechanical malfunctions by servicing certain vehicle systems and components at specified intervals. Learn as much as possible about your car and follow these suggested preventive procedures. Your chances of having car trouble will drop sharply.

2. *Give thought to the appointment time.* Knowing when to take your car in for service is as important as knowing where. Avoid Mondays like the plague if you're going to a new car dealer. Not only is everybody jamming the dealer's service drive following a weekend, but you have to compete for time with repair jobs left over from the previous week. Fridays are not much better. Mechanics are trying to

finish all those cars promised "for the weekend." Save yourself some grief and target Tuesday, Wednesday, or Thursday as appointment day at dealerships.

3. *Prepare for the appointment.* If you're having warranty work done on a new car, be sure to have the right papers with you. Take your warranty folder. The writeup man needs your Vehicle Identification Number (VIN) for processing your work. Keep a service log on your car and bring it with you. This gives the service people your car's maintenance history and can often provide clues to possible causes of your current problem. Don't keep secrets. If you've had an accident or something done to your car that's not on your maintenance log, let him know.

4. *Prepare a list.* Make a written list of your car's problems or the specific work you want done. Your car is only one of hundreds a busy shop sees in a week, and it's impossible for him to remember each detail of every conversation with a car owner. Help the mechanic (and yourself) with a written list.

5. *Be specific in your requests.* "I'm going on a trip; do what needs to be done." This is an open invitation to misunderstandings and contested service bills. Write down what *you* think needs to be done, then ask for the service writer's suggestions. When you leave the car, leave with it a mutually agreed upon list of items to be serviced, and a mutually agreed upon cost estimate.

6. *Be reasonable in your requests.* Don't leave a list of twenty items needing attention and then expect to have your car back by five o'clock. Larger repair facilities have specialists, and your car may need the attention of several service technicians. If you list multiple items, and you must have your car at day's end, discuss the situation with the service writer and list the items in order of priority. Expect to make a second appointment for work not completed during the first.

7. *Leave no living creatures for service.* Ridiculous as it may seem, people will leave small animals in their car, saying to the repairman, "Just ignore him, he won't bite." They'll also park their children in the waiting room. Repair shops service automobiles; very few provide babysitting service.

8. *Don't insist on watching.* Don't be offended when you're told you can't watch the work. Insurance requirements usually bar the admission of customers to vehicle repair areas. Plus, the service technician is like most of us . . . he doesn't like working with someone looking over his shoulder. With the complexity of today's automobiles, any distraction during a servicing procedure is one too many.

9. *Make complaints promptly.* Check out the service or repair job as soon after picking up your car as possible, and notify the service manager of any dissatisfaction then—not six weeks later. If circumstances

prevent your returning for immediate corrective work, make an appointment for as early a date as practical.

10. *Cherish your service professional.* A good mechanic deserves your continuing business. If you've received a good job on a previous maintenance or service trip, return to that shop for more service. Like your doctor or dentist, those professionals will get to know you and your requirements. You'll benefit from the long-time relationship and be surprised at how far a little bit of thought and preparation will take you.

8

Warranties

Loosely defined, a warranty is a guarantee of the integrity of a product, the manufacturer's expression of good faith that he will repair or replace defective parts or workmanship for a stated period of time. The warranty may apply to cars, parts, or services purchased by the consumer.

There are basically two kinds of warranties—expressed and implied. An expressed warranty is that which is stated, either in black and white or as an assurance by the salesperson. An implied warranty is intended, suggested, or understood, though it is not specifically stated. It is usually these implied warranties that manufacturers are guarding against when they say words to the effect that "there are no warranties, either expressed or implied, other than those stated herein. . . ." But the implied warranty that the car do what can be reasonably expected is firmly grounded in law.

◆ New/Used Car Warranties

Find out about the warranty on any new or used car in detail. There is considerable variation in warranties, but virtually all car warranties will *not* cover:

- Tires (these are warranted for detects by the tire manufacturer)
- Travel outside U.S. and Canada (regulations applying to the manufacture of cars and light trucks are practically identical in both countries, while regulations in other countries, including Mexico, are quite different)
- Abuse (most warranties state that the car must be properly maintained)

Car warranties are a lot like contracts, insofar as they're valid only as long as both parties abide by the provisions. "Normal maintenance" as spelled out in the owner's manual is your part of the bargain. It includes such things as oil changes, filters, and tune-ups, to keep the car in good condition. The dealer's part of the bargain is to repair or replace any defective parts or workmanship covered by the warranty.

The wording of most warranties implies that you should have the maintenance and repair work performed by the local dealer. However, you can take your vehicle to any competent garage or service establishment to have work done, or you can do the work yourself. You can also buy parts and lubricants of any quality brand, as long as they meet the manufacturer's specifications. Just make sure to save the receipts and bills for any parts or work that you have done. Documentation is the key to successful resolution of warranty or service problems in general.

New car warranties generally run for 12 months or 12,000 miles, whichever comes first, from the date of purchase, though a few new car warranties run longer. For an extra fee that varies with manufacturers, you can purchase an extended warranty plan, which amounts to buying insurance. As an example, Ford's extended warranty covers a new car or truck for 36 months/36,000 miles, provided the warranty is purchased within 90 days from date of car purchase. It is available only to the original buyer or lessee. Cost of the plan varies from $150 for small cars to $275 for big cars.

No two used-car warranties are the same, so read them carefully. A dealer selling a used car will probably offer a 30-day or 1,000-mile warranty. Some dealers will want to split the cost of repairs 50/50 with you, while others will offer a 100% warranty. Be sure that you get the warranty in writing and signed by the seller before you buy the car.

◆ Parts and Repair Warranties

Almost all repair shops guarantee their work and parts, and most parts manufacturers warrant their parts to perform as expected. The guarantee from a repair shop should be in writing, or printed on the repair bill itself. It should specify the length of time for which it is valid, or the amount of mileage during which it is effective. Usually repair work and parts are warranted for 90 days or 3,000 miles, whichever comes first, though this will vary depending on the part or the shop.

In the case of repair work, be sure you understand whether only parts or labor is covered, or both. The guarantee may last as long as you own your car or it may void itself if the car is sold, as is the case with the warranty offered by major muffler chains.

Some work will not be warranted at all, for instance, custom installations of exhaust systems, installation of nonstandard parts, or the installation of parts that are not considered original equipment. The latter could apply to custom exhaust systems, speed or high-performance equipment, or work which requires altering the emission system.

◆ Emission Control Systems Warranty

The emission control and related system parts are warranted differently than other parts of the car. According to federal law, if:

- Your car is less than five years old and has less than 50,000 miles, *and*
- An original engine part fails because of a defect in materials or workmanship, *and*
- The part failure causes your car to exceed federal emissions standards,

then the car manufacturer must repair or replace the defective part. This protection is afforded by the Emissions Design and Defect Warranty required by the Clean Air Act.

The emissions warranty applies to all motor vehicles manufactured since 1972, including cars, pick-ups, recreational vehicles, trucks, and motorcycles. However, the length of the warranty coverage, as expressed by a time or mileage limitation called "useful life," is different for each type of vehicle. The length of warranty coverage or useful life that applies to your vehicle is stated in the emissions warranty description in your owner's manual or warranty booklet (beginning with 1972 models). For most cars this is five years or 50,000 miles, whichever comes first.

Parts that do not have a stated replacement interval in the maintenance instructions are warranted for the useful life of the vehicle. Parts with a stated replacement interval, such as, "replace at 15,000 miles or 12 months," are warranted up to the first replacement point only. Finally, parts that are the subject of some maintenance instruction that requires them to be "checked and replaced if necessary" are warranted for the entire period of warranty coverage.

Under the law, each manufacturer must honor the warranty if the three conditions listed above are met. It does not matter if you brought your car new or used, from a dealer or from anyone else. As long as your vehicle has not exceeded the warranty time or mileage limitations, the warranty applies.

What Parts Are Covered?

Coverage of parts under the emission control systems warranty includes: (1) any part whose primary purpose is to control emissions, and (2) any part that has an effect on emissions. These parts are listed in the sections below. Parts are often given different names by different manufacturers, and one manufacturer may use more parts than another, so the following lists may not be complete for all vehicles.

If you or a mechanic can show that a part in one of the listed systems is defective, it is probably covered under the emissions warranty. When you believe you have identified a defective part that may be covered you should make a warranty claim to the manufacturer using the procedures in your owner's manual or warranty booklet.

EMISSIONS CONTROL PARTS

These are parts which the manufacturer has included in the car to control emissions. If one of these parts fails because of a defect in materials or workmanship, it should be repaired or replaced under the emissions warranty:

Exhaust Gas Recirculation (EGR) System
  EGR valve
  EGR spacer plate
  Thermal vacuum switch
  EGR backpressure transducer
Evaporative Emissions Control System
  Evaporative canister
Crankcase Emissions Control System
  PCV valve
Early Fuel Evaporative (EFE)/Heat Riser Systems
  EFE valve
  Thermal vacuum switch
  Heat riser valve
Air Injection System
  Air pump
  Anti-backfire (diverter) valve
  Reed valve
Catalytic and Exhaust Gas Conversion Systems
  Catalytic converter
  Thermal reactor
  Oxygen sensor
Spark Advance Control System
  Vacuum advance unit
  Transmission controlled spark switches
  Electronic spark controls
Hoses, gaskets, brackets, clamps, and other accessories used in the
  above systems.

EMISSIONS RELATED PARTS

There are other parts of your car which have significant effects on your car's emissions. When any of these parts are defective in materials or workmanship and have failed in a way that would be likely to cause your car's emissions to exceed federal standards, they should be repaired or replaced under the emissions warranty:

Carburetion System
  Carburetor
  Choke
Fuel Injection System
  Fuel injectors
  Fuel distributor
Air Induction System
  Thermostatically controlled air cleaner
  Air box
Ignition System
  Distributor
  Electronic controls
  Spark plugs
  Ignition wires and coil
Hoses, gaskets, brackets, clamps, and other accessories used in the above systems.

Lack of Scheduled Maintenance

Performance of scheduled maintenance is your responsibility. You are expected to perform scheduled maintenance yourself or have a qualified mechanic perform it for you. If a part failure is a direct result of your car not being maintained or used according to the manufacturer's recommendations, the manufacturer may not be required to repair or replace the failed part under the emissions warranty.

Proof of maintenance is not required in order to obtain coverage under the emissions warranty. However, when lack of scheduled maintenance could have caused the particular part failure, you may be asked to show that scheduled maintenance was performed.

Use of Leaded Gas

When leaded gas is used in cars requiring unleaded fuel, the emission controls (particularly the catalytic converter) may be affected. In addition, lead deposits will form inside the engine and, under certain circumstances, may contribute to the failure of an engine part. The emissions warranty does not cover any part failures that result from the use of leaded fuel in a car that requires unleaded fuel.

CHAPTER

9

Buying a New Car

Remember the first snowy day of the season when you couldn't get the engine in the family car to turn over? You needed a new battery that time. And just last week the fuel pump went. For the past couple of months you've been dreaming of a shiny new car, with at least a year's worth of warranty coverage and a minimum of upkeep. Maybe a compact this time.

If a good car is high on your list of life's priorities, you wouldn't buy a used one any more than you would buy a used hairpiece. You're going to order a new car, one meeting your specifications. Although the price is going to be high (the average price of a new car is currently around $6,500), you have to consider it in the relative scheme of things.

In 1980, the $6,500 average purchase price of a new car represents about 36% of the median national income of approximately $18,000. That's a bargain, when you figure that in 1970, a new car was 38% of the national median income, and in 1960, a new car cost even more dearly—about 50% of the average Americans' wages. And in 1950, the figure was a whopping 66% of the median income.

Though the absolute cost of new cars has increased considerably, so has the value of used cars. If you've kept yours in good running condition, you may be pleasantly surprised at how much trade-in value it actually has.

Give careful consideration to any leftover models your dealer has before you pass them by. It's true that a leftover model is technically a year old when you buy it, but three years from now, when it's competing with the even more expensive new cars, it may not do badly at all.

Or, if you're considering an economy car this time, maybe you can get by with standard transmission and brakes. And if you want the versatility of a station wagon but don't like the high prices of full-size models, maybe you can get by with a hatchback or wagon model in the compact line.

◆ Decide What You Want

Since the family cars we buy add up over time to the largest investment next to housing that most of us ever make, it's a good idea to spend some time and thought before you spend any money. Car salesmen tell amazing stories about sales concluded for the most inconsequential, even ridiculous reasons after only a few minutes in the showroom or on the lot. Not that buying a car from the dealer's stock may not be justified under certain circumstances. In most cases, though, it will be to your benefit to consider your needs very carefully and order your new car accordingly.

Naturally, everyone is influenced to some degree by brand loyalty, advertising, or reputation, but the important point is to buy what you really need. A subcompact will not pull a camping trailer, but you probably don't need a full-size car if most of your driving consists of relatively short trips by two or three people.

After you have decided that you want or need another car, set down some definite criteria—subcompact or intermediate, room for four people, type of engine, and so on. Only then is it time to start making the rounds of dealers. Some factors to consider are described below.

SIZE (WEIGHT)

If maximum fuel economy is your goal, weight of the car is the single most important factor. Roughly, each 500-pounds gain in weight over 2,000 pounds will cost you 2 to 5 mpg. On the other hand, the fuel economy penalty for heavier cars is less if most of your driving is at sustained highway speeds.

BODY STYLE

Body style will be determined largely by your needs and the way you use a car or truck. Generally, the smallest car that fits your needs will be most economical.

ENGINES

All other factors being equal, smaller engines are considered more economical to operate, but this can be deceiving. One of the biggest mistakes new car buyers make is to underpower their car. This is particularly true with intermediate and larger-size cars. Although manufacturers advertise the smaller engines to make their fleet average

Table 9-1
What Size Car is Best for You?

Size	Advantages	Disadvantages
Subcompact	Costs least Best gas mileage Easiest to handle Simpler engines Cheapest to run, maintain	Stiff ride Very limited space All options not available
Compact	Costs a little more Good gas mileage Good for commuting Easy to handle Cheap to run, maintain	Somewhat stiff ride Limited space Options somewhat limited

Intermediate	Good room and comfort
	Fairly easy to handle
	Good choice of engines,
	    options*
	Fairly cheap to run, maintain
		Costs quite a bit more
		Lower gas mileage
		Not as good for big families,
		    heavy loads as full-size

Full-size	Most comfortable
	Widest choice of engines,
	    options*
	Best long-trip car
	Best for heavy loads
		Costs most to buy, run,
		    maintain
		Hardest to handle
		Lowest gas mileage

*It is worthwhile to note that many of the options previously reserved for full-size and luxury cars are beginning to be offered on intermediate and compact models, as these cars become more popular.

economy as high as possible, in fact, compared to weight, engine size is not a significant factor in fuel economy *at highway speeds.*

Depending on the use of the car, it may be to your advantage to have a slightly larger engine. While a larger engine will almost invariably use slightly more fuel in urban-type driving, you may need the extra power to run a car laden with accessories or to haul heavy loads. A smaller engine may have to work much harder to do the same job, requiring more frequent maintenance and service.

EASE OF SERVICE

If you plan to maintain the car yourself, look for easy accessibility of parts frequently replaced (plugs, filters, lube fittings, and so on). Even if you don't want dirty hands, an unavoidable price of working on the car, easy accessibility can mean cheaper mechanic's bills.

◆ **When to Shop**

New car prices vary according to supply and demand, just as those of other products. The best time to look for a deal on a new car is the end of the month when salesmen are looking for sales to make their quotas.

Many dealerships run monthly sales incentive programs, and many salesmen have quotas to meet each month. Depending on the circumstances, the salesman may be willing to take a slightly lower commission, somewhere between what you want to pay and what the sales manager will accept, to sell a car. During the winter months when sales are traditionally slow, and near the end of the model year when dealers are trying to clear out overstocks of the previous year's models, are also good times to shop for a new car. Keep in mind that if you buy a new car in August or September, it will be considered a year old and depreciate accordingly in a few months.

Fig. 9-1 One of the best times to buy a new car is in the fall, when dealers are trying to clear out their stocks to make way for the new models.

In addition to the ideal buying times, there are other factors to consider. If you're shopping for a mileage-maker economy car, do not try to find a good time to look for a "deal"—there *is* none. Dealers can move all of the economy cars they can get their hands on at the price they are asking. On the other hand, prices for full-size cars or cars the public perceives as gas guzzlers have seldom been lower. These cars are extremely difficult to move, and you can almost always work some kind of a deal on them.

Some manufacturers have resorted to offering rebates on selected models of cars in an effort to reduce inventories or move certain models. The rebate is a one-time cash refund from the manufacturer and is the equivalent of a discount. Rebates are usually in effect for a stated time period and apply only to stated models, so you have to be aware of the manufacturers' advertising.

◆ Car Brokers

New-car dealers are the traditional source of new cars. A much more limited source and a thorn in the side of the dealer is a car buying service, such as a broker. Brokers, unlike new-car dealers, are not limited to handling certain manufacturers although they rarely have access to all makes and models. They buy a selection of new cars from a variety of dealers and sell them through various organizations and associations. Because they usually buy in volume, their big advantage is that they can offer an attractive price on given makes and models. Their disadvantages are inconvenient locations that may make it difficult to test-drive a particular car or to inspect the car you wish to purchase and the lack of facilities for servicing the car after you buy it. While it is under warranty, the manufacturer's dealers are obligated to service the car, but they may wonder out loud why the car is being brought to them for service when they did not sell it to you.

Some brokers, such as Car Puter, operate slightly differently. You send the broker a small fee, usually $5 to $10, along with the list of options you want. Car Puter will send you a computer printout of the car you want to buy listing the dealer cost of the car, including options, and the list price. Comparing the two prices will give you a good idea of just how much the dealer is making on the deal, and you can haggle with the dealer from there.

If you can't get the deal you want from the dealer, you can then buy the car from the broker, who will deliver the car to a participating dealer in your area and make a commission on the sale.

For service, you can consider that the car was bought from the dealer, since he made a profit on the sale (although, as mentioned above, the dealer is *obligated* to handle warranty work no matter where the car was purchased).

◆ Selecting Your Options

After much soul searching and shopping around, you've finally narrowed your choices down to a few models. How do you decide which car is really going to give you the most for your money?

Start by comparing the sticker prices of the models and paying close attention to exactly what equipment each includes. "Standard equipment" is a flexible term, and there is a lot of difference in its meaning from one domestic car maker to another. What one car maker offers as standard equipment may easily be considered an option by others.

Beyond the essential parts needed to make the car run, the more equipment you get for the same money, the better off you are. Options can add up fast, and can drive up the price of your car by the hundreds before you know it. But there are many options well worth the extra cost. If you pull a trailer or haul heavy loads, options such as the trailer pulling package (heavy duty components matched to your car model), auxiliary transmission oil coolers, or air-adjustable, load-leveling shock absorbers are relatively inexpensive and worth the extra cost.

Some options that you can probably do without, except in special circumstances, include grossly oversized tires, fender flares, spoilers, power mirrors, power seats, power windows, and the like. Unless you have a real need for or just can't live without convenience or stylized accessories such as these, skip them, as they're only going to drive the price of the car sky-high and add to your fuel costs as well.

Performance-Related Parts

These are "extras" like radial tires, disc brakes, and overdrive transmission, which no one will know you have but will make all the difference in the way your car handles and performs. And they can help you achieve the maximum degree of economy. Radial tires and disc brakes may be either standard or optional equipment.

Manual overdrive transmission is a great thing to have if you do a lot of highway driving, saving you gas and reducing wear and tear on your car. If you plan to use your car for quick jaunts around town, forget it. Look at it as one of those things that are nice to have if the manufacturer throws them in free, but don't order it unless you really need it.

Comfort/Convenience Accessories

Usually optional on domestic models, these accessories are an area where import cars have a definite edge. It's not unusual to find tinted glass, radio, and rear-window defogger as standard equipment on one of the imported models. You probably shouldn't let the presence or lack of a radio influence your decision very much, especially since you can always buy one later and install it in your car for a lot less.

Air conditioning is almost never considered standard equipment. Where you live plays an important part in your decision as to whether you need it or not. And remember that the performance and the fuel economy of your car are probably going to suffer if you have air conditioning—but you will be comfortable.

Style/Trim Accessories

These have no real function, except for body side moldings that protect your car from parking lot dents. Body moldings are usually inexpensive and worth the extra cost, although there are many excellent do-it-yourself kits on the market that are both inexpensive and every bit as protective as the factory equipment. In fact, several major manufacturers of body molding kits supply the original equipment to the car manufacturer.

Most style accessories are usually described in glowing terms like "deluxe custom interior," "custom wheel covers," and "sport package." If you're really shopping for a bargain, forget about these. There are many kits available to the do-it-yourselfer that can allow you to customize your car nicely without the expense of having the factory do it for you.

◆ Getting What You Want

By choosing wisely, you can tailor your car for maximum performance, economy, durability, comfort, or any combination of these. But don't let the salesman sell you a car that's *almost* like the one you want, unless the price is so good that you can't refuse.

Car salesmen are notorious for not knowing the option list of the cars they sell as well as some of their customers do. And for special-order cars, they also tend to get nervous about cancellations and the resulting loss of commissions. The salesman will not want to order a rare combination of equipment and options on a car that he will have trouble unloading if you back out of the deal. Both of these facts can conspire to prevent you from getting exactly the car you want, so you have to know how to go about ordering.

All salesmen have a book that lists the available options and list prices for any given model. Since it does not include any dealer costs, there is nothing confidential about the book and there is no reason you shouldn't be allowed to see it. In fact, if you are special-ordering a car, insist on seeing it. Don't take the salesman's word that the only transmissions available on the model you want are the automatic and three-speed manual or that you can get bucket seats only on the two-door model.

You should also check for free or low-cost promotional package deals offered by the factory to sell slow-moving options or combinations. Certain combinations may be offered at bargain prices, but these are bargains *only* if you really want the options in the first place and if they cost substantially below the list price.

Another thing you should be aware of is something called the "mandatory options." These are options that are required by various states or localities, or options that are required with certain equipment. There is, for example, the California Emission Certification Test, and even though it *is* required, you'll find it listed as an "option" on the invoice, because it's required only of cars sold in California. Similarly, New York State requires that all cars sold there be equipped with a rear-window defogger, and New York City requires that all cars sold there be equipped with both "city" and "country" horns that produce different sounds.

Other mandatory options are those required by the manufacturer when you order a car with certain equipment. For example, depending on the manufacturer, you may have to purchase a heavy-duty cooling system when you purchase air conditioning, because the heavy-duty cooling system allows the car to handle the added burden of air conditioning. Other manufacturers may simply include the cooling system with the air conditioning option.

Before you sign on the dotted line, it's wise to check all the equipment that you ordered, to be sure you are getting exactly the equipment you want.

◆ EPA Mileage Estimates

How realistic are the EPA mileage estimates? There is no question that a driver's fuel economy in a particular car will vary widely. Complicating the estimate is the fact that cars are even more variable than drivers.

There has been considerable criticism of the EPA fuel consumption figures as being too optimistic. The EPA procedure is useful as a simplified representation of the wide variation in conditions that affect customer fuel consumption. In addition to the driving cycle itself, it establishes many standard test conditions for variables such as type of fuel, ambient temperature, and "soak time" (elapsed time since vehicle was last operated, which affects warm-up conditions). Though the specifications are meant to be representative, each introduces into the

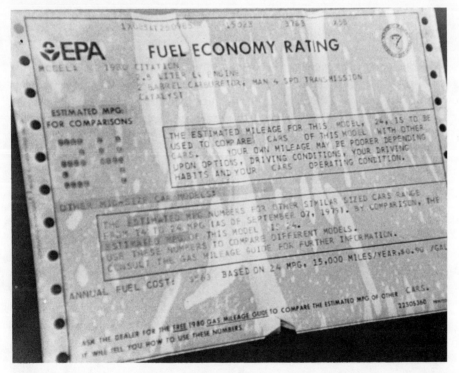

Fig. 9-2 All new cars must display an EPA mileage estimate for combined city/highway driving. Mileage will vary with many factors, including the way the car is equipped and your driving habits.

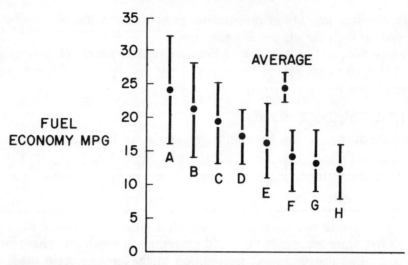

Fig. 9-3 This chart shows the results of tests, published by the Society of Automotive Engineers, that measured the real-world fuel economy of eight different kinds of cars (identified A through H). Drivers of these cars recorded their fuel mileage for three successive tank fillings. The range of fuel economy indicated by the highs and lows is compared to the EPA estimates, shown by the dots.

measurement of fuel consumption a variable which tends to make it higher or lower than customer usage indicates.

As an example, look at the dynamometer tests. The car is run in a stationary position on large rollers that allow the wheels to spin, simulating road speed. Tire rolling resistance is affected by vehicle weight distribution and tire pressure, among other factors. But only one pair of tires (front or rear) is cradled on the dynamometer rollers. Because of this, front-wheel-drive cars can experience higher losses due to tire rolling resistance than rear-wheel-drive cars. Tire pressure also influences rolling resistance, and the EPA specifies an artificially high tire pressure to increase durability during the tests.

Other factors contributing small biases toward the final EPA economy number include road surface type, road state of repair, wind, weather conditions, altitude, engine accessory loads, and customer maintenance. All will affect the actual in-use fuel economy number.

Fuel economy labels are meant to be useful in comparing *relative* economy of cars and in *estimating* the actual fuel consumption experienced in use. Obviously the in-use fuel economy obtained by any given driver/vehicle combination is subject to many variables and cannot be determined exactly.

◆ Depreciation

It is almost impossible to tell with certainty how much your car will depreciate or what it will be worth several years after you have owned it. Determining your car's trade-in value are such factors as gasoline availability vs. your car's fuel economy, frequency of repairs, general public acceptance (popularity), and whether it is an import or American made.

In general, import cars have been holding their value slightly better than their American counterparts, and due to the uncertain gasoline situation, small cars are faring much better than big cars come trade-in time. There are also individual variances within makes/models, depending on individual car condition and equipment. Tables 1-3 and 1-4 give a good idea of the general depreciation rates. Table 9-2 shows percentages of 1975 new-car prices of specific models retained in their 1979 trade-in values.

Table 9-2
1975 New-Car Values Retained in 1979

Type of Car	Percentage of Value Retained (1975 to 1979)
FULL-SIZE LUXURY	
Continental Mark IV	43.1
Buick Riviera	42.4
Buick Le Sabre	41.7
Oldsmobile Delta 88 Royale	41.3
Cadillac Coupe deVille	40.8
Chevrolet Impala	40.7
Oldsmobile 98	39.3
Buick Electra	38.7
Ford LTD	38.3
Cadillac Eldorado	38.1
Pontiac Catalina	37.6
Mercury Marquis	37.2
Lincoln Continental	34.4
Chrysler Newport	34.4
Chrysler New Yorker Brougham	33.6
Oldsmobile Toronado	32.6
COMPACT/SUBCOMPACT	
Chevrolet Corvette	82.1
Pontiac Firebird Trans Am	67.0
Chevrolet Camaro	66.6
Ford Mustang II	54.5
Oldsmobile Omega	52.5
Ford Maverick	51.9
Chevrolet Nova	51.6
Buick Skylark	51.1
Oldsmobile Starfire	50.9
Dodge Dart	50.5
Pontiac Ventura	50.5
Mercury Comet	50.1
Buick Skyhawk	48.9
Plymouth Valiant	48.3
Mercury Bobcat	47.3
Chevrolet Monza 2 + 2	47.2

Table 9-2 (continued)

Type of Car	Percentage of Value Retained (1975 to 1979)
AMC Hornet	47.1
Mercury Monarch	46.7
Ford Granada	46.2
Ford Pinto	44.9
AMC Gremlin	43.4
AMC Pacer	40.7
Pontiac Astre	35.5
MID-SIZE	
Oldsmobile Cutlass Supreme	55.6
Chevrolet Monte Carlo	53.0
Buick Century Regal	51.2
Pontiac Grand Prix	48.9
Pontiac LeMans Sport Coupe	48.8
Ford Elite	47.8
Mercury Cougar XR-7	47.7
Chevrolet Malibu Classic	43.7
Chrysler Cordoba	42.6
Dodge Charger	41.4
Ford Torino	34.7
Mercury Montego	33.9
FOREIGN	
Porsche 9115	82.8
Mercedes-Benz 450SL	79.7
Mercedes-Benz 300D	71.1
BMW 530i	69.6
BMW (320i)	66.7
Datsun 280Z	64.3
Honda Civic	63.8
Volkswagen convertible	62.7
Toyota Celica	61.8
Datsun B210	58.0
Volkswagen Rabbit	57.9
Volkswagen Dasher wagon	55.7
Volvo 245	55.5
Dodge Colt	52.5
Toyota Corona	51.9
Volkswagen Scirocco	51.7
Datsun 610	50.3
Audi Fox	47.8
Subaru wagon	47.1
Fiat 131	41.4
Fiat 128	41.2
Mazda RX-4	35.9
Mazda 808	33.4

◆ Extended Service Contracts

Although virtually all manufacturer's warranties expire at 12 months or 12,000 miles, whichever comes first, extended service contracts can stretch the warranty to as long as 5 years or 50,000 miles, for an extra fee. Most extended service warranties cover basically the same items, with minor differences, so the availability of such a warranty probably will not be a factor in influencing your choice of manufacturer. The extended contract itself, however, may be worthwhile, depending on the use you give the car. Bear in mind that, since the manufacturer is warranting certain parts of the car for a longer interval, he probably expects them to last at least that long anyway. But, if you pile up a very large number of miles in a relatively short period of time (as a traveling salesperson would), the extended service warranty can be beneficial because of the extra mileage allowance.

Almost all U.S. manufacturers and many independent firms offer this extended protection, most of which includes the drive train and air conditioner, which are the big-bucks repairs; other plans cover these in addition to brakes and electrical systems.

Boosters of the extended warranties claim that they reduce the risk of a huge repair bill resulting from a blown engine or transmission, that could easily run as high as $1,000. Critics respond that the extended warranty protects you when you're least likely to need it and won't offer any protection at 80,000 or 100,000 miles, when you're more likely to need it. All of these contracts require that you maintain

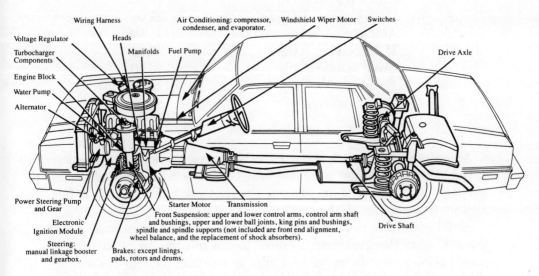

Fig. 9-4 These are some of the typical components covered by extended warranty plans. Note especially what is not covered in this particular plan.

your car "by the book," leading other critics to note that you shouldn't experience driveline problems during the term of the contract if the car is properly maintained. Moreover, manufacturers aren't entirely free of liability for some malfunctions, even after 12 months/12,000 miles (see the section on Emission Control Warranties in Chapter 8).

The best thing is to consider each policy individually and read everything carefully to see what you are responsible for and what the contract will pay for and when.

◆ Getting the Best Price

Now that you have your choice narrowed down, it's time to shop for the best deal. A dealer has to make between $125 and $300 on each car to stay in business. But that doesn't mean that the sticker price on the window reflects this profit margin—it's probably much more. You can easily figure the approximate cost of the car to the dealer by looking in any of several publications available on newsstands or by using Table 9-3.

The suggested retail price is shown on the window and probably looks something like this mythical car:

Base price includes:	$4,295.00
Front disc brakes	no charge
Color-keyed wheel covers	no charge
Bright side molding	no charge
Outside rear-view mirror	no charge
Air-conditioning	$ 482.00
2.73:1 rear axle	16.00
Rear-window defogger	21.00
Automatic transmission	184.00
H.D. cooling system	27.00
Front stabilizer bar	16.00
Hi-torque V-8 engine	120.00
Power steering	84.00
	$5,245.00

According to Table 9-3, if this hypothetical car were an intermediate it would cost the dealer about $4,445. To this you have to add dealer preparation, transportation, taxes and tags. A good deal on a car is that bottom line plus the dealer profit of $125–$300.

Arriving at what you consider a fair price is relatively easy. But that doesn't mean the dealer or salesman has to sell the car at that price. Get the salesman to put his best offer in writing, then go to different dealers and try to bargain for a lower price. Remember, too, that no price a salesman quotes is binding until the sales manager accepts it.

Table 9-3
Typical Dealer Mark-Up

Size	Dealer Mark-up	To find dealer cost, divide sticker price by
Subcompact	13%	1.13
Compact	14%	1.14
Intermediate	18%	1.18
Full-size	20%	1.20
Luxury	22%	1.22
Specialty	15%	1.15

◆ Salesmen's Tricks of the Trade

Most car salespeople are basically honest, but let's face it—we all have to eat and pay the bills, so they do not want to let you get away "unsold." Salespeople make a living by convincing you to buy one car rather than another. In shopping for a car, you have to be alert. Be polite, but don't expect the seller to be your pal. There are a few common ploys you should know about and avoid.

THE HIGHEST TRADE-IN PROMISE

This is the dealer's assurance that he can offer you the highest trade-in anywhere, because he sells so many used cars that he constantly has to restock his lot. To check his figures, check with the finance company, bank, or local newspaper classified ads to find out what your car is really worth and read the section in this chapter on trade-ins.

VERBAL DEALS

Make sure that any deal is put in writing and included in the sales agreement—and be sure the sales manager signs the agreement. If they don't want to put the agreement in writing—BEWARE!

LOWBALLING

The salesperson will quote you a price for the car you want. It will probably be an excellent price, but when it comes time for the deal to be approved the sales manager invariably will explain that the agreed-on price is too low; the dealership just can't stay in business selling cars at such a low price. The sales manager, the villain in this piece, will send you back to renegotiate the price with the salesperson. At this point you will be told something to the effect that the few hundred dollars more that the car will cost you amount to only "pennies more a month."

The other approach to lowballing is for the salesman to quote you "his best price" because he really needs the sale this month. He feels he can convince the sales manager to accept the deal. Eventually the sales manager is going to come down heavily on the salesman (in your presence) for making such a stupid deal, and you hopefully will feel bad enough about the whole situation to be willing to spend the few hundred extra that the sales manager will accept.

HIGHBALLING

The salesman quotes you a fantastic trade-in price on your old car, building the car up to be a wonderful car in excellent condition that they can sell off the lot tomorrow. After you've agreed to the deal, the sales manager (the culprit again) will void the deal by declaring that they can't possibly give you that much for your old car on a trade for the car you want to buy. They may find something wrong with the car you're trading in, or they may say that they can give you the money you want for your old car, but only if you buy this other, higher priced car.

BUSHING

The dealer raises the price after you have made a deposit or lowers a generous trade-in allowance that had been offered previously. Bushing often takes the form of padding the bill with last-minute extras, such as undercoating or rustproofing tacked on as an apparent afterthought.

BAIT AND SWITCH

You may often find that the fully equipped car advertised at a ridiculously low price is unavailable. Usually, this car was "just sold yesterday." But a higher-priced model with much the same equipment is available and right there on the lot.

◆ Trade-Ins

If you plan to trade in your old car, don't discuss this until you have arrived at a price for your new car. This avoids a lot of confusion about what the car is costing and how much trade you're allowed.

There's little chance the dealer is going to pay you more than wholesale for your used car. All car dealers subscribe to one of several used-car valuation books that list the average finance value (the maximum loan that can be obtained) and the average wholesale and retail values for a car, depending on condition. If he offers a lot more than wholesale, he's beating you out of money somewhere else. If the dealer can't make money on selling you a new car, he may try to get your excellent-condition used car at rock-bottom trade-in.

A good rule of thumb is to accept a dealer's trade-in offer if it is within $200 of the price your car commands in the local papers. The annoyance and cost of selling your car yourself are worth at least that much. But if the dealer can't come closer than $200, sell it privately.

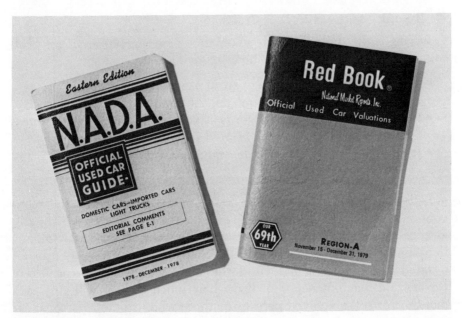

Fig. 9-5 These are some of the trade-in guides that are used to determine the worth of a used car.

CHEVROLET 1976

Avg. Fin.	Avg. Whsl.	Mod. No.	Body Type	Engine	Ins. Sym.	Avg. Retail	O P
ADD "Optional Equipment" on 1976 VEGA, MONZA:							
45	50		Custom Interior Vega			75	
15	20		Custom Exterior Vega			25	
135	150		GT			175	
20	25		2.3 Liter 2 Bbl			35	
90	100		4.3 Liter 2 Bbl			125	
ADD "Optional Equipment" on 1976 NOVA, CAMARO:							
15	20		Positraction			25	
30	35		Exterior Decor Pkg. (Nova)			50	
65	75		SS (Nova)			100	
90	100		Bucket Seats (Nova)			125	
110	125		Rally Sport (Camaro)			150	
30	35		Custom (Concours)			50	
65	75		Bucket Seats, Concours			100	
ADD "Optional Equipment" on 1976 MALIBU, MONTE CARLO:							
15	20		Positraction			25	
45	50		Swing Out Seats, Malibu			75	
ADD "Optional Equipment" on 1976 (Full Size) CHEVROLET:							
15	20		Positraction			25	
90	100		Reclining Seat & 50/50			125	
ADD "Optional Equipment" on 1976 CORVETTE: A/T or 4 Spd. Std. Equip.							
200	225		350/L82 210 Hp Eng			275	

CHEVROLET 1975

Chevrolet (Full Size) Power Brakes Steering and Auto. Trans. Std. Eq.

Avg. Fin.	Avg. Whsl.	Mod. No.	Body Type	Engine	Ins. Sym.	Avg. Retail	O P
1975-4-VEGA-							
855	950	V11	Coupe		4	1450	A
990	1100	V11	Coupe LX		4	1600	A
945	1050	V77	Coupe Hatchback		4	1550	A
990	1100	V15	Wagon		4	1600	A
1125	1250	V15	Estate Wagon		4	1750	A
—	—	V77	Coupe H/B Cosworth		6	—	A
1975-4-MONZA-							
1415	1575	R07	Coupe S		5	2075	A
1595	1775	R07	Coupe 2+2		5	2275	A
1325	1475	M27	Coupe TOWNE		5	1975	A
1975-8-MONZA-							
1505	1675	R07	Coupe S		5	2175	A
1685	1875	R07	Coupe 2+2		5	2375	A
1415	1575	M27	Coupe TOWNE		5	2075	A
1975-6-NOVA-							
1415	1575	X27	Coupe S		4	2075	B
1505	1675	X27	Coupe		4	2175	B
1460	1625	X69	Sedan, 4dr		4	2125	B
1550	1725	X17	Coupe Hatchback		5	2225	B

CHEVROLET 1975

Avg. Fin.	Avg. Whsl.	Mod. No.	Body Type	Engine	Ins. Sym.	Avg. Retail	O P
1975-8-NOVA-							
1550	1725	X27	Coupe S		4	2225	B
1640	1825	X27	Coupe		5	2325	B
1595	1775	X69	Sedan, 4dr		5	2275	B
1685	1875	X17	Coupe Hatchback		5	2375	B
1975-6-NOVA CUSTOM-							
1640	1825	Y27	Coupe		5	2325	B
1595	1775	Y69	Sedan, 4dr		5	2275	B
1685	1875	Y17	Coupe Hatchback		5	2375	B
1975-8-NOVA CUSTOM-							
1730	1925	Y27	Coupe		5	2425	B
1685	1875	Y69	Sedan, 4dr		5	2375	B
1775	1975	Y17	Coupe, Hatchback		5	2475	B
1975-6-NOVA LN-							
1910	2125	Y27	Coupe		5	2625	B
1955	2175	Y69	Sedan, 4dr		5	2675	B
1975-8-NOVA LN-							
2000	2225	Y27	Coupe		5	2725	B
2045	2275	Y69	Sedan, 4dr		5	2775	B
1975-6-CAMARO-							
2205	2450	Q87	Coupe		5	2950	B
1975-8-CAMARO-							
2295	2550	Q87	Coupe		5	3050	B
2430	2700	S87	Coupe 'LT'		5	3200	B
1975-6-MALIBU-							
1260	1400	C37	Coupe		5	1900	B
1125	1250	C29	Sedan, 4dr		5	1750	B
1975-8-MALIBU-							
1350	1500	C37	Coupe		5	2000	B
1215	1350	C29	Sedan, 4dr		5	1850	B
1975-6-MALIBU CLASSIC-							
1440	1600	D37	Coupe		5	2100	B
1305	1450	D29	Sedan, 4dr		5	1950	B
1575	1750	D37	Coupe, LANDAU		5	2250	B
1975-8-MALIBU CLASSIC-							
1530	1700	D37	Coupe		5	2200	B
1395	1550	D29	Sedan, 4dr		5	2050	B
1665	1850	D37	Coupe, LANDAU		5	2350	B
1975-8-LAGUNA-TYPE S3-							
1845	2050	E37	Coupe			2550	B
1975-8-MALIBU STATION WAGONS-							
1235	1375	C35	4dr, 2-Seat		5	1875	B
1370	1525	C35	4dr, 3-Seat		5	2025	B
1370	1525	D35	4dr, 2-Seat CLASSIC		5	2025	B
1505	1675	D35	4dr, 3-Seat CLASSIC		5	2175	B
1460	1625	G35	4dr, 2-Seat ESTATE		5	2125	B
1595	1775	G35	4dr, 3-Seat ESTATE		5	2275	B

SEE INSIDE FRONT COVER FOR OPTION CODE DEFINITION.
19

CHEVROLET 1975

Avg. Fin.	Avg. Whsl.	Mod. No.	Body Type	Engine	Ins. Sym.	Avg. Retail	O P
1975-8-MONTE CARLO'S"-							
1980	2200	H57	Coupe 'S'		6	2800	B
2115	2350	H57	Coupe LANDAU		6	2950	B
1975-8-BEL AIR-							
1010	1125	K69	Sedan, 4dr		5	1725	B
1975-8-IMPALA-							
1415	1575	L47	Coupe, Custom		5	2175	B
1505	1675	L47	Coupe, Landau		5	2275	B
1325	1475	L57	Coupe, Sport		5	2075	B
1235	1375	L39	Sedan, 4dr Sport		5	1975	B
1145	1275	L69	Sedan, 4dr		5	1875	B
1975-8-CAPRICE CLASSIC-							
1595	1775	N47	Coupe		5	2375	B
1685	1875	N47	Coupe, Landau		5	2475	B
1530	1700	N39	Sedan, 4dr Sport		5	2300	B
1460	1625	N69	Sedan, 4dr		5	2225	B
2405	2675	N67	Convertible		5	3275	B
1975-8-CHEVROLET STATION WAGONS-							
1100	1225	K35	4dr 2-Seat BEL AIR		5	1825	B
1235	1375	K45	4dr 3-Seat BEL AIR		6	1975	B
1235	1375	L35	4dr 2-Seat IMPALA		6	1975	B
1370	1525	L45	4dr 3-Seat IMPALA		6	2125	B
1395	1550	N35	4dr 2-Seat CAPRICE		6	2150	B
1530	1700	N45	4dr 3-Seat CAPRICE		6	2300	B
1975-8-CORVETTE-							
5085	5650	Z37	Coupe		7	6450	B
5085	5650	Z67	Convertible		7	6450	B
ADD "Optional Equipment" on 1975 VEGA, MONZA:							
45	50		Custom Interior Vega			75	
30	35		Custom Exterior Vega			50	
135	150		GT			175	
ADD "Optional Equipment" on 1975 NOVA, CAMARO:							
15	20		Positraction			25	
20	25		Exterior Decor Pkg. Nova			50	
65	75		SS Nova			100	
45	50		Bucket Seats (Nova)			75	
35	40		Spoiler Camaro			50	
65	75		Cabriolet (Nova)			100	
ADD "Optional Equipment" on 1975 MALIBU, MONTE CARLO:							
15	20		Positraction			25	
45	50		Swing Out Seats			75	
ADD "Optional Equipment" on 1975 (Full Size) CHEVROLET:							
15	20		Positraction			25	
45	50		Reclining Seat			75	

CHEVROLET 1975

Avg. Fin.	Avg. Whsl.	Mod. No.	Body Type	Engine	Ins. Sym.	Avg. Retail	O P
ADD "Optional Equipment" on 1975 CORVETTE:							
155	175		350 205 H.P. Eng.			225	
155	175		Off Road Pkg.			225	
200	225		Aux. Top Inc. Vinyl Roof			275	

CHEVROLET 1974

Power Strg., Disc Brakes, Auto. Trans. Std. Equip. Chevrolet
Power Steering, Brakes Std. Equip. Monte Carlo
4 Speed Trans. Manual Disc Brakes Std. Corvette

Avg. Fin.	Avg. Whsl.	Mod. No.	Body Type	Engine	Ins. Sym.	Avg. Retail	O P
1974-4-VEGA-							
515	575	V11	Coupe		3	1075	A
605	675	V11	Coupe, LX		3	1175	A
630	700	V77	Coupe, Hatchback		3	1200	A
585	650	V15	Sta. Wagon, 2dr		4	1150	A
785	875	V15	Cpe., Htchbk Estate		4	1375	A
1974-6-NOVA-							
1170	1300	X27	Coupe		4	1800	B
1125	1250	X69	Sedan, 4dr		4	1750	B
1215	1350	X17	Coupe, Hatchback		4	1850	B
1974-8-NOVA-							
1260	1400	X27	Coupe		4	1900	B
1215	1350	X69	Sedan, 4dr		4	1850	B
1305	1450	X17	Coupe Hatchback		4	1950	B
1974-6-NOVA CUSTOM-							
1305	1450	Y27	Coupe		4	1950	B
1260	1400	Y69	Sedan, 4dr		4	1900	B
1325	1475	Y17	Coupe Hatchback		4	1975	B
1974-8-NOVA CUSTOM-							
1395	1550	Y27	Coupe		4	2050	B
1350	1500	Y69	Sedan, 4dr		4	2000	B
1415	1575	Y17	Coupe Hatchback		4	2075	B
1974-6-CAMARO-							
1640	1825	Q87	Coupe		4	2325	B
1974-8-CAMARO-							
1775	1975	Q87	Coupe		4	2475	B
1935	2150	S87	Coupe LT		4	2650	B
1974-6-MALIBU-							
990	1100	C29	Sedan, 4dr		4	1600	B
1035	1150	C37	Coupe		4	1650	B
1974-8-MALIBU-							
1125	1250	C29	Sedan, 4dr		4	1750	B
1170	1300	C37	Coupe		4	1800	B
1974-6-MALIBU CLASSIC-							
1125	1250	D29	Sedan, 4dr		4	1750	B
1170	1300	D37	Coupe		4	1800	B
1350	1500	D37	Coupe, Landau			2000	B

SEE INSIDE FRONT COVER FOR OPTION CODE DEFINITION.
20

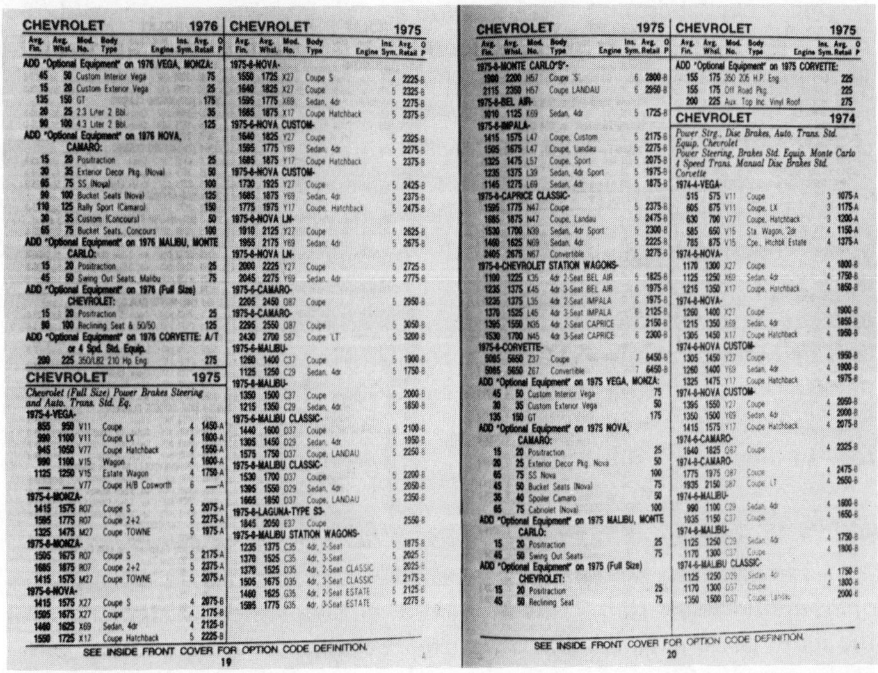

Fig. 9-6 The trade-in guides used by dealers and lending institutions usually list models for the previous six to seven years and give an average finance value, wholesale value, and retail value. These figures are averages and depend largely on the condition of the car and the way the car is equipped.

◆ Buying vs. Leasing

Buying is the traditional way to obtain a new car, but leasing is gaining in popularity and offers some attractive advantages:

- It can free capital, enabling you to use your cash in other ways.
- It can help you stabilize your monthly transportation expenses.
- It can simplify your tax records if you use your car for business purposes.
- It avoids some of the hassles inherent in buying, owning, and selling a car.

Leasing generally requires less down-payment cash outlay than conventional buying—and the more expensive the car, the greater the difference between the two becomes. This allows you to use your money in other ways. The lease also fixes the amount of your car expenses for a stated period of time, and within the terms of the lease, regardless of repairs and maintenance, you know how much the car will cost each month. For self-employed persons or those who use their personal car for business purposes on a regular basis, the leasing arrangement provides a quick and easy method of documenting car expenses over a period of time. Many drivers simply want to avoid the complications of buying a car, shopping, applying for a loan, and being responsible for the car's service needs. They prefer instead to deal with one person or firm to make all the arrangements and handle routine service and repairs.

You will, of course, have to pay for some of these advantages. For starters, while the money you pay to lease a car entitles you to use the car, ownership stays with the lessor, although you may be able to apply your lease amount toward the purchase price at the end of the lease term. Second, your use of the car may be restricted in terms of a mileage limit, or you may be required to return the car to a particular service center for maintenance or repair. And third, while the amount of cash you need to lease a given car is less than the cash required to buy the same car, most lessors will require a more extensive credit history to meet their standards.

Types of Leases

Leases fall into two main categories—open end and closed end. An open-ended lease states the estimated worth of the car at the end of the lease period. This is known as the "residual" or "bring-back" value of the car. If at the end of the lease the car is judged to be worth less than this stated amount, you may be held responsible for the difference, although it cannot be more than the total of three monthly payments, unless you have exceeded a mileage limit or given the car more than normal use or abuse. A closed-end lease does not specify a residual value for the car. Your responsibility ends at the end of the lease period, provided the car's condition meets the lease requirements at that time. It is up to the lessor to sell the car and absorb the profit or loss.

Most leases offer you an opportunity to buy the car at the end of the lease period or to renew the lease.

Figuring the Lease Cost

The cost of the lease will be determined by four factors:

1. Value of the car at the beginning of the lease (if it's a new car, this is the capitalized cost)

2. How many miles you plan to drive over the term of the lease

3. How much the lessor expects the car to be worth at the end of the lease (its residual value)

4. Who will absorb any loss from the sale of the car

The "capitalized cost" (or new car cost) represents the price the lessor paid for the car, including options, plus the business expenses the lessor has added to stay in business and make a profit. The lessor's capitalized cost can be compared to current market values by consulting *Edmund's New Car Price Guide* or any of the comparable new-car pricing books available on newsstands, or by visiting a new-car showroom.

The residual value of the car is typically the amount that the lessor expects the car to be worth at the end of the lease. It will be influenced by number of miles driven, normal wear and tear, and the amount the particular make/model depreciates. The residual value can be compared to any of the used-car pricing guidebooks, keeping in mind the car's probable mileage and condition or you can get a general idea of depreciation on popular cars from Table 1-3.

If the lease states that it is the responsibility of the lessor to absorb any loss on the resale of the car, the monthly lease payment will probably be higher. On the other hand, if *you* agree to absorb any of the loss, the lessor will not be taking as great a risk and will offer a lower monthly payment.

Though all the advantages and disadvantages figure into the decision to buy or lease, the largest factor is the cost of leasing compared to the cost of buying a car outright. There are no hard-and-fast rules for determining which is less expensive and each person's situation is different. You'll have to work out your own expenses yourself, but you should be able to make a fairly accurate comparison by projecting your operating expenses if you buy a car, using the data in Chapter 1 as a base of comparison, to the cost of leasing a comparable vehicle. Be sure to include financing charges in your operating costs to get an accurate comparison.

Before You Sign

These are some of the questions you'll want to answer regarding any lease you may contemplate signing.

1. Will you have to pay a penalty if you exceed the mileage limit? If so, how is the penalty assessed? Does it begin with the first mile over the limit or with the 1,000th?

2. If you drive less mileage than anticipated, will you receive a rebate?

3. What will happen if you break the lease before it expires?

4. Can the lessor end the lease?

5. How much cash do you owe at the beginning of the lease?

6. Can you put up a "capitalized cost reduction" or "cash reduction of original value"? This cash payment allows you to obtain a lower monthly payment or meet lessor's stiffer credit history.

7. Who pays for licenses and maintenance? Leasing arrangements vary in these areas, but responsibility should be stated plainly.

8. Does the lease make a distinction between maintenance expenses and repairs? Frequently the lessee is required to keep the car in good working order throughout the period of the lease. If so, you should carefully read the chapter on warranties and know your responsibilities where routine maintenance is concerned.

9. Will the lessor require you to take the car to a designated service center for work?

10. Who is responsible for scheduling maintenance appointments?

11. What is considered "unreasonable" wear?

12. What happens if the car needs repairs away from home?

13. What is the minimum acceptable insurance coverage?

14. What are your obligations at the end of the lease?

15. Can you buy the car? What is the price?

16. Will you be allowed to sell the car? If so, you will probably be allowed to keep the difference between the selling price and the residual value.

17. Can you renew the lease on the same car.? If so, will the lease conditions stay the same?

CHAPTER

10

Buying a Used Car

Some car buyers wouldn't buy a new car regardless of price. They are convinced that the quality used car is a better buy than a new one.

Approximately 13 to 14 million used cars are sold every year in the United States by dealers, private sellers, and renting/leasing agencies, totaling more than $21 billion. Almost 75% of all passenger cars purchased for private use are previously owned.

Obviously, there are a lot of buyers who are convinced that a quality used car is a bargain. The Hertz Corporation annually publishes its compilation of car operating costs. Among the reams of statistics in this tome is the following information, which tends to support the used car argument. (The figures are rounded off to the nearest cent per mile.)

Age of Car when Purchased (in Years)	Ownership/Operating Cost	
	Cents per Mile	Percent Saved
New	28	—
One	25	10
Two	20	30
Three	15	48
Four	14	51
Five	13	52
Six	13	53
Seven	13	53

With new-car prices skyrocketing and no end in sight, many car buyers are turning to used cars. The old saw that you're only buying someone else's trouble was never less true. People sell or trade cars for all kinds of reasons, and if you're willing to compromise a little on the car of your dreams, you may get a good buy.

First decide what kind of car you want and start looking for it, either privately or on new- or used-car lots. Cars on used-car lots are easier to find, but frequently cost more than those offered for sale privately in newspapers. The reason is simple—the dealer has to make money over what he paid for the car. But although private cars may be less expensive, they require considerably more leg work to track down and weed out the clunkers. You are also strictly on your own when buying a used car from a private party. True, you don't have to deal with a used-car salesman who's a pro, but there's no law requiring honesty from private citizens selling used cars, either.

◆ Shopping Hints

Once you've located a promising car, how can you lessen the chances that you're buying someone else's trouble? Start by following these shopping rules:

1. Never shop for used cars at night. The glare of bright lights make it easy to overlook body imperfections.

2. Take along a small magnet. Casually try the magnet in locations all along the fenders. Anywhere the magnet doesn't stick—BEWARE! The fender probably has been filled with plastic. This isn't always bad. The panel could have suffered minor damage and been repaired in the traditonal manner using plastic body filler. On the other hand, the car could have been involved in a major accident and suffered extensive damage beneath the neatly plastic-filled exterior. The worst possibility is that a rust hole was repaired using body plastic. This is a temporary solution only—the rust will always come back.

3. Ask to see the title. Many states identify cars that were bought out of state with a code, and the codes are usually explained somewhere on the title. Cars on a lot were frequently bought at an auction. Occasionally, a used-car dealer may get an exceptional car at auction, but for the most part, the auction is a dumping ground for cars that other dealers took in trade and were not worth reselling. As a general rule, you should beware of a car that was bought out of state or at an auction.

4. Try to contact the former owner. Get the name and address from the title. No reputable dealer will refuse the information. If he does, walk away.

5. Write down the year, model, and serial number before you buy any used car. Then dial 1-800-424-9393, the toll-free number of the NHTSA (National Highway Traffic Safety Administration) and ask the clerk if the car has ever been included on any manufacturer's recall list. If so, make sure the needed repairs were made.

◆ Understand the Ads

Private purchases rank second to dealers as a source for used cars. A private purchase can be a profitable buy, but it can take time and care to track a good one down. The most common way to track down a used car is to look in the classified ads in your local newspaper, and to read the ads, you have to know "used-car shorthand":

> OLDS 98 '73 lo mi, Orig own, 4 dr,
> PW-L-Sts air, cruise, am-fm, tilt
> str, rdls, showrm cond. dk red/whte
> rf, best offer

Here's the translation: The original owner is selling a four-door 1973 Oldsmobile 98 with low mileage, power seats, air conditioning, cruise control, am-fm radio, tilt steering wheel, radial tires, in excellent condition, dark red with white roof.

Some other frequently used abbreviations are:

a/c—air conditioning
a/t, at, auto—automatic transmission
cb—citizens band radio
cass—cassette tape player
conv—convertible
cpe—coupe
cruise—cruise control
cu in—cubic inches
cyl—cylinders (four, five, six, eight)
dk—dark (color)
dlr—dealer
dr—doors (two or four)
exc—excellent
full pwr—all power options (brakes, seats, steering, etc.)
h/back—hatchback
hdtp—hardtop
hd—heavy duty
man trans, mt—manual transmission
mint—superb, like-new condition
mpg—miles per gallon
orig owr—original owner
pb—power brakes
ps—power steering
pow seats—power seats
pw—power windows
rdls—radial tires
rear dfg—rear defogger

rf—roof
sac—sacrifice
sed—sedan
spd—speed (3, 4, 5)
snrf—sunroof
tape—tape player
vnyl—vinyl top
wrnty—warranty
wgn—station wagon

◆ Used Car Inspection Checklist

You should check all the items listed below on any used car you are considering. All items are indicative of the general condition of the car, how long it probably will last, and how much it should cost you in ownership expenses. Depending on the use you plan to give the car and how much money you plan to spend on it, you may consider some items more serious than others. Parts replacement is usually a negotiable matter at purchase time. Replacement of parts that do not affect the operation and performance of the car will not seriously affect future, long-term operating costs, although it can significantly alter the purchase price. Beware, however, of signs of trouble in areas that will affect operation, performance, safety, or emissions.

The column headed "Illustration Number" refers to Figure 10-1.

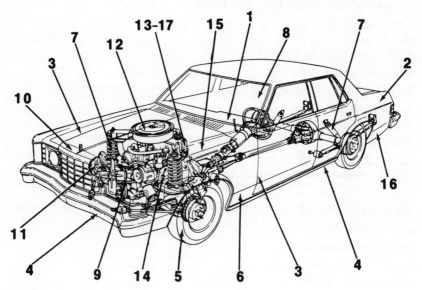

Fig. 10-1 You should check these points when purchasing a used car. Refer to the chart for an explanation of the numbered items.

Table 10-1
Used Car Checklist

Illustration Number	Area or Component	What to Look For
1	Mileage	Average mileage is about 12,000 miles per year. The numbers should be straight across the odometer. If a 1975 or later car is near 50,000 miles, the catalytic converter probably needs service.
2	Paint	Check around tailpipe, molding, and windows for overspray indicating the car has been repainted.
	Body rust (see also No. 6)	Check fenders, doors, rocker panels, rain gutters, window moldings, and wheelwells for signs of rust. Any rust at all will be a problem. There is no inexpensive way to check the spread of rust. The only 100% sure way is to replace the rusted part.
	Moldings, bumpers, grille	Check overall condition of parts and sheetmetal.
	Vinyl roof	Check for good condition. There should be no signs of rust underneath.
	Glass	Look for scratches or cracks in all glass.
3	Doors, trunk lid	Check where the body panels meet. Severe misalignment indicates crash work. Sight down the contours of the body panels. Ripples indicate body work.
4	Leaks	Get down and look under the car. There are no normal "leaks," other than water from the A/C condenser.
5	Tires	Check the tire pressure. A common used-car trick is to pump the tire pressure up to make the car easier to roll. Check the tread wear. Uneven wear is a clue that the front end needs alignment.
6	Rust	Check all around the car (inside wheelwells, under floor mats, in the trunk) for signs of rust.
7	Shocks	Check the shock absorbers by bouncing each corner of the car. Good shocks will not bounce more than twice after you let go.
8	Interior	Check the entire interior. You're looking for an interior condition that doesn't agree with the overall condition of the car. Reasonable wear is expected, but be suspicious of new seatcovers on sagging seats, new pedal pads, and worn armrests. These indicate an attempt to cover up hard use. Pull back the carpets and look for evidence of water leaks or flooding.
	Trunk interior	Look for evidences of a leak or rust. New welds indicate recent crash work.
	Hardware	Look for missing door handles, control knobs, and other miscellaneous pieces.
	Lights, signals	Check for proper operation.

Table 10-1 (continued)

Illustration Number	Areas or Component	What to Look For
	Air conditioning	Check for proper operation.
	Heater/ defroster	Check for proper operation.
	Gauges	Check for proper operation.
	Radio/tape player	Check for proper operation.
	Windshield wiper/washer	Check for proper operation.
9	Hoses, blets	Check all belts and hoses for wear or weak spots.
10	Battery terminals	Low electrolyte level, corroded terminals, and/or cracked case indicate a lack of maintenance.
11	Radiator/ coolant	Look for corrosion or rust around the radiator, signifying a leak. Rust in the coolant indicates a lack of maintenance.
12	Air filter	A dirty air filter usually means a lack of preventive maintenance.
13	Ignition wires	Check the ignition wires for cracks, burned spots, or wear. Worn wires will have to be replaced.
14	Oil level	If the oil level is low, chances are even that the engine uses oil. Beware of water in the oil (cracked block), excessively thick oil (used to quiet a noisy engine), or thin dirty oil with a distinct gasoline smell (internal problems in the engine).
15	Automatic transmission	Pull the automatic transmission dipstick out when the engine is running. The level should read "Full," and the fluid should be clear and bright red. Dark brown or black fluid, or fluid that has a distinct burnt odor, signals a transmission in need of repair or overhaul.
16	Exhaust	Check the color of the exhaust smoke. Blue smoke indicates worn rings; black smoke can indicate burnt valves or that a tune-up is needed.
17	Spark plugs	Remove one of the spark plugs (the most accessible will do). An engine in good condition will show plugs with a light tan or gray firing tip.

Once you have checked the car out thoroughly and taken careful note of any problems as outlined above, you can come to a fairly reliable initial evaluation of the condition of the car and the care it has received. Below is a guide to help you. If your inspection turns up problems in two of the areas below, or in only one of them but a problem shows up in your road test, proceed with caution. That car is in less than excellent condition.

Illustration numbers 1–8: Problems in more than two areas indicate a lack of maintenance, and you should beware.

Illustration numbers 9–13: Problems in any of these areas indicate a lack of proper care, too, but can usually be corrected with a tune-up or relatively simple parts replacement.

Illustration numbers 14–17: Be very wary of problems in either the engine or automatic transmission. These can mean major expense. Walk away from any car with problems in *both* areas.

◆ Road Test and Mechanic's Opinion

If you are satisfied with the apparent condition of the car, take it out on a road test. The results of the road test should agree with your original evaluation. Check for these things on the road:

Engine performance: Should be peppy whether cold or warm, with plenty of power and good pickup. It should respond smoothly through all the gears.

Brakes: Should provide quick, firm stops with no signs of noise, pulling, or fading pedal.

Steering: Should provide sure control with no binding, harshness, or looseness and no shimmy in the wheel. Noise or vibration from the steering wheel when turning the car means trouble.

Clutch, manual transmission: Should give quick, smooth response with easy shifting. The clutch pedal should have about 1–1½" play before it disengages the clutch. Start engine, set parking brake, put in first gear, and slowly release the clutch pedal. Engine should stall when pedal is one-half to three-quarters of the way up.

Automatic transmission: Should shift rapidly and smoothly, with no hesitation and no noise.

Differential: No noise or thumps.

Driveshaft, universal joints: Vibration and shimmy could mean driveshaft problems. Clicking sound at low speeds means worn U-joints.

Suspension: Hit bumps going slow and fast. A car that bounces has weak shocks. Shimmying may be due to driveshaft problems.

Frame: Wet the tires and drive in a straight line on concrete. Tracks should show two straight lines, not four.

It won't take a good mechanic more than an hour to check the car over. If your opinion coincides with that of a trusted mechanic, that's about the best you can expect. The rest is up to you.

11

Financing and Insurance

♦ **Financing a Car**

One of the major expenses in purchasing a car is borrowing the money to buy it. It used to be true that the cheapest way to purchase a car was for cash, but with the prices of new cars averaging around $6,500 and with no ceiling in sight, that's not usually very feasible these days. But even if you can afford to pay cash for a car, it may be to your advantage to take a loan anyway. The interest you pay on a loan can be deducted from your income tax, and assuming that the inflation rate remains in double digits, you're going to be repaying the loan in cheaper, inflation-ridden dollars. Let's say that you are the average consumer and borrow $5,800 from a dealer for three years to buy a new car. At 11% interest, you will have repaid only $5,450 in 1979 dollars, assuming that inflation is no lower than 9% each year.

Auto loans are generally for 24 to 36 months, but with the higher prices for new cars, loans of longer duration are becoming more common, often running to 48 months. There are even some five-year loans available, but these are infrequent and usually reserved for expensive cars and cars that traditionally hold their value extremely well. In addition, lenders are generally unwilling to commit their money for a longer period of time on an auto loan, unless it is for a lot of money.

The easiest measure of what a loan will cost you is the Annual Percentage Rate (APR). This represents the interest that you will pay the lender to use his money. It will vary considerably, depending on where you borrow money, even in the same geographical area. Other major factors that will affect the cost are the loan term length, the down payment, and the lender.

The kind of car (new or used) and the amount of money borrowed will determine the length of the loan. Obviously, the lending institution wants to recover its money as soon as possible without imposing a hardship on the borrower and, since a new car is worth more than a used one, will generally finance a greater portion of a new car. For purposes of comparison shopping, ask various lending institutions to quote you figures for a loan based on the same repayment period.

◆ Sources for Loans

Banks

Local banks are the most common sources of car loans. The annual percentage rate will vary widely, depending on the bank and how eager it is to make car loans. Try your own bank first. You'll usually have a better chance if the bank wants to keep your business, and it may even offer a small discount for automatic deductions of payments from your account. Also, smaller banks are better choices for car loans than larger commercial, account-oriented banks. Although the car you're buying serves as collateral for the loan, obtaining the loan may be slightly easier from a bank where you're known, especially if you have a savings account there or have had another type of account for a period of time.

Dealer Financing

In return for the convenience of one-stop shopping for both car and credit, and for making loans to those that banks might consider a poor risk, the new-car dealer or its affiliate will command a higher percentage rate. The advantage, to some, lies in the availability of money with few of the inconveniences of shopping for a loan. Naturally, the car dealer is interested in selling cars and is willing to work with you in obtaining a loan. Sometimes the dealer will obtain the loan from a commercial lending institution (GMAC Finance or Chrysler Credit, for example) and sometimes will refer all auto loans to a local bank, from whom they may obtain a slightly favored rate or loans for higher-risk applicants.

Credit Unions

Credit unions are usually among the less expensive lending institutions, but you must be a member of one before you can borrow money. Many also require that you have a minimum amount on deposit in order to borrow specified sums of money. But because they are nonprofit, credit unions frequently offer the lowest interest rates, and a few will even offer an interest refund in a profit-making year. Company credit unions also offer the convenience of repaying by payroll deduction, and some of the larger ones may be affiliated with group purchase plans, enabling you to buy a new car even less expensively.

Other sources of money include personal loans and life insurance loans.

◆ Down Payment and Security

No matter where you borrow money for a car, the down payment is going to vary from the amount required to cover taxes and licensing to up to 25% of the cost of the car. No matter where you apply for a car loan, be sure the loan application specifies that the down payment is refundable if the loan is refused.

Normally, the car you are purchasing will be security for the loan— the lender retaining title, "encumbered" by the amount of the loan. When the loan is repaid, the "encumbrance" is satisfied, and title to the car is returned to the purchaser of the vehicle. The encumbrance allows the financing institution to repossess (take the car back, subject to state limitations) if you fail to repay the loan, then sell the car to recover their money. If they sell the car for less than the amount of the loan, you could be liable for the difference.

◆ Loan Comparison Checklist

Here's a form to use to help you compare the costs of several loans.

	Lender A	Lender B	Lender C
1. Car's price, including taxes	_____	_____	_____
2. Down payment	_____	_____	_____
3. Remaining price (subtract 2 from 1)	_____	_____	_____
4. Trade-in allowance	_____	_____	_____
5. Amount to be financed (subtract 4 from 3)	_____	_____	_____
6. Amount of monthly payments	_____	_____	_____
7. Number of monthly payments	_____	_____	_____
8. Sum of monthly payments	_____	_____	_____
9. *Total* cost (down payment less trade-in, plus sum of monthly payments).	_____	_____	_____

◆ Insurance

There are nearly 132 million motorists driving more than 90 million insured cars on the nation's highways. But millions of other cars, in violation of state laws, are not insured, simply because owners cannot afford it.

Car insurance is a $15-billion business that is essentially a huge bookmaking operation. Insurance companies collect premiums from the people they insure, betting that they will not have to pay off for bodily injury or property damage claims. It's a risky business with a small profit margin (less than 5%, according to the Insurance Institute), and the cost that you pay (your premium) is determined by the degree of risk.

◆ How Your Rate is Determined

The business of insuring cars is based on statistics and probabilities, and much more goes into assigning a premium rate than you might think. Pennsylvania's rating plan is not unusual, with close to 300 separate categories that could apply to your rate in a single territory. And forty different modifications are possible for application to those categories, for an unbelievable total of nearly 12,000 separate factors! Basically seven factors are taken into consideration by an insurer.

1. Geographic environment. Rates vary because statistics show that most accidents occur within twenty-five miles of your residence. So, if you live in a risk territory, your chance of being involved in an accident is statistically greater and your premium higher. No matter where an insured person has an accident, if he is at fault or if a claim is paid, it is statistically recorded in the area in which he resides. The territories are rated high or low depending on the experience of the company with drivers living in the territory. If your territory has a high accident record, high medical costs, or high repair costs, your insurance will cost more.

2. Who uses the car. The age of each person regularly driving the car will affect the amount of the premium. Drivers under the age of 24 are involved in 25% of all accidents and are therefore higher risks. The statistics also reveal that male drivers are involved in accidents more than female drivers and that married males under 30 and married females under 25 are less likely to be involved in an accident than their single counterparts, but more likely than married males and females over 30 and 25 but under 65.

3. How the car is used. You will usually be charged a higher premium if you drive your car more than 10 miles to work, less if it is used for pleasure purposes only. Cars not driven to and from work are usually subject to lower premiums.

4. Driving record. Statistics prove that the drivers who have had accidents previously or have been convicted of serious traffic violations are more likely to be involved in an accident than drivers with clean

records. Many companies surcharge traffic violations and "at-fault" accidents within the last three years.

5. Type of car. The car's make, model, and engine size are prime rate determining factors. Studies by the Insurance Institute for Highway Safety show that: Within each size group, two-door models have more injury claims than four-door models. Subcompacts have the highest percentage of collision claims. Among cars of the same size, sports and specialty models have larger collision claims than other models.

6. Cost of each claim. Car repair charges, hospital bills, and financial awards vary greatly from area to area. Inflation in these charges result in higher premiums to cover them.

7. Discounts. Most companies will offer discounts from rates established by the above factors to young drivers who have successfully completed a driver education course, owners of compact cars, and families with more than one car (on the theory that each car is driven less).

How to Drive Your Rates Sky-High

You're probably already aware that most states will slap you with points against your license for accidents and traffic violations you incur. And that if you get too many points against you during a specified amount of time, you may even lose your license.

But did you know that insurance companies have a "points system" of their own? And that a major motor vehicle offense like drunk driving can boost your premiums by 150%?

Here's how it works:

Number of Points	Rate Increase	Point Schedule
1	40%	A moving violation resulting in suspension or requirement to file a Financial Responsibility Certificate
		An accident with any injury, or over $200 damage to property of any one person if you are at fault
		Two accidents, each with less than $200 damage and no injuries if you are at fault
		For each driver with less than three years' driving experience
2	90%	Filing a Financial Responsibility Certificate because of an accumulation of points under the Motor Vehicle code
3	150%	Conviction of drunk driving
		Conviction of homicide or assault
		Driving during suspension of driver's license

◆ Types of Car Insurance

Car insurance protects you against three kinds of risks: (1) In case someone is hurt in a car accident in which you are involved (liability); (2) in case you destroy someone else's property (property damage); and (3) in case your car is stolen or damaged (collision or comprehensive).

Liability Insurance

Until 1970, in the event someone was hurt in an accident, insurance policies protected you through "bodily injury" liability and "medical payments" insurance. If the accident was judged your fault, the bodily injury portion of your policy covered the medical payments of those you injured. Your medical payments insurance covered your own medical bills and those of any passengers in your car. If the accident was the other person's fault, you collected from his insurance policy under the same arrangement. This system is known as "fault-based," since it involves a question of who was at fault; it has often resulted in interminable court cases.

Since 1971, twenty-six states have adopted what has come to be known as no-fault insurance. Basically, this means that persons involved in an accident submit claims to, and collect from, their own insurance company, regardless of who is at fault. On the surface, this seems a smooth and equitable way of handling things. But there is a hitch: in some states, under certain circumstances, even if you are covered under a no-fault policy, persons who are badly injured in accidents can take you to court and sue for additional amounts. The threshold for determining the right to sue when damages exceed a designated amount varies among states, but is as low as $400.

But no-fault applies only in certain circumstances. Mainly, it covers only personal injury, not property damage. Other factors that determine whether no-fault applies (depending on the state in which you reside) and would allow you to bring suit, include:

- An accident resulting in death or serious or permanent injury
- Medical expenses in excess of a predetermined amount
- Physical or mental impairment that keeps you from performing your normal daily activities
- Cosmetic disfigurement injury

Significantly, when no-fault does apply, you cannot recover damages for what is commonly referred to as "pain and suffering." Normally when you bring suit for an injury, you sue for recovery of actual expenses and compensation for the "pain and suffering" endured as a result of the injury. Under no-fault, you are limited to recovering monetary losses only. Each state in which no-fault applies has detailed and specific applications of the no-fault provisions. Be sure to check with your insurance company or state insurance commissioner for exact coverages and requirements in your state.

Typical liability coverage is $10,000/$20,000/$5,000, which means that if you have an accident, you are covered for $10,000 for any one person you injure, $20,000 for more than one person, and $5,000 for property damage. Bodily injury liability is the $10,000/$20,000 portion of the policy. Property damage liability is the $5,000 portion.

For maximum protection, even though you have no fault insurance, you may decide you need extra bodily injury coverage. Higher liability coverage will protect you from losing any assets you may have, such as savings accounts or property, should you lose a lawsuit and the person you injured is awarded a sum higher than that covered by no fault.

Before you decide on the coverage you want, be sure to check your state laws. Some require a minimum.

Personal Injury Insurance

Personal injury protection (PIP) pays for reasonable medical expense and loss of income or earning capacity. PIP is usually available with deductibles which generally range from $100 to $400. Your premiums will be lower if you choose one of these deductibles. Check with the state insurance department for specific details on any minimum coverage requirements.

Property Damage Insurance

As the name implies, this part of the policy covers damages caused other people's property by your car. It usually covers you if you are driving your own car, someone else's car (with their permission), or if someone else is driving your car with your permission.

Collision Insurance

Collision insurance pays the bills if your car is damaged in an accident with another car or if you damage your car by backing into a telephone pole, for example. It is sold on a deductible basis, which means that for any claim you submit, you must pay the deductible amount yourself before the insurance takes over. On most cars, damage from almost any accident costs more to repair than the common $100 or $200 deductibles. But if your car is old enough that a major accident would cost more to repair than the car is worth, you should consider raising the deductible, which will lower your premiums.

Carrying collision insurance is usually voluntary, but if you don't want it, you will be required to reject it in writing.

Comprehensive Insurance

Comprehensive insurance covers damage to your car that results from anything other than a collision. It is also usually sold on a deductible basis. Common losses such as fire, theft, windstorm, hail, flood, vandalism and glass breakage, malicious mischief, or riot are covered under comprehensive.

Fire, theft and combined additional coverage is an alternative to comprehensive coverage. It usually covers the same things as comprehensive except for glass breakage. It applies to "named perils" which are specifically listed in your insurance policy.

Other Coverage

Towing and labor cost coverage pays a stated amount for towing and labor costs in an emergency.

Medical payments insurance pays for medical, surgical, and dental expenses. It will pay up to the limits you have chosen regardless of fault.

Uninsured motorist coverage pays if you are hit by an uninsured motorist and your loss of income and medical bills total more than the $5,000 paid under your personal injury protection portion of your no-fault policy.

◆ Parts of the Policy

Most auto insurance policies follow a regular form, with each part setting down specific information and conditions.

1. Declarations. This includes information about the person taking out the policy, the amount of the policy, the kind of coverage, cost, the date and time coverage begins, and the date the policy expires.

2. Insuring agreements. This states what the policy will cover.

3. Exclusions. This states what the policy will *not* pay for, sometimes referred to as the "fine print." Some usual exclusions are:

- Intentional damage to your own automobile
- Damages caused when your automobile is being used as a public or delivery vehicle unless the declarations portion of your policy states that it will be used for this purpose
- Damages caused while your automobile is being driven by employees of a garage, parking lot, or auto sales agency

4. Conditions. This gives the policy rules and your duties in case of a loss, such as:

- Report a loss to the company as soon as possible
- Use reasonable care to prevent further damage to your car
- Provide the company with information to assist them in settling claims
- File proper proof of loss
- Forward all documents concerning suits under your policy to your company

5. Endorsements. Sometimes changes must be made in your insurance policy. When this happens, changes are typed on a form called an

endorsement, signed by a company official, and attached to your policy.

◆ Insuring Old Cars

Most old-car owners don't carry collision or comprehensive coverage. But on an old or antique car that is worth considerably more than the average for its year and model, the little extra for special coverage is well worth it. You can usually arrange with an insurance broker or company for special comprehensive coverage of such cars. Normally you will need a written evaluation from a car appraiser, specifying why your car is worth more than average and accompanied by photos substantiating the condition of the car.

Some insurance carriers will amend a good customer's policy upon submission of an appraisal, but most companies are not that accommodating. If your normal auto insurance carrier does not offer such coverage, you should go to one of the several companies specializing in old-car insurance.

◆ Shaving Insurance Costs

With auto insurance rates taking a big bite of the family budget, especially when young drivers are involved, your car insurance shopping should include a close scrutiny of all discounts and rate structures available. Here are a few suggestions on how to save money on your policy.

First, you might consider buying collision and comprehensive coverage with higher deductibles. Collision coverage can be reduced about 17% when the deductible is changed from $100 to $200, and going from $50 to $100 deductible for comprehensive could work out to a 20% savings. Carefully evaluate the need for collision and the amount of deductible, but don't skimp on bodily injury or property damage liability.

Another possibility is to drop collision insurance entirely on an older car, because regardless of how much coverage you carry, the insurance company will pay only up to the car's "book value." For example, if your car requires $1,000 in repairs but its "book value" is only $500, the insurance company is required to pay only $500.

Investigate special discounts offered by some companies in some states. They are available for young drivers who have successfully completed driver education courses. There also are special discounts for those with good driving records, or for college students attending a school more than a hundred miles from home, as well as discounts for women over 30 and for families with two or more cars.

The lowest premium should not be your only goal. You should con-

Table 11-1
Rate Comparison Worksheet

Company Names				
Type of Coverage	Amount of Coverage	Annual Rates	Annual Rates	Annual Rates
Liability	$_____	$_____	$_____	$_____
Medical payments				
Property damage				
Uninsured motorist				
Collision				
Comprehensive	(Deductible)			
Other	(Deductible)			
TOTAL		$_____	$_____	$_____

sider that you want to get the satisfaction you're entitled to when you make a claim.

If you are getting good service from your present company, making a switch may not be to your advantage in the long run. If you stay with your present company and have an accident, your company will take your previous record into consideration.

Table 11-1, Rate Comparison Worksheet, can help you compare the cost of several different policies.

PART

II

Parts & Labor Guide

In the Labor Guide which begins on page 149, the following American cars are listed under each operation. Datsun, Honda Toyota, and Volkswagen are dealt with in separate sections beginning on page 245.

American Motors
AMC/Jeep
Buick LeSabre, Electra, Riviera (1974–78)
Buick Riviera (1979–80)
Buick Apollo, Century, Gran Sport, Regal, Skylark
Buick Skyhawk
Cadillac
Cadillac Seville
Cadillac Eldorado
Camaro, Chevelle, Malibu, Monte Carlo, Nova
Capri & Mustang (1979–80)
Chevrolet & Corvette
Chevette
Citation, Omega, Phoenix, Skylark—All 1980
Chrysler, Cordoba, Imperial
Comet, Cougar, Monarch, Montego, Lincoln Versailles
Dodge
Elite, Granada, Maverick, Torino, LTD II, Thunderbird (1977–79)
Ford
Horizon & Omni
Lincoln Continental, Mark IV, Mark V
Mercury
Mustang II, Bobcat, Pinto, Fairmont, Zephyr
Oldsmobile
Olds Cutlass, Omega (1974–79)
Olds Toronado
Olds Starfire
Plymouth
Pontiac, Grand Prix
Pontiac Astre, Sunbird
Pontiac Firebird, LeMans, Phoenix (1978–79), Ventura (1974–77)
Thunderbird (1974–76)
Valiant, Dart, Barracuda, Challenger, Aspen, Volare, LeBaron, Diplomat
Vega & Monza

Labor Guide
to Common Auto Repairs

If you're the average car owner, you have little idea of what any given automotive service job may cost you. How can you or a mechanic know what to charge or how long a specific job will take? The answer is provided for service shop operators, mechanics, and car owners like yourself in an automotive service labor guide, sometimes called a "flat rate" book. These labor guides are an aid to the mechanic/businessman in managing his business in a professional, reputable manner.

In the automotive service business, the charge for labor makes up a large part of the customer's bill. Knowing the expected charge for labor in advance is especially important to the service manager or independent mechanic/businessman, because, in almost all cases, he will be asked or required by law to provide an estimate of the total bill as part of the normal transaction. Human nature being what it is, this estimate will usually become fixed in the consumer's mind as the final amount of the bill, regardless of whatever unanticipated complications arise.

◆ What Is a Labor Guide?

Most professional service managers and mechanics refer to an automotive labor guide to get a handle on what the job is going to cost. Most labor guides, except those published by the vehicle manufacturer for use in dealerships, are compiled and published independently. They usually appear annually, and are available to professional automotive shop owners, service managers, and mechanics. While most labor guides do not carry a suggested price for individual service jobs, they do list the recognized time to perform each job. By multiplying the suggested time by the individual shop's hourly rate, the service manager or mechanic will be able to give you an accurate estimate of the cost of the work to do a given job.

Chilton's Professional Labor Guide and Parts Manual is a good example of these labor guides. Published since 1926, it is an 1800-page book, listing over 100,000 part numbers for all makes of domestic cars for the last seven years. It also provides a guide to the amount of work involved in diagnosing a problem and making the repair, given in hours and tenths of an hour. A typical entry might read as follows:

	Chilton
(Factory Time)	**Time**

(G) Clutch Assembly, Renew
Includes: R&R trans and adjust free play.

1975–76 (2.4)	3.2
1977–79 (1.8)	2.6
w/5 speed add (.4)	.5

The labor guide includes a time specified by the vehicle manufacturer (factory time) for authorized dealers to use in settling warranty claims. The "Chilton time" is an adjusted time that allows for the variables that greatly affect the time it takes to repair a car that has aged since it was covered by warranty. Some of these variables are:

- Need for special tools and equipment that are not always part of the mechanic's toolbox
- Accumulation of dirt, rust, corrosion, and grease that make repairs more difficult
- Lack of maintenance
- Unauthorized modifications that complicate diagnosis and repair
- Time spent in repairing broken or stripped bolts resulting from age
- Special options or equipment that affect service time on given repairs
- Inclusion of other repairs or maintenance that should be done at the time work is performed

All of these factors are obviously not for every individual job, but all have a bearing on determining an adjusted work time representative of actual field service conditions. There is a great difference between an old car and a new one, and it takes longer and costs more to repair an older, even slightly deteriorated car.

The labor guide is a consumer protection device, and it is a necessity for today's service outlets. It enables the service personnel to accurately quote the price of a job, and in most cases it is the customer's assurance of reasonable, fair labor charges for almost any kind of automotive service. It sets up guidelines for a fair time to aid the mechanic/businessman in competitively pricing his services. Most mechanics rely on it as a guide and are reasonable in adjusting labor charges to reflect time actually spent on the job.

The labor guide also serves as a check, by the consumer, on the efficiency of the shop that he or she chooses to deal with. If the shop you deal with does not use a labor guide to price major automotive services, you could be getting set up for an inflated estimate.

◆ Understanding Labor Charges

There are two ways of computing charges for automotive service—the clock-hour and the "flat-rate" hour methods. Under the clock-hour method of billing, the shop will calculate labor charges for the time a mechanic actually takes to complete a job. If the shop rate is $14 per hour and the job takes 1½ hours, you will be billed for $21.00 labor. If the job takes 3 hours, you will be billed for $42.00 labor, and so forth. Unfortunately, you have no way of checking on the amount of time it took to do a job, so the possibilities for padding the time are endless. And what if your work is done by a slow or inexperienced mechanic?

Under the rate-per-job system, used in the great majority of shops, you can check to see that the charge is correct. Since it would be impossible for the shop owner or mechanic to instantly recall how long it ought to take any given mechanic to perform any one of the over 7500 auto service or diagnostic procedures on any of the approximately 3000 different combinations of years/makes/models, he must rely on the average time listed in the labor guide. If he were to bill you for actual time, he would have to know which mechanic will be assigned to the job, the exact condition of the car, and the exact equipment to be repaired. And since more competent mechanics can demand a higher pay scale, the labor rate on each job would have to vary accordingly. The record-keeping task would be enormous, overhead would be much higher, and the customer would be totally confused.

The net result would be that the customer would wind up paying for the increased overhead and would be less able to compare the services of different shops. To simplify things, the shop owner or mechanic could bill on the average time of all mechanics, but all this does is recreate the labor guide, which brings us back where we started.

◆ Estimating Your Repair Bill

You, the consumer, who pays the repair bills, can actually pre-price the cost of many repairs using the guide that follows. It lists the labor times from *Chilton's Professional Labor Guide and Parts Manual* for many of the common automotive services that your car will require. If the shop you deal with uses *Chilton's Professional Parts and Labor Guide* (most do, and you can check by asking them) what is listed below will be the same time as is listed in your mechanic's book. By knowing his hourly labor rate you can estimate the labor charges. Add in the cost of any parts and you'll be pretty close to the actual estimate from your local mechanic.

This will give you a good idea of what the bill is going to be. Take your car to the shop and get an estimate of the total bill for the work required. Make sure that it is a written estimate and that you specify that if the bill is going to be any higher someone call you and get your OK before doing the work. Leave a phone number where you can be reached.

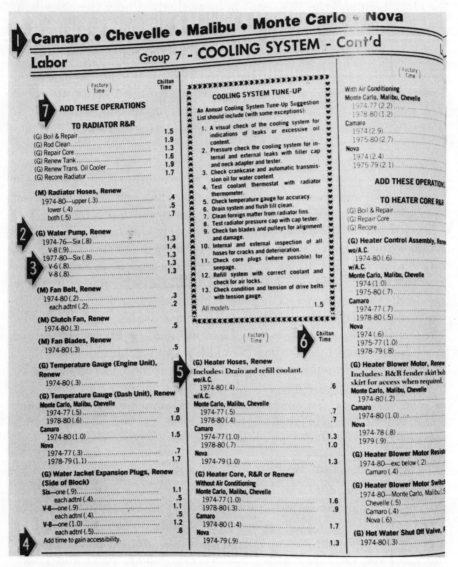

The accompanying illustration shows an actual page from *Chilton's Professional Labor Guide and Parts Manual*. The key shows you how to read the information.

1. Section name—These are the cars included in each section.

2. Operation—These are the individual operations. Each job is graded with a letter (P, G, or M) in parentheses preceding each operation. The grading suggests a skill level for each operation that can be defined as follows:

P—Precision indicates a highly skilled operation requiring the use of precision measuring devices. The mechanic must be highly skilled and possess a thorough understanding of complex components. Examples of precision repair are automatic transmission overhaul, engine overhaul, and axle overhaul.

G—General means that a normally skilled mechanic is needed to perform jobs requiring simpler measuring devices such as feeler gauges or tach/dwell meters. The mechanic must have a thorough knowledge of the component involved. Examples of general repairs are linkage adjustments, brake overhaul, fuel/ignition system adjustments, or axle shaft replacement.

M—Maintenance means that a semi-skilled mechanic is needed to replace parts that generally require no adjustments. Examples of maintenance operations are oil and filter change, replacing belts or hoses, or other routinely performed operations.

3. Years/Models—These are the individual years and/or models listed for each operation.

4. Footnotes—Be sure to check the footnotes (if there are any) for special notes or cautions. These frequently indicate individual differences among models that affect the time required to perform a given job.

5. Inclusions—Where necessary, it is stated exactly what procedures the time for the operation includes.

6. Chilton Time—This is the time required to perform the operation in hours and $1/10$th's of an hour and takes many factors into account, as described in the text.

7. Adds—These are called "adds" because they are times for general operations that may or may not have to be performed. If they are performed, the time should be added to the time required to remove and replace the component.

TUNE-UP

(G) Engine Tune Up, (Minor)
Includes: Clean or renew spark plugs, renew ignition points and condenser, set ignition timing, set carburetor idle mixture and idle speed. Service carburetor air cleaner.

(G) Engine Tune Up, (Major)
Includes: Check engine compression, clean or renew and adjust spark plugs. Test battery, clean terminals. Renew and adjust distributor points and condenser. Check distributor cap and rotor. Set ignition timing, test coil. Free up manifold heat control valve. Tighten manifold and carburetor mounting bolts. Adjust carburetor idle speed. Inspect and tighten all hose connections.

(G) Engine Tune Up, (Electronic Ignition)
Includes: Test battery and clean connections. Tighten manifold and carburetor mounting bolts. Check engine compression, clean and adjust or renew spark plugs. Test resistance of spark plug cables. Inspect distributor cap and rotor. Adjust air gap. Check vacuum advance operation. Reset ignition timing. Adjust idle mixture and idle speed. Service air cleaner. Inspect crankcase ventilation system. Inspect and adjust drive belts. Inspect choke operation and adjust or free up. Check operation of EGR valve.

(Factory Time)	Chilton Time

American Motors

(G) Compression Test

Four (.3)	.7
Six (.3)	.7
V-8 (.6)	.8

(Factory Time)	Chilton Time
(G) Engine Tune Up, (Minor)	
Four—1977–80 (.9)	1.2
Six—1974 (1.0)	1.2
V-8—1974 (1.3)	1.6
w/A.C. add	.6
(G) Engine Tune Up (Major)	
Four—1977–80 (1.4)	1.8
Six—1974 (1.7)	2.3
V-8—1974 (2.4)	2.9
w/A.C. add	.6
(G) Engine Tune Up (Electronic Ingition)	
Six—1975–80	2.0
V-8—1975–80	2.5
w/A.C. add	.6

AMC/Jeep

(G) Compression Test	
Six (.3)	.6
V-8 (.6)	.8
(G) Engine Tune Up, (Minor)	
Six (1.1)	1.4
V-8 (1.2)	1.5
w/A.C. add	.6
(G) Engine Tune Up (Major)	
Six (2.4)	3.0
V-8 (2.8)	3.5
w/A.C. add	.6
(G) Engine Tune Up (Electronic)	
1975–80	2.5
w/A.C. add	.6

| | Chilton |
| (Factory Time) | Time |

| | Chilton |
| (Factory Time) | Time |

Buick Apollo, Century, Gran Sport, Regal, Skylark (1974–79)

(G) Compression Test

Six—1974–75	.6
V-6—1975–80	*.8
V-8—1974–80	.9
w/A.C. add	.3
*w/Turbocharger add (.2)	.2

(G) Engine Tune Up, (Minor)

Six—1974 (1.2)	1.4
V-8—1974 (1.5)	1.9
w/A.C. add	.6

Engine Tune Up (Electronic)

V-6—1975–80	*2.0
V-8—1974–80	2.7
w/A.C. add	.6
*w/Turbocharger add	1.2

Buick LeSabre, Electra, Riviera (1974–78)

(G) Compression Test

V-6—1976–80	.8
V-8—1974–80	.9
w/A.C. add	.3
w/Turbocharger add (.2)	.3

(G) Engine Tune Up, (Minor)

V-8—1974 (1.5)	1.9
w/A.C. add	.6

(G) Engine Tune Up (Major)

V-8—1974 (2.9)	3.5
w/A.C. add	.6

(G) Engine Tune Up, (Electronic Ignition)

V-6—1976–80	*2.0
V-8—1974–80	2.7
w/A.C. add	.6
*w/Turbocharger add	1.2

Buick Riviera (1979–80)

(G) Compression Test

V-6—1979–80	.8
V-8—1979–80	.9
w/A.C. add	.3
w/Turbocharger add (.2)	.3

(G) Engine Tune Up, (Electronic Ignition)

V-6—1979–80	*2.0
V-8—1979–80	2.7
w/A.C. add	.6
*w/Turbocharger add	1.2

Buick Skyhawk

(G) Compression Test

1975–80	.8
w/A.C. add	.3

(G) Engine Tune Up, (Electronic Ignition)

V-6—1975–80	2.0
w/A.C. add	.6

Cadillac

(G) Engine Tune Up, (Minor)

1974 (1.6)	1.9
w/A.I.R. add	.2
w/A.C. add	.6

(G) Engine Tune Up, (Major)

1974 (3.2)	4.0
w/A.I.R. add	.2
w/A.C. add	.6

(G) Engine Tune Up, (Electronic Ignition)

1974–80	3.0
Test and adjust fuel injection system add	1.5
w/A.I.R. add	.2
w/A.C. add	.6

Cadillac Seville

(G) Compression Test

1976–80	.8
w/A.I.R. ádd	.2
w/A.C. add	.3

(G) Engine Tune Up

1976–80	3.0
Test and adjust fuel injection system, add	1.5
w/A.I.R. add	.2
w/A.C. add	.6

Cadillac Eldorado

(G) Compression Test

1974–80	.8
w/A.I.R. add	.2
w/A.C. add	.3

(G) Engine Tune Up, (Minor)

1974 (1.6)	1.9
w/A.I.R. add	.2
w/A.C. add	.6

(G) Engine Tune Up, (Major)

1974 (3.2)	4.0
w/A.I.R. add	.2
w/A.C. add	.6

(G) Engine Tune Up, (Electronic Ignition)

1974–80	3.0
Test and adjust fuel injection system add	1.5
w/A.I.R. add	.2
w/A.C. add	.6

Camaro, Chevelle, Malibu, Monte Carlo, Nova

(G) Compression Test

Six—1974–80 (.5)	.6
V-6—1978–80 (.5)	.7
V-8—1974–80 (.8)	.9
w/A.C. add	.3

(G) Engine Tune Up, (Minor)

Six—1974 (2.0)	2.4
V-8—1974 (2.6)	3.1
w/A.C. add	.6

	(Factory Time)	Chilton Time
(G) Engine Tune Up, (Electronic Ignition)		
	Six—1975–80	1.8
	V-6—1978–80	2.1
	V-8—1975–80	2.5
	w/A.C. add	.6

Chevrolet & Corvette

(G) Compression Test
Chevrolet
	Six—1977–80 (.5)	.6
	V-8—1974–80 (.7)	.9

Corvette
	1974–80—350 eng (1.2)	1.5
	1974—454 eng (1.0)	1.3
	w/A.C.—V-8 add	.3

(G) Engine Tune Up, (Minor)
Chevrolet
	V-8—1974 (1.4)	1.8

Corvette
	1974—350 eng (2.0)	2.6
	1974—454 eng (1.8)	2.4
	w/A.C.—V-8 add	.6

(G) Engine Tune Up, (Major)
Chevrolet
	V-8—1974 (2.6)	3.1

Corvette
	1974—350 eng (3.1)	3.6
	1974—454 eng (2.9)	3.4
	w/A.C. add	.6

(G) Engine Tune Up, (Electronic Ignition)
Chevrolet
	Six—1977–80	1.8
	V-8—1975–80	2.5

Corvette
	V-8—1975–80	3.0
	w/A.C. add	.6

Capri & Mustang 1979–80

(G) Compression Test
	Four—1979–80 (.3)	.6
	V-6—1979–80 (.4)	1.2
	V-8—1979–80 (.5)	.9
	w/A.C. add	.2

(G) Engine Tune Up, (Electronic Ignition)
	Four—1979–80	1.5
	V-6—1979–80	1.7
	V-8—1979–80	2.4
	w/A.C. add	.2

Comet, Cougar, Monarch, Montego, Lincoln Versailles, Elite, Granada, Maverick, Torino, LTD II, Thunderbird (1977–79)

(G) Compression Test
	Six—1974–80 (.3)	.7
	V-8—1974–80 (.5)	.9
	w/A.C. add	.3

(G) Engine Tune Up, (Minor)
	Six—1974 (1.4)	1.6

	(Factory Time)	Chilton Time
	V-8—1974 (1.6)	1.8
	w/A.C. add	.6
(G) Engine Tune Up, (Major)		
	Six—1974 (2.2)	2.8
	V-8—1974 (2.6)	3.4
	w/A.C. add	.6

(G) Engine Tune Up, (Electronic Ignition)
	Six—1974–80	2.1
	V-8—1974–80	2.7
	w/A.C. add	.6

Chevette

(G) Compression Test
	1976–80	.6

(G) Engine Tune Up, (Electronic Ignition)
	1976–80	2.0
	w/A.C. add	.6

Citation, Omega, Phoenix & Skylark—All 1980

(G) Compression Test
1980
	Four (.3)	.5
	V-6 (.5)	.8
	w/Cruise control add	.3

(G) Engine Tune Up, (Electronic Ignition)
	FOUR—1980	1.6
	V-6—1980	2.1
	w/A.C. add	.6
	w/Cruise control add	.3

Dodge

(G) Compression Test
	Six—1974–80 (.5)	.6
	V-8—1974–80—318, 360 engs (.6)	.8
	400,440 engs (1.0)	1.2
	w/A.C. add (.3)	.3

(G) Engine Tune Up, (Electronic Ignition)
	Six—1974–80	2.0
	V-8—1974–80	2.5
	w/A.C. add	.6

Horizon & Omni

(G) Compression Test
	1978–80	.5

(G) Engine Tune Up, (Electronic Ignition)
	1978–80	1.5

Ford

(G) Compression Test
	1974–80 (.4)	.9
	w/A.C. add	.3

(Factory Time)	Chilton Time
(G) Engine Tune Up (Minor)	
V-8—1974 (1.6)	1.8
w/A.C. add	.6
(G) Engine Tune Up, (Major)	
V-8—1974 (2.6)	3.4
w/A.C. add	.6
(G) Engine Tune Up, (Electronic Ignition)	
V-8—1974–80	2.7
w/A.C. add	.6

Lincoln Continental, Mark IV, Mark V, Mark VI

(G) Compression Test	
1974–80 (.5)	1.0
w/A.C. add	.3
(G) Engine Tune Up, (Minor)	
1974 (1.5)	2.0
w/A.C. add	.6
(G) Engine Tune Up (Major)	
1974 (2.6)	4.0
w/A.C. add	.6
(G) Engine Tune Up (Electronic)	
1974–80	3.0
w/A.C. add	.6

Mercury

(G) Compression Test	
1974–80 (.4)	1.0
w/A.C. add	.3
(G) Engine Tune Up, (Minor)	
V-8—1974 (1.9)	2.4
w/A.C. add	.6
(G) Engine Tune Up, (Major)	
V-8—1974 (3.0)	3.7
w/A.C. add	.6
(G) Engine Tune Up, (Electronic Ignition)	
V-8—1974–80	3.0
w/A.C. add	.6

Mustang II, Bobcat, Pinto, Fairmont, Zephyr

(G) Compression Test	
Four—1974–80 (.3)	.6
Six—1977–80 (.3)	.6
V-6—1974–80 (.5)	.7
V-8—1975–80 (.9)	1.1
w/A.C. add	.2
(G) Engine Tune Up, (Minor)	
Four—1974	1.0
V-6—1974	1.5
V-8—1974	1.8
w/A.C. add	.2
(G) Engine Tune Up, (Major)	
Four—1974	2.0
V-6—1974	2.2
V-8—1974	2.5
w/A.C. add	.2
(G) Engine Tune Up, (Electronic Ignition)	
Four—1974–80	1.5
Six—1977–80	2.0

(Factory Time)	Chilton Time
V-6—1974–80	1.7
V-8—1974–80	2.4
w/A.C. add	.2

Oldsmobile

(G) Compression Test	
V-6—1977–80 (.5)	.7
V-8—1974–80 (.6)	.8
w/A.C. add (.3)	.3
(G) Engine Tune Up, (Minor)	
V-8—1974 (1.4)	1.8
w/P.S. add (.2)	.2
w/A.C. add	.6
(G) Engine Tune Up, (Major)	
V-8—1974 (2.5)	3.0
w/P.S. add (.2)	.2
w/A.C. add	.6
(G) Engine Tune Up, (Electronic Ignition)	
V-6—1977–80	2.0
V-8—1974–80	2.5
w/A.C. add	.6

Olds Cutlass, Omega (1974–79)

(G) Compression Test	
Six—1974–76 (.5)	.7
V-6—1977–80 (.5)	.7
V-8—1974–80 (.8)	1.0
w/A.C. add	.1
(G) Engine Tune Up, (Minor)	
Six—1974 (1.0)	1.2
V-8—1974 (1.3)	1.6
w/A.C. add	.6
(G) Engine Tune Up, (Major)	
Six—1974 (2.0)	2.5
V-8—1974 (2.5)	3.0
w/A.C. add	.6
(G) Engine Tune Up, (Electronic)	
Six—1974–76	1.5
V-6—1977–80	1.5
V-8—1974–80	2.5
w/A.C. add	.5

Olds Toronado

(G) Compression Test	
1974–76 (.6)	.8
1977–80 (.7)	.9
w/A.C. add	.3
(G) Engine Tune Up, (Minor)	
1974 (1.4)	2.0
w/A.C. add	.6
(G) Engine Tune Up, (Major)	
1974 (2.5)	3.0
w/A.C. add	.6
(G) Engine Tune Up, (Electronic Ignition)	
1974–80	2.5
w/A.C. add	.6

Olds Starfire

(G) Compression Test	
Four—1976–80 (.5)	.7
V-6—1975–80 (.5)	.7

(Factory Time)	Chilton Time
V-8—1977–80 (1.0)	1.3
w/A.C. add	.2
(G) Engine Tune Up, (Electronic Ignition)	
Four—1976–80	1.5
V-6—1975–80	2.0
V-8—1977–80	2.5
w/A.C. add	.6

Plymouth

(G) Compression Test	
Six—1974–78 (.5)	.6
V-8—1974–78—318, 360 engs (.6)	.8
400, 440 engs (1.0)	1.2
w/A.C. add (.3)	.3
(G) Engine Tune Up, (Electronic Ignition)	
Six—1974–78	2.0
V-8—1974–78	2.5
w/A.C. add	.6

Pontiac & Grand Prix

(G) Compression Test	
V-6—1977–80 (.5)	.8
V-8—1974–80 (.6)	.9
w/A.C. add	.3
(G) Engine Tune Up, (Minor)	
V-8—1974 (1.1)	1.7
w/A.C. add	.6
(G) Engine Tune Up, (Major)	
V-8—1974 (2.7)	3.3
w/A.C. add	.6
(G) Engine Tune Up, (Electronic Ignition)	
V-6—1977–80	2.0
V-8—1974–80	2.5
w/A.C. add	.6

Pontiac Astre & Sunbird

(G) Compression Test	
Four—1975–80 (.4)	.7
V-6—1976–80 (.5)	.8
V-8—1979–80 (.6)	.9
w/A.C. add	.3
(G) Engine Tune Up, (Electronic Ignition)	
Four—1975–80	1.5
V-6—1976–80	2.0
V-8—1979–80	2.5
w/A.C. add	.6

Pontiac Firebird, LeMans, 1978–79 Phoenix, 1974–77 Ventura

(G) Compression Test	
Four—1977–80 (.4)	.7
Six—1974–76 (.5)	.8
V-6—1977–80 (.5)	.8
V-8—1974–80 (.6)	.9
w/A.C. add	.3

(Factory Time)	Chilton Time
(G) Engine Tune Up, (Minor)	
Six—1974 (.9)	1.2
V-8—1974 (1.1)	1.7
w/A.C. add	.6
(G) Engine Tune Up (Major)	
Six—1974 (2.3)	2.9
V-8—1974 (2.7)	3.3
w/A.C. add	.6
(G) Engine Tune Up (Electronic)	
Four—1977–80	1.4
Six—1974–76	1.7
V-6—1977–80	2.0
V-8—1974–80	2.5
w/A.C. add	.6

Thunderbird (1974–76)

(G) Compression Test	
1974–76 (.7)	1.0
(G) Engine Tune Up, (Minor)	
1974–76 (1.5)	2.0
w/A.C. add	.6
(G) Engine Tune Up, (Major)	
1974–76 (2.3)	4.0
w/A.C. add	.6
(G) Engine Tune Up, (Electronic)	
1974–76—V-8	3.0
w/A.C. add	.6

Valiant, Dart, Barracuda, Challenger, Aspen, Volare, LeBaron, Diplomat

(G) Compression Test	
Six—1974–80 (.5)	.6
V-8—1974–80 (.6)	.8
w/A.C. add (.3)	.3
(G) Engine Tune Up, (Electronic Ignition)	
Six—1974–80	2.0
V-8—1974–80	2.5
w/A.C. add	.6

Vega & Monza

(G) Compression Test	
1974–80	
Four (.3)........................	.5
V-6 (.5)	.7
V-8 (.6)	.8
(G) Engine Tune Up, (Minor)	
Four—1974	1.0
V-8—1974	2.0
w/A.C. add	.6
(G) Engine Tune Up, (Major)	
Four—1974	2.0
V-8—1974	3.1
w/A.C. add	.6
(G) Engine Tune Up, (Electronic Ignition)	
Four—1975–80	1.6
V-6—1975–80	2.1
V-8—1975–80	*2.5
w/A.C. add	.6

*If necessary to raise engine, add appropriate time.

FUEL SYSTEM

	Chilton
(Factory Time)	Time

American Motors

(G) Fuel Pump, Test
Includes: Disconnect line at carburetor, attach pressure gauge.
All models	.2

(G) Carburetor, Renew
Includes: Necessary adjustments.
Four—1977–80 (.5)	.7
Six—1974–80 (.5)	.8
V-8—1974–80 (.6)	.8

(G) Carburetor, R&R and Clean or Recondition
Includes: Necessary adjustments.
Four—1977–80 (1.0)	1.5
Six & V-8—1974–80	
1 bbl (1.0)	1.3
2 bbl (1.1)	1.6
4 bbl (1.0)	1.9

(G) Fuel Pump, Renew
Four—1977–80 (.4)	.6
Six—1974–80 (.4)	.6
V-8—1974–80 (.7)	.9
Add pump test if performed.	

(G) Intake Manifold or Gasket, Renew
Four—1977–80 (1.2)	1.9
V-8—1974–80 (1.8)	2.4

(G) Intake and Exhaust Manifold or Gaskets, Renew
Six—1974–76 (1.6)	2.2
1977–80 (2.4)	3.0
w/Air guard and/or P.S. add (.3)	.3

AMC/Jeep

(G) Fuel Pump, Test
Includes: Disconnect line at carburetor, attach pressure gauge.
All models (.2)	.3

(G) Carburetor, Renew
Includes: Necessary adjustments.
1974–80 (.5)	.8

(G) Carburetor, R&R and Clean or Recondition
Includes: Necessary adjustments.
1974–80—1 bbl (1.3)	1.6
2 bbl (1.5)	2.1
4 bbl (1.5)	2.1

(G) Intake Manifold or Gaskets, Renew
Six (1.2)	1.6
V-8 (1.7)	2.2
w/Air Guard add (.2)	.2

Buick LeSabre, Electra, Riviera (1974–78)

(G) Fuel Pump, Test
Includes: Disconnect line at carburetor, attach pressure gauge.
All models	.2

	Chilton
(Factory Time)	Time

(G) Carburetor, Renew
Includes: All necessary adjustments.
1974–76 (.7)	1.1
1977–80 (.5)	.9

(G) Carburetor, R&R and Clean or Recondition
Includes: All necessary adjustments.
1974–76 (1.8)	2.5
1977–80 (1.3)	2.2

(G) Fuel Pump, Renew
1974–80 (.3)	.6
w/P.S. add (.2)	.3
Add pump test if performed.	

(G) Intake Manifold Gaskets and/or Seals, Renew
Includes: Drain and refill cooling system. Make all necessary adjustments.
V-6—1976–80 (1.0)	1.5
w/Turbocharger add (1.3)	1.4
V-8—1974–76 (1.2)	1.7
1977–80	
350 eng, code J (1.0)	1.5
350–403 engs, code R or K (1.4)	1.9
305–350 engs, code U or L (1.9)	2.4
350 eng, code X (1.0)	1.5
301 eng, code Y (1.4)	1.9
Renew manif add (.4)	.5
w/A.C. add (.4)	.4
w/Cruise control add (.1)	.1

(G) Turbocharger Assembly, Renew
Includes: Transfer all necessary parts.
V-6—1978–80 (1.7)	2.3

Buick Riviera (1979–80)

(G) Fuel Pump, Test
Includes: Disconnect line at carburetor, attach pressure gauge.
All models	.2

(G) Carburetor, Renew
Includes: All necessary adjustments.
1979–80 (.5)	.9

(G) Carburetor, R&R and Clean or Recondition
Includes: All necessary adjustments.
1979–80 (1.3)	2.2

(G) Fuel Pump, Renew
1979–80 (.3)	.6
w/A.C. add (.5)	.5
w/P.S. add (.3)	.3
Add pump test if performed.	

(G) Intake Manifold Gaskets and/or Seals, Renew
Includes: Drain and refill cooling system. Make all necessary adjustments.
V-6—1979–80 (1.8)	2.9
V-8—1979–80	
350 eng, Code R (1.4)	1.9
Renew manif add (.4)	.5
w/A.C. add (.4)	.4

(G) Turbocharger Assembly, Renew
Includes: Transfer all necessary parts.
V-6—1979–80 (1.6)	2.3

	Chilton
(Factory Time)	Time

Buick Apollo, Century, Gran Sport, Regal, Skylark (1974–79)

(G) Fuel Pump, Test
Includes: Disconnect line at carburetor, attach pressure gauge.
All models 2

(G) Carburetor, Renew
Includes: All necessary adjustments.
Six—1974–75 (.5)	.9
V-6—1975–76 (.7)	1.1
1977–80 (.5)	.9
V-8—1974–76 (.7)	1.1
1977–80 (.5)	.9

(G) Carburetor, R&R and Clean or Recondition
Includes: All necessary adjustments.
Six—1974–75 (1.5)	2.2
V-6—1975–76 (1.9)	2.6
1977–80 (1.1)	2.0
V-8—1974–76 (1.8)	2.5
1977–80 (1.3)	2.0

(G) Fuel Pump, Renew
| 1974–80 (.3) .... | .6 |
| w/P.S. add (.2) .... | .3 |
Add pump test if performed.

(G) Intake Manifold Gaskets and/or Seals, Renew
Includes: Drain and refill cooling system. Make all necessary adjustments.
Six—1974–75 (1.4)	1.9
V-6—1975–80 (1.0)	1.5
w/Turbocharger add (1.3)	1.4
V-8—1974–76 (1.2)	1.7
1977–80	
350 eng, Code J (1.0)	1.5
350–403 engs, Code R or K (1.4) .	1.9
305–350 engs, Code U, H or L (1.9)	2.4
Renew manif add (.4)	.5
w/A.C. add (.4)	.4
w/A.I.R. add (.1)	.1

(G) Turbocharger Assembly, Renew
Includes: Transfer all necessary parts.
| **V-6**—1978–80 (1.7) .... | 2.3 |

Buick Skyhawk

(G) Fuel Pump, Test
Includes: Disconnect line at carburetor, attach pressure gauge.
All models 2

(G) Carburetor, Renew
Includes: All necessary adjustments.
| 1975–76 (.7) .... | 1.1 |
| 1977–80 (.5) .... | .9 |

(G) Carburetor, R&R and Clean or Recondition
Includes: All necessary adjustments.
| 1975–76 (1.9) .... | 2.5 |
| 1977–80 (1.1) .... | 1.8 |

(G) Fuel Pump, Renew
Includes: R&R gas tank.
| 1975–80 (.9) .... | 1.3 |
Add pump test if performed.

	Chilton
(Factory Time)	Time

(G) Intake Manifold Gaskets and/or Seals, Renew
Includes: Drain and refill cooling system. Make all necessary adjustments.
| 1975–80 (1.0) .... | 1.5 |
| Renew manif add (.4) .... | .5 |

Cadillac

(G) Fuel Pump, Test
Includes: Disconnect line at carburetor, attach pressure gauge.
All models 2

(G) Carburetor, Renew
Includes: Necessary adjustments.
| 1974 (.8) .... | 1.1 |
| 1975–80 (.6) .... | 1.0 |

(G) Carburetor, R&R and Clean or Recondition
Includes: Necessary adjustments.
| 1974 (2.3) .... | 3.0 |
| 1975–80 (2.1) .... | 3.0 |

(G) Fuel Pump, Renew
| 1974–80 (.5) .... | .8 |
Add pump test if performed.

(G) Intake Manifold or Gaskets, Renew
1974 (1.0)	1.4
1975–80 (1.3)	1.7
Renew manif add (.2)	.5
w/A.C. add	.3

ELECTRONIC FUEL INJECTION

(G) E.F.I. System, Test
Includes: Complete testing of system using analyzer.
| 1975–76 (.8) .... | 1.0 |
| 1977–80 (.9) .... | 1.1 |

(G) Electronic Control Unit, Renew
| 1975–80 (.4) .... | .7 |

DIESEL FUEL INJECTION

(G) Fuel Supply Pump, Renew
Includes: Vacuum, pressure, and volume test.
| 1979–80 (.5) .... | .9 |

(G) Fuel Pump, Renew
| 1975–80 (.4) .... | .7 |

(G) Intake Manifold or Gasket, Renew
Includes: R&R oil fill pipe, injection pump and lines. R&R all wires, hoses, and linkage. Drain and refill cooling system.
| 1979–80 (2.3) .... | 3.0 |
| Renew manif add (.2) .... | .5 |

(G) Exhaust Manifold, Renew
| 1979–80—right side (.8) .... | 1.2 |
| left side (.7) .... | 1.1 |

Cadillac Seville

ELECTRONIC FUEL INJECTION

(G) E.F.I. System, Test
Includes: Complete testing of system using analyzer.
| 1976–80 (.8) .... | 1.1 |

(Factory Time)	Chilton Time
(G) Electronic Control Unit, Renew	
1976–80 (.3)	.7
(G) Fuel Pump, Renew	
1976–80 (.4)	.7
(G) Intake Manifold or Gasket, Renew	
1976–80 (1.6)	2.3
Renew manif add (.2)	.5

DIESEL FUEL INJECTION

(G) Fuel Supply Pump, Renew
Includes: Vacuum, pressure, and volume test.

1978–80 (.5)	.9
(G) Intake Manifold or Gasket, Renew	

Includes: R&R oil fill pipe, injection pump and lines. R&R all wires, hoses, and linkage. Drain and refill cooling system.

1978–80 (2.3)	3.0
Renew manifold add (.2)	.5
(G) Exhaust Manifold, Renew	
1978–80—right side (.8)	1.2
left side (.7)	1.1

Cadillac Eldorado

(G) Fuel Pump, Test
Includes: Disconnect line at carburetor, attach pressure gauge.

All models	.2
(G) Carburetor, Renew	

Includes: Necessary adjustments.

1974 (.8)	1.1
1975–78 (.6)	1.0

(G) Carburetor, R&R and Clean or Recondition
Includes: Necessary adjustments.

1974 (2.3)	3.0
1975–78 (2.1)	3.0
(G) Fuel Pump, Renew	
1974–80 (.6)	.8
Add pump test if performed.	
(G) Intake Manifold or Gaskets, Renew	
1974 (1.0)	1.4
1975–78 (1.3)	1.7
Renew manif add (.2)	.5
w/A.C. add	
1974 (.3)	.3

ELECTRONIC FUEL INJECTION

(G) E.F.I. System, Test
Includes: Complete testing of system using analyzer.

1975–80 (.8)	1.1
(G) Electronic Control Unit, Renew	
1975–77 (.4)	.7
1978–80 (.3)	.7
(G) Fuel Pump, Renew	
1975–80 (.4)	.7

DIESEL FUEL INJECTION

(M) Air Cleaner, Service

1979–80 (.2)	.2

(G) Air Intake Crossover and/or Gasket, Renew

1979–80 (.3)	.5

(G) Fuel Supply Pump, Renew
Includes: Vacuum, pressure, and volume test.

1979–80 (.5)	.9

(Factory Time)	Chilton Time
(G) Intake Manifold or Gasket, Renew	

Includes: R&R oil fill pipe, injection pump and lines. R&R all wires, hoses, and linkage. Drain and refill cooling system.

1979–80 (2.3)	3.0
Renew manif add (.2)	.5
(G) Exhaust Manifold, Renew	
1979–80—right side (.8)	1.2
left side (.7)	1.1

Camaro, Chevelle, Malibu, Monte Carlo, Nova

(G) Fuel Pump, Test
Includes: Disconnect line at carburetor, attach pressure gauge.

All models	.3
(G) Carburetor, Renew	

Includes: Necessary adjustments.

1974–80 (.5)	.7

(G) Carburetor, R&R and Clean or Recondition
Includes: Necessary adjustments.

1974–80—1 bbl (1.1)	1.8
2 bbl (1.4)	2.0
4 bbl (1.7)	2.8
(G) Fuel Pump or Push Rod, Renew	
Six—1974–80 (.3)	.5
V-6—1978–80 (.4)	.6
V-8—1974–77 (.7)	.9
1978–80 (.5)	.9
w/P.S. add (.2)	.2
w/A.I.R. add (.5)	.5
(G) Intake Manifold or Gaskets, Renew	
Six—1974 (1.0)	1.4
1975–80 (1.2)	1.7
V-6—1978–80	
200 eng (1.8)	2.2
231 eng (1.3)	1.7
V-8—1974 (1.8)	2.2
1975–80 (2.0)	2.4
w/P.S. add (.3)	.3
w/A.C. add (.2)	.2
w/A.I.R. add (.1)	.1
(G) Exhaust to Intake Manifold Gasket, Renew	
Six—1975–80 (1.1)	1.6
w/P.S. add (.7)	.7
w/A.I.R. add (.7)	.7
(G) Intake and Exhaust Manifold Gaskets, Renew	
Six—1979–80 (1.0)	1.5
w/P.S. or A.I.R. add (.5)	.5

Chevrolet & Corvette

(G) Fuel Pump, Test
Includes: Disconnect line at carburetor, attach pressure gauge.

All models	.3
(G) Carburetor, Renew	

Includes: Necessary adjustments.

1974–80 (.5)	.8

(G) Carburetor, R&R and Clean or Recondition
Includes: Necessary adjustments.

1974–80 (1.5)	2.4

| | Chilton |
| (Factory Time) | Time |

(G) Fuel Pump or Push Rod, Renew
Chevrolet
1974–80—Six (.3) 5
V-8 (.6) 9
Corvette
1974–80 (.7) 1.1
(G) Intake Manifold or Gaskets, Renew
Chevrolet
Six—1979–80 (1.2) 1.7
w/P.S. or A.I.R. add (.5) 5
V-8—1974 (1.8) 2.2
1975–80 (2.0) 2.6
Corvette
1974 (2.0) 2.5
1975–80 (1.9) 2.5
Renew manif add 5
w/A.C. add 3
w/Air inj add 2
(G) Exhaust to Intake Manifold Gasket, Renew
Six—1977–80 (1.1) 1.6
w/P.S. or A.I.R. add (.7) 7
(G) Intake and Exhaust Manifold Gasket, Renew
Six—1979–80 (1.0) 1.5
w/P.S. or A.I.R. add (.5) 5

Chevette

(G) Fuel Pump, Test
Includes: Disconnect line at carburetor, attach pressure gauge.
All models 3
(G) Carburetor, Renew
Includes: Necessary adjustments.
1976–80 (.5) 8
(G) Carburetor, R&R and Clean or Recondition
Includes: Necessary adjustments.
1976–80 (1.2) 1.5
(G) Fuel Pump or Push Rod, Renew
1976–80 (.5) 1.0
w/A.C. add (.6) 6
(G) Intake Manifold or Gaskets, Renew
1976–80 (1.8) 2.5
w/A.C. add (1.0) 1.0

Citation, Omega, Phoenix, Skylark—All 1980

(G) Fuel Pump, Test
Includes: Disconnect line at carburetor, attach pressure gauge.
All models 2
(G) Carburetor, Renew
Includes: Necessary adjustments.
1980 (.6)........................ 1.0
(G) Carburetor, R&R and Clean or Recondition
Includes: Necessary adjustments.
1980 .... 1.9
(G) Fuel Pump or Push Rod, Renew
1980 (.6)........................ .9
(G) Intake Manifold Gasket, Renew
1980—Four (1.3) 1.9
V-6 (2.7) 3.3

| | Chilton |
| (Factory Time) | Time |

w/Cruise control add (.3) 3
Renew manif add (.3) 5

Chrysler, Cordoba, Imperial

(G) Fuel Pump, Test
Includes: Disconnect line at carburetor, attach pressure gauge.
All models 2
(G) Carburetor, Renew
Includes: Adjust idle speed and mixture with analyzer.
1 bbl—1979–80 (.9).............. 1.3
2 bbl—1974–77 (.7).............. 1.1
1978–80 (.9) 1.3
4 bbl—1974–76 (.9) 1.3
1977–80 (.7) 1.3
(G) Carburetor, R&R and Clean or Recondition
Includes: Adjust idle speed and mixture with analyzer.
1 bbl—1979–80 (.8).............. 2.5
2 bbl—1974–77 (1.7)............. 2.8
1978–80 (.9) 2.8
4 bbl—1974–80 (1.5) 2.5
Thermo-Quad (2.4) 4.0
(G) Fuel Pump, Renew
Six—1979–80 (.6) 1.0
V-8—1974–80
318–360 engs (.4) 8
400–440 engs (.6) 1.0
Add pump test if performed. .....
(G) Intake Manifold or Gaskets, Renew
V-8—1974–80
318–360 engs (2.1) 2.7
400–440 engs (1.4) 2.0
w/A.C add (.4) 4
w/Air inj add (.2) 3
(G) Intake and Exhaust Manifold Gaskets, Renew
Six—1979–80 (1.7) 2.3
w/A.C. add (.4) 4

Dodge

(G) Fuel Pump, Test
Includes: Disconnect line at carburetor, attach pressure gauge.
All models 2
(G) Carburetor, Renew
Includes: Adjust idle speed and mixture with analyzer.
1974–80—exc below (.7) 1.1
1976—4 bbl (.9) 1.3
(G) Carburetor, R&R and Clean or Recondition
Includes: Adjust idle speed and mixture with analyzer.
1974–80—1 bbl (1.4) 2.5
2 bbl (1.7) 2.8
4 bbl (1.5) 2.5
Thermo-Quad (2.4) 4.0
(G) Fuel Pump, Renew
Six—1974–80 (.4) 8
V-8—1974–80—318, 360 engs (.4) .8
400, 440 engs (.5) 9
Add fuel pump test if performed.

(Factory Time)	Chilton Time
(G) Intake Manifold or Gaskets, Renew	
Six—1974–76 (2.1)	2.5
1977–80 (1.9)	2.4
V-8—1974–75	
318, 360 engs (1.9)	2.4
400, 400 engs (1.5)	1.9
1976–80—318, 360 engs (2.1)	2.7
400, 440 engs (1.6)	2.0
w/A.C. add (.4)	.4
w/Air inj add (.3)	.3
(G) Intake and Exhaust Manifold Gaskets, Renew	
Six—1974–80 (1.7)	2.3
w/A.C. add (.4)	.4

Horizon & Omni

	Chilton Time
(G) Fuel Pump, Test	
Includes: Disconnect line at carburetor, attach pressure gauge.	
All models	.3
(G) Carburetor, Renew	
Includes: Adjust idle speed and mixture.	
1978–80 (1.1)	1.6
(G) Carburetor, R&R and Clean or Recondition	
Includes: Adjust idle speed and mixture.	
1978–80	3.0
(G) Fuel Pump, Renew	
1978–80 (.5)	.9
Add pump test if performed.	
(G) Intake Manifold, Renew	
1978–80 (2.6)	3.8
w/P.S. add (.2)	.2
(G) Intake and Exhaust Manifold Gaskets, Renew	
1978–80 (2.6)	3.4
w/P.S. add (.2)	.2

Capri & Mustang (1979–80)

	Chilton Time
(G) Fuel Pump, Test	
Includes: Disconnect line at carburetor, attach pressure gauge.	
All models	.3
(G) Carburetor, Renew	
Includes: Necessary adjustments.	
1979–80—Four (.4)	.8
V-6 (.5)	.9
V-8 (.5)	.9
(G) Carburetor, R&R and Clean or Recondition	
Includes: Necessary adjustments.	
1979–80—Four (1.0)	1.7
V-6 (1.3)	2.2
V-8 (1.5)	2.4
Renew spacer add (.2)	.2
(G) Fuel Pump, Renew	
1979–80 (.4)	.8
Add pump test if performed.	
(G) Intake Manifold or Gaskets, Renew	
1979–80—Four (1.1)	1.6
V-6 (2.4)	3.0
V-8 (1.9)	2.4
Renew manif add (.4)	.5

Comet, Cougar, Monarch, Montego, Lincoln Versailles

(Factory Time)	Chilton Time
(G) Fuel Pump, Test	
Includes: Disconnect line at carburetor, attach pressure gauge.	
All models	.3
(G) Carburetor, Renew	
Includes: Necessary adjustments.	
Six—1974–80 (.4)	.7
V-8—1974–80 (.5)	.9
(G) Carburetor, R&R and Clean or Recondition	
Includes: Necessary adjustments.	
Six—1974–80 (1.2)	1.8
V-8—1974–80 (1.5)	2.4
Renew spacer add (.2)	.2
Transfer choke add (.1)	.1
(G) Fuel Pump, Renew	
Six—1974–80 (.3)	.5
V-8—1974–80 (.5)	.8
w/A.C. add	.2
Add pump test if performed.	
(G) Intake Manifold or Gaskets, Renew	
Six—1974–80 (1.1)	1.6
V-8—1974–80—exc below (1.8) ..	2.3
429, 460 engs (2.3)	2.8
Renew manif add (.4)	.5
w/Six cyl A.C. comp add (.2)	.2

Elite, Granada, Maverick, Torino, LTD II, Thunderbird (1977–79)

	Chilton Time
(G) Fuel Pump, Test	
Includes: Disconnect line at carburetor, attach pressure gauge.	
All models	.3
(G) Fuel Pump, Renew	
Six—1974–80 (.3)	.5
V-8—1974–80 (.5)	.8
(G) Carburetor, Renew	
Includes: Necessary adjustments.	
Six—1974–80 (.4)	.7
V-8—1974–80 (.5)	.9
(G) Carburetor, R&R and Clean or Recondition.	
Includes: Necessary adjustments.	
Six—1974–80 (1.2)	1.8
V-8—1974–80 (1.5)	2.4
Renew spacer add (.2)	.2
Transfer choke add (.1)	.1
w/A.C. add	.2
Add pump test if performed.	
(G) Intake Manifold or Gaskets, Renew	
Six—1974–80 (1.1)	1.6
V-8—1974–80—exc below (1.8) ..	2.3
429, 460 engs (2.3)	2.8
Renew manif add (.4)	.5
w/Six cyl A.C. comp add (.2)	.2

Ford

	Chilton Time
(G) Fuel Pump, Test	
Includes: Disconnect line at carburetor, attach pressure gauge.	
All models	.3

(Factory Time)	Chilton Time
(G) Carburetor, Renew	
Includes: Necessary adjustments.	
1974–80 (.5)	.8
(G) Carburetor, R&R and Clean or Recondition	
Includes: Necessary adjustments.	
1974–80 (1.5)	2.7
Renew spacer add (.2)	.2
Transfer choke add (.1)	.1
(G) Fuel Pump, Renew	
302–351 Wengs	
1974–78 (.4)	.7
1979–80 (.5)	.9
351C/M-400 engs	
1974–76 (.5)	.9
1977–80 (.4)	.9
460 eng	
1974–78 (.5)	.9
w/A.C. add	.2
Add pump test if performed.	
(G) Intake Manifold or Gaskets, Renew	
1974 (1.7)	2.2
1975–80—exc below (1.6)	2.1
460 eng (2.3)	2.7
Renew manif add (.4)	.5

Lincoln Continental, Mark IV, Mark V

(Factory Time)	Chilton Time
(G) Fuel Pump, Test	
Includes: Disconnect line at carburetor, attach pressure gauge.	
All models	.3
(G) Carburetor, Renew	
Includes: Necessary adjustments.	
1974–80—Continental (.4)	.8
Mark IV, V (.5)	.9
(G) Carburetor, R&R and Clean or Recondition	
Includes: Necessary adjustments.	
1974–80—Continental (1.4)	2.7
Mark IV, V (1.5)	2.8
Renew spacer add (.2)	.2
Transfer choke add (.1)	.1
(G) Fuel Pump, Renew	
1974–80—Continental (.5)	.8
Mark IV, V (.4)	.8
w/A.C. add	.1
Add pump test if performed.	
(G) Intake Manifold or Gaskets, Renew	
1974–80 (2.3)	3.0
Renew manif add (.4)	.5

Mercury

(Factory Time)	Chilton Time
(G) Fuel Pump, Test	
Includes: Disconnect line at carburetor, attach pressure gauge.	
All models	.3
(G) Carburetor, Renew	
Includes: Necessary adjustments.	
1974–80 (.5)	.8
(G) Carburetor, R&R and Clean or Recondition	
Includes: Necessary adjustments.	
1974–80 (1.5)	2.7

(Factory Time)	Chilton Time
Renew spacer add (.2)	.2
Transfer choke add (.1)	.1
(G) Fuel Pump, Renew	
302—351W engs	
1974–78 (.4)	.7
1979–80 (.5)	.9
351 C/M—400 engs	
1974–76 (.5)	.9
1977–80 (.4)	.9
460 eng	
1974–78 (.5)	.9
wo/A.C. add	.2
Add pump test if performed.	
(G) Intake Manifold or Gaskets, Renew	
1974 (1.7)	2.2
1975–80—exc below (1.6)	2.1
460 eng (2.3)	2.7
Renew manif add (.4)	.5

Mustang II, Bobcat, Pinto, Fairmont, Zephyr

(Factory Time)	Chilton Time
(G) Fuel Pump, Test	
Includes: Disconnect line at carburetor, attach pressure gauge.	
All models	.3
(G) Carburetor, Renew	
Includes: Necessary adjustments.	
1974–80 (.5)	.9
(G) Carburetor, R&R and Clean or Recondition	
Includes: Necessary adjustments.	
1974–80—Four (1.1)	1.7
Six (1.5)	2.4
V-6 (1.5)	2.4
V-8 (1.5)	2.4
Renew spacer add (.2)	.2
Transfer choke add (.1)	.1
(G) Fuel Pump, Renew	
1974–80—Four (.4)	.7
Six (.3)	.6
V-6 (.6)	.9
V-8 (.4)	.7
Add pump test if performed.	
(G) Intake Manifold or Gaskets, Renew	
1974–80—Four (1.1)	1.6
Six (1.1)	1.7
V-6 (2.2)	2.7
V-8—exc below (1.9)	2.4
Mustang II (2.4)	3.0
Renew manif add (.4)	.5

Oldsmobile

GASOLINE ENGINES

(Factory Time)	Chilton Time
(G) Fuel Pump, Test	
Includes: Disconnect line at carburetor, attach pressure gauge.	
All models	.2
(G) Carburetor, Renew	
Includes: Transfer parts, make all necessary adjustments.	
1974–80 (.5)	.8

	(Factory Time)	Chilton Time

(G) Carburetor, R&R and Clean or Recondition
Includes: All necessary adjustments.

1974–80—2 bbl (1.8)	2.3
4 bbl (2.1)	2.8

(G) Fuel Pump, Renew

1974–75 (.3)	.5
1976–80—V-6 (.6)	.8
V-8 (.4)	.6
wo/A.C. add (.1)	.1
w/A.C. and A.I.R. add (.4)	.4
Add pump test if performed.	

(G) Intake Manifold or Gaskets, Renew
Includes: Adjust carburetor and linkage as necessary. Drain and refill radiator. Adjust timing.

1974–76 (1.4)	1.9
1977–80—V-6 (1.0)	1.5
1977–80—V-8—exc below (1.4)	1.9
350 eng—Code G or L (1.9)	2.4
Renew manif add (.3)	.5
w/A.C. add (.4)	.4
w/A.I.R. add (.1)	.1

DIESEL ENGINE

(G) Fuel Supply Pump, Renew

1978–80 (.5)	.8

(G) Intake Manifold or Gaskets, Renew

1978–80 (2.0)	2.8
Renew manif add (.3)	.5

Olds Cutlass, Omega (1974–79)

GASOLINE ENGINES

(G) Fuel Pump, Test
Includes: Disconnect line at carburetor, attach pressure gauge.

All models	.2

(G) Carburetor, Renew
Includes: Transfer parts, make all necessary adjustments.

1974–80 (.5)	.7

(G) Carburetor, R&R and Clean or Recondition
Includes: All necessary adjustments.

1974–80—1 bbl (1.6)	2.1
2 bbl (1.8)	2.3
4 bbl (2.0)	2.6

(G) Fuel Pump, Renew

Six—1974–76 (.3)	.5
V-6—1977–80 (.6)	.8
V-8—1974–75 (.3)	.5
1976–80 (.4)	.6
w/A.C. and A.I.R. add (.4)	.4
Add pump test if performed.	

(G) Intake Manifold or Gaskets, Renew
Includes: Adjust carburetor and linkage as necessary. Drain and refill radiator. Adjust timing.

Six—1974–76 (.8)	1.2
V-6—1977–80 (1.0)	1.5
V-8—1974–76 (1.4)	1.9
1977–80—exc below (1.4)	1.9
305–350 engs, Code G, H, L or U (1.9)	2.4
Renew manif add (.3)	.3
w/A.C. add (.4)	.4
w/A.I.R. add (.1)	.1

DIESEL ENGINE

(G) Fuel Supply Pump, Renew

1979–80 (.5)	.8

(G) Intake Manifold or Gaskets, Renew

1979–80 (2.0)	2.8
Renew manif add (.3)	.5

Olds Toronado

GASOLINE ENGINES

(G) Fuel Pump, Test
Includes: Disconnect line at carburetor, attach pressure gauge.

All models	.2

(G) Carburetor, Renew
Includes: Transfer parts, make all necessary adjustments.

1974–80 (.5)	.8

(G) Carburetor, R&R and Clean or Recondition
Includes: All necessary adjustments.

1974–80 (2.1)	2.6

(G) Fuel Pump, Renew

1974–75 (.5)	.7
1976–80 (.6)	.8
Add pump test if performed.	

(G) Intake Manifold or Gaskets, Renew
Includes: Adjust carburetor and linkage as necessary. Drain and refill radiator. Adjust timing.

1974–80 (1.4)	1.9
Renew manif add (.3)	.5
w/A.C. add (.4)	.4
w/A.I.R. add (.1)	.1

DIESEL ENGINES

(G) Fuel Supply Pump, Renew

1979–80 (1.0)	1.4

(G) Intake Manifold or Gaskets, Renew

1979–80 (2.0)	2.8
Renew manif add (.3)	.3

Olds Starfire

(G) Fuel Pump, Test
Includes: Disconnect line at carburetor, attach pressure gauge.

All models	.2

(G) Carburetor, Renew
Includes: Transfer parts, make all necessary adjustments.

Four—1976–80 (.4)	.7
V-6—1975–80 (.5)	.8
V-8—1977–80 (.5)	.8

(G) Carburetor, R&R and Clean or Recondition
Includes: All necessary adjustments.

Four—1976–80 (1.7)	2.2
V-6—1975–80 (1.8)	2.3
V8—1977–80 (1.8)	2.3

(G) Fuel Pump, Renew

Four—1976–80 (.8)	1.0
V-6—1975–80 (.8)	1.0
V-8—1977–80 (.6)	*.8
*w/A.C. add (.5)	.5
Add pump test if performed.	

(Factory Time)	Chilton Time

(G) Intake Manifold or Gaskets, Renew
*Includes: Adjust carburetor and linkage
as necessary. Drain and refill radiator.
Adjust timing.*

Four—1976–77 (1.3)	1.8
1978–80 (1.3)	1.8
V-6—1975–80 (1.0)	1.5
V-8—1977–80 (1.9)	*2.4
Renew manif add (.3)	.5
*w/A.C. add (.9)	.9
*w/A.I.R. add (.5)	.5

Plymouth

(G) Fuel Pump, Test
*Includes: Disconnect line at carburetor,
attach pressure gauge.*

All models	.2

(G) Carburetor, Renew
*Includes: Adjust idle speed and mixture
with analyzer.*

1974–78—exc below (.7)	1.1
1976—4 bbl (.9)	1.3

**(G) Carburetor, R&R and Clean or
Recondition**
*Includes: Adjust idle speed and mixture
with analyzer.*

1974–78—1 bbl (1.4)	2.5
2 bbl (1.7)	2.8
4 bbl (1.5)	2.5
Thermo-Quad (2.4)	4.0

(G) Fuel Pump, Renew

Six—1974–78 (.4)	.8
V-8—1974–78—318, 360 engs (.4) . .	.8
400, 440 engs (.5)	.9
Add fuel pump test if performed.	

(G) Intake Manifold or Gaskets, Renew

Six—1974–78 (2.0)	2.5
V-8—1974–75	
318, 360 engs (1.9)	2.4
400, 440 engs (1.5)	1.9
1976–78—318, 360 engs (2.1)	2.7
400, 440 engs (1.6)	2.0
w/A.C. add (.4)	.4
w/Air inj pump add (.3)	.3

**(G) Intake and Exhaust Manifold
Gaskets, Renew**

Six—1974–78 (1.7)	2.3
w/A.C. add (.4)	.4

Pontiac & Grand Prix

(G) Fuel Pump, Test
*Includes: Disconnect line at carburetor,
attach pressure gauge.*

All models	.2

(G) Carburetor, Renew
Includes: All necessary adjustments.

V-6—1977–80 (.3)	.7
V-8—1974–80 (.5)	.9

(G) Idle Stop Solenoid, Renew
Includes: Adjust.

1975–80 (.2)	.3

**(G) Carburetor, R&R and Clean or
Recondition**
Includes: All necessary adjustments.

V-6—1977–80 (1.8)	2.5

(Factory Time)	Chilton Time

V-8—1974–80—2 bbl (1.8)	2.5
4 bbl (1.9)	2.6

(G) Fuel Pump, Renew

V-6—1977–80 (.3)	.6
V-8—1974–80 (.4)	.7
Add pump test if performed.	

(G) Intake Manifold or Gaskets, Renew

V-6—1977–80 (1.0)	1.5
V-8—1974–76 (1.5)	2.0
1977–80	
350 eng, Code X (1.0)	1.5
305–350 engs, Code H-U-L (1.9) . .	2.4
350–403 engs—Code R-K (1.4) . . .	1.9
301-350-400 engs,	
Code W-Y-P-Z (1.4)	1.9
w/A.C. add (.4)	.4
w/A.I.R. add (.2)	.2
Renew manif add (.4)	.5

Pontiac Astre & Sunbird

(G) Fuel Pump, Test
*Includes: Disconnect line at carburetor,
attach pressure gauge.*

All models	.2

(G) Carburetor, Renew
Includes: All necessary adjustments.

1975–76—1 bbl (.5)	.8
2 bbl (.4)	.8
1977–80 (.3)	.7

**(G) Carburetor, R&R and Clean or
Recondition**
Includes: All necessary adjustments.

1975–76—1 bbl (1.2)	1.9
2 bbl (1.1)	1.9
1977–80 (1.8)	2.5

(G) Fuel Pump, Renew

1975–76 (.9)	1.3
1977–80	
140 eng (.9)	1.3
151 eng (.5)	.8
V-6 (.9)	1.3
V-8 (.5)	.8
Add pump test if performed.	

(G) Intake Manifold or Gaskets, Renew

1975–80	
Four—140 eng (1.7)	2.2
151 eng (1.3)	1.8
V-6 (1.0)	1.5
V-8 (1.9)	2.4
Renew manif add (.4)	.5
w/A.C. add (.1)	.1
w/P.S. add (.3)	.3

**(G) Intake and Exhaust Manifold
Gaskets, Renew**

1977–80	
Four—151 eng code 1 (1.4)	1.9

Firebird, Phoenix (1978–79), LeMans, Ventura (1974–77)

(G) Fuel Pump, Test
*Includes: Disconnect line at carburetor,
attach pressure gauge.*

All models	.2

(G) Carburetor, Renew
Includes: All necessary adjustments.

1974–76—1 bbl (.5)	.9

(Factory Time)	Chilton Time
2 bbl (.6)	1.0
4 bbl (.6)	1.0
1977–80—Four (.3)	.7
V-6 (.3)	.7
V-8 (.5)	.9

(G) Carburetor, R&R and Clean or Recondition
Includes: All necessary adjustments.

1974–76—1 bbl (1.9)	2.6
2 bbl (1.8)	2.5
4 bbl (1.8)	2.5
1977–80—Four (1.5)	2.2
V-6 (1.8)	2.5
V-8 (1.8)	2.5

(G) Fuel Pump, Renew

Four—1977–80 (.4)	.7
Six—1974–76 (.3)	.6
V-6—1977–80 (.3)	.6
V-8—1974–80 (.4)	.7
Add pump test if performed.	

(G) Intake Manifold or Gaskets, Renew

Four—1977–80 (1.3)	1.8
Six—1974–76 (1.2)	1.7
V-6—1977–80 (1.0)	1.5
V-8—1974–76 (1.6)	2.1
1977–80	
305-350 engs	
Code G-H-U-L (1.9)	2.4
350–403 engs	
Code R-K (1.4)	1.9
301–350–400 engs	
Code W-Y-P-Z (1.4)	1.9
w/A.C. add (.4)	.4
w/P.S. add (.3)	.3
w/A.I.R. add (.2)	.2

Thunderbird (1974–76)

(G) Fuel Pump, Test
Includes: Disconnect line at carburetor, attach pressure gauge.

All models	.2

(G) Carburetor, Renew
Includes: Necessary adjustments.

1974–76 (.5)	.8

(G) Carburetor, R&R and Clean or Recondition
Includes: Necessary adjustments.

1974–76 (1.7)	2.7
Renew Spacer add (.2)	.2
Transfer Choke add (.1)	.1

(G) Fuel Pump, Renew

1974–76 (.5)	.7

(G) Intake Manifold or Gaskets, Renew

1974–76 (2.4)	3.0
Renew manif add (.4)	.5
w/Thermactor add (.2)	.2

Valiant, Dart, Barracuda, Challenger, Aspen, Volare, LeBaron, Diplomat

(G) Fuel Pump, Test
Includes: Disconnect line at carburetor, attach pressure gauge.

All models	.2

(Factory Time)	Chilton Time

(G) Carburetor, Renew
Includes: Adjust idle speed and mixture with analyzer.

1974–80—exc below (.7)	1.1
1976—4 bbl (.9)	1.3

(G) Carburetor, R&R and Clean or Recondition
Includes: Adjust idle speed and mixture with analyzer.

1974–80—1 bbl (1.4)	2.5
2 bbl (1.7)	2.8
4 bbl (1.5)	2.5
Thermo-Quad (2.4)	4.0

(G) Fuel Pump, Renew

Six—1974–80 (.6)	.8
V-8—1974–80 (.4)	.8
Add fuel pump test if performed.	

(G) Intake and Exhaust Manifold Gaskets, Renew

Six—1974–76 (1.7)	2.3
w/A.C. add (.4)	.4

(G) Intake Manifold or Gaskets, Renew

Six—1974–80 (2.1)	2.4
1977–80 (2.0)	2.4
V-8—1974–80 (2.1)	2.7
w/A.C. add (.4)	.4
w/Air inj add (.3)	.3

Vega & Monza

(G) Fuel Pump, Test
Includes: Disconnect line at carburetor, attach pressure gauge.

All models	.2

(G) Carburetor, Renew
Includes: Necessary adjustments.

1974–80 (.5)	.7

(G) Carburetor, R&R and Clean or Recondition
Includes: Necessary adjustments.

1974–80—1 bbl (1.2)	1.5
2 bbl (1.4)	2.0

(G) Fuel Pump or Push Rod, Renew

1974–77 (.9)	1.2
1978–80—Four (.3)	.5
V-6 (.9)	*1.4
V-8 (.9)	*1.4
*Includes: R&R fuel tank.	
V-8—w/A.I.R. add (.5)	.5

(G) Intake Manifold or Gaskets, Renew

Four—1974–77 (1.7)	2.1
1978–80 (1.7)	2.1
w/P.S. add (.3)	.3
V-6—1978–80 (1.3)	1.7
V8—1975–80 (2.0)	2.5
Vega w/A.C. add (.2)	.2
Monza w/A.C. add (.9)	.9
w/A.I.R add (.5)	.5

(G) Exhaust to Intake Manifold Gasket, Renew

Four—1978–80 (1.4)	1.8
w/P.S. add (.3)	.3

ALTERNATOR AND REGULATOR

American Motors

	(Factory Time)	Chilton Time

(G) Alternator, Renew
Four—1977–80 (.6)	.9
Six—1974–30 (.4)	.7
V-8—1974–78 (.5)	.8
1979–80 (.4)	.8
w/A.C. add (.1)	.1
Add circuit test if performed.	

(G) Alternator, R&R and Recondition
Four—1977–80 (1.0)	1.3
Six—1974–76	
Delco (.7)	1.0
Motorola (.9)	1.2
Motorcraft (.8)	1.1
1977–79 (.7)	1.0
w/A.C. add (.1)	.1
V8—1974–76	
Delco (.8)	1.1
Motorola (1.0)	1.3
Motorcraft (.9)	1.2
1977–80 (.9)	1.2
Add circuit test if performed.	

AMC/Jeep

(G) Alternator, Renew
Six—1974–80—Delco (.4)	.6
Motorola (.6)	.8
V8—1974–80 (.5)	.8
Add circuit test if performed.	

(G) Alternator, R&R & Recondition
1974–80—Delco (.7)	1.0
Motorola (.9)	1.2
Motorcraft (.8)	1.1
w/A.C. add (.1)	.1
Add circuit test if performed.	

Buick LeSabre, Electra, Riviera (1974–78)

(G) Delcotron Assembly, Renew
Includes: Transfer pulley and fan.
1974–80 (.4)	.6
w/A.C. and Turbocharger add (.2)	.3
Add circuit test if performed.	

(G) Delcotron, R&R and Recondition
Includes: Complete disassembly, inspect, test, replace parts as required, reassemble.
1974–80 (1.1)	1.7
w/A.C. and Turbocharger add (.2)	.3

Buick Riviera (1979–80)

(G) Delcotron, R&R and Recondition
Includes: Complete disassembly, inspect, test, replace parts as required, reassemble.
1979–80 (1.1)	1.7
w/A.C. and Turbocharger add (.2)	.3

	(Factory Time)	Chilton Time

(G) Delcotron Assembly, Renew
Includes: Transfer fan and pulley.
1979–80 (.4)	.6
w/A.C. and Turbocharger add (.2)	.3

Buick Apollo, Century, Gran Sport, Regal, Skylark (1974–79)

(G) Delcotron Assembly, Renew
Includes: Transfer pulley and fan.
1974–80 (.4)	.6
w/A.C. and Turbocharger add (.2)	.3
Add circuit test if performed.	

(G) Delcotron, R&R and Recondition
Includes: Complete disassembly, inspect, test, replace parts as required, reassemble.
1974–80 (1.1)	1.7
w/A.C. and Turbocharger add (.2)	.3

Buick Skyhawk

(G) Delcotron Assembly, Renew
Includes: Transfer pulley and fan.
1975–80 (.4)	.6
Add circuit test if performed.	

(G) Delcotron, R&R and Recondition
Includes: Complete disassembly, inspect, test, replace parts as required, reassemble.
1975–80 (1.1)	1.7

Cadillac

(G) Delcotron Assembly, Renew
1974–80 (.5)	.7

(G) Delcotron, R&R and Recondition
Includes: Complete disassembly, replacement of parts as required.
1974–80 (1.2)	1.9

Cadillac Seville

(G) Delcotron, Renew
1976–77 (.5)	.7
1978–80 (.3)	.7

(G) Delcotron, R&R and Recondition
Includes: Complete disassembly, replacement of parts as required.
1976–77 (1.2)	1.9
1978–80 (1.0)	1.9

Cadillac Eldorado

(G) Delcotron Assembly, Renew
1974–78 (.5)	.7
1979–80 (.4)	.7

(Factory Time)	Chilton Time

(G) Delcotron, R&R and Recondition
Includes: Complete disassembly, replacement of parts as required.

1974–78 (1.2)	1.9
1979–80 (1.1)	1.9

Camaro, Chevelle, Malibu, Monte Carlo, Nova

(G) Delcotron Assembly or Fan Pulley, Renew

1974–77—Six (.4)	.7
V-8 (.5)	.8
1978–80 (.4)	.7

(G) Delcotron, R&R and Recondition
Includes: Complete disassembly, replacement of parts as required, reassemble.

1974—Six (1.0)	1.5
V-8 (1.2)	1.7
1975–77 (1.0)	1.5
1978–80—Six (.5)	.9
V-6 (.6)	1.0
V-8 (.6)	1.0

Chevrolet & Corvette

(G) Delcotron Assembly or Fan Pulley, Renew

1974—Six (.4)	.6
V-8 (.6)	.8
1975–77—Six (.4)	.6
V-8 (.5)	.8
1978–80 (.4)	.6

(G) Delcotron, R&R and Recondition
Includes: Complete disassembly, replacement of parts as required, reassemble.

1974—Six (1.0)	1.5
V-8 (1.2)	1.7
1975–77 (1.1)	1.6
1978–80—Six (1.2)	1.7
V-8 (1.1)	1.7

Chevette

(G) Delcotron Assembly or Fan Pulley, Renew

1976–77 (.4)	.6
1978–80 (.3)	.6

(G) Delcotron, R&R and Recondition
Includes: Complete disassembly, replacement of parts as required, reassemble.

1976–77 (1.1)	1.5
1978–80 (1.2)	1.6

Citation, Omega, Phoenix, Skylark—All 1980

(G) Delcotron Assembly, Renew

1980—Four (.5)	.7
V-6 (.4)	.6
w/P.S. add (.3)	.3

(G) Delcotron, R&R and Recondition
Includes: Complete disassembly, replacement of parts as required, reassemble.

1980—Four (1.4)	1.9

(Factory Time)	Chilton Time

V-6 (1.2)	1.7
w/P.S. add (.3)	.3

Chrysler, Cordoba, Imperial

(G) Alternator, Renew
Includes: Transfer pulley if required.

1974–76 (.6)	.8
1977–80 (.4)	.6
w/A.C. add (.1)	.1
w/Air inj add (.2)	.2
w/100 amp alter add (.1)	.1
Add circuit test if performed.	

(G) Alternator, R&R and Recondition
Includes: Test and disassemble.

1974 (1.5)	2.2
1975–76 (2.0)	2.7
1977–80 (1.9)	2.7
w/A.C. add (.1)	.1
w/Air inj add (.2)	.2
w/100 amp alter add (.1)	.1

Dodge

(G) Alternator, Renew
Includes: Transfer pulley if required.

1974–76 (.6)	.8
1977–80 (.4)	.6
w/A.C. add (.1)	.1
w/Air inj add (.2)	.2
w/100 amp alter add (.1)	.1
Add circuit test if performed.	

(G) Alternator, R&R and Recondition
Includes: Test and disassemble.

1974 (1.5)	2.2
1975–76 (2.0)	2.7
1977–80 (1.9)	2.7
w/A.C. add (.1)	.1
w/Air inj add (.2)	.2
w/100 amp alter add (.1)	.1

Horizon & Omni

(G) Alternator, Renew
Includes: Transfer pulley if required.

1978–80 (1.0)	1.4
w/A.C. add (.5)	.5
Add circuit test if performed.	

(G) Alternator, R&R and Recondition
Includes: Test and disassemble, renew parts as required.

1978–80 (1.7)	2.4
w/A.C. add (.5)	.5

Capri & Mustang (1979–80)

(G) Alternator, Renew

1979–80 (.4)	.8
Transfer pulley add (.1)	.1
Circuit test add	.6

(G) Alternator, R&R and Recondition
Includes: Complete disassembly, replacement of parts as required. Test validity of rotor fields, stator and diodes.

1979–80 (1.0)	2.0
Circuit test add	.6

	Chilton Time		Chilton Time
(Factory Time)		(Factory Time)	

Comet, Cougar, Monarch, Montego, Lincoln Versailles

(G) Alternator, Renew

1974–80 (.4)	.8
w/A.C. add	.2
Transfer pulley add (.1)	.1
Circuit test add	.6

(G) Alternator, R&R and Recondition
Includes: Complete disassembly, replacement of parts as required. Test validity of rotor fields, stator and diodes.

1974–80 (1.0)	2.0
w/A.C. add	.2
Circuit test add	.6

Elite, Granada, Maverick, Torino, LTD II, Thunderbird (1977–79)

(G) Alternator, Renew

1974–80 (.4)	.8
w/A.C. add	.2
Transfer pulley add (.1)	.1
Circuit test add	.6

(G) Alternator, R&R and Recondition
Includes: Complete disassembly, replacement of parts as required. Test validity of rotor fields, stator and diodes.

1974–80 (1.0)	2.0
w/A.C. add	.2
Circuit test add	.6

Ford

(G) Alternator, R&R and Recondition
Includes: Complete disassembly, replacement of parts as required. Test validity of rotor fields, stator and diodes.

| 1974–80 (1.0) .... | 2.0 |
| Circuit test add (.4) .... | .6 |

(G) Alternator, Renew

1974–80 (.4)	.8
Transfer pulley add (.1)	.1
Circuit test add (.4)	.6

Lincoln Continental, Mark IV, Mark V

(G) Alternator, Renew

1974 (.5)	.9
1975–80 (.6)	1.0
Transfer pulley add (.1)	.1
Circuit test add (.4)	.6

(G) Alternator, R&R and Recondition
Includes: Complete disassembly, replacement of parts as required. Test validity of rotor fields, stator and diodes.

1974 (1.1)	2.1
1975–80 (1.2)	2.2
Circuit test add (.4)	.6

Mercury

(G) Alternator, Renew

1974–80 (.4)	.8
Transfer pulley add (.1)	.1
Circuit test add (.4)	.6

(G) Alternator, R&R and Recondition
Includes: Complete disassembly, replacement of parts as required. Test validity of rotor fields, stator and diodes.

| 1974–80 (1.0) .... | 2.0 |
| Circuit test add (.4) .... | .6 |

Mustang II, Bobcat, Pinto, Fairmont, Zephyr

(G) Alternator, Renew

1974–80 (.4)	.8
Transfer pulley add (.1)	.1
Circuit test add	.6

(G) Alternator, R&R and Recondition
Includes: Complete disassembly, replacement of parts as required. Test validity of rotor fields, stator and diodes.

| 1974–80 (1.0) .... | 2.0 |
| Circuit test add .... | .6 |

Oldsmobile

(G) Delcotron Assembly or Fan Pulley, Renew

| 1974–75 (.3) .... | .5 |
| 1976–80 (.5) .... | .7 |

(G) Delcotron, R&R and Recondition
Includes: Complete disassembly, replacement of parts as required.

| 1974–80 (1.1) .... | 1.6 |
| w/Diesel eng add (.1) .... | .1 |

Olds Cutlass, Omega (1974–79)

(G) Delcotron Assembly or Fan Pulley, Renew

Six—1974–76 (.3)	.5
V-6—1977–80 (.5)	.7
V-8—1974–75 (.3)	.5
1976–80 (.5)	.7

(G) Delcotron, R&R and Recondition
Includes: Complete disassembly, replacement of parts as required. Reassemble.

| 1974–80 (1.0) .... | 1.6 |
| w/Diesel eng add (.1) .... | .1 |

Olds Toronado

(G) Delcotron Assembly or Fan Pulley, Renew

| 1974–75 (.3) .... | .6 |
| 1976–80 (.5) .... | .8 |

(G) Delcotron, R&R and Recondition
Includes: Complete disassembly, replacement of parts as required. Reassemble.

| 1974–80 (1.1) .... | 1.6 |

(Factory Time)	Chilton Time

Olds Starfire

(G) Delcotron Assembly or Fan Pulley, Renew
1975–80 (.5) 7
(G) Delcotron, R&R and Recondition
Includes: Complete disassembly, replacement of parts as required.
1975–80 (1.0) 1.6

Plymouth

(G) Alternator, Renew
Includes: Transfer pulley if required.
1974–76 (.6) 8
1977–78 (.4) 6
w/A.C. add (.1) 1
w/Air inj add (.2) 2
w/100 amp alter add (.1) 1
Add circuit test if performed.
(G) Alternator, R&R and Recondition
Includes: Test and disassemble.
1974 (1.5) 2.2
1975–76 (2.0) 2.7
1977–78 (1.9) 2.7
w/A.C. add (.1) 1
w/Air inj add (.2) 2
w/100 amp alter add (.1) 1

Pontiac & Grand Prix

(G) Delcotron Assembly, Renew
Includes: Transfer pulley and fan.
1974–80 (.4) 6
Add circuit test if performed.
(G) Delcotron, R&R and Recondition
Includes: Complete disassembly, inspect, test, replace parts as required. Reassemble.
1974–80 (1.5) 2.2

Pontiac Astre & Sunbird

(G) Delcotron Assembly, Renew
Includes: Transfer pulley and fan.
1975–80 (.4) 6
Add circuit test if performed.
(G) Delcotron, R&R and Recondition
Includes: Complete disassembly, inspect, test, replace parts as required. Reassemble.
1975–80 (1.1) 2.0

Firebird, Phoenix (1978–79), LeMans, Ventura (1974–77)

(G) Delcotron Assembly, Renew
Includes: Transfer pulley and fan.
1974–80 (.4) 6
Add circuit test if performed.

(Factory Time)	Chilton Time

(G) Delcotron, R&R and Recondition
Includes: Complete disassembly, inspect, test, replace parts as required. Reassemble.
1974–80 (1.5) 2.2

Thunderbird (1974–76)

(G) Alternator, Renew
1974–76 (.5) 9
Transfer pulley add (.1) 1
Circuits test add (.6) 6
(G) Alternator, R&R and Recondition
Includes: Complete disassembly, replacement of parts as required. Test validity of rotor fields, stator and diodes.
1974–76 (1.1) 2.1

Valiant, Dart, Barracuda, Challenger, Aspen, Volare, LeBaron, Diplomat

(G) Alternator, Renew
Includes: Transfer pulley if required.
1974–76 (.6) 8
1977–80 (.4) 6
w/A.C. add (.1) 1
w/Air inj add (.2) 2
w/100 amp alter add (.1) 1
Add circuit test if performed.
(G) Alternator, R&R and Recondition
Includes: Test and disassemble.
1974 (1.5) 2.2
1975–76 (2.0) 2.7
1977–80 (1.9) 2.7
w/A.C. add (.1) 1
w/Air inj add (.2) 2
w/100 amp alter add (.1) 1

Vega & Monza

(G) Delcotron Assembly or Fan Pulley, Renew
Four—1974–77 (.4) 6
1978–80 (.3) 6
V-6—1978–80 (.4) 6
V-8—1975–77 (.5) 7
1978–80 (.4) 7
(G) Delcotron, R&R and Recondition
Includes: Complete disassembly, replacement of parts as required, reassemble.
Four—1974–77 (1.0) 1.6
1978–80 (.5) 1.1
V-6—1978–80 (.6) 1.2
V-8—1975–77 (1.1) 1.7
1978–80 (.6) 1.2

STARTING SYSTEM

(Factory Time)	Chilton Time

American Motors

(G) Starter, Renew
1974–80 (.3) 6
Add draw test if performed.
(G) Starter, R&R and Recondition
Includes: Turn down armature.
1974–80 (1.1) 2.3
Renew fields add (.3) 5
Add draw test if performed.
(G) Starter Drive, Renew
Includes: R&R starter.
1974–80 (.4) 8
(G) Starter Solenoid, Renew
1974–80 (.2) 4

AMC/Jeep

(G) Starter, Renew
1974–80 (.3) 6
Add draw test if performed.
(G) Starter, R&R and Recondition
Includes: Turn down armature.
1974–80 (1.1) 2.3
New fields add (.3) 5
Add draw test if performed.
(G) Starter Drive, Renew
1974–80 (.4) 8

Buick LeSabre, Electra, Riviera (1974–78)

(G) Starter, Renew
V-6—1976–80 (.4) 7
V-8—1974–80 (.6) 9
(G) Starter, R&R and Recondition
Includes: Turn down armature.
V-6—1976–80 (1.2) 1.7
V-8—1974–80 (1.4) 1.9
Renew field coils add (.2) 2
(G) Starter Drive, Renew
V-6—1976–80 (.5) 9
V-8—1974–80 (.7) 1.1
(G) Starter Solenoid Switch, Renew
Includes: R&R starter.
V-6—1976–80 (.4) 7
V-8—1974–80 (.6) 9

Buick Riviera (1979–80)

(G) Starter, Renew
V-6—1979–80 (.4) 7
V-8—1979–80 (.3) 9
(G) Starter, R&R and Recondition
Includes: Turn down armature.
V-6—1979–80 (1.2) 1.7
V-8—1979–80 (1.2) 1.9
Renew field coils add (.2) 2
(G) Starter Drive, Renew
V-6—1979–80 (.5) 9
V-8—1979–80 (.5) 1.1

(Factory Time)	Chilton Time

(G) Starter Solenoid Switch, Renew
Includes: R&R starter.
V-6—1979–80 (.4) 7
V-8—1979–80 (.4) 9

Buick Apollo, Century, Gran Sport, Regal, Skylark (1974–79)

(G) Starter, Renew
Six—1974–75 (.4) 7
V-6—1975–80 (.4) 7
V-8—1974–80 (.6) 9
(G) Starter, R&R and Recondition
Includes: Turn down armature.
Six—1974–75 (1.2) 1.7
V-6—1975–80 (1.2) 1.7
V-8—1974–80 (1.4) 1.9
Renew field coils add (.2) 2
(G) Starter Drive, Renew
Six—1974–75 (.5) 9
V-6—1975–80 (.5) 9
V-8—1974–80 (.7) 1.1
(G) Starter Solenoid Switch, Renew
Includes: R&R starter.
Six—1974–75 (.4) 7
V-6—1975–80 (.4) 7
V-8—1974–80 (.6) 9

Buick Skyhawk

(G) Starter, Renew
1975—w/M.T. (3.1) *4.0
w/A.T. (1.0) 1.6
1976–80—w/M.T. (1.1) 1.6
w/A.T. (.9) 1.5
Includes R&R trans and clutch housing.
(G) Starter, R&R and Recondition
Includes: Turn down armature.
1975—w/M.T. (3.7) *5.0
w/A.T. (1.6) 2.1
1976–80—w/M.T. (1.8) 2.3
w/A.T. (1.7) 2.2
Renew field coils add (.2) 2
Includes R&R trans and clutch housing.
(G) Starter Drive, Renew
1975—w/M.T. (3.2) *4.3
w/A.T. (1.1) 1.7
1976–80—w/M.T. (1.1) 1.7
w/A.T. (1.0) 1.6
Includes R&R trans and clutch housing.
(G) Starter Solenoid Switch, Renew
Includes: R&R starter.
1975—w/M.T. (3.1) *4.1
w/A.T. (1.0) 1.6
1976–80—w/M.T. (1.0) 1.6
w/A.T. (.9) 1.5
Includes R&R trans and clutch housing.

	Chilton Time
(Factory Time)	

Cadillac

(G) Starter, Renew
1974–80 (.6)	1.0
Add draw test if performed.	

(G) Starter, R&R and Recondition
Includes: Turn down armature.
1974–80 (1.5)	2.4
Renew fields add (.4)	.5
Add draw test if performed.	

(G) Starter Drive, Renew
1974–80 (1.1)	1.5

(G) Starter Solenoid, Renew
Includes: R&R starter.
1974–80 (.9)	1.2

Cadillac Seville

(G) Starter, Renew
1976–77 (.5)	.9
1978–80 (.4)	.9
Add draw test if performed.	

(G) Starter, R&R and Recondition
Includes: Turn down armature.
1976–77 (1.4)	2.3
1978–80 (1.3)	2.3
Renew fields add (.4)	.5

(G) Starter Drive, Renew
1976–77 (1.1)	1.5
1978–80 (.9)	1.5

(G) Starter Solenoid, Renew
Includes: R&R starter.
1976–77 (.7)	1.0
1978–80 (.6)	1.0

Cadillac Eldorado

(G) Starter, Renew
1974–77 (.6)	1.0
1978–80 (.4)	1.0
Add draw test if performed.	

(G) Starter, R&R and Recondition
Includes: Turn down armature.
1974–77 (1.5)	2.4
1978–80 (1.3)	2.4
Renew fields add (.4)	.5
Add draw test if performed.	

(G) Starter Drive, Renew
1974–77 (1.1)	1.5
1978–80 (.9)	1.5

(G) Starter Solenoid, Renew
Includes: R&R starter.
1974–77 (.9)	1.2
1978–80 (.7)	1.2

Camaro, Chevelle, Malibu, Monte Carlo, Nova

(G) Starter, Renew
Six—1974–80 (.4)	.6
V-6—1978–80 (.4)	.6
V-8—1974—80 (.6)	.9

(G) Starter, R&R and Recondition
Includes: Turn down armature.
Six—1974–80 (1.2)	2.2

	Chilton Time
(Factory Time)	

V-6—1978–80 (1.2)	2.2
V-8—1974–80 (1.4)	2.4
Renew fields add (.2)	.5

(G) Starter Drive, Renew
Six—1974–80 (.7)	1.0
V-6—1978–80 (.7)	1.0
V-8—1974–80 (.9)	1.2

(G) Starter Solenoid Switch, Renew
Includes: R&R starter.
Six—1974–80 (.6)	.9
V-6—1978–80 (.6)	.9
V-8—1974–80 (.8)	1.1

Chevrolet & Corvette

(G) Starter, Renew
Six—1977–80 (.4)	.6
V-8—1974–76 (.5)	.8
1977–80 (.6)	.9

(G) Starter, R&R and Recondition
Includes: Turn down armature.
Six—1977–80 (1.4)	2.2
V-8—1974–76 (1.5)	2.4
1977–80 (1.6)	2.6
Renew fields add (.2)	.5

(G) Starter Drive, Renew
Six—1977–80 (.7)	1.0
V-8—1974–76 (.8)	1.2
1977–80 (.9)	1.3

(G) Starter Solenoid Switch, Renew
Includes: R&R starter.
Six—1977–80 (.5)	.8
V-8—1974–76 (.6)	.9
1977–80 (.7)	1.1

Chevette

(G) Starter, Renew
1976–80 (.6)	1.0
w/P.B. add (.8)	.8
w/A.C. add (.8)	.8

(G) Starter, R&R and Recondition
Includes: Turn down armature.
1976–80 (1.4)	2.1
w/P.B. add (.8)	.8
w/A.C. add (.8)	.8
Renew fields add (.2)	.4

(G) Starter Drive, Renew
1976–80 (.9)	1.3
w/P.B. add (.8)	.8
w/A.C. add (.8)	.8

(G) Starter Solenoid Switch, Renew
Includes: R&R starter.
1976–80 (.7)	1.2
w/P.B. add (.8)	.8
w/A.C. add (.8)	.8

Citation, Omega, Phoenix, Skylark—All 1980

(G) Starter, Renew
1980—Four (.4)	.7
V-6 (.6)	.9
Add draw test if performed.	

(Factory Time)	Chilton Time
(G) Starter, R&R and Recondition	
Includes: Turn down armature.	
1980—Four (1.2)	**2.0**
V-6 (1.4)	**2.2**
Renew fields add (.2)	**.2**
Add draw test if performed.	
(G) Starter Drive, Renew	
Includes: R&R starter.	
1980—Four (.7)	**1.0**
V-6 (.9)	**1.2**
(G) Starter Motor Solenoid, Renew	
Includes: R&R starter on V-6.	
1980—Four (.3)	**.5**
V-6 (.6)	**1.0**

Chrysler, Cordoba, Imperial

(G) Starter, Renew	
Includes: Test starter relay, starter solenoid and amperage draw.	
Six—1979–80 (.5)	**.9**
V-8—1974–80	
318–360 engs (.7)	**1.2**
400–440 engs (.7)	**1.2**
(G) Starter, R&R and Recondition	
Includes: Test relay, starter solenoid and amperage draw.	
Six—1979–80 (2.1)	**2.9**
V-8—1974–80	
318–360 engs (2.3)	**3.1**
400–440 engs (2.3)	**3.1**
Renew fields add (.5)	**.5**
(G) Starter Drive, Renew	
Six—1979–80 (.9)	**1.4**
V-8—1974–80	
318–360 engs (1.1)	**1.6**
400–440 engs (1.1)	**1.6**
(G) Starter Relay, Renew	
1974–76 (.3)	**.4**
1977–80 (.2)	**.4**
(G) Starter Solenoid, Renew	
Includes: R&R starter.	
Six—1979–80 (.9)	**1.4**
V-8—1974–80	
318–360 engs (1.1)	**1.6**
400–440 engs (1.1)	**1.6**

Dodge

(G) Starter, Renew	
Includes: Test starter relay, starter solenoid and amperage draw.	
Six—1974–76 (.4)	**.6**
1977–80 (.5)	**.7**
V-8—1974—318, 360 engs (.5)	**.7**
400, 440 engs (.7)	**1.2**
1975–80 (.7)	**1.2**
(G) Starter, R&R and Recondition	
Includes: Test relay, starter solenoid and amperage draw.	
Six—1974–80 (2.0)	**2.5**
V-8—1974–80—318, 360 engs (2.1)	**2.7**
400, 440 engs (2.3)	**2.9**
New fields add (.5)	**.5**

(Factory Time)	Chilton Time
(G) Starter Drive, Renew	
Six—1974–75 (1.4)	**1.7**
1976 (.8)	**1.1**
1977–80 (.9)	**1.2**
V-8—1974–75—318, 360 engs	
(1.5)	**1.8**
400, 440 engs (1.7)	**2.0**
1976—318, 360 engs (.9)	**1.2**
400, 440 engs (1.7)	**2.0**
1977–80 (1.1)	**1.4**
(G) Starter Relay, Renew	
1974–76 (.3)	**.4**
1977–80 (.2)	**.4**
(G) Starter Solenoid, Renew	
Six—1974–76 (1.3)	**1.6**
1977–80 (1.0)	**1.3**
V-8—1974–76—318, 360 engs	
(1.4)	**1.7**
400, 440 engs (1.6)	**1.8**
1977–80 (1.1)	**1.4**

Capri & Mustang (1979–80)

(G) Starter, Renew	
1979–80 (.3)	**.6**
(G) Starter Solenoid Relay, Renew	
1979–80 (.3)	**.4**
(G) Starter, R&R and Recondition	
Includes: Turn down armature.	
1979–80	
positive engagement starter (1.8) .	**2.4**
solenoid actuated starter (1.6) . . .	**2.2**
New fields add	**.5**
Add draw test if performed.	
(G) Starter Drive, Renew	
Includes: R&R starter.	
1979–80 (.5)	**.8**
(G) Starter Solenoid, Renew	
Includes: R&R starter.	
1979–80 (.4)	**.7**

Horizon & Omni

(G) Starter, Renew	
Includes: Test starter relay, starter solenoid and amperage draw.	
1978–80—w/M.T. (.8)	**1.4**
w/A.T. (1.0)	**1.6**
(G) Starter, R&R and Recondition	
Includes: Test relay, starter solenoid and amperage draw.	
1978–80—w/M.T. (1.5)	**2.5**
w/A.T. (1.8)	**2.8**
Renew fields add (.5)	**.5**
(G) Starter Drive, Renew	
Includes: R&R starter.	
1978–80—w/M.T. (1.2)	**1.8**
w/A.T. (1.6)	**2.0**
(G) Starter Relay, Renew	
1978–80 (.2)	**.3**
(G) Starter Solenoid, Renew	
Includes: R&R starter.	
1978–80—w/M.T. (.9)	**1.6**
w/A.T. (1.1)	**1.8**

(Factory Time)	Chilton Time

Comet, Cougar, Monarch, Montego, Lincoln Versailles

(G) Starter, Renew
1974–80—exc below (.3) 7
1976–80—Monarch—V-8 (.5) 9
1977–80—Versailles (.5) 9
Add draw test if performed.
(G) Starter Solenoid Relay, Renew
1974–80 (.3) 4
(G) Starter, R&R and Recondition
Includes: Turn down armature.
1974–80
positive engagement starter (1.8) . 2.5
solenoid actuated starter (1.6) ... 2.3
New fields add 5
Add draw test if performed.
(G) Starter Drive, Renew
1973–79—exc below (.6) 1.2
1977–80—Cougar (.4) 8
(G) Starter Solenoid, Renew
Includes: R&R starter.
1974–80—exc below (.4) 8
1976–80—Monarch—V-8 (.6) 1.0
1977–80—Versailles (.6) 1.0

Elite, Granada, Maverick, Torino, LTD II, Thunderbird (1977–79)

(G) Starter, Renew
1974–80—exc below (.3) 7
1976–80—Granada V-8 (.5) 9
Add draw test if performed.
(G) Starter, R&R and Recondition
Includes: Turn down armature.
1974–80
positive engagement starter (1.8) . 2.5
solenoid actuated starter (1.6) ... 2.3
New fields add 5
Add draw test if performed
(G) Starter Drive, Renew
1974–80—exc below (.6) 1.2
LTD II (.4) 8
Granada 6 cyl (.4) 8
(G) Starter Solenoid, Renew
1974–80—exc below (.4) 8
1976–80—Granada V-8 (.6) 1.0
(G) Starter Solenoid Relay, Renew
1974–80 (.3) 4

Ford

(G) Starter, Renew
1974–80 (.3) 7
Add draw test if performed
(G) Starter Drive, Renew
1974–80 (.4) 1.0
(G) Starter Solenoid, Renew
Includes: R&R starter.
1974–80 (.4) 9
(M) Starter Solenoid Relay, Renew
1974–80 (.3) 4

(Factory Time)	Chilton Time

(G) Starter, R&R and Recondition
Includes: Turn down armature.
1974–80
positive engagement starter (1.6) . 2.3
solenoid actuated starter (1.4) ... 2.1
New fields add 5
Add draw test if performed.

Lincoln Continental, Mark IV, Mark V

(G) Starter, Renew
Continental
1974 (.6)........................ 1.2
1975–76 (.4) 9
1977–80 (.3) 9
Mark IV, V
1974–80 (.7) 1.3
Add draw test if performed.
(G) Starter, R&R and Recondition
Includes: Turn down armature.
Continental
1974 (1.9) 3.0
1975–76 (1.7) 2.7
1977–80 (1.6) 2.7
Mark IV, V
1974–80 (2.0) 3.0
New fields add 5
Add draw test if performed
(G) Starter Drive, Renew
Continental
1974 (.8)........................ 1.4
1975–76 (.6) 1.1
1977–80 (.5) 1.1
Mark IV, V
1974–80 (.9) 1.4
(G) Starter Solenoid, Renew
Includes: R&R starter.
Continental
1974 (.9)........................ 1.5
1975–76 (.7) 1.2
1977–80 (.6) 1.2
Mark IV, V
1974–80 (1.0) 1.5
(G) Starter Solenoid Relay, Renew
1974–80 (.3) 4

Mercury

(G) Starter, Renew
1974–80 (.3) 7
Add draw test if performed.
(G) Starter, R&R and Recondition
Includes: Turn down armature.
1974–80
positive engagement starter (1.6) . 2.3
solenoid actuated starter (1.4) ... 2.1
New fields add 5
Add draw test if performed.
(G) Starter Drive, Renew
1974–80 (.4) 1.0
(G) Starter Solenoid, Renew
Includes: R&R starter.
1974–80 (.4) 9
(G) Starter Solenoid Relay, Renew
1974–80 (.3) 4

(Factory Time)	Chilton Time

Mustang II, Bobcat, Pinto, Fairmont, Zephyr

(G) Starter, Renew
1974–80—exc below (.5)	.9
Mustang II (.6)	1.0

(G) Starter Solenoid Relay, Renew
1974–80 (.3)	.4

(G) Starter, R&R and Recondition
Includes: Turn down armature.
1974–80
positive engagement starter (1.9) .	2.6
solenoid actuated starter (1.7) ...	2.4
New fields add	.5
Add draw test if performed.	

(G) Starter Drive, Renew
1974–80—exc below (.7)	1.3
Mustang II (.8)	1.4

(G) Starter Solenoid, Renew
Includes: R&R starter.
1974–80—exc below (.6)	1.1
Mustang II (.7)	1.2

Oldsmobile

(G) Starter, Renew
Includes: R&R solenoid.
1974–76 (.5)	.8
1977–80—V-6 (.5)	.8
1977–80—V-8—exc below (.5)	.8
350 eng, Code G or L (.7)	1.0
1978–80—diesel (.5)	.8
Add draw test if performed.	

(G) Starter, R&R and Recondition
Includes: Turn down armature.
1974–76 (1.5)	2.3
1977–80—V-6 (1.5)	2.3
1977–80—V-8—exc below (1.5) ..	2.3
350 eng, Code G or L (1.7)	2.5
1978–80—diesel (1.4)	2.3
Renew fields add (.2)	.2
Add draw test if performed.	

(G) Starter Drive, Renew
Includes: R&R starter and solenoid.
1974–76 (.8)	1.2
1977–80—V-6 (.8)	1.2
1977–80—V-8—exc below (.8)	1.2
350 eng, Code G or L (1.0)	1.4
1978–80—diesel (.7)	1.2

Olds Cutlass, Omega (1974–79)

(G) Starter, Renew
Includes: R&R solenoid.
Six—1974–76 (.4)	.7
V-6—1977–80 (.5)	.8
V-8—1974–76 (.5)	.8
1977–80—exc below (.5)	.8
305–350 engs, Code G, H, L or U (.7)	1.0
1979–80—Diesel (.5)	.8
Add draw test if performed.	

(G) Starter, R&R and Recondition
Includes: Turn down armature.
Six—1974–76 (1.4)	1.9
V-6—1977–80 (1.5)	2.0

(Factory Time)	Chilton Time

V-8—1974–76 (1.3)	1.9
1977–80—exc below (1.5)	2.0
305–350 engs, Code G, H, L or U (1.7)	2.2
1979–80—Diesel (1.4)	2.3
Renew fields add (.2)	.2
Add draw test if performed.	

(G) Starter Drive, Renew
Includes: R&R starter and solenoid.
Six—1974–76 (.7)	1.2
V-6—1977–80 (.8)	1.3
V-8—1974–76 (.7)	1.2
1977–80—exc below (.8)	1.3
305–350 engs, Code G, H, L or U (1.0)	1.5
1979–80—Diesel (.7)	1.2

Olds Toronado

(G) Starter, Renew
Includes: R&R solenoid.
1974–80 (.5)	.8
Add draw test if performed.	

(G) Starter, R&R and Recondition
Includes: Turn down armature.
Gasoline
1974–80 (1.5)	2.3
Diesel—1979–80 (1.4)	2.3
Renew fields add (.2)	.2
Add draw test if performed.	

(G) Starter Drive, Renew
Includes: R&R starter and solenoid.
Gasoline
1974–80 (.8)	1.2
Diesel—1979–80 (.7)	1.2

Olds Starfire

(G) Starter, Renew
Includes: R&R solenoid.
Four—1976–77 (.4)	.7
1978–80 (.6)	.9
V-6—1975–80—w/A.T. (1.2)	1.5
w/M.T. (1.3)	1.6
V-8—1977–80 (1.4)	1.7
Add draw test if performed.	

(G) Starter, R&R and Recondition
Includes: Turn down armature.
Four—1976–77 (1.4)	2.2
1978–80 (1.5)	2.3
V-6—1975–80—w/A.T. (1.9)	2.7
w/M.T. (2.0)	2.8
V-8—1977–80 (2.4)	3.2
Renew fields add (.2)	.2
Add draw test if performed.	

(G) Starter Drive, Renew
Includes: R&R starter and solenoid.
Four—1976–77 (.7)	1.1
1978–80 (.9)	1.3
V-6—1975–80—w/A.T. (1.2)	1.6
w/M.T. (1.3)	1.7
V-8—1977–80 (1.7)	2.1

Plymouth

(G) Starter Relay, Renew
1974–76 (.3)	.4
1977–78 (.2)	.4

	Chilton Time
(Factory Time)	

(G) Starter, Renew
Includes: Test starter relay, starter solenoid and amperage draw.

Six—1974–76 (.4)	.6
1977–78 (.5)	.7
V-8—1974—318, 360 engs (.5)....	.7
400, 440 engs (.7)	1.2
1975–78 (.7)	1.2

(G) Starter, R&R and Recondition
Includes: Test relay, starter solenoid and amperage draw.

Six—1974–78 (2.0)	2.5
V-8—1974–78—318, 360 engs	
(2.1)	2.7
400, 440 engs (2.3)	2.9
New fields add (.5)	.5

(G) Starter Drive, Renew

Six—1974–75 (1.4)	1.7
1976 (.8).........................	1.1
1977–78 (.9)	1.2
V-8—1974–75—318, 360 engs	
(1.5)	1.8
400, 440 engs (1.7)	2.0
1976—318, 360 engs (.9)	1.2
400, 440 engs (1.7)	2.0
1977–78 (1.1)	1.4

(G) Starter Solenoid, Renew

Six—1974–76 (1.3)	1.6
1977–78 (1.0)	1.3
V-8—1974–76—318, 360 engs	
(1.4)	1.7
400, 440 engs (1.6)	1.8
1977–78 (1.1)	1.4

Pontiac & Grand Prix

(G) Starter, Renew
Includes: Separate solenoid, clean and inspect plunger and spring.

1974–80 (.6)	1.0
Add draw test if performed.	

(G) Starter Drive, Renew
Includes: R&R starter

1974–80 (.9)	1.3

(G) Starter, R&R and Recondition
Includes: Turn down armature.

1974–80 (1.5)	2.0
Renew field coils add (.2)	.2

(G) Starter Solenoid, Renew
Includes: R&R starter.

1974–80 (.7)	1.0

Pontiac Astre & Sunbird

(G) Starter, Renew
Includes: Separate solenoid, clean and inspect plunger and spring.

1975–76 (.4)	.8
1977–80—Four (.6)	1.0
V-6 (.8)	1.2
V-8 (.6)	1.0
Add draw test if performed.	

(G) Starter, R&R and Recondition
Includes: Turn down armature.

1975–76 (1.5)	2.0

	Chilton Time
(Factory Time)	

1977–80—Four (1.5)	2.0
V-6 (1.7)	2.2
V-8 (1.5)	2.0
Renew field coils add (.2)	.2
Add draw test if performed.	

(G) Starter Drive, Renew
Includes: R&R starter.

1975–76 (.7)	1.1
1977–80—Four (.9)	1.3
V-6 (1.1)	1.5
V-8 (.9)	1.3

(G) Starter Solenoid, Renew
Includes: R&R starter.

1975–76 (.5)	.8
1977–80—Four (.7)	1.0
V-6 (.9)	1.2
V-8 (.7)	1.0

Firebird, Phoenix (1978–79), LeMans, Ventura (1974–77)

(G) Starter, Renew
Includes: Separate solenoid, clean and inspect plunger and spring.

1974–80 (.6)	1.0
Add draw test if performed.	

(G) Starter, R&R and Recondition
Includes: Turn down armature.

1974–80 (1.5)	2.0
Renew field coils add (.2)	.2
Add draw test if performed.	

(G) Starter Drive, Renew
Includes: R&R starter.

1974–80 (.9)	1.3

(G) Starter Solenoid, Renew
Includes: R&R starter.

1974–80 (.7)	1.0

Thunderbird (1974–76)

(G) Starter, Renew

1974–76 (.7)	1.0

(G) Starter, R&R and Recondition
Includes: Turn down armature.

1974–76 (2.1)	2.8
Add draw test if performed.	

(G) Starter Drive, Renew

1974–76 (.9)	1.1

(G) Starter Solenoid, Renew

1974–76 (.8)	1.1

(G) Starter Solenoid Relay, Renew

1974–76 (.3)	.4

Vega & Monza

(G) Starter, Renew

Four—1974–80—exc below (.4) ..	.7
Vega Cosworth (1.0)	1.3
V-6—1978–80 (.4)	.8
V-8—1975–80 (1.4)	1.8
w/A.C. add (.2)	.2

(G) Starter, R&R and Recondition
Includes: Turn down armature.

Four—1974–80—exc below (1.4) .	2.1

(Factory Time)	Chilton Time		(Factory Time)	Chilton Time
Vega Cosworth (2.0)	2.7		**V-8**—1975–80 (1.7)	2.1
V-6—1978–80 (1.4)	2.2		w/A.C. add (.2)	.2
V-8—1975–80 (2.4)	3.1		**(G) Starter Solenoid Switch, Renew**	
Renew fields add (.2)	.2		*Includes: R&R starter.*	
w/A.C. add (.2)	.2		**Four**—1974–80—exc below (.5) ..	.7
(G) Starter Drive, Renew			Vega Cosworth (1.1)	1.6
Four—1974–80—exc below (.7) ..	1.0		**V-6**—1978–80 (.5)	.8
Vega Cosworth (1.3)	1.6		**V-8**—1975–80 (1.5)	2.0
V-6—1978–80 (.7)	1.1		w/A.C. add (.2)	.2

BRAKE SYSTEM

(Factory Time)	Chilton Time		(Factory Time)	Chilton Time
American Motors			rear-drum (.7)	1.4
			all four wheels (1.2)	2.5
(G) Bleed Brakes (Four Wheels)			Resurface front disc rotor, add-	
Includes: Add fluid.			each	.9
1974–80 (.3)	.6		Resurface rear brake drum, add-	
(G) Brake Shoes, Renew			each	.5
Includes: Install new or exchange shoes,			**(G) Disc Brake Rotor, Renew (One)**	
adjust brakes and bleed system.			*Includes: Repack and adjust bearings.*	
1974–76—front-drum (.6)	1.3		1974 (.8)	1.0
1974–79—rear-drum (.7)	1.4		1975–80 (.6)	1.0
all four wheels (1.2)	2.3		**(G) Caliper Assembly, Renew (One)**	
Resurface brake drum add, each .	.5		*Includes: Bleed system.*	
(G) Brake Shoes and/or Pads, Renew			1974–76 (.6)	1.1
Includes: Install new or exchange shoes			1977–80 (.4)	1.1
or pads, adjust service and hand brake.			**(G) Caliper Assy., R&R and Recondition**	
Bleed system.			**(One)**	
1974–80—front-disc (.6)	1.2		*Includes: Bleed system.*	
rear-drum (.7)	1.4		1974–80 (.6)	1.5
all four wheels (1.2)	2.5			
Resurface front disc rotor, add-				
each	.9		**AMC/Jeep**	
Resurface rear brake drum, add-				
each	.5		**(G) Bleed Brakes, (Four Wheels)**	
(G) Brake Drum, Renew (One)			*Includes: Add fluid.*	
front—1974–76 (.4)	.6		All models (.3)	.6
rear—1974–80 (.3)	.5		**(G) Brake Shoes, Renew**	
			Includes: Install new or exchange shoes.	
BRAKE HYDRAULIC SYSTEM			*Adjust brakes and bleed system.*	
(G) Wheel Cylinders, Renew			1974–80—front (.7)	1.0
Includes: Bleed system.			rear (.8)	1.1
1974–80—one (.7)	1.0		all four wheels (1.4)	2.0
each additional (.3)	.5		**(G) Brake Shoes and/or Pads, Renew**	
(G) Wheel Cylinder, R&R and			*Includes: Install new or exchange shoes*	
Recondition			*or pads, adjust service and hand brake.*	
Includes: Hone cyl. and bleed system.			*Bleed system.*	
1974–80—one (.7)	1.2		1974–80—front—disc (.5)	1.2
each additional (.3)	.5		rear—drum (.8)	1.5
(G) Master Cylinder, Renew			all four wheels (1.2)	2.6
Includes: Bleed system.			Resurface front disc rotor, add-	
1974–80 (.8)	1.0		each	.9
(G) Master Cylinder, R&R and Rebuild			Resurface rear brake drum, add-	
Includes: Hone cyl and bleed system.			each	.5
1974–80 (1.1)	1.7		**(G) Brake Drum, Renew**	
			1974–80—front—one (.3)	.5
DISC BRAKES			both (.8)	.8
(G) Brake Shoes and/or Pads, Renew			Front hub replace add (.2)	.2
Includes: Install new or exchange shoes			rear—one (.5)	*.7
or pads, adjust service and hand brake.			both (.7)	*1.0
Bleed system.			*Includes: Adjust parking brake.*	
1974–80—front-disc (.6)	1.2			

	Chilton Time
(Factory Time)	

BRAKE HYDRAULIC SYSTEM

(G) Wheel Cylinders, Renew
Includes: Bleed system.

1974–80—exc below—one (.8) ...	1.1
each adtnl (.4)	.6
full floating rear axle—one (1.1) ..	1.4
each adtnl (.7)	.9

(G) Wheel Cylinder, R&R and Recondition
Includes: Hone cylinder and bleed system.

1974–80—exc below—one (1.1) ..	1.4
each adtnl (.5)	.7
full floating rear axle—one (1.4) ..	1.7
each adtnl (.8)	1.0

(G) Master Cylinder, Renew
Includes: Bleed system.

1974–80 (.8)	1.4

(G) Master Cylinder, R&R and Rebuild
Includes: Hone cylinder and bleed system.

1974–80 (1.1)	1.7

DISC BRAKES

(G) Disc Brake Rotor, Renew
Includes: Renew seals, repack and adjust wheel bearings.

1974–80—one (.8)	1.3
both (1.5)	1.9

(G) Brake Shoes and/or Pads, Renew
Includes: Install new or exchange shoes or pads, adjust service and hand brake. Bleed system.

1974–80—front—disc (.5)	1.2
rear—drum (.8)	1.5
all four wheels (1.2)	2.6
Resurface front disc rotor, add- each	.9
Resurface rear brake drum, add- each	.5

(G) Caliper Assembly, Renew
Includes: Bleed system and repack bearings.

1974–80—one (.9)	1.5

(G) Caliper Assembly, R&R and Recondition
Includes: Bleed system and repack bearings.

1974–80 (1.1)	1.8

Buick LeSabre, Electra, Riviera (1974–78)

(G) Bleed Brakes (Four Wheels)
Includes: Fill master cylinder.

All models (.3)	.5

(G) Brake Shoes and/or Pads, Renew
Includes: Install new or exchange shoes or pads, adjust service and hand brake. Bleed system.

1974–80—front—disc (.8)	1.2
rear—drum (.9)	1.4
all four wheels	2.5
Resurface front disc rotor add, each	.9
Resurface rear brake drum add, each	.5

(G) Brake Drum, Renew (One)

1974–80 (.3)	.5

BRAKE HYDRAULIC SYSTEM

(G) Wheel Cylinder, Renew (Rear)
Includes: Bleed system.

1974–80—one (.6)	.9
both (1.0)	1.5

(G) Wheel Cylinder, Rebuild
Includes: Hone cylinder and bleed system.

1974–80—one (.8)	1.3
both (1.4)	2.1

(G) Master Cylinder, Renew
Includes: Bleed complete system.

1974–77—manual (.6)	1.0
power (.5)	.9
1978–80 (.6)	1.0

(G) Master Cylinder, R&R and Rebuild
Includes: Hone cylinder and bleed sys-plete system.

1974–77—manual (1.4)	2.0
power (1.3)	1.9
1978–80 (1.4)	2.0

DISC BRAKES

(G) Brake Shoes and/or Pads, Renew
Includes: Install new or exchange shoes or pads, adjust service and hand brake. Bleed system.

1974–80—front—disc (.8)	1.2
rear—drum (.9)	1.4
all four wheels	2.5
Resurface front disc brake rotor add, each	.9
Resurface rear brake drum add, each	.5

(G) Disc Brake Pads, Renew
Includes: Install new or exchange brake pads only.

1974–80—front (.8)	1.2
1977–80—rear (.7)	1.2
all four wheels	2.3

(G) Disc Brake Rotor, Renew
Includes: R&R wheel, transfer bearings and races. Clean and repack wheel bearings.

1974–80—front—one (.7)	.9
both (1.2)	1.4
1977–80—rear—one (.6)	.9
both (.9)	1.4
all four wheels	2.5

(G) Caliper Assembly, Renew
Includes: Remove brake shoes. Bleed complete system.

1974–80—front—one (.6)	.9
both (.9)	1.3
1977–80—rear—one (.6)	.9
both (.9)	1.3
all four wheels	2.3

(G) Caliper Assembly, R&R and Recondition
Includes: Remove brake shoes, renew parts as required and bleed complete system.

1974–80—front—one (1.1)	1.6
both (1.9)	2.9
1977–80—rear—one (1.1)	1.6

	Chilton Time			Chilton Time
(Factory Time)			(Factory Time)	

both (1.9) **2.9**
all four wheels **4.4**

Buick Riviera (1979–80)

(G) Bleed Brakes (Four Wheels)
Includes: Fill master cylinder.
All models (.3) .... **.5**

(G) Brake Shoes·and/or Pads, Renew
Includes: Install new or exchange shoes or pads, adjust service and hand brake. Bleed system.
1979–80—front—disc (.6) **1.2**
rear—drum (.9) **1.4**
All four wheels **2.5**
Resurface front disc rotor add,
each .... **.9**
Resurface rear brake drum add,
each .... **.5**

(G) Brake Drum, Renew (One)
1979–80 (.3) .... **.5**

BRAKE HYDRAULIC SYSTEM

(G) Wheel Cylinder, Renew
Includes: Bleed system.
1979–80—one (.6) .... **.9**
both (1.0) **1.5**

(G) Wheel Cylinder, R&R and Rebuild
Includes: Hone cylinder and bleed system.
1979–80—one (.8) **1.3**
both (1.4) **2.1**

(G) Master Cylinder, Renew
Includes: Bleed complete system.
1979–80 (.6) **1.0**

(G) Master Cylinder, R&R and Rebuild
Includes: Hone cylinder and bleed complete system.
1979–80 (1.4) **2.0**

DISC BRAKES

(G) Brake Shoes and/or Pads, Renew
Includes: Install new or exchange shoes or pads, adjust service and hand brake. Bleed system.
1979–80—front—disc (.6) **1.2**
rear—drum (.9) **1.4**
All four wheels **2.5**
Resurface front disc rotor add,
each .... **.9**
Resurface rear brake drum add,
each .... **.5**

(G) Disc Brake Pads, Renew
Includes: Install new or exchange brake pads only.
1979–80—front (.6) **1.2**
rear (.7) **1.2**
All four wheels **2.3**

(G) Disc Brake Rotor, Renew
Includes: R&R wheel, transfer bearings and races. Clean and repack wheel bearings.
1979–80—front—one (.5) .... **.9**
both (.7) **1.4**
rear—one (.6) .... **.9**
both (.9) **1.4**
All four wheels **2.5**

(G) Caliper Assembly, Renew
Includes: Remove brake shoes. Bleed complete system.
1979–80—front—one (.6) .... **.9**
both (.9) **1.3**
rear—one (.6) .... **.9**
both (.9) **1.3**
All four wheels **2.3**

(G) Caliper Assy., R&R and Recondition
Includes: Remove brake shoes, renew parts as required and bleed system.
1979–80—front—one (1.1) **1.6**
both (1.9) **2.9**
rear—one (1.1) **1.6**
both (1.9) **2.9**
All four wheels **4.4**

Buick Apollo, Century, Gran Sport, Regal, Skylark (1974–79)

(G) Bleed Brakes (Four Wheels)
Includes: Fill master cylinder.
All models (.3) .... **.5**

(G) Brake Shoes, Renew
Includes: Install new or exchange shoes, service self adjustors. Adjust service and hand brake. Bleed system.
1974—front (.9) **1.6**
rear (.9) **1.5**
all four wheels **3.0**
Resurface brake drum add, each . **.4**

(G) Brake Shoes and/or Pads, Renew
Includes: Install new or exchange shoes or pads, adjust service and hand brake. Bleed system.
1974–80—front—disc (.8) **1.2**
rear—drum (.9) **1.5**
all four wheels **2.6**
Resurface front disc rotor add,
each .... **.9**
Resurface rear brake drum add,
each .... **.4**

(G) Brake Drum Assembly, Renew (One)
1974—front (.5) .... **.7**
1974–80—rear (.3) .... **.5**

(G) Brake Combination Valve, Renew
1974–80 (.7) **1.1**

BRAKE HYDRAULIC SYSTEM

(G) Wheel Cylinder, Renew
Includes: Bleed system.
1974—front—one (.8) **1.3**
both (1.5) **2.1**
1974–80—rear—one (.6) .... **.9**
both (1.0) **1.5**
all four wheels **3.6**

(G) Wheel Cylinder, Rebuild
Includes: Hone cylinder and bleed system.
1974—front—one (1.0) **1.5**
both (1.9) **2.5**
1974–80—rear—one (.8) **1.3**
both (1.4) **2.1**
all four wheels **4.4**

	Chilton Time
(Factory Time)	

	Chilton Time
(Factory Time)	

(G) Master Cylinder, Renew
Includes: Bleed complete system.

1974–77—manual (.6)	**1.0**
power (.5)	**.9**
1978–80 (.6)	**1.0**

(G) Master Cylinder, R&R and Rebuild
Includes: Hone cylinder and bleed complete system.

1974—manual (1.4)	**2.0**
power (1.3)	**1.9**
1978–80 (1.4)	**2.0**

(G) Brake System, Flush and Refill

All models	**1.2**

DISC BRAKES

(G) Brake Shoes and/or Pads, Renew
Includes: Install new or exchange shoes or pads, adjust service and hand brake. Bleed system.

1974–80—front—disc (.8)	**1.2**
rear—drum (.9)	**1.5**
all four wheels	**2.6**
Resurface front disc rotor add, each	**.9**
Resurface rear brake drum add, each	**.4**

(G) Disc Brake Rotor, Renew
Includes: R&R wheel, transfer bearings and races. Clean and repack wheel bearings.

1974–80—one (.7)	**.9**
both (1.2)	**1.4**

(G) Caliper Assembly, Renew
Includes: Remove brake shoes. Bleed complete system.

1974–80—one (.6)	**.9**
both (.9)	**1.3**

(G) Caliper Assembly, R&R and Recondition
Includes: Remove brake shoes, renew parts as required and bleed complete system.

1974–80—one (1.1)	**1.6**
both (1.9)	**2.9**

Buick Skyhawk

(G) Bleed Brakes (Four Wheels)
Includes: Fill master cylinder.

All models (.3)	**.5**

(G) Brake Shoes and/or Pads, Renew
Includes: Install new or exchange shoes or pads, adjust service and hand brake. Bleed system.

1975–80—front—disc (.8)	**1.2**
rear—drum (.9)	**1.4**
all four wheels	**2.5**
Resurface front disc rotor add, each	**.9**
Resurface rear brake drum add, each	**.5**

(G) Brake Drum, Renew (One)

1975–80 (.3)	**.5**

BRAKE HYDRAULIC SYSTEM

(G) Wheel Cylinder, Renew (Rear)
Includes: Bleed system.

1975–80—one (.6)	**.9**

both (1.0) ... **1.5**

(G) Wheel Cylinder, Rebuild
Includes: Hone cylinder and bleed system.

1975–80—one (.8)	**1.3**
both (1.4)	**2.1**

(G) Master Cylinder, Renew
Includes: Bleed complete system.

1975–80 (.6)	**1.0**

(G) Master Cylinder, R&R and Rebuild
Includes: Hone cylinder and bleed complete system.

1975–80 (1.4)	**2.0**

DISC BRAKES

(G) Disc Brake Rotor, Renew
Includes: R&R wheel, transfer bearings and races. Clean and repack wheel bearings.

1975–80—one (.7)	**.9**
both (1.2)	**1.4**

(G) Brake Shoes and/or Pads, Renew
Includes: Install new or exchange shoes or pads, adjust service and hand brake. Bleed system.

1975–80—front—disc (.8)	**1.2**
rear—drum (.9)	**1.4**
all four wheels	**2.5**
Resurface front disc rotor add, each	**.9**
Resurface rear brake drum add, each	**.5**

(G) Caliper Assembly, Renew
Includes: Remove brake shoes. Bleed complete system.

1975–80—one (.6)	**.9**
both (.9)	**1.3**

(G) Caliper Assembly, R&R and Recondition
Includes: Remove brake shoes, renew parts as required and bleed complete system.

1975–80—one (1.1)	**1.6**
both (1.9)	**2.9**

Cadillac

(G) Brake Shoes and/or Pads, Renew
Includes: Install new or exchange shoes or pads, adjust service and hand brake. Bleed system.

1974–80—front—disc (.7)	**1.1**
rear—drum (1.0)	**1.5**
all four wheels	**2.5**
Resurface front disc rotor add, each	**.9**
Resurface rear brake drum add, each	**.5**

(G) Brake Drum, Renew

1974–80—one (.3)	**.4**
both (.5)	**.6**

BRAKE HYDRAULIC SYSTEM

(G) Wheel Cylinder, Renew
Includes: Bleed system.

1974–80—one (.7)	**1.0**
both (1.3)	**1.9**

(Factory Time)	Chilton Time

(G) Wheel Cylinder, Rebuild
Includes: Hone cylinder and bleed system.

1974–80—one (.8)	1.2
both (1.5)	2.3

(G) Brake Hose, Renew
Includes: Bleed system.

1974–80—each (.4)	.6

(G) Master Cylinder, Renew
Includes: Bleed at cylinder.

1974–80 (.4)	.6
Bleed system add (.4)	.5

(G) Master Cylinder, R&R and Rebuild
Includes: Bleed at cylinder.

1974–80 (1.1)	1.5
Bleed system add (.4)	.5

DISC BRAKES

(G) Disc Brake Pads, Renew

1974–80—front (.7)	1.1
1977–80—rear (.7)	1.1
all four wheels	2.0

(G) Hub, Rotor and Bearing Assy., Renew
Includes: Install new bearings and seals.
Front

1974–76—one (.9)	1.3
both (1.4)	2.0
1977–80—one (.7)	1.3
both (1.2)	2.0

Rear

1977–80—one (1.5)	2.0
both (2.1)	3.1
all four wheels	4.8

(G) Caliper Assembly, Renew
Includes: Bleed system.

Front—1974–80—one (.5)	.8
both (.9)	1.5
Rear—1977–80—one (.9)	1.2
both (1.2)	1.8
all four wheels	3.0

(G) Caliper Assy., R&R and Recondition
Includes: Bleed system.

Front—1974–80—one (.8)	1.2
both (1.4)	2.1
Rear—1977–80—one (1.2)	1.6
both (1.7)	2.4
all four wheels	4.2

Cadillac Seville

(G) Bleed Brakes (Four Wheels)
Includes: Fill master cylinder.

All models (.4)	.6

(G) Brake Shoes and/or Pads, Renew
Includes: Install new or exchange shoes or pads, adjust service and hand brake. Bleed system.

1976—front—disc (.7)	1.1
rear—drum (1.0)	1.5
all four wheels	2.5
Resurface front disc rotor add, each	.9
Resurface rear brake drum add, each	.5

(G) Brake Drum, Renew

1976—one (.3)	.4
both (.5)	.6

(Factory Time)	Chilton Time

BRAKE HYDRAULIC SYSTEM

(G) Wheel Cylinder, Renew
Includes: Bleed system.

1976—one (.7)	1.0
both (1.3)	1.9

(G) Wheel Cylinder, Rebuild
Includes: Hone cylinder and bleed system.

1976—one (.8)	1.2
both (1.5)	2.3

(G) Master Cylinder, Renew
Includes: Bleed at cylinder.

1976–80 (.4)	.6
Bleed system add (.4)	.5

(G) Master Cylinder, R&R and Robuild
Includes: Bleed at cylinder.

1976–80 (1.1)	1.5
Bleed system add (.4)	.5

DISC BRAKES

(G) Disc Brake Pads, Renew

1976–80—front (.5)	1.1
rear (.6)	1.1
all four wheels	2.0

(G) Hub, Rotor and Bearing Assy., Renew
Includes: Install new bearings and seals
Front

1976–80—one (.7)	1.3
both (1.2)	2.0

Rear

1977–80—one (1.5)	2.0
both (2.1)	3.1
all four wheels	4.8

(G) Caliper Assembly, Renew
Includes: Bleed system.

Front—1976–80—one (.5)	.8
both (.8)	1.5
Rear—1977—one (.9)	1.2
both (1.2)	1.8
all four wheels	3.0
1978–80—one (.5)	1.2
both (.8)	1.8
all four wheels	3.0

(G) Caliper Assembly, R&R and Recondition
Includes: Bleed system.

Front—1976–80—one (.8)	1.2
both (1.4)	2.1
Rear—1977—one (1.2)	1.6
both (1.7)	2.4
all four wheels	4.2
1978–80—one (.8)	1.6
both (1.4)	2.4
all four wheels	4.2

Cadillac Eldorado

(G) Bleed Brakes (Four Wheels)
Includes: Fill master cylinder.

All models (.4)	.6

(G) Brake Shoes and/or Pads, Renew
Includes: Install new or exchange shoes or pads, adjust service and hand brake. Bleed system.

1974–75—front—disc (.7)	1.1
rear—drum (1.0)	1.5

(Factory Time)	Chilton Time
all four wheels	2.5
Resurface front disc rotor add, each	.9
Resurface rear brake drum add, each	.5
(G) Disc Brake Pads, Renew	
1976–80—front (.5)	1.1
rear (.7)	1.1
all four wheels	2.0
Resurface disc brake rotor add, each	.9
(G) Brake Drum, Renew	
1974–75—one (.3)	.4
both (.5)	.6

BRAKE HYDRAULIC SYSTEM

(G) Wheel Cylinder, Renew	
Includes: Bleed system.	
1974–75—one (.7)	1.0
both (1.3)	1.9
(G) Wheel Cylinder, R&R and Rebuild	
Includes: Hone cylinder and bleed system.	
1974–75—one (.8)	1.2
both (1.5)	2.3
(G) Master Cylinder, Renew	
Includes: Bleed at cylinder.	
1974–80 (.4)	.6
Bleed system add (.4)	.5
(G) Master Cylinder, R&R and Rebuild	
Includes: Bleed at cylinder.	
1974–80 (1.1)	1.5
Bleed system add (.4)	.5

DISC BRAKES

(G) Disc Brake Pads, Renew	
1974–77—front (.7)	1.1
1978–80—front (.5)	1.1
1976–77—rear (.7)	1.1
1978–80—rear (.5)	1.1
all four wheels	2.0
(G) Hub, Rotor and Bearing Assy., Renew	
Includes: Install new bearings and seals.	
Front	
1974–80—one (1.8)	2.2
both (2.4)	3.0
Rear	
1976–80—one (1.1)	1.6
both (1.7)	2.5
all four wheels	5.2
(G) Caliper Assembly, Renew	
Includes: Bleed system.	
Front—1974–78—one (.9)	1.2
both (1.1)	1.5
1979–80—one (.4)	1.2
both (.6)	1.5
Rear—1976–78—one (.9)	1.2
both (1.2)	1.8
1979–80—one (.6)	1.2
both (.9)	1.8
all four wheels	3.0
(G) Caliper Assy., R&R and Recondition	
Includes: Bleed system.	
Front—1974–78—one (1.2)	1.6
both (1.6)	2.3
1979–80—one (.7)	1.6
both (1.1)	2.3

(Factory Time)	Chilton Time
Rear—1976–78—one (1.2)	1.6
both (1.7)	2.4
1979–80—one (1.0)	1.6
both (1.6)	2.4
all four wheels	4.5

Chevrolet & Corvette

(G) Bleed Brakes (Four Wheels)	
Includes: Fill master cylinder.	
All models (.3)	.5
(G) Brake Shoes and/or Pads, Renew	
Includes: Install new or exchange shoes or pads, adjust service and hand brake. Bleed system.	
Chevrolet	
1974–80—front—disc (.8)	1.3
rear—drum (1.0)	1.6
all four wheels	2.7
Corvette	
1974–80—front—disc (.6)	1.2
rear—disc (.6)	1.2
all four wheels	2.0
Resurface disc rotor, add-each ..	.9
Resurface brake drum, add-each .	.5
(G) Brake Drum, Renew (One)	
1974–80—rear (.4)	.6

BRAKE HYDRAULIC SYSTEM

(G) Wheel Cylinder, Renew (Rear)	
Includes: Bleed system.	
1974–80—one (.6)	1.0
both (1.0)	1.6
(G) Wheel Cylinder, Rebuild	
Includes: Hone cylinder and bleed system.	
1974–80—rear—one (.8)	1.4
both (1.2)	2.2
(G) Master Cylinder, Renew	
Includes: Bleed complete system.	
1974–80 (.5)	.8
(G) Master Cylinder, R&R and Rebuild	
Includes: Hone cylinder and bleed complete system.	
1974–77 (1.1)	1.4
1978–80 (.9)	1.4

DISC BRAKES

(G) Disc Brake Pads, Renew	
Chevrolet	
1974–80 (.8)	1.3
Corvette	
1974–80—front (.6)	1.2
rear (.6)	1.2
all four wheels	2.0
(G) Brake Rotor, Renew	
Chevrolet	
1974–80—one (.6)	1.0
both (1.1)	1.5
Corvette	
1974–80—front—one (.6)	1.0
both (1.1)	1.5
rear—one (1.0)	1.4
both (1.8)	2.6
all four wheels	4.1

	Chilton Time		Chilton Time
(Factory Time)		(Factory Time)	

(G) Caliper Assembly, Renew
Includes: Bleed complete system.
  Chevrolet
    1974–80—one (.9) **1.3**
    both (1.5) **1.9**
  Corvette
    1974–80—front—one (.9) **1.3**
    both (1.5) **1.9**
    rear—one (.8) **1.4**
    both (1.1) **1.8**
    all four wheels **3.5**
(G) Caliper Assembly, R&R and Recondition
Includes: Bleed complete system.
  Chevrolet
    1974–80—one (1.1) **1.7**
    both (1.7) **2.4**
  Corvette
    1974–80—front—one (1.1) **1.7**
    both (1.9) **2.6**
    rear—one (1.3) **1.9**
    both (2.1) **2.8**
    all four wheels **5.0**

Chevette

(G) Bleed Brakes (Four Wheels)
Includes: Fill master cylinder.
    1976–80 (.3) .... **.5**
(G) Brake Shoes and/or Pads, Renew
Includes: Install new or exchange shoes or pads, adjust service and hand brake. Bleed system.
    1976–80—front—disc (.7) **1.2**
    rear—drum (1.0) **1.6**
    all four wheels **2.5**
    Resurfaced disc rotor, add-each . **.9**
    Resurfaced brake drum, add-each **.5**
(G) Brake Drum, Renew (One)
    1976–80—rear (.3) .... **.5**

BRAKE HYDRAULIC SYSTEM
(G) Wheel Cylinder, Renew (Rear)
Includes: Bleed system.
    1976–80—one (.6) **1.2**
    both (1.0) **2.0**
(G) Wheel Cylinder, Rebuild
Includes: Hone cylinder and bleed system.
    1976–80—one (.8) **1.6**
    both (1.2) **2.6**
(G) Master Cylinder, Renew
Includes: Bleed complete system.
    1976–80 (.5) .... **.8**
    w/A.C. & P.B. (1.0) **1.6**
(G) Master Cylinder, R&R and Rebuild
Includes: Hone cylinder and bleed complete system.
    1976–80 (.9) **1.6**
    w/A.C. & P.B. (1.4) **2.2**

DISC BRAKES
(G) Disc Brake Pads, Renew
    1976–80 (.7) **1.2**

(G) Brake Rotor, Renew
    1976–80—one (.6) **1.1**
    both (.9) **1.9**
(G) Caliper Assembly, Renew
Includes: Bleed complete system.
    1976–80—one (.9) **1.2**
    both (1.5) **1.9**
(G) Caliper Assembly, R&R and Recondition
Includes: Bleed complete system.
    1976–80—one (1.1) **1.5**
    both (1.7) **2.4**

Citation, Omega, Phoenix, Skylark—All 1980

(G) Bleed Brakes (Four Wheels)
Includes: Fill master cylinder.
    All models (.4) .... **.5**
(G) Brake Shoes and/or Pads, Renew
Includes: Install new or exchange shoes or pads, adjust service and hand brake. Bleed system.
    1980—front—disc (.8) **1.2**
    rear—drum (.9) **1.5**
    all four wheels **2.5**
    Resurface front disc rotor add-
      each .... **.9**
    Resurface rear brake drum add-
      each .... **.5**
(G) Brake Drum, Renew (One)
    1980—rear (.3) .... **.5**

BRAKE HYDRAULIC SYSTEM
(G) Wheel Cylinder, Renew (Rear)
Includes: Bleed system.
    1980—one (.7) **1.1**
    both (1.0) **1.6**
(G) Wheel Cylinder, R&R and Rebuild
Includes: Hone cylinder and bleed system.
    1980—one (.9) **1.4**
    both (1.4) **2.0**
(G) Master Cylinder, Renew
Includes: Bleed complete system.
    1980 (.7) **1.0**
(G) Master Cylinder, R&R and Rebuild
Includes: Hone cylinder and bleed complete system.
    1980 (1.5) **1.9**

DISC BRAKES
(G) Disc Brake Pads, Renew
    1980 (.8) **1.2**
(G) Disc Brake Rotor, Renew
    1980—one (.5) .... **.7**
    both (.8) **1.3**
(G) Caliper Assembly, Renew
Includes: Bleed complete system.
    1980—one (.6) .... **.8**
    both (.9) **1.4**
(G) Caliper Assembly, R&R and Recondition
Includes: Bleed complete system.
    1980—one (1.1) **1.3**
    both (1.9) **2.4**

	Chilton
	Time
(Factory Time)	

	Chilton
	Time
(Factory Time)	

Chrysler, Cordoba, Imperial

(G) Bleed Brakes (Four Wheels)
Includes: Add fluid.
| All models (.4) .... | .6 |
| w/P.B. add .... | .2 |

(G) Brakes Shoes and/or Pads, Renew
Includes: Install new or exchange shoes or pads, adjust service and hand brake. Bleed system.
1974–80—front—disc (.6)	1.2
rear—drum (.7)	1.7
all four wheels (1.3)	2.9
Resurface front disc rotor, add-	
each	.9
Resurface rear brake drum, add-	
each	.5

(G) Brake Drum, Renew (One)
| 1974–80—rear (.3) .... | .4 |

BRAKE HYDRAULIC SYSTEM

(G) Wheel Cylinder, Renew (Rear)
Includes: Bleed system.
| 1974–75—one (.9) .... | 1.2 |
| 1977–80—one (.7) .... | 1.2 |

(G) Wheel Cylinder, Rebuild
Includes: Hone cylinder & bleed system.
| 1974–80—rear—one .... | 1.5 |
| both .... | 2.3 |

(G) Master Cylinder, Renew
Includes: Bleed complete system.
| 1974–78 (.6) .... | .9 |
| 1979–80 (.7) .... | 1.0 |

(G) Master Cylinder, R&R and Rebuild
Includes: Bleed complete system.
| 1974–80 .... | 2.1 |

DISC BRAKES

(G) Brake Shoes and/or Pads, Renew
Includes: Install new or exchange shoes or pads, adjust service and hand brake. Bleed system.
1974–80—front—disc (.6)	1.2
rear—drum (.7)	1.7
all four wheels (1.3)	2.9
Resurface front disc rotor, add-	
each	.9
Resurface rear brake drum, add-	
each	.5

(G) Rear Brake Disc Pads, Renew
| 1974–75—Imperial (.6) .... | 1.3 |

(G) Caliper Assembly, Renew
Includes: Bleed system.
1974–80—one (.7)	1.3
both (1.2)	1.9
1974–75—Imperial—rear—one	
(.6)........................	1.3
both (1.1)	1.9

(G) Caliper Assembly, R&R and Recondition
Includes: Bleed system.
1974–80—one (1.0)	1.8
both (1.9)	2.9
1974–75—Imperial—rear—one	
(1.0)	1.8
both (1.7)	2.9

Dodge

(G) Bleed Brakes (Four Wheels)
Includes: Add fluid.
| All models (.4) .... | .6 |
| w/Pwr brks add (.2) .... | .2 |

(G) Brakes, Renew
Includes: Install new or exchange shoes and adjust brakes.
| 1974–80—2 rear whls (.7) .... | 1.7 |
| Bleed system add .... | .3 |

(G) Brake Shoes and/or Pads, Renew
Includes: Install new or exchange shoes or pads, adjust service and hand brake. Bleed system.
1974–80—front—disc (.6)	1.3
rear—drum (.7)	1.7
all four wheels (1.3)	2.9
Resurface front disc rotor, add-	
each	.9
Resurface rear brake drum, add-	
each	.5

(G) Brake Drum, Renew (One)
| 1974–80—rear (.3) .... | .4 |

BRAKE HYDRAULIC SYSTEM

(G) Wheel Cylinder, Renew (Rear)
Includes: Bleed system.
| 1974–75—one (.9) .... | 1.2 |
| 1976–80—one (.7) .... | 1.2 |

(G) Wheel Cylinder, Rebuild
Includes: Hone cylinder & bleed system.
| 1974–80—rear—one .... | 1.5 |
| both .... | 2.3 |

(G) Master Cylinder, Renew
Includes: Bleed complete system.
1974–80—exc below (.5)	.8
1978–80—w/Alum housing (.7) ...	1.0
w/P.B. add (.1)	.1

(G) Master Cylinder, R&R and Rebuild
Includes: Bleed complete system.
| 1974–80 .... | 2.1 |
| w/P.B. add .... | .1 |

DISC BRAKES

(G) Front Brake Disc Pads, Renew
Includes: Install new or exchange disc brake pads only.
| 1974–76 (.7) .... | 1.3 |
| 1977–80 (.6) .... | 1.3 |

(G) Brake Shoes and/or Pads, Renew
Includes: Install new or exchange shoes or pads, adjust service and hand brake. Bleed system.
1974–80—front—disc (.6)	1.3
rear—drum (.7)	1.7
all four wheels (1.3)	2.9
Resurface front disc rotor, add-	
each	.9
Resurface rear brake drum, add-	
each	.5

(G) Disc Brake Rotor, Renew
Includes: Replace inner and outer bearings if necessary.
| 1974–80—each (.6) .... | .9 |

(G) Caliper Assembly, Renew
Includes: Bleed system.
| 1974–80—one (.7) .... | 1.2 |

(Factory Time)	Chilton Time
both (1.2)	1.8

(G) Caliper Assembly, R&R and Recondition
Includes: Bleed system.

1974–80—one (1.0)	1.8
both (1.9)	2.9

Horizon & Omni

(G) Bleed Brakes (Four Wheels)
Includes: Fill master cylinder.

All models (.4)	.6

(G) Brake Shoes and/or Pads, Renew
Includes: Install new or exchange shoes or pads, adjust service and hand brake. Bleed system.

1978–80—front—disc (.5)	.9
rear—drum (1.0)	1.6
all four wheels	2.5
Resurface front disc rotor, add— each	.9
Resurface rear brake drum, add— each	.5

(G) Brake Drum, Renew

1978–80—one (.3)	.4

BRAKE HYDRAULIC SYSTEM

(G) Wheel Cylinder, Renew
Includes: Bleed system.

1978–80—each (.6)	.9

(G) Wheel Cylinder, R&R and Recondition
Includes: Bleed system.

1978–80—one	1.3
both	2.5

(G) Master Cylinder, Renew
Includes: Bleed complete system.

1978–80 (.6)	.9

(G) Master Cylinder, R&R and Recondition
Includes: Bleed complete system.

1978–80	1.7

DISC BRAKES

(G) Brake Shoes and/or Pads, Renew
Includes: Install new or exchange shoes or pads, adjust service and hand brake. Bleed system.

1978–80—front—disc (.5)	.9
rear—drum (1.0)	1.6
all four wheels	2.5
Resurface front disc rotor, add— each	.9
Resurface rear brake drum, add— each	.5

(G) Disc Brake Rotor w/Hub, Renew

1978–80—each (1.0)	1.4

(G) Disc Brake Rotor, Renew

1978–80—each (.4)	.7

(G) Caliper Assembly, Renew
Includes: Bleed system.

1978–80—each (.5)	.9

(G) Caliper Assembly, R&R and Recondition
Includes: Bleed system.

1978–80—each (1.1)	1.6

Capri & Mustang (1979–80)

(G) Bleed Brakes (Four Wheels)
Includes: Fill master cylinder.

All models (.3)	.5

(G) Brake Shoes and/or Pads, Renew
Includes: Install new or exchange shoes or pads. Adjust service and hand brake. Bleed system.

1979–80—front—disc (.8)	1.3
rear—drum (1.2)	1.7
all four wheels (1.6)	2.6
Resurface front disc rotor, add— each	.9
Resurface rear brake drum, add— each	.5

(G) Brake Drum, Renew
Includes: Remove wheel and adjust brakes.

1979–80—one (.4)	.7
both (.5)	1.0

BRAKE HYDRAULIC SYSTEM

(G) Wheel Cylinder, Renew
Includes: Bleed system.

1979–80—one (.9)	1.4
both (1.6)	2.1

(G) Wheel Cylinder, R&R and Rebuild
Includes: Hone cylinder and bleed system.

1979–80—one (.9)	1.7
both (1.6)	2.7

(G) Master Cylinder, Renew
Includes: Bleed complete system.

1979–80 (.6)	1.0

(G) Master Cylinder, R&R and Rebuild
Includes: Hone cylinder and bleed complete system.

1979–80	1.6

DISC BRAKES

(G) Disc Brake Pads, Renew

1979–80 (.8)	1.3
Resurface disc brake rotor, add— each	.9

(G) Caliper Assembly, Renew
Includes: Bleed complete system.

1979–80—one (.7)	1.2
both (.9)	1.7

(G) Caliper Assy., R&R and Recondition
Includes: Bleed complete system.

1979–80—one (1.2)	2.0
both (1.5)	3.2

(G) Brake Rotor, Renew
Includes: Renew wheel bearings and grease retainer and repack bearings.

1979–80—one (.5)	1.1
both (.7)	1.6

Comet, Cougar, Monarch, Montego, Lincoln Versailles

(G) Bleed Brakes (Four Wheels)
Includes: Fill master cylinder.

All models (.3)	.5

	Chilton Time
(Factory Time)	

(G) Brake Shoes, Renew
Includes: Install new or exchange shoes, service self adjustors, adjust service and hand brake. Bleed system.

1974–75—front (1.0)	1.5
rear (1.3)	1.8
all four wheels (1.9)	2.7
Resurface brake drum add—each	.5

(G) Brake Shoes and/or Pads, Renew
Includes: Install new or exchange shoes or pads. Adjust service and hand brake. Bleed system.

1974–80—front—disc (1.0)	1.4
rear—drum (1.3)	1.7
all four wheels (1.8)	2.6
Resurface front disc rotor, add— each	.9
Resurface rear brake drum, add— each	.5

(G) Brake Drum, Renew
Includes: Replace front bearings and grease retainer, pack bearings and adjust conventional brakes.

1974–75—front—one (.5)	.8
1974–80—rear—one (.4)	.7

BRAKE HYDRAULIC SYSTEM

(G) Wheel Cylinder, Renew
Includes: Bleed system.

1974–75—front—one (.8)	1.3
both (1.4)	1.9
1974–80—rear—one (1.0)	1.4
both (1.7)	2.1
all four wheels (2.6)	3.4

(G) Wheel Cylinder, R&R and Rebuild
Includes: Hone cylinder and bleed system.

1974–75—front—one (.8)	1.6
both (1.4)	2.5
1974–80—rear—one (1.0)	1.7
both (1.7)	2.7
all four wheels (2.5)	4.6

(G) Master Cylinder, Renew
Includes: Bleed complete system.

1974–80 (.6)	1.0

(G) Master Cylinder, R&R and Rebuild
Includes: Hone cylinder and bleed complete system.

1974–80	1.6

DISC BRAKES

(G) Disc Brake Pads, Renew

1974–80—front (1.0)	1.6
rear (1.0)	1.6
all four wheels (1.5)	2.8
Resurface disc brake rotor, add— each	.9

(G) Caliper Assembly, Renew
Includes: Bleed complete system.

1974–80—front—one (.7)	1.2
both (.9)	1.7
rear—one (.7)	1.5
both (1.0)	2.1

(G) Caliper Assembly, R&R and Recondition
Includes: Bleed complete system.

1974–80—front—one (1.2)	2.0
both (1.7)	3.2

	Chilton Time
(Factory Time)	

rear—one (1.4)	2.3
both (2.0)	3.5

(G) Brake Rotor, Renew
Includes: Renew front wheel bearings and grease retainer and repack bearings. Remove rear wheel assembly.

1974–80—front—one (.5)	1.1
both (.8)	1.6
rear—one (.4)	1.0
both (.6)	1.5

Elite, Granada, Maverick, Torino, LTD II, Thunderbird (1977–79)

(G) Bleed Brakes (Four Wheels)
Includes: Fill master cylinder.

All models (.3)	.5

(G) Brake Shoes, Renew
Includes: Install new or exchange shoes, service self adjustors, adjust service and hand brake. Bleed system.

1974–75—front (1.0)	1.5
rear (1.3)	1.8
all four wheels (1.9)	2.7
Resurface brake drum add-each	.5

(G) Brake Shoes and/or Pads, Renew
Includes: Install new or exchange shoes or pads. Adjust service and hand brake. Bleed system.

1974–80—front—disc (1.0)	1.4
rear—drum (1.3)	1.7
all four wheels (1.8)	2.6
Resurface front disc rotor, add- each	.9
Resurface rear brake drum, add- each	.5

(G) Brake Drum, Renew
Includes: Replace front bearings and grease retainer, pack bearings and adjust conventional brakes.

1974–75—front—one (.5)	.8
1974–80—rear—one (.4)	.7

BRAKE HYDRAULIC SYSTEM

(G) Wheel Cylinder, Renew
Includes: Bleed system.

1974–75—front—one (.8)	1.3
both (1.4)	1.9
1974–80—rear—one (1.0)	1.4
both (1.7)	2.1
all four wheels (2.6)	3.4

(G) Wheel Cylinder, R&R and Rebuild
Includes: Hone cylinder and bleed system.

1974–75—front—one (.8)	1.6
both (1.4)	2.5
1974–80—rear—one (1.0)	1.7
both (1.7)	2.7
all four wheels (2.5)	4.6

(G) Master Cylinder, Renew
Includes: Bleed complete system.

1974–80 (.6)	1.0

(Factory Time)	Chilton Time

(G) Master Cylinder, R&R and Rebuild
Includes: Hone cylinder and bleed complete system.

1974–80	1.6

DISC BRAKES

(G) Disc Brake Pads, Renew

1974–80—front (1.0)	1.6
rear (1.0)	1.6
all four wheels (1.5)	2.8
Resurface disc brake rotor, add—each	.9

(G) Caliper Assembly, Renew
Includes: Bleed complete system.

1974–80—front—one (.7)	1.2
both (.9)	1.7
rear—one (.7)	1.5
both (1.0)	2.1

(G) Caliper Assembly, R&R and Recondition
Includes: Bleed complete system.

1974–80—front—one (1.2)	2.0
both (1.7)	3.2
rear—one (1.4)	2.3
both (2.0)	3.5

(G) Brake Rotor, Renew
Includes: Renew front wheel bearings and grease retainer and repack bearings. Remove rear wheel assembly.

1974–80—front—one (.5)	1.1
both (.8)	1.6
rear—one (.4)	1.0
both (.6)	1.5

Ford

(G) Bleed Brakes (Four Wheels)
Includes: Fill master cylinder.

All models (.3)	.5

(G) Brake Shoes and/or Pads, Renew
Includes: Install new or exchange shoes or pads. Adjust rear brakes and hand brake. Bleed system.

1974–80—front—disc (1.0)	1.9
rear—drum (1.3)	2.1
all four wheels (1.8)	3.4
Resurface front disc rotor add—each	.9
Resurface rear brake drum add—each	.5

(G) Brake Drum, Renew

1974–80—one (.4)	.6
both (.5)	.8

BRAKE HYDRAULIC SYSTEM

(G) Wheel Cylinder, Renew
Includes: Bleed system.

1974–80—one (1.6)	2.1
both (1.7)	2.5

(G) Wheel Cylinder, R&R and Rebuild
Includes: Hone cylinder and bleed system.

1974–80—one (1.6)	2.4
both (1.7)	3.4

(Factory Time)	Chilton Time

(G) Master Cylinder, Renew
Includes: Bleed complete system.

1974–80 (.6)	1.0

(G) Master Cylinder, R&R and Rebuild
Includes: Hone cylinder and bleed complete system.

1974–80	1.6

DISC BRAKES

(G) Disc Brake Pads, Renew

1975–80—front (1.0)	1.6
rear (1.0)	1.6
all four wheels (1.5)	2.8
Resurface disc brake rotor add—each	.9

(G) Caliper Assembly, Renew
Includes: Bleed complete system.

1974–80—front-one (.7)	1.2
both (.9)	1.7
rear—one (.7)	1.5
both (1.0)	2.1

(G) Caliper Assembly, R&R and Recondition
Includes: Bleed complete system.

1974–80—front—one (1.2)	2.0
both (1.7)	3.2
rear—one (1.4)	2.3
both (2.0)	3.5

(G) Brake Rotor, Renew
Includes: Renew front wheel bearings and grease retainer and repack bearings. Remove rear wheel assembly.

1974–80—front—one (.5)	1.1
both (.8)	1.6
rear—one (.4)	1.0
both (.6)	1.5

Lincoln Continental, Mark IV, Mark V

(G) Bleed Brakes (Four Wheels)
Includes: Fill master cylinder.

All models (.3)	.5

(G) Brake Shoes and/or Pads, Renew
Includes: Install new or exchange shoes or pads. Adjust rear brakes and hand brake. Bleed system.

1974–80—front—disc (1.0)	1.9
rear—drum (1.3)	2.1
all four wheels (1.8)	3.4
Resurface front disc rotor add—each	.9
Resurface rear brake drum add—each	.5

(G) Brake Drum, Renew

1974–80—one (.4)	.6
both (.5)	.8

BRAKE HYDRAULIC SYSTEM

(G) Wheel Cylinder, Renew
Includes: Bleed system.

1974–80—one (1.6)	2.1
both (1.7)	2.5

	(Factory Time)	Chilton Time

(G) Wheel Cylinder, R&R and Rebuild
Includes: Hone cylinder and bleed system.

1974–80—one (1.6)	2.4
both (1.7)	3.4

(G) Master Cylinder, Renew
Includes: Bleed complete system.

1974–80 (.6)	1.1

(G) Master Cylinder, R&R and Rebuild
Includes: Hone cylinder and bleed complete system.

1974–80	1.8

DISC BRAKES

(G) Disc Brake Pads, Renew

1975–80—front (1.0)	1.6
rear (1.0)	1.6
all four wheels (1.5)	2.8
Resurface disc brake rotor add-each	.9

(G) Caliper Assembly, Renew
Includes: Bleed complete system.

1974–80—front—one (.7)	1.2
both (.9)	1.7
rear—one (.7)	1.5
both (1.0)	2.1

(G) Caliper Assembly, R&R and Recondition
Includes: Bleed system.

1974–80—front—one (1.2)	2.0
both (1.7)	3.2
rear—one (1.4)	2.3
both (2.0)	3.5

(G) Brake Rotor, Renew
Includes: Renew front wheel bearings and grease retainer and repack bearings. Remove rear wheel assembly.

1974–80—front—one (.5)	1.1
both (.8)	1.6
rear—one (.4)	1.0
both (.6)	1.5

Mercury

(G) Bleed Brakes (Four Wheels)
Includes: Fill master cylinder.

All models (.3)	.5

(G) Brake Shoes and/or Pads, Renew
Includes: Install new or exchange shoes or pads. Adjust rear brakes and hand brake. Bleed system.

1974–80—front—disc (1.0)	1.9
rear—drum (1.3)	2.1
all four wheels (1.8)	3.4
Resurface front disc rotor add-each	.9
Resurface rear brake drum add-each	.5

(G) Brake Drum, Renew

1974–80—one (.4)	.6
both (.5)	.8

BRAKE HYDRAULIC SYSTEM

(G) Wheel Cylinder, Renew
Includes: Bleed system.

1974–80—one (1.6)	2.1
both (1.7)	2.5

	(Factory Time)	Chilton Time

(G) Wheel Cylinder, R&R and Rebuild
Includes: Hone cylinder and bleed system.

1974–80—one (1.6)	2.4
both (1.7)	3.4

(G) Master Cylinder, Renew
Includes: Bleed complete system.

1974–80 (.6)	1.0

(G) Master Cylinder, R&R and Rebuild
Includes: Hone cylinder and bleed complete system.

1974–80.	1.6

DISC BRAKES

(G) Disc Brake Pads, Renew

1974–80—front (1.0)	1.6
rear (1.0)	1.6
all four wheels (1.5)	2.8
Resurface disc brake rotor add-each	.9

(G) Caliper Assembly, Renew
Includes: Bleed complete system.

1974–80—front—one (.7)	1.2
both (.9)	1.7
rear—one (.7)	1.5
both (1.0)	2.1

(G) Caliper Assembly, R&R and Recondition
Includes: Bleed complete system.

1974–80—front—one (1.2)	2.0
both (1.7)	3.2
rear—one (1.4)	2.3
both (2.0)	3.5

(G) Brake Rotor, Renew
Includes: Renew front wheel bearings and grease retainer and repack bearings. Remove rear wheel assembly.

1974–80—front—one (.5)	1.1
both (.8)	1.6
rear—one (.4)	1.0
both (.6)	1.5

Mustang II, Bobcat, Pinto, Fairmont, Zephyr

(G) Bleed Brakes (Four Wheels)
Includes: Fill master cylinder.

All models (.3)	.5

(G) Brake Shoes, Renew
Includes: Install new or exchange shoes, service self adjustors, adjust service and hand brake. Bleed system.

1974–75—front (1.0)	1.5
rear (1.3)	1.8
all four wheels (1.9)	2.7
Resurface brake drum add-each .	.5

(G) Brake Shoes and/or Pads, Renew
Includes: Install new or exchange shoes or pads. Adjust service and hand brake. Bleed system.

1974–80—front—disc (.9)	1.3
rear—drum (1.3)	1.7
all four wheels (1.8)	2.6

	Chilton Time
(Factory Time)	

	Chilton Time
(Factory Time)	

Resurface front disc rotor, add—
each 9

Resurface rear brake drum, add—
each 5

(G) Brake Drum, Renew
Includes: Replace front bearings and grease retainer, pack bearings and adjust conventional brakes.

1974–75—front—one (.5) 8
1974–80—rear—one (.4) 7

BRAKE HYDRAULIC SYSTEM

(G) Wheel Cylinder, Renew
Includes: Bleed system.

1074–75—front—one (.8) 1.3
both (1.4)...................... 1.9
1974–80—rear—one (1.0) 1.4
both (1.7)...................... 2.1
all four wheels (2.6) 3.4

(G) Wheel Cylinder, R&R and Rebuild
Includes: Hone cylinder and bleed system.

1974–75—front—one (.8) 1.6
both (1.4)...................... 2.5
1974–80—rear—one (1.0) 1.7
both (1.7)...................... 2.7
all four wheels (2.5) 4.6

(G) Master Cylinder, Renew
Includes: Bleed complete system.

1974–80 (.6) 1.0

(G) Master Cylinder, R&R and Rebuild
Includes: Hone cylinder and bleed complete system.

1974–80 .... 1.6

DISC BRAKES

(G) Disc Brake Pads, Renew

1974–80 (.9) 1.3
Resurface disc brake rotor, add—
each 9

(G) Caliper Assembly, Renew
Includes: Bleed complete system.

1974–80—one (.7) 1.2
both (.9)...................... 1.7

(G) Caliper Assembly, R&R and Recondition
Includes: Bleed complete system.

1974–80—one (1.2).............. 2.0
both (1.7)...................... 3.2

(G) Brake Rotor, Renew
Includes: Renew front wheel bearings and grease retainer and repack bearings. Remove rear wheel assembly.

1974–80—one (.5) 1.1
both (.8)...................... 1.6

Oldsmobile

(G) Bleed Brakes (Four Wheels)
Includes: Fill master cylinder.

All models 5

(G) Brake Shoes and/or Pads, Renew
Includes: Install new or exchange shoes

or pads, adjust service and hand brake. Bleed system.

1974–80—front—disc (.8) 1.2
rear—drum (.8) 1.2
all four wheels 2.3
Resurface front disc rotor add,
each 9
Resurface rear brake drum add,
each 5

(G) Brake Drum, Renew (One)

1974–80 (.3) 4

BRAKE HYDRAULIC SYSTEM

(G) Wheel Cylinder, Renew (Rear)
Includes. Bleed system.

1974–75—one (.8) 1.2
both (1.3)...................... 1.9
1976–80—one (.6) 1.2
both (.9)...................... 1.9

(G) Wheel Cylinder, Rebuild
Includes: Hone cylinder and bleed system.

1974–75—one (1.0) 1.5
both (1.5)............... 2.4
1976–80—one (.8) 1.5
both (1.3)...................... 2.4

(G) Master Cylinder, Renew
Includes: Bleed complete system.

1974–80 (.6) 1.0

(G) Master Cylinder, R&R and Rebuild
Includes: Hone cylinder and bleed complete system.

1974–80 (1.2) 1.8

DISC BRAKES

(G) Brake Shoes and/or Pads, Renew
Includes: Install new or exchange shoes or pads, adjust service and hand brake. Bleed system.

1974–80—front—disc (.8) 1.2
rear—drum (.8) 1.2
all four wheels 2.3
Resurface front disc rotor add,
each 9
Resurface rear brake drum add,
each 5

(G) Disc Brake Rotor, Renew
Includes: R&R wheel, brake shoes and bearings.

1974–80—one (.7) 8
both (1.2)...................... 1.2

(G) Caliper Assembly, Renew
Includes: Remove brake shoes. Bleed complete system.

1974–75—one (.9) 1.3
both (1.2)...................... 1.7
1976–80—one (.6) 1.0
both (.9)...................... 1.4

(G) Caliper Assembly, R&R and Recondition
Includes: Remove brake shoes, renew parts as required and bleed complete system.

1974–75—one (1.2).............. 1.7
both (1.8)...................... 2.6
1976–80—one (.9) 1.4
both (1.5)...................... 2.3

| | Chilton | | | Chilton |
| (Factory Time) | Time | | (Factory Time) | Time |

Olds Cutlass, Omega (1974–79)

(G) Bleed Brakes (Four Wheels)
Includes: Fill master cylinder.
All models 5
(G) Brake Shoes, Renew
Includes: Install new or exchange shoes, service self adjustors. Adjust service and hand brake. Bleed system.
1974–75—front (.8)	1.3
rear (.6)	1.1
all four wheels (1.2)	2.0
Resurface brake drum add, each .	.4

(G) Brake Drum, Renew (One)
| **Front**—1974–75 (.3) . . . . | .5 |
| **Rear**—1974–80 (.3) . . . . | .4 |

BRAKE HYDRAULIC SYSTEM

(G) Wheel Cylinder, Renew
Includes: Bleed system.
Front—1974–75—one (.7)	1.1
both (1.1)	1.7
Rear—1974–80—one (.6)	1.0
both (.9)	1.6
all four (1.8)	2.8

(G) Wheel Cylinder, Rebuild
Includes: Hone cylinder and bleed system.
Front—1974–75—one (.9)	1.4
both (1.5)	2.2
Rear—1974–80—one (.8)	1.3
both (1.3)	2.1
all four (2.6)	4.0

(G) Master Cylinder, Renew
Includes: Bleed system.
| 1974–80 (.6) . . . . | 1.0 |

(G) Master Cylinder, R&R and Rebuild
Includes: Hone cylinder and bleed system
| 1974–80 (1.2) . . . . | 1.8 |

DISC BRAKES

(G) Brake Shoes and/or Pads, Renew
Includes: Install new or exchange shoes or pads, adjust service and hand brake. Bleed system.
1974–80—front—disc (.8)	1.2
rear—drum (.6)	1.1
all four wheels	2.2
Resurface front disc rotor add, each	.9
Resurface rear brake drum add, each	.4

(G) Disc Brake Rotor, Renew
Includes: R&R wheel, brake shoes and bearings.
| 1974–80—one (.7) . . . . | .8 |
| both (1.2) . . . . | 1.2 |

(G) Caliper Assembly, Renew
Includes: Remove brake shoes. Bleed complete system.
1974–75—one (.9)	1.3
both (1.2)	1.7
1976–80—one (.6)	1.0
both (.9)	1.4

(G) Caliper Assembly, R&R and Recondition
Includes: Remove brake shoes, renew

parts as required and bleed complete system.
1974–75—one (1.2)	1.7
both (1.8)	2.6
1976–80—one (.9)	1.4
both (1.5)	2.3

Olds Toronado

(G) Bleed Brakes (Four Wheels)
Includes: Fill master cylinder.
All models 5
(G) Brake Shoes and/or Pads, Renew
Includes: Install new or exchange shoes or pads, adjust service and hand brake. Bleed system.
1974–80—front—disc (.8)	1.2
rear—drum (.8)	1.2
all four wheels	2.3
Resurface front disc rotor add, each	.9
Resurface rear brake drum add, each	.5

(G) Brake Drum, Renew (One)
| 1974–80 (.3) . . . . | .5 |

BRAKE HYDRAULIC SYSTEM

(G) Wheel Cylinder, Renew (Rear)
Includes: Bleed system.
1974–75—one (.7)	1.0
both (1.1)	1.4
1976–80—one (.6)	1.0
both (.9)	1.4

(G) Wheel Cylinder, Rebuild
Includes: Hone cylinder and bleed system.
1974–75—one (.9)	1.2
both (1.5)	1.8
1976–80—one (.8)	1.2
both (1.3)	1.8

(G) Master Cylinder, Renew
Includes: Bleed complete system.
| 1974–80 (.6) . . . . | 1.0 |

(G) Master Cylinder, R&R and Rebuild
Includes: Hone cylinder and bleed complete system.
| 1974–80 (1.2) . . . . | 1.8 |

DISC BRAKES

(G) Brake Shoes and/or Pads, Renew
Includes: Install new or exchange shoes or pads, adjust service and hand brake. Bleed system.
1974–80—front—disc (.8)	1.2
rear—drum (.8)	1.2
all four wheels	2.3
Resurface front disc rotor add, each	.9
Resurface rear brake drum add, each	.5

(G) Disc Brake Pads, Renew
Includes: Install new or exchange disc brake pads only.
| 1979–80—front—disc (.8) . . . . | 1.2 |

(Factory Time)	Chilton Time
rear—disc (.8)	1.2
all four wheels	2.3
Resurface disc brake rotor add, each	.9

(G) Disc Brake Rotor, Renew
Includes: R&R wheel, brake shoes and bearings.

Front—1974—one (.6)	.8
both (.8)	1.2
1975–80—one (.4)	.7
both (.7)	1.1
Rear—1979–80—one (.8)	1.2
both (1.1)	1.6

(G) Caliper Assembly, Renew
Includes: Remove brake shoes. Bleed complete system.

Front—1974–75—one (.8)	1.2
both (1.1)	1.6
1976–80—one (.6)	1.0
both (.9)	1.4
Rear—1979–80—one (.9)	1.3
both (1.1)	1.7

(G) Caliper Assembly, R&R and Recondition
Includes: Remove brake shoes, renew parts as required and bleed complete system.

Front—1974–75—one (1.1)	1.6
both (1.7)	2.5
1976–80—one (.9)	1.4
both (1.5)	2.3
Rear—1979–80—one (1.4)	1.8
both (2.1)	2.7

Olds Starfire

(G) Bleed Brakes (Four Wheels)
Includes: Fill master cylinder.

All models	.5

(G) Brake Shoes and/or Pads, Renew
Includes: Install new or exchange shoes or pads, adjust service and hand brake. Bleed system.

1975–80—front—disc (.8)	1.2
rear—drum (.8)	1.2
all four wheels	2.3
Resurface front disc rotor, each	.9
Resurface rear brake drum add, each	.4

(G) Brake Drum, Renew (One)

1975–80 (.3)	.4

BRAKE HYDRAULIC SYSTEM

(G) Wheel Cylinder, Renew (Rear)
Includes: Bleed system.

1975–80—one (.6)	1.2
both (.9)	1.9

(G) Wheel Cylinder, Rebuild
Includes: Hone cylinder and bleed system.

1975–80—one (.8)	1.5
both (1.3)	2.4

(Factory Time)	Chilton Time

(G) Master Cylinder, Renew
Includes: Bleed complete system.

1975–80 (.5)	.9

(G) Master Cylinder, R&R and Rebuild
Includes: Hone cylinder and bleed complete system.

1975–80 (1.0)	1.6

DISC BRAKES

(G) Brake Shoes and/or Pads, Renew
Includes: Install new or exchange shoes or pads, adjust service and hand brake. Bleed system.

1975–80—front—disc (.8)	1.2
rear—drum (.8)	1.2
all four wheels	2.3
Resurface front disc rotor add, each	.9
Resurface rear brake drum add, each	.4

(G) Disc Brake Rotor, Renew
Includes: R&R wheel, brake shoes and bearings.

1975–80—one (.7)	.8
both (1.2)	1.2

(G) Caliper Assembly, Renew
Includes: Remove brake shoes. Bleed complete system.

1975—one (.9)	1.3
both (1.2)	1.7
1976–80—one (.6)	1.0
both (.9)	1.4

(G) Caliper Assembly, R&R and Recondition
Includes: Remove brake shoes, renew parts as required and bleed complete system.

1975—one (1.2)	1.7
both (1.8)	2.6
1976–80—one (.9)	1.4
both (1.5)	2.3

Plymouth

(G) Bleed Brakes (Four Wheels)
Includes: Add fluid.

All models (.4)	.6
w/Power brks add (.2)	.2

(G) Brake Shoes and/or Pads, Renew
Includes: Install new or exchange shoes or pads, adjust service and hand brake. Bleed system.

1974–78—front—disc (.6)	1.3
rear—drum (.7)	1.7
all four wheels (1.3)	2.9
Resurface front disc rotor, add- each	.9
Resurface rear brake drum, add- each	.5

(G) Brake Drum, Renew (One)

1974–78—rear (.3)	.4

BRAKE HYDRAULIC SYSTEM

(G) Wheel Cylinder, Renew (Rear)
Includes: Bleed system.

1974–75—one (.9)	1.2
1976–78—one (.7)	1.2

	Chilton
(Factory Time)	Time

(G) Wheel Cylinder, Rebuild
Includes: Hone cylinder and bleed system.

1974–78—rear—one	1.5
both	2.3

(G) Master Cylinder, Renew
Includes: Bleed complete system.

1974–78—exc below (.5)	.8
1978—w/Alum housing (.7)	1.0
w/P.B. add (.1)	.1

(G) Master Cylinder, R&R and Rebuild
Includes: Bleed complete system.

1974–78	2.1
w/P.B. add	.1

DISC BRAKES

(G) Brake Shoes and/or Pads, Renew
Includes: Install new or exchange shoes or pads, adjust service and hand brake. Bleed system.

1974–78—front—disc (.6)	1.3
rear—drum (.7)	1.7
all four wheels (1.3)	2.9
Resurface front disc rotor, add-each	.9
Resurface rear brake drum, add-each	.5

(G) Disc Brake Rotor, Renew
Includes: Replace inner and outer bearings if necessary.

1974–78—each (.6)	.9

(G) Caliper Assembly, Renew
Includes: Bleed system.

1974–78—one (.7)	1.2
both (1.2)	1.8

(G) Caliper Assembly, R&R and Recondition
Includes: Bleed system.

1974–78—one (1.0)	1.8
both (1.9)	2.9

Pontiac & Grand Prix

(G) Bleed Brakes (Four Wheels)
Includes: Fill master cylinder.

All models	.5

(G) Brake Shoes and/or Pads, Renew
Includes: Install new or exchange shoes or pads, adjust service and hand brake. Bleed system.

1974–80—front-disc (.8)	1.2
rear-drum (.9)	1.4
all four wheels	2.5
Resurface front disc rotor add, each	.9
Resurface rear brake drum add, each	.5

(G) Brake Drum, Renew

1974–80—each (.3)	.5

BRAKE HYDRAULIC SYSTEM

(G) Wheel Cylinder, Renew
Includes: Bleed system.

1974–80—one (.7)	1.0

	Chilton
(Factory Time)	Time

(G) Wheel Cylinder, R&R and Rebuild
Includes: Hone cylinder, bleed system.

1974–80—one (.9)	1.4

(G) Master Cylinder, Renew
Includes: Bleed cylinder.

1974–80—std brake (.5)	.9
power brake (.3)	.7

(G) Master Cylinder, R&R and Rebuild
Includes: Bleed cylinder.

1974–80—std brake (1.3)	1.9
power brake (1.1)	1.7

DISC BRAKES

(G) Brake Shoes and/or Pads, Renew
Includes: Install new or exchange shoes or pads, adjust service and hand brake. Bleed system.

1974–80—front-disc (.8)	1.2
rear-drum (.9)	1.4
all four wheels	2.5
Resurface front disc rotor add, each	.9
Resurface rear brake drum add, each	.5

(G) Disc Brake Rotor, Renew

1974–80—one (.7)	.9

(G) Caliper Assembly, Renew
Includes: Remove brake shoes, bleed system.

1974–80—one (.6)	.9
both (.9)	1.3

(G) Caliper Assembly, R&R and Recondition
Includes: Remove brake shoes, renew parts as required and bleed system.

1974–80—one (1.1)	1.6
both (1.9)	2.9

Pontiac Astre & Sunbird

(G) Bleed Brakes (Four Wheels)
Includes: Fill master cylinder.

All models	.5

(G) Brake Shoes and/or Pads, Renew
Includes: Install new or exchange shoes or pads, adjust service and hand brake. Bleed system.

1975–80—front-disc (.8)	1.2
rear-drum (.9)	1.4
all four wheels	2.5
Resurface front disc rotor add, each	.9
Resurface rear brake drum add, each	.5

(G) Brake Drum, Renew

1975–80—each (.4)	.6

BRAKE HYDRAULIC SYSTEM

(G) Wheel Cylinder, Renew
Includes: Bleed system.

1975–80—one (.6)	.9

(G) Wheel Cylinder, Rebuild
Includes: Hone cylinder, bleed system.

1975–80—one (.8)	1.3

(Factory Time)	Chilton Time		(Factory Time)	Chilton Time

(G) Master Cylinder, Renew
Includes: Bleed cylinder.
    1975–80 (.5) .... **.9**

(G) Master Cylinder, Rebuild
Includes: Bleed cylinder.
    1975–80 (1.1) **1.7**

DISC BRAKES

(G) Disc Brake Rotor, Renew
    1975–80—one (.7) .... **.9**

(G) Brake Shoes and/or Pads, Renew
Includes: Install new or exchange shoes or pads, adjust service and hand brake. Bleed system.
    1975–80—front—disc (.8) **1.2**
    rear–drum (.9) **1.4**
    all four wheels **2.5**
    Resurface front disc rotor add,
        each .... **.9**
    Resurface rear brake drum add,
        each .... **.5**

(G) Caliper Assembly, Renew
Includes: Remove brake shoes, bleed system.
    1975–80—one (.6) .... **.9**
    both (.9) **1.3**

(G) Caliper Assembly, R&R and Recondition
Includes: Remove brake shoes, renew parts as required and bleed system.
    1975–80—one (1.1) **1.6**
    both (1.9) **2.9**

Firebird, Phoenix (1978–79), LeMans, Ventura (1974–77)

(G) Bleed Brakes (Four Wheels)
Includes: Fill master cylinder.
    All models .... **.5**

(G) Brake Shoes and/or Pads, Renew
Includes: Install new or exchange shoes or pads, adjust service and hand brake. Bleed system.
    1974–80—front—disc (.8) **1.2**
    rear—drum (.9) **1.4**
    all four wheels **2.5**
    Resurface front disc rotor add,
        each .... **.9**
    Resurface rear brake drum add,
        each .... **.5**

(G) Brake Shoes, Renew
Includes: Install new or exchange shoes. Service self adjustors, adjust service and hand brake. Bleed system.
    1974—front (1.0) **1.5**
    rear (1.0) **1.6**
    all four wheels **3.0**
    Resurface brake drum add, each . **.5**

(G) Brake Drum, Renew
    Front—1974—each (.6) .... **.8**
    Rear—1974–80—each (.3) .... **.5**

BRAKE HYDRAULIC SYSTEM

(G) Wheel Cylinder, Renew
Includes: Bleed system.
    Front—1974—one (.8) **1.3**
    Rear—1974–80—one (.7) **1.2**
    all four wheels **3.6**

(G) Wheel Cylinder, Rebuild
Includes: Hone cylinder, bleed system.
    Front—1974—one (1.0) **1.6**
    Rear—1974–80—one (.9) **1.5**
    all four wheels **4.4**

(G) Master Cylinder, Renew
Includes: Bleed cylinder.
    1974–80—std brake (.5) .... **.9**
    power brake (.3) .... **.7**

(G) Master Cylinder, Rebuild
Includes: Bleed cylinder.
    1974–80—std brake (1.3) **1.9**
    power brake (1.1) **1.7**

DISC BRAKES

(G) Brake Shoes and/or Pads, Renew
Includes: Install new or exchange shoes or pads, adjust service and hand brake. Bleed system.
    1974–80—front-disc (.8) **1.2**
    rear-drum (.9) **1.4**
    all four wheels **2.5**
    Resurface front disc rotor add,
        each .... **.9**
    Resurface rear brake drum add,
        each .... **.5**

(G) Disc Brake Pads, Renew
Includes: Install new or exchange disc brake pads. R&R calipers and bleed system.
    1979–80—front—disc (.8) **1.2**
    rear—disc (1.2) **1.6**
    all four wheels **2.7**
    Resurface disc brake rotor add,
        each .... **.9**

(G) Disc Brake Rotor, Renew
    Front—1974–80—one (.7) .... **.9**
    Rear—1979–80—one (.7) **1.0**

(G) Caliper Assembly, Renew
Includes: Remove brake shoes, bleed system.
    Front—1974–80—one (.6) .... **.9**
    both (.9) **1.3**
    Rear—one (.6) .... **.9**
    both (.9) **1.3**

(G) Caliper Assembly, R&R and Recondition
Includes: Remove brake shoes, renew parts as required and bleed system.
    Front—1974–80—one (1.1) **1.6**
    both (1.9) **2.9**
    Rear—one (1.1) **1.6**
    both (1.9) **2.9**

Thunderbird (1974–76)

(G) Brake Drum, Renew
    1974–76—rear—each (.4) .... **.6**

(G) Bleed Brakes (Four Wheels)
Includes: Fill master cylinder.
    All models (.3) .... **.5**

(G) Brake Shoes and/or Pads, Renew
Includes: Install new or exchange shoes

| | Chilton |
| (Factory Time) | Time |

or pads. *Adjust rear brakes and hand brake. Bleed system.*

1974–76—front—disc (1.1)	2.1
rear—drum (1.5)	2.1
all four wheels (2.1)	3.4

BRAKE HYDRAULIC SYSTEM

(G) Wheel Cylinders, Renew
Includes: Bleed system.

| 1974–76—rear—one (1.1) | 1.4 |
| both (1.8) | 2.1 |

(G) Wheel Cylinder, R&R and Rebuild
Includes: Hone cylinder and bleed system.

| 1974–76—rear—one (1.1) | 1.7 |
| both (1.8) | 2.7 |

(G) Master Cylinder, Renew
Includes: Bleed complete system.

| 1974–76 (.5) | .9 |

(G) Master Cylinder, R&R and Rebuild
Includes: Hone cylinder and bleed complete system.

| 1974–76 | 1.5 |

DISC BRAKES

(G) Disc Brake Pads, Renew

| 1974–76 (1.1) | 2.1 |

(G) Caliper Assembly, Renew
Includes: Bleed complete system.

1974–76—front—one (.7)	1.2
both (.9)	1.7
rear—one (1.0)	1.5
both (1.3)	2.1

(G) Caliper Assembly, R&R and Recondition
Includes: Bleed complete system.

1974–76—front—one (1.4)	2.0
both (2.0)	3.2
rear—one (1.7)	2.3
both (2.3)	3.5

(G) Brake Rotor, Renew
Includes: Renew front wheel bearings and grease retainer and repack bearings. Remove rear wheel assembly.

| 1974–76—one (.5) | .8 |
| both (.8) | 1.4 |

Valiant, Dart, Barracuda, Challenger

(G) Bleed Brakes (Four Wheels)
Includes: Add fluid.

| All models (.4) | .6 |
| w/Pwr brks add | .2 |

(G) Brake Shoes, Renew
Includes: Install new or exchange brake shoes. Adjust service and hand brake. Bleed system.

1974–76—front (.9)	1.5
rear (.9)	1.7
all four wheels	2.9
Resurface brake drum, add-each .	.5

(G) Brakes Shoes and/or Pads, Renew
Includes: Install new or exchange shoes or pads, adjust service and hand brake. Bleed system.

| 1974–80—front—disc (.6) | 1.2 |

| | Chilton |
| (Factory Time) | Time |

rear—drum (.7)	1.7
all four wheels (1.3)	2.9
Resurface front disc rotor, add-each	.9
Resurface rear brake drum, add-each	.5

(G) Brake Drum, Renew (One)

| 1974–80—front (.4) | .5 |
| rear (.3) | .4 |

BRAKE HYDRAULIC SYSTEM

(G) Wheel Cylinders, Renew
Includes: Bleed system.

1974–76—front one (1.0)	1.2
both (1.6)	1.9
rear one (.9)	1.2
both (1.6)	1.9
all four (2.6)	3.4
1977–80—rear one (.7)	1.2
both (1.3)	1.9

Aspen, Volare, LeBaron, Diplomat, Valiant, Dart, Barracuda, Challenger

(G) Wheel Cylinder, Rebuild
Includes: Hone cylinder and bleed system.

1974–76—front—one	1.5
both	2.3
rear one	1.5
both	2.3
1977–80—rear one	1.5
both	2.3
all four	4.0

(G) Master Cylinder, Renew
Includes: Bleed complete system.

1974–80—exc below (.5)	.8
1978–80—w/Alum housing (.7)	1.0
w/P.B. add (.1)	.1

(G) Master Cylinder, R&R and Rebuild
Includes: Bleed complete system.

| 1974–80 | 2.1 |
| w/P.B. add | .2 |

DISC BRAKES

(G) Disc Brake Rotor, Renew
Includes: Replace inner and outer bearings if necessary.

| 1974–80—each (.6) | .9 |

(G) Brake Shoes and/or Pads, Renew
Includes: Install new or exchange shoes or pads, adjust service and hand brake. Bleed system.

1974–80—front—disc (.6)	1.2
rear—drum (.7)	1.7
all four wheels (1.3)	2.9
Resurface front disc rotor, add-each	.9
Resurface rear brake drum, add-each	.5

(G) Caliper Assembly, Renew
Includes: Bleed system.

| 1974–80—one (.7) | 1.2 |
| both (1.2) | 1.8 |

(Factory Time)	Chilton Time	(Factory Time)	Chilton Time

(G) Caliper Assembly, R&R and Recondition
Includes: Bleed system.

1974–80—one (1.0)		**1.8**
both (1.9)		**2.9**

Vega & Monza

(G) Bleed Brakes (Four Wheels)
Includes: Fill master cylinder.

All models (.3)		**.5**

(G) Brake Shoes and/or Pads, Renew
Includes: Install new or exchange shoes or pads, adjust service and hand brake. Bleed system.

1974–80—front—disc (.8)		**1.2**
rear—drum (1.0)		**1.6**
all four wheels		**2.5**
Resurface disc rotor, add-each		**.9**
Resurface brake drum, add-each		**.5**

(G) Brake Drum, Renew (One)

1974–80—rear (.3)		**.5**

BRAKE HYDRAULIC SYSTEM

(G) Wheel Cylinder, Renew (Rear)
Includes: Bleed system.

1974–77—one (.8)		**1.2**
both (1.3)		**1.8**
1978–80—one (.6)		**1.0**
both (1.0)		**1.6**

(G) Wheel Cylinder, Rebuild
Includes: Hone cylinder and bleed system.

1974–77—one (.8)		**1.5**
both (1.3)		**2.3**
1978–80—one (.8)		**1.5**
both (1.2)		**2.3**

(G) Master Cylinder, Renew
Includes: Bleed complete system.

1974–80 (.5)		**.8**

(G) Master Cylinder, R&R and Rebuild
Includes: Hone cylinder and bleed complete system.

1974–77 (1.1)		**1.7**
1978–80 (.9)		**1.7**

DISC BRAKES

(G) Disc Brake Pads, Renew
Includes: Install new or exchange disc brake pads only.

1974–80 (.8)		**1.2**

(G) Disc Brake Rotor, Renew

1974–80—one (.6)		**.9**
both (1.1)		**1.5**

(G) Caliper Assembly, Renew
Includes: Bleed complete system.

1974–80—one (.7)		**1.1**
both (1.0)		**1.5**

(G) Caliper Assembly, R&R and Recondition
Includes: Bleed complete system.

1974–80—one (1.1)		**1.6**
both (1.7)		**2.5**

COOLING SYSTEM

(Factory Time)	Chilton Time	(Factory Time)	Chilton Time

All Cars

ADD THESE OPERATIONS TO RADIATOR R&R

(G) Boil & Repair		**1.5**
(G) Rod Clean		**1.9**
(G) Repair Core		**1.3**
(G) Renew Tank		**1.6**
(G) Renew Trans. Oil Cooler		**1.9**
(G) Recore Radiator		**1.7**

American Motors

(G) Winterize Cooling System
Includes: Run engine to check for leaks, tighten all hose connections. Test radiator pressure cap, drain radiator and engine block. Add anti-freeze and refill system.

All models		**.5**

(M) Thermostat, Renew

1974–80 (.4)		**.5**

(G) Radiator Assembly, Remove and Reinstall or Renew

1974–76 (.5)		**.8**
1977–80—Four (.4)		**.7**
Six (.5)		**.8**
V-8 (.5)		**.8**
w/A.C. add (.1)		**.1**
w/A.T. add (.1)		**.1**

(G) Water Pump, Renew

Four—1977–80 (1.1)		**1.6**
w/P.S. add (.1)		**.1**
Six—1974–76 (.6)		**1.1**
1977–80—Pacer (.9)		**1.3**
all other models (.7)		**1.1**
w/P.S. add (.1)		**.1**
w/Air guard add (.1)		**.1**
w/A.C. add (.3)		**.3**
V-8—1974–80 (1.1)		**1.6**
w/P.S. add (.1)		**.1**
w/A.C. add (.6)		**.6**

(M) Fan Belt, Renew

Four—1977–80 (.2)		**.3**
Six—1974–80 (.2)		**.3**
V-8—1974–80 (.3)		**.4**
w/P.S., A.C. or Air guard add (.1)		**.1**

	Chilton		Chilton
(Factory Time)	Time	(Factory Time)	Time

AMC/Jeep

(M) Winterize Cooling System
Includes: Run engine to check for leaks, tighten all hose connections. Test radiator and pressure cap, drain radiator and engine block. Add anti-freeze and refill system.
All models 5
(M) Thermostat, Renew
All models (.3) 4
w/A.C. add .5
(M) Radiator Assembly, R&R or Renew
1974–80 (.4) 9
w/A.C. add (.1) 1
w/A.T. add (.1) 1
(M) Radiator Hoses, Renew
1974–80—Six—upper or lower (.3) .5
V-8—upper (.3) 5
lower (.4) 6
(G) Water Pump, Renew
1974–80—Six (.6) 8
V-8 (1.1) 1.4
w/P.S. or Air Guard add (.2) 2
w/A.C. add (.6) 6
(M) Fan Belt, Renew
1974–80 (.3) 3

Buick LeSabre, Electra, Riviera (1974–78)

(M) Winterize Cooling System
Includes: Run engine to check for leaks, tighten all hose connections. Test radiator and pressure cap, drain radiator and engine block. Add anti-freeze and refill system.
All models 5
(M) Thermostat, Renew
V-6—1976–77 (.4) 6
1978–80 (.6) 8
V-8—1974–80 (.4) 6
w/Turbocharger and A.I.R. add
(.4) 4
(M) Radiator Assembly, R&R or Renew
Includes: Drain and refill cooling system.
1974–80 (.7) 1.1
(M) Radiator Hoses, Renew
1974–80—upper (.3) 4
lower (.4) 5
both (.6) 7
by-pass (.4) .5
w/Turbocharger and A.I.R. add
(.3) 4
(M) Fan Belt, Renew
1974–80 (.3) 4
w/A.C. add (.1) 1
w/P.S. add (.1) 1
w/A.I.R. add (.1) 1
(G) Water Pump, Renew
Includes: R&R fan and pulleys.
V-6—1976–77 (.6) 9
1978–80 (.8) 1.1
V-8—1974–76 (1.1) 1.4
1977–80 (.9) 1.2
w/A.C. add (.2) 2
w/P.S. add (.1) 1
w/A.I.R. add (.1) 1

Buick Riviera (1979–80)

(M) Winterize Cooling System
Includes: Run engine to check for leaks, tighten all hose connections. Test radiator and pressure cap, drain radiator and engine block. Add anti-freeze and refill system.
All models 5
(M) Thermostat, Renew
V-6—1979–80 (.6) 8
V-8—1978–80 (.4) 6
w/Turbocharger and A.I.R. add
(.4) 6
(M) Radiator Assembly, R&R or Renew
Includes: Drain and refill cooling system.
1979–80 (.7) 1.1
(M) Radiator Hoses, Renew
1979–80—upper (.3) 4
lower (.4) 5
both (.6) 7
by-pass (.4) .5
w/Turbocharger and A.I.R. add
(.3) 4
(M) Fan Belt, Renew
1979–80 (.3) 5
w/P.S. add (.1) 1
w/A.I.R. add (.1) 1
(G) Water Pump, Renew
Includes: R&R fan and pulleys.
V-6—1979–80 (.8) 1.1
V-8—1979–80 (1.0) 1.4
w/P.S. add (.1) 1
w/A.C. add (.2) 2
w/A.I.R. add (.1) 1

Buick Apollo, Century, Gran Sport, Regal, Skylark (1974–79)

(M) Winterize Cooling System
Includes: Run engine to check for leaks, tighten all hose connections. Test radiator and pressure cap, drain radiator and engine block. Add anti-freeze and refill system.
All models 5
(M) Thermostat, Renew
Six—1974–75 (.4) 6
V-6—1975–77 (.4) 6
1978–80 (.6) 8
V-8—1974–80 (.4) 6
w/Turbocharger and A.I.R. add
(.4) 4
(M) Radiator Assembly, R&R or Renew
Includes: Drain and refill cooling system
1974–77 (.4) 7
1978–80 (.5) 8
w/A.T. add (.2) 2
(M) Radiator Hoses, Renew
1974–80—upper (.3) 4
lower (.4) 5
both (.6) 7
by-pass (.4) .5
w/Turbocharger and A.I.R. add
(.3) 4
(M) Fan Belt, Renew
1974–80 (.3) 4

(Factory Time)	Chilton Time		(Factory Time)	Chilton Time

w/A.C. add (.1) 1

w/P.S. add (.1) 1

w/A.I.R. add (.1) 1

(G) Water Pump, Renew

Includes: R&R fan and pulleys.

Six—1974–75 (.8) 1.1

V-6—1975–77 (.6) 9

1978–80 (.8) 1.1

V-8—1974–76 (1.1) 1.4

1977–80 (.9) 1.2

w/A.C. add (.2) 2

w/P.S. add (.1) 1

w/A.I.R. add (.1) 1

Buick Skyhawk

(M) Winterize Cooling System

Includes: Run engine to check for leaks, tighten all hose connections. Test radiator and pressure cap, drain radiator and engine block. Add anti-freeze and refill system.

All models 5

(M) Thermostat, Renew

1975–76 (.4) 6

1978–80 (.6) 8

(M) Radiator Assembly, R&R or Renew

Includes: Drain and refill cooling system.

1975–76 (.6) 9

1977–80 (.5) 9

w/A.T. add (.2) 2

(G) Radiator Hoses, Renew

1975–80—upper (.3) 4

lower (.4) 5

both (.6) 7

by-pass (.4) 5

(M) Fan Belt, Renew

1975–80 (.3) 4

w/P.S. add (.1) 1

w/A.I.R. add (.1) 1

(G) Water Pump, Renew

Includes: R&R fan and pulleys.

1975–76 (.8) 1.1

1977–80 (.6) 9

w/A.C. add (.1) 1

w/P.S. add (.1) 1

w/A.I.R. add (.1) 1

Cadillac

(M) Winterize Cooling System

Includes: Run engine to check for leaks, tighten all hose connections. Test radiator and pressure cap, drain radiator and engine block. Add anti-freeze and refill system.

All models 5

(G) Thermostat, Renew

1974–80 (.4) 6

(M) Radiator Assembly, R&R or Renew

1974–80 (.6) 1.1

(M) Radiator Hoses, Renew

1974–80—upper (.2) 3

lower (.3) 4

both (.4) 5

(G) Water Pump, Renew

1974–80 (1.0) 1.5

Recond pump add (.3) 4

w/A.I.R. add (.2) 2

(M) Fan Belt, Renew

1974–80 (.3) 4

w/A.I.R. add (.2) 2

Cadillac Seville

(M) Winterize Cooling System

Includes: Run engine to check for leaks, tighten all hose connections. Test radiator and pressure cap, drain radiator and engine block. Add anti-freeze and refill system.

All models 5

(G) Thermostat, Renew

1976–80 (.4) 6

(M) Radiator Assembly, R&R or Renew

1976–80 (.6) 1.1

(M) Radiator Hoses, Renew

1976–80—upper (.2) 3

lower (.3) 4

both (.4) 5

(G) Water Pump, Renew

1976–77 (1.3) 1.8

1978–80 (1.5) 2.1

Recond pump add (.3) 4

w/A.I.R. add (.2) 2

(M) Fan Belt, Renew

1976–80 (.3) 5

Cadillac Eldorado

(M) Winterize Cooling System

Includes: Run engine to check for leaks, tighten all hose connections. Test radiator and pressure cap, drain radiator and engine block. Add anti-freeze and refill system.

All models 5

(G) Thermostat, Renew

1974–80 (.4) 6

(M) Radiator Assembly, R&R or Renew

1974–78 (.6) 1.1

1979–80 (.9) 1.4

(M) Radiator Hoses, Renew

1974–80—upper (.2) 3

lower (.3) 4

both (.4) 5

(G) Water Pump, Renew

1974–78 (1.0) 1.5

1979–80 (1.5) 2.1

Recond pump add (.3) 4

w/A.I.R. add (.2) 2

(M) Fan Belt, Renew

1974–80 (.4) 5

w/A.I.R. add (.2) 2

Camaro, Chevelle, Malibu, Monte Carlo, Nova

(M) Winterize Cooling System

Includes: Run engine to check for leaks, tighten all hose connections. Test radia-

	Chilton		Chilton
(Factory Time)	Time	(Factory Time)	Time

tor and pressure cap, drain radiator and engine block. Add anti-freeze and refill system.

All models	.5	w/Air inj add (.2)	.2

(M) Thermostat, Renew

1974 (.4)	.6		
1975–80—Six (.3)	.6		
V-6 (.6)	.8		
V-8 (.3)	.6		

(M) Fan Belt, Renew

1974–80 (.2)	.3
each adtnl (.2)	.2

Chevette

(M) Winterize Cooling System
Includes: Run engine to check for leaks, tighten all hose connections. Test radiator and pressure cap, drain radiator and engine block. Add anti-freeze and refill system.

All models	.5

(M) Thermostat, Renew

1976 (.6)	.8
1977–80 (.3)	.5

(M) Radiator Assembly, R&R or Renew
Includes: Drain and refill cooling system.

1976–80 (.5)	.8
w/A.T. add (.2)	.2

(M) Radiator Hoses, Renew

1976–80—upper (.3)	.4
lower (.4)	.5
both (.5)	.7

(G) Water Pump, Renew

1976–80 (1.2)	1.5
w/P.S. add (.2)	.2

(M) Fan Belt, Renew

1976–80 (.2)	.3
each adtnl belt (.2)	.2

(M) Radiator Assembly, R&R or Renew
Includes: Drain and refill cooling system.

1974–76 (.6)	.9
1977–80 (.5)	.9
w/A.T. add (.2)	.2

(M) Radiator Hoses, Renew

1974–80—upper (.3)	.4
lower (.4)	.5
both (.5)	.7

(G) Water Pump, Renew

1974–76—Six (.8)	1.3
V-8 (.9)	1.4
1977–80—Six (.8)	1.3
V-6 (.8)	1.3
V-8 (.8)	1.3

(M) Fan Belt, Renew

1974–80 (.2)	.3
each adtnl (.2)	.2

Chevrolet & Corvette

(M) Winterize Cooling System
Includes: Run engine to check for leaks, tighten all hose connections. Test radiator and pressure cap, drain radiator and engine block. Add anti-freeze and refill system.

All models	.5

(M) Thermostat, Renew

1974–80 (.3)	.6

(M) Radiator Assembly, R&R or Renew
Includes: Drain and refill cooling system.

Chevrolet

1974–76 (.6)	.9
1977–80 (.5)	.9

Corvette

1974–76 (2.1)	2.5
1977–80 (.8)	1.4
w/A.C. add	.3
w/A.T. add	.2

(M) Radiator Hoses, Renew

Chevrolet

upper (.3)	.4
lower (.4)	.5
both (.6)	.7

Corvette

upper (.3)	.5
lower (.5)	.6
both (.6)	.8

(G) Water Pump, Renew

Chevrolet

Six—1977–80 (.8)	1.2
V-8—1974–76 (.9)	1.3
1977–80 (.8)	1.2

Corvette

1974 (.9)	1.4
1975–80 (.7)	1.2
w/A.C. add (.5)	.5
w/P.S. add (.2)	.2

Citation, Omega, Phoenix, Skylark—All 1980

(M) Winterize Cooling System
Includes: Run engine to check for leaks, tighten all hose connections. Test radiator and pressure cap, drain radiator and engine block. Add anti-freeze and refill system.

All models	.5

(G) Thermostat, Renew

1980 (.3)	.5

(G) Radiator Assembly, R&R or Renew
Includes: Drain and refill cooling system.

1980 (.7)	1.1
w/A.T. add (.2)	.2

(M) Radiator Hoses, Renew

1980—upper (.3)	.4
lower (.4)	.5

(M) Drive Belt, Renew

1980 (.2)	.3
each adtnl (.2)	.2

(G) Water Pump and/or Gasket, Renew

1980 (.8)	1.3
w/P.S. add (.2)	.2
w/A.C. add	
Four (.6)	.6
V-6 (.2)	.2

Chrysler, Cordoba, Imperial

(M) Winterize Cooling System
Includes: Run engine to check for leaks, tighten all hose connections. Test radia-

(Factory Time)	Chilton Time

tor and pressure cap, drain radiator and engine block. Add anti-freeze and refill system.

All models	.5
(M) Thermostat, Renew	
1974–80 (.4)	.6
w/A.C. add (.3)	.3
(M) Radiator Assembly, R&R or Renew	
1974–76 (.6)	1.0
1977–80 (.8)	1.2
w/A.C. add (.1)	.2
w/A.T. add (.1)	.2
(M) Radiator Hoses, Renew	
1974–80—upper (.4)	.6
lower (.4)	.8
by-pass—Six (.6)	.9
V-8 (.3)	.6
(G) Water Pump, Renew	
Includes: Drain and refill coolant.	
Six—1979–80 (.9)	1.3
V-8—1974–80	
318–360 engs (1.0)	1.4
400–440 engs (.8)	1.2
w/P.S. add (.2)	.2
w/A.C. add (.4)	.4
(M) Fan Belt, Renew	
1974–80 (.2)	.4
w/A.C. add (.1)	.1
w/Air inj add (.2)	.2
w/P.S. add (.1)	.1

Dodge

(M) Winterize Cooling System
Includes: Run engine to check for leaks, tighten all hose connections. Test radiator pressure cap, drain radiator and engine block. Add anti-freeze and refill system.

All models	.5
(M) Thermostat, Renew	
1974–80 (.4)	.6
w/A.C. add (.3)	.3
(M) Radiator Assembly, R&R or Renew	
1974–76 (.6)	1.0
1977–80 (.8)	1.2
w/A.C. add (.1)	.2
w/A.T. add (.1)	.2
(M) Radiator Hoses, Renew	
1974–80—upper (.3)	.6
lower (.4)	.8
by-pass—Six (.9)	1.4
V-8 (.3)	.6
(G) Water Pump, Renew	
Includes: Drain and refill coolant.	
Six—1974–80 (.9)	1.3
w/A.C. add (.4)	.4
V-8—1974–80 (1.0)	1.3
w/P.S. add (.2)	.2
w/A.C. add (.4)	.4
(M) Fan Belt, Renew	
1974–80 (.2)	.4
w/A.C. add (.1)	.1
w/Air inj add (.2)	.2
w/P.S. add (.1)	.1

Horizon & Omni

(M) Winterize Cooling System
Includes: Run engine to check for leaks, tighten all hose connections. Test radiator and pressure cap, drain radiator and engine block. Add anti-freeze and refill system.

All models	.5
(M) Thermostat, Renew	
1978–80 (.4)	.5
(M) Radiator Assembly, R&R or Renew	
1978–80 (.8)	1.1
w/A.T. add (.1)	.1
(M) Radiator Hoses, Renew	
1978–80—upper (.3)	.4
lower (.5)	.6
(G) Water Pump, Renew	
Includes: Drain and refill coolant.	
1978–80 (1.5)	1.9
w/P.S. add (.2)	.2
w/A.C. add (.7)	.7
w/Air inj add (.4)	.4
(M) Fan Belt, Renew	
1978–80 (.5)	.6

Capri & Mustang (1979–80)

(M) Winterize Cooling System
Includes: Run engine to check for leaks, tighten all hose connections. Test radiator and pressure cap, drain radiator and engine block. Add anti-freeze and refill system.

All models	.5
(M) Thermostat, Renew	
1979–80—Four (.5)	.7
V-6 (.5)	.7
V-8 (.6)	.8
w/A.C. add	.2
(M) Radiator Assembly, R&R or Renew	
Includes: Drain and refill cooling system.	
1979–80 (.5)	1.0
(M) Radiator Hoses, Renew	
1979–80—upper (.4)	.5
lower (.4)	.5
both (.5)	.8
(G) Water Pump, Renew	
Four—1979–80 (1.0)	1.7
V-6—1979–80 (1.1)	1.8
V-8—1979–80 (.9)	1.6

Comet, Cougar, Monarch, Montego, Lincoln Versailles

(M) Winterize Cooling System
Includes: Run engine to check for leaks, tighten all hose connections. Test radiator and pressure cap, drain radiator and engine block. Add anti-freeze and refill system.

All models	.5
(M) Thermostat, Renew	
1974–80—exc below (.4)	.6
302, 351W engs (.5)	.8
w/P.S. add (.1)	.1
w/A.C. add (.1)	.2

(Factory Time)	Chilton Time

(M) Radiator Assembly, R&R or Renew
Includes: Drain and refill cooling system.

1974–80—exc below (.6)	**1.0**
Comet & Monarch (.8)	**1.2**
Versailles (.9)	**1.3**

(M) Radiator Hoses, Renew
1974–80—exc below

upper (.3)	**.4**
lower (.5)	**.6**
both (.6)	**.8**
429, 460 engs	
upper (.4)	**.6**
lower (.6)	**.8**
both (.7)	**.9**

(G) Water Pump, Renew

Six—1974–80—wo/A.C. (.8)	**1.5**
w/A.C. (1.2)	**1.9**
V-8—1974–80	
302, 351W engs—wo/A.C. (1.1) . . .	**1.6**
w/A.C. (1.5)	**2.1**
351, 400 engs—wo/A.C. (1.4)	**1.9**
w/A.C. (1.6)	**2.1**
429, 460 engs—wo/A.C. (1.8)	**2.7**
w/A.C. (2.1)	**3.0**
w/P.S. add	**.2**

(M) Fan Belt, Renew

1974–80 (.3)	**.4**
w/P.S. add	**.1**
w/A.C. add	**.1**

Elite, Granada. Maverick, Torino, LTD II, Thunderbird (1977–79)

(M) Winterize Cooling System
Includes: Run engine to check for leaks, tighten all hose connections. Test radiator and pressure cap, drain radiator and engine block. Add anti-freeze and refill system.

All models	**.5**

(M) Thermostat, Renew

1974–80—exc below (.5)	**.6**
302, 351W engs (.6)	**.8**
w/A.C. add	**.2**

(M) Radiator Assembly, R&R or Renew
Includes: Drain and refill cooling system.

1974–80—exc below (.6)	**1.1**
Maverick & Granada (.5)	**1.0**
V-8 add (.2)	**.2**
w/A.C. add (.1)	**.1**

(M) Radiator Hoses, Renew
1974–80—exc below

upper (.4)	**.4**
lower (.5)	**.5**
both (.6)	**.7**
429, 460 engs	
upper (.4)	**.6**
lower (.6)	**.8**
both (.7)	**.9**

(G) Water Pump, Renew

Six—1974–80—wo/A.C. (.8)	**1.5**
w/A.C. (1.2)	**1.9**
V-8—1974–80	
302, 351W engs—wo/A.C. (1.1) . . .	**1.6**
w/A.C. (1.5)	**2.4**
351, 400 engs—wo/A.C. (1.4)	**1.9**

(Factory Time)	Chilton Time

w/A.C. (1.6)	**2.1**
429, 460 engs—wo/A.C. (1.8)	**2.7**
w/A.C. (2.1)	**3.0**
w/P.S. add	**.2**

(M) Fan Belt, Renew

1974–80 (.3)	**.4**
w/P.S. add	**.1**
w/A.C. add	**.1**

Ford

(M) Winterize Cooling System
Includes: Run engine to check for leaks, tighten all hose connections. Test radiator and pressure cap, drain radiator and engine block. Add anti-freeze and refill system.

All models	**.5**

(M) Thermostat, Renew

1974–80 (.5)	**.8**
w/Thermactor add	**.2**
w/A.C. add	**.2**

(M) Radiator Assembly, R&R or Renew
Includes: Drain and refill cooling system.

1974–78 (.7)	**1.0**
1979–80 (.5)	**1.0**
w/A.C. add	**.2**

(M) Radiator Hoses, Renew
1974–80

upper (.3)	**.6**
lower (.5)	**.8**
both (.6)	**.9**

(G) Water Pump, Renew

1974–80—302, 351 engs (1.1)	**1.9**
429, 460 engs (1.9)	**2.5**
w/A.C. or P.S. add (.1)	**.2**

(M) Fan Belt, Renew

1974–80 (.3)	**.4**
w/Thermactor add	**.2**
w/A.C. add	**.2**

Lincoln Continental, Mark IV, Mark V

(M) Winterize Cooling System
Includes: Run engine to check for leaks, tighten all hose connections. Test radiator and pressure cap, drain radiator and engine block. Add anti-freeze and refill system.

All models	**.5**

(M) Thermostat, Renew

1974–80 (.4)	**.6**

(M) Radiator Assembly, R&R or Renew
Includes: Drain and refill cooling system.

1974–80 (.7)	**1.4**
w/A.C. add	**.4**

(M) Radiator Hoses, Renew
1974–80

upper (.4)	**.5**
lower (.6)	**.8**
both (.7)	**1.0**

(G) Water Pump, Renew
Continental

1974 (1.8)	**3.0**
1975–80—460 eng (1.9)	**3.0**
400 eng (1.5)	**2.8**

(Factory Time)	Chilton Time
Mark IV, V	
1974–80—460 eng (2.3)	3.2
400 eng (1.5)	2.8
(M) Fan Belt, Renew	
1974–80 (.3)	.4
w/Thermactor add	.2
w/A.C. add	.2

Mercury

(M) Winterize Cooling System
Includes: Run engine to check for leaks, tighten all hose connections. Test radiator and pressure cap, drain radiator and engine block. Add anti-freeze and refill system.

All models	.5
(M) Thermostat, Renew	
1974–80 (.5)	.8
w/Thermactor add	.2
w/A.C. add	.2
(M) Radiator Assembly, R&R or Renew	

Includes: Drain and refill cooling system.

1974–78 (.7)	1.0
1979–80 (.5)	1.0
w/A.C. add	.2
(M) Radiator Hoses, Renew	
1974–80	
upper (.3)	.6
lower (.5)	.8
both (.6)	.9
(G) Water Pump, Renew	
1974–80—302, 351 engs (1.1)	1.9
429, 460 engs (1.9)	2.5
w/A.C. or P.S. add (.1)	.2
(M) Fan Belt, Renew	
1974–80 (.3)	.4
w/Thermactor add	.2
w/A.C. add	.2

Mustang II, Bobcat, Pinto, Fairmont, Zephyr

(M) Winterize Cooling System
Includes: Run engine to check for leaks, tighten all hose connections. Test radiator and pressure cap, drain radiator and engine block. Add anti-freeze and refill system.

All models	.5
(M) Thermostat, Renew	
1974–80 (.6)	.8
Mustang II w/302 eng (.9)	1.3
w/A.C. add	.2
(M) Radiator Assembly, R&R or Renew	

Includes: Drain and refill cooling system.

1974–80—exc below (.6)	1.1
Pinto & Bobcat (.8)	1.3
(M) Radiator Hoses, Renew	
1974–80	
upper (.4)	.4
lower (.5)	.6
both (.6)	.7
(G) Water Pump, Renew	
Four—1974 (.8)	1.5
1975–80 (1.0)	1.7

(Factory Time)	Chilton Time
Six—1977–80 (.9)	1.6
V-6—1975–80 (1.0)	1.7
V-8—1975–77 (1.6)	2.1
1978–80 (1.2)	2.0
w/A.C. add (.2)	.3
w/P.S. add	.2
(M) Fan Belt, Renew	
1974–80 (.5)	.8
w/A.C. add	.2

Oldsmobile

(M) Winterize Cooling System
Includes: Run engine to check for leaks, tighten all hose connections. Test radiator and pressure cap, drain radiator and engine block. Add anti-freeze and refill system.

All models	.5
(M) Thermostat, Renew	

Includes: Test thermostat.

1974–76 (.4)	.6
1977–80—V-6 (.6)	* .7
V-8 (.5)	.6
Diesel (.5)	.6
* w/A.C. add (.1)	.1
(M) Radiator Assembly, R&R or Renew	

Includes: Drain and refill cooling system.

1974–76 (.5)	.8
1977–80—V-6 (.5)	.8
V-8 (.6)	.9
Diesel (.7)	1.0
Renew lower insulators add (.1)	.1
(M) Radiator Hoses, Renew	
1974–80—one (.3)	.4
both (.4)	.5
by-pass (.3)	.4
all (.5)	.7
w/A.C. add (.1)	.1
(G) Water Pump, Renew	

Includes: R&R fan blade and pulley. Drain and refill radiator. Adjust belts.

1974–76 (1.0)	1.3
1977–80—V-6 (.7)	.9
V-8—exc below (1.0)	1.3
350 eng, Code G or L (.8)	1.1
Diesel (1.0)	1.3
w/A.C. add (.1)	.1
w/A.I.R. add (.1)	.1
(M) Fan Belt, Renew	
1974–80 (.2)	.3
w/A.C. add (.1)	.1
(G) Temperature Gauge (Engine Unit), Renew	
1974–80 (.3)	.4

Olds Cutlass, Omega (1974–79)

(M) Winterize Cooling System
Includes: Run engine to check for leaks, tighten all hose connections. Test radiator and pressure cap, drain radiator and engine block. Add anti-freeze and refill system.

All models	.5

| | Chilton |
| (Factory Time) | Time |

(M) Thermostat, Renew
Includes: Test thermostat.

Six—1974–76 (.4)	.6
V-6—1977–80 (.6)	.8
V-8—1974–75 (.4)	.6
1976–80 (.5)	.7
1979–80—Diesel (.5)	.6

(M) Radiator Assembly, R&R or Renew
Includes: Drain and refill cooling system.
Cutlass

| 1974–80—gas (.5) | .7 |
| 1979–80—Diesel (.7) | 1.0 |

Omega

1974–79 (.4)	.6
w/A.T. add (.1)	.2
Renew lower insulators add (.1)	.1

(M) Radiator Hoses, Renew

1974–80—one (.3)	.4
both (.4)	.5
by-pass (.3)	.4
all (.5)	.7

(G) Water Pump, Renew
Includes: R&R fan blade and pulley. Drain and refill radiator. Adjust belts.

Six—1974–76 (.8)	1.1
V-6—1977–80 (.7)	1.0
1979–80—Diesel (1.0)	1.3

Cutlass V-8

1974–76 (1.0)	1.3
1977–80—exc below (1.0)	1.3
305–350 engs, Code G, H, L or U (.8)	1.1

Omega V-8

1974–77 (.7)	1.0
1978–79 (.8)	1.1
w/A.C. add (.1)	.1
w/P.S. add (.3)	.3
w/A.I.R. add (.1)	.1

(M) Fan Belt, Renew

| 1974–80 (.3) | .3 |
| w/A.C. add | .1 |

Olds Toronado

(M) Winterize Cooling System
Includes: Run engine to check for leaks, tighten all hose connections. Test radiator and pressure cap, drain radiator and engine block. Add anti-freeze and refill system.

| All models | .5 |

(M) Thermostat, Renew
Includes: Test thermostat.
Gasoline

1974–76 (.4)	.5
1977–80 (.5)	.6
Diesel—1979–80 (.5)	.6

(M) Radiator Assembly, R&R or Renew
Includes: Drain and refill cooling system.
Gasoline

| 1974–80 (.4) | .8 |
| Diesel—1979–80 (.7) | 1.0 |

(M) Radiator Hoses, Renew

1974–80—one (.3)	.4
both (.4)	.5
by-pass (.3)	.4
all (.5)	.7

| | Chilton |
| (Factory Time) | Time |

(M) Fan Belt, Renew

| 1974–80 (.3) | .4 |
| w/A.C. add | .1 |

(G) Water Pump, Renew
Includes: R&R fan blade and pulley. Drain and refill radiator. Adjust belts.
Gasoline

1974–76 (1.0)	1.3
1977 (1.3)	*1.6
1978–80 (1.0)	1.3
Diesel—1979–80 (1.4)	1.8

*Includes R&R crankshaft sensor.

| w/A.C. add (.2) | .2 |

Olds Starfire

(M) Winterize Cooling System
Includes: Run engine to check for leaks, tighten all hose connections. Test radiator and pressure cap, drain radiator and engine block. Add anti-freeze and refill system.

| All models | .5 |

(M) Thermostat, Renew
Includes: Test thermostat.

Four—1976–77 (.6)	.7
1978–80 (.5)	.6
V-6—1975–80 (.6)	.7
V-8—1977–80 (.5)	.6
w/A.C. add (.1)	.1

(M) Radiator Assembly, R&R or Renew
Includes: Drain and refill cooling system.

Four—1976–80 (.6)	.9
w/A.T. add (.2)	.2
V-6—1975–80 (.5)	.8
V-8—1977–80 (.5)	.8
w/A.T. add (.1)	.1
Renew lower insulators add (.1)	.1

(M) Radiator Hoses, Renew

1975–80—one (.3)	.4
both (.4)	.5
by-pass (.3)	.4
all (.5)	.7
w/A.C. add (.1)	.1

(G) Water Pump, Renew
Includes: R&R fan blade and pulley. Drain and refill radiator. Adjust belts.

Four—1976–77 (1.0)	1.3
1978–80 (.7)	1.0
w/A.C. add (.2)	.2
w/P.S. add (.2)	.2
V-6—1975–80 (.6)	.9
V-8—1977–80 (.8)	1.1
w/A.C. add (.9)	.9
w/P.S. add (.3)	.3
w/A.I.R. add (.1)	.1

(M) Fan Belt, Renew

| 1975–80 (.2) | .3 |

Plymouth

(M) Winterize Cooling System
Includes: Run engine to check for leaks, tighten all hose connections. Test radiator and pressure cap, drain radiator and engine block. Add anti-freeze and refill system.

| All models | .5 |

(Factory Time)	Chilton Time
(M) Thermostat, Renew	
1974–78 (.4)	.6
w/A.C. add (.3)	.3
(M) Radiator Assembly, R&R or Renew	
1974–76 (.6)	1.0
1977–78 (.8)	1.2
w/A.C. add (.1)	.2
w/A.T. add (.1)	.2
(M) Radiator Hoses, Renew	
1974–78—upper (.3)	.6
lower (.4)	.8
by-pass—Six (.9)	1.4
V-8 (.3)	.6
(G) Water Pump, Renew	
Includes: Drain and refill coolant.	
Six—1974–78 (.9)	1.3
w/A.C. add (.4)	.4
V-8—1974–78 (1.0)	1.3
w/P.S. add (.2)	.2
w/A.C. add (.4)	.4
(M) Fan Belt, Renew	
1974–78 (.2)	.4
w/A.C. add (.1)	.1
w/Air inj add (.2)	.2
w/P.S. add (.1)	.1

Pontiac & Grand Prix

(M) Winterize Cooling System
Includes: Run engine to check for leaks, tighten all hose connections. Test radiator and pressure cap, drain radiator and engine block. Add anti-freeze and refill system.

	Chilton Time
All models	.5
(G) Thermostat, Renew	
1974 (.4)	.6
1975–76 (.5)	.7
1977–80 (.3)	.5
(M) Radiator, R&R or Renew	
Includes: Drain and refill cooling system.	
1974–80—w/M.T. (.6)	.9
w/A.T. (.7)	1.1
(M) Radiator Hoses, Renew	
1974–80—upper (.3)	.4
lower (.3)	.5
both (.4)	.7
by-pass (.3)	.4
(M) Fan Belt, Renew	
1974–80 (.2)	.3
w/A.C. add (.2)	.2
w/P.S. add (.1)	.1
(G) Water Pump, Renew	
V-6—1977–80 (.6)	.9
V-8—1974–80 (.8)	1.1
w/A.C. add (.2)	.2
w/P.S. add (.1)	.1

Pontiac Astre & Sunbird

(M) Winterize Cooling System
Includes: Run engine to check for leaks, tighten all hose connections. Test radiator and pressure cap, drain radiator and

(Factory Time)	Chilton Time
engine block. Add anti-freeze and refill system.	
All models	.5
(G) Thermostat, Renew	
1975–80 (.4)	.6
w/140 eng add (.3)	.3
(M) Radiator, R&R or Renew	
Includes: Drain and refill cooling system.	
1975–80 (.6)	.9
w/A.T. add (.2)	.2
(M) Radiator Hoses, Renew	
1975–80—upper (.3)	.4
lower (.3)	.5
both (.4)	.7
by-pass (.3)	.4
(M) Fan Belt, Renew	
1975–80 (.2)	.3
w/P.S. add (.1)	.1
(G) Water Pump, Renew	
Four—1975–80 (.7)	1.0
V-6—1975–77 (.8)	1.1
1978–80 (.6)	.9
V-8—1979–80 (.8)	1.1
w/A.C. add (.2)	.2
w/P.S. add (.2)	.2

Firebird, Phoenix (1978–79), LeMans, Ventura (1974–77)

(M) Winterize Cooling System
Includes: Run engine to check for leaks, tighten all hose connections. Test radiator and pressure cap, drain radiator and engine block. Add anti-freeze and refill system.

	Chilton Time
All models	.5
(G) Thermostat, Renew	
1974 (.4)	.6
1975–76 (.5)	.7
1977–80 (.3)	.5
(M) Radiator, R&R or Renew	
Includes: Drain and refill cooling system.	
1974–80—Four—w/M.T. (.4)	.7
w/A.T. (.5)	.8
Six & V-6—w/M.T. (.6)	1.0
w/A.T. (.7)	1.1
V-8—w/M.T. (.6)	1.0
w/A.T. (.7)	1.1
(M) Radiator Hoses, Renew	
1974–80—upper (.3)	.4
lower (.3)	.5
both (.4)	.7
by-pass (.3)	.4
(M) Fan Belt, Renew	
1974–80 (.2)	.3
w/A.C. add (.2)	.2
w/P.S. add (.1)	.1
(G) Water Pump, Renew	
Four—1977–80 (.6)	.9
Six—1974–76 (.8)	1.1
V-6—1977–80 (.6)	.9
V-8—1974–80 (.8)	1.1
w/A.C. add (.2)	.2
w/P.S. add (.2)	.2
w/A.I.R. add (.2)	.2

(Factory Time)	Chilton Time

Thunderbird (1974–76)

(M) Winterize Cooling System
Includes: Run engine to check for leaks, tighten all hose connections. Test radiator and pressure cap, drain radiator and engine block. Add anti-freeze and refill system.

All models	.5

(M) Thermostat, Renew

1974–76 (.4)	.6

(M) Radiator Assembly, R&R or Renew
Includes: Drain and refill cooling system.

1974–76 (.7)	1.0
w/A.C. add	.2

(M) Radiator Hoses, Renew

1974–76 (1.8)	2.1
w/A.C. (2.1)	2.5

(G) Water Pump, Renew

1974–76—wo/A.C. (1.8)	2.7
w/A.C. (2.2)	3.0
w/Thermactor add (.2)	.2

(M) Fan Belt, Renew

1974–76 (.3)	.3

Valiant, Dart, Barracuda Challenger, Aspen, Volare, LeBaron, Diplomat

(M) Winterize Cooling System
Includes: Run engine to check for leaks, tighten all hose connections. Test radiator and pressure cap, drain radiator and engine block. Add anti-freeze and refill system.

All models	.5

(M) Thermostat, Renew

1974–80 (.4)	.6
w/A.C. add (.3)	.3

(M) Radiator Assembly, R&R or Renew

1974–76 (.6)	1.0
1977–80 (.8)	1.2
w/A.C. add (.1)	.2
w/A.T. add (.1)	.2

(M) Radiator Hoses, Renew

1974–80—upper (.3)	.6
lower (.4)	.8
by-pass—Six (.9)	1.4
V-8 (.3)	.6

(Factory Time)	Chilton Time

(G) Water Pump, Renew
Includes: Drain and refill coolant.

Six—1974–80 (.9)	1.3
w/A.C. add (.4)	.4
V-8—1974–80 (1.0)	1.3
w/P.S. add (.2)	.2
w/A.C. add (.4)	.4

(M) Fan Belt, Renew

1974–80 (.2)	.4
w/A.C. add (.1)	.1
w/Air inj add (.2)	.2
w/P.S. add (.1)	.1

Vega & Monza

(M) Winterize Cooling System
Includes: Run engine to check for leaks, tighten all hose connections. Test radiator and pressure cap, drain radiator and engine block. Add anti-freeze and refill system.

All models	.5

(M) Thermostat, Renew

Four—1974–77 (.6)	.9
1978 (.4)	.9
1979–80 (.7)	1.0
V-6—1978–80 (.6)	.8
V-8—1975–80 (.3)	.6

(M) Radiator Assembly, R&R or Renew
Includes: Drain and refill cooling system.

1974–76—Vega (.5)	.8
Monza (.6)	.9
1977–80 (.5)	.8
w/A.T. add (.2)	.2

(M) Radiator Hoses, Renew

1974–80—upper (.3)	.4
lower (.4)	.5
both (.5)	.7

(G) Water Pump, Renew

Four—1974–77 (1.0)	1.3
1978–80 (.7)	1.0
V-6—1978–80 (.8)	1.3
V-8—1975–80 (.7)	1.2
w/P.S. add (.2)	.2
w/A.C. add (.9)	.9
w/A.I.R. add (.4)	.4

(M) Fan Belt, Renew

1974–80 (.2)	.3
each adtnl (.2)	.2

EXHAUST SYSTEM

(Factory Time)	Chilton Time

American Motors

(G) Muffler, Renew

1974–80—one (.5)	.9

(G) Tail Pipe, Renew

1974–80—one (.3)	.6

(G) Exhaust Pipe, Renew
1974–80

front (.4)	.8

(Factory Time)	Chilton Time

rear (.4)	.8
intermediate (.5)	.9

(G) Exhaust Manifold or Gaskets, Renew

Four—1977–80 (1.2)	1.9

V-8—1974–76
Hornet-Gremlin

right side (1.4)	1.8
left side (1.1)	1.5

	Chilton Time
(Factory Time)	

Javelin
right side (1.0) **1.4**
left side (1.1) **1.5**
Matador-Ambassador
right side (1.0) **1.4**
left side (1.0) **1.4**
1977–80—all models
right side (.7) **1.2**
left side (.6) **1.1**
(G) Intake and Exhaust Manifold or Gaskets, Renew
Six—1974–76 (1.6) **2.2**
1977–80 (2.4) **3.0**
w/Air guard and/or P.S. add (.3) .. **.3**

AMC/Jeep

(G) Muffler, Renew
1974–80 (.5) .... **.8**
(G) Tail Pipe, Renew
1974–80 (.6) .... **.9**
(G) Exhaust Pipe, Renew
1974–80—Six (.7) **1.1**
V-8—exc below
left side (.5) .... **.9**
right side (.6) **1.0**
CJ series
left side (.7) **1.1**
right side (.6) **1.0**
(G) Exhaust Manifold or Gaskets, Renew
1974–80—Six (1.2) **2.0**
V-8—left side (.4) .... **.9**
right side (.6) **1.3**

Buick LeSabre, Electra, Riviera (1974–78)

(G) Muffler, Renew
1974—one—exc below (.6) ...... **.9**
Riviera (.7) **1.0**
1975–77 (.6) .... **.9**
1978–80 (.5) .... **.9**
(G) Tail Pipe, Renew
1975–80 (.4) .... **.6**
(G) Exhaust Crossover Pipe, Renew
1974–76 (.5) .... **.8**
1977–80 (.4) .... **.7**
(G) Exhaust Intermediate Pipe, Renew
Includes: Cut at muffler.
1974–80 (.4) .... **.7**
(G) Exhaust Rear Pipe and Resonator Assembly, Renew
1974–80 (.4) .... **.7**
(G) Front Exhaust Pipe, Renew
1976–80 (.4) .... **.7**
(G) Exhaust Manifold, Renew
V-6—1976–80—each (.7) **1.1**
w/Turbocharger add (.6) .... **.6**
V-8—1974–76—each (1.1) **1.5**
1977–80
350 eng Code J-each (.8) **1.2**
350–403 engs, code R or K-each (.8) **1.2**
350 eng, Code X-each (.8) **1.2**
301 eng, Code Y-each (.7) **1.1**

	Chilton Time
(Factory Time)	

305–350 engs, Code U or L
right side (1.2) **1.6**
left side (.8) **1.2**
w/A.C. add (.4) .... **.4**
w/P.S. add (.2) .... **.2**

Buick Riviera (1979–80)

(G) Muffler, Renew
1979–80 (.5) .... **.9**
(G) Exhaust Crossover Pipe, Renew
1979–80 (1.8) **2.4**
(G) Front Exhaust Pipe, Renew
1979–80 (.5) .... **.9**
(G) Exhaust Intermediate Pipe, Renew
Includes: Cut at muffler.
1979–80 (.4) .... **.7**
(G) Rear Exhaust Pipe and Resonator Assy., Renew
1979–80 (.4) .... **.8**
(G) Resonator Assembly, Renew
1979–80 (.4) .... **.7**
(G) Exhaust Manifold, Renew
V-6—1979–80
right side (1.3) **1.7**
left side (.6) **1.0**
w/A.C. add (.3) .... **.3**
V-8—1979–80
350 eng Code R
right side (.9) **1.3**
left side (.6) **1.0**
w/A.C. add (.4) .... **.4**

Buick Apollo, Century, Gran Sport, Regal, Skylark (1974–79)

(G) Muffler, Renew
1974—Century (.6) .... **.9**
Apollo (.8) **1.1**
1975–80 (.5) .... **.9**
(G) Tail Pipe, Renew
1974–80 (.5) .... **.7**
(G) Exhaust Crossover Pipe, Renew
1974–76 (.5) .... **.9**
1977–80 (.4) .... **.8**
(G) Exhaust Intermediate Pipe, Renew
Includes: Cut at muffler.
1974–80 (.4) .... **.7**
(G) Front Exhaust Pipe, Renew
1976–80 (.4) .... **.7**
(G) Exhaust Manifold, Renew
Six—1974–75 (1.0) **1.4**
V-6—1975–80—each (.7) **1.1**
w/Turbocharger add (.6) .... **.6**
V-8—1974–76—each (.6) **1.0**
1977–80
350 eng, Code J—each (.8) **1.2**
350–403 engs, Code R or K each (.8) **1.2**
305–350 engs, Code U, H or L
right side (1.2) **1.6**
left side (.8) **1.2**
w/A.C. add (.4) .... **.4**
w/P.S. add (.2) .... **.2**

	(Factory Time)	Chilton Time

Buick Skyhawk

(G) Muffler, Renew		
1975–77 (.6)		.9
1978–80 (.5)		.9
(G) Tail Pipe, Renew		
1975–80 (.5)		.7
(G) Exhaust Crossover Pipe, Renew		
1975–76 (.5)		.8
1977–80 (.4)		.7
(G) Exhaust Intermediate Pipe, Renew		
Includes: Cut at muffler.		
1975–80 (.4)		.7
(G) Front Exhaust Pipe, Renew		
1976–80 (.4)		.7
(G) Exhaust Manifold, Renew		
1975–80—right side (.7)		1.1
left side (.9)		1.5
w/A.C. add (.3)		.4
w/P.S. add (.2)		.2

Cadillac

(G) Muffler, Renew		
1974–80 (.5)		.9
(G) Resonator, Renew		
1974–80 (.4)		.8
(G) Exhaust 'Y' Pipe, Renew		
1974–80 (.4)		.8
(G) Exhaust Manifold, Renew		
1974–80—right side (.8)		1.4
1974–80—left side (.7)		1.3

Cadillac Seville

(G) Muffler, Renew		
1976–80 (.5)		.9
(G) Resonator, Renew		
1976–80 (.5)		.9
(G) Exhaust Crossover Pipe, Renew		
1976–80 (.4)		.8
(G) Exhaust Pipe, Renew		
1976–80 (.4)		.8
(G) Intermediate Pipe, Renew		
1976–80 (.5)		.9
(G) Exhaust Manifold, Renew		
1976–80—right side (.8)		1.4
left side (.6)		1.2

Cadillac Eldorado

(G) Muffler, Renew		
1974–80 (.5)		.9
(G) Resonator, Renew		
1974–80 (.6)		.8
(G) Exhaust 'Y' Pipe, Renew		
1974–80—one side (.4)		.6
both sides (.7)		1.0
(G) Intermediate Pipe, Renew		
1974–80 (.5)		.7
(G) Exhaust Manifold, Renew		
1974—right side (.8)		1.4
1975–80—right side (.5)		1.1
1974–80—left side (.7)		1.3

	(Factory Time)	Chilton Time

Camaro, Chevelle, Malibu, Monte Carlo, Nova

(G) Muffler, Renew		
1974–80—exc below (.6)		.9
1974—Camaro, Nova (.8)		1.0
(G) Tail Pipe, Renew		
1974–80 (.4)		.6
(G) Resonator Assy., Renew		
1974–80 (.5)		.8
(G) Exhaust Pipe (Rear), Renew		
1974–80 (.5)		.8
(G) Exhaust Pipe (Front), Renew		
1974–80—Six (.5)		.8
V-6 (.6)		.9
V-8 (.6)		.9
(G) Exhaust Manifold, Renew		
Six—1974 (1.0)		1.4
1975–80 (1.2)		1.5
V-6—1978–80		
200 eng—right (.6)		1.0
left (.5)		.9
231 eng—right (.7)		1.1
left (.6)		1.0
V-8—1974—right (.8)		1.3
left (.8)		1.3
Monte Carlo, Malibu		
1975–77—right (1.0)		1.5
left (.8)		1.3
1978–80—right (1.3)		1.8
left (.8)		1.3
Chevelle		
1975–77—right (1.2)		1.7
left (.8)		1.3
Camaro, Nova		
1975–80—right (1.4)		1.9
left (.8)		1.3
w/A.C. add (.5)		.5
w/P.S. add (.2)		.2
w/A.I.R. add (.2)		.2

Chevrolet & Corvette

(G) Muffler, Renew		
1974 (.6)		1.0
1975–80—Chev. (.6)		1.0
Corv. (.4)		.8
(G) Tail Pipe, Renew		
1974–80 (.4)		.8
(G) Resonator Assy., Renew		
1974–77 (.5)		.8
(G) Exhaust Pipe (Rear), Renew		
1974–80—Chev. (.5)		.9
Corv. (.8)		1.2
(G) Exhaust Pipe (Front), Renew		
Six—1977–80 (.5)		.8
V-8—1974–80 (.6)		.9
(G) Exhaust Manifold, Renew (One)		
Six—1977–80 (1.2)		1.6
w/P.S. or Air inj add (.6)		.6
V-8—1974 (.7)		1.2
1975–76 (1.0)		1.5
1977–80—right (1.3)		1.8
left (.8)		1.3
w/A.C. add (.6)		.6
w/Air inj add (.2)		.2

(Factory Time)	**Chilton Time**

Chevette

(G) Muffler, Renew
1976–80 (.7) 9
(G) Tail Pipe, Renew
1976–80 (.6) 9
(G) Exhaust Pipe (Rear), Renew
1976–80 (.5) 8
(G) Exhaust Pipe (Front), Renew
1976–80 (.5) 8
(G) Exhaust Manifold, Renew
1976–80 (.6) 1.1

Citation, Omega, Phoenix, Skylark—All 1980

(G) Muffler, Renew (Right or Transverse)
1980 (.6) 9
(G) Tail Pipe, Renew
1980—right (.5) 7
(G) Front Exhaust Pipe, Renew
1980—right (.5) 8
crossover (.6) 9
(G) Front Crossover Extension Pipe, Renew
1980 (.4) 7
(G) Rear Exhaust Pipe, Renew
1980—right (.5) 7
(G) Exhaust Manifold or Gasket, Renew
1980—Four (.8) 1.2
w/A.C. add (.5) 5
V-6—each (.8) 1.2
w/Cruise control add (.2) 2

COMBINATIONS

(G) Muffler, Exhaust and Tail Pipe, Renew
All models 1.6
(G) Muffler and Tail Pipe, Renew
All models 1.1

Chrysler, Cordoba, Imperial

(G) Muffler, Renew
1974–76—each (.7) 9
1977–80—each (.6) 9
(G) Tail Pipe, Renew
1974–80—one (.4) 6
(G) Exhaust Pipe, Renew
1974–76—single (.8) 1.0
dual, one (.5) 8
1977–80—single (.6) 1.0
dual, one (.5) 8
Cut at muffler add (.2) 2
(G) Exhaust Manifold or Gaskets, Renew
Six—1979–80 (1.7) 2.5
V-8—1974–80
318–360 engs
right side (.7) 1.0
left side (.6) 9
400–440 engs
right side (.8) 1.1
left side (.9) 1.2

---

w/Air inj add (.4) 4
w/A.C. add (.4) 4

Dodge

(G) Muffler, Renew
1974–76—each (.7) 9
1977–80—each (.6) 9
(G) Tail Pipe, Renew
1974–80—one (.4) 6
(G) Exhaust Pipe, Renew
Six—1974–76 (.7) 9
1977–80 (.5) 7
V-8—1974–76—single (.8) 1.0
dual one (.5) 8
1977–80—single (.6) 1.0
dual one (.5) 8
Cut at muffler add (.2) 2
(G) Exhaust Manifold or Gaskets, Renew
Six—1974–76 (2.0) 3.0
1977–80 (1.7) 3.0
V-8—1974–76
318 eng
right (.6) 9
left (.7) 1.0
360 eng
right (1.0) 1.4
left (.7) 1.0
400, 440 engs
right (.8) 1.1
left (1.0) 1.4
1977–80
318, 360 engs
right (.7) 1.0
left (.6) 9
400, 440 engs
right (.8) 1.1
left (1.3) 1.6
w/Air inj add (.4) 4
w/A.C. add (.4) 4

Horizon & Omni

(G) Muffler, Renew
1978–80 (.6) 8
Cut exhaust pipe add (.2) 2
(G) Tail Pipe, Renew
1978–80 (.4) 5
Cut at muffler add (.2) 2
(G) Exhaust Pipe, Renew
1978–80 (.6) 8
Cut at muffler add (.2) 2
(G) Exhaust Manifold, Renew
1978–80 (2.6) 3.8
w/P.S. add (.2) 2

Capri & Mustang (1979–80)

(G) Muffler, Renew
1979–80—Four (.4) 8
V-6 (.7) 1.2
V-8 (.7) 1.2
Welded type add 3

	(Factory Time)	Chilton Time

(G) Exhaust Pipe, Renew
Includes: Replace exhaust control valve if required.

1979–80 (.6)	.9

(G) Exhaust Manifold, Renew

1979–80—Four (.8)	1.5
V-6—right (.8)	1.4
left (.9)	1.5
V-8—right (.7)	1.3
left (.6)	1.1

Comet, Cougar, Monarch, Montego, Lincoln Versailles

(G) Muffler, Renew

1974–80—one (.6)	.9
both (.9)	1.4
Welded type add	.3

(G) Tail Pipe, Renew

1974–80—one (.2)	.5
both (.3)	.8
Welded type add	.3

(G) Resonator, Renew

1974–76—one (.6)	.8
1977–80—one (.4)	.8

(G) Exhaust Pipe, Renew
Includes: Replace exhaust control valve if required.

1974–80—exc below (.6)	.9
Versailles (.8)	1.1

(G) Exhaust Manifold, Renew

Six—1974–80 (1.2)	1.8
w/A.C. add (.5)	.6
V-8—1974–80	
302 eng—right (.9)	1.5
left (.9)	1.4
351C/M, 400 engs—right (1.2)	2.0
left (.9)	1.5
351W eng—right (1.4)	2.0
left (1.8)	2.4
429, 460 engs—right (.8)	1.4
left (.9)	1.5

Elite, Granada, Maverick, Torino, LTD II, Thunderbird (1977–79)

(G) Muffler, Renew

1974–80—one (.6)	.9
both (.9)	1.4
Welded type add	.3

(G) Tail Pipe, Renew

1974–80—one (.2)	.5
both (.3)	.8
Welded type add	.3

(G) Resonator, Renew

1974–80—one (.5)	.7
both (.7)	1.2

(G) Exhaust Pipe, Renew
Includes: Replace exhaust control valve if required.

1974–77 (.6)	.9
1977–80 (.4)	.9

(G) Exhaust Manifold, Renew

Six—1974–80 (1.2)	1.8
w/A.C. add (.5)	.6

	(Factory Time)	Chilton Time

V-8—1974–80

302 eng—right (.9)	1.5
left (.9)	1.4
351C/M, 400 engs—right (1.2)	2.0
left (.9)	1.5
351W eng—right (1.4)	2.0
left (.9)	1.5
429, 460 engs—right (.8)	1.4
left (.9)	1.5

Ford

(G) Muffler, Renew

1974–78—one (.6)	.9
both (.9)	1.4
1979–80—one (.8)	1.4
Welded type add	.3

(G) Tail Pipe, Renew

1974–80—one (.2)	.5
both (.3)	.8
Welded type add	.3

(G) Exhaust Pipe, Renew
Includes: Replace exhaust control valve if required.

1974–76—one (.6)	.9
both (.7)	1.1
1977–78—each (.4)	.7
1979–80 (.6)	.9

(G) Exhaust Manifold, Renew
1974–80

302 eng—right (.7)	1.1
left (.9)	1.3
both (1.3)	2.0
351W eng—right (.7)	1.1
left (.6)	1.0
both (1.0)	1.9
351C/M–400 engs—right (1.1)	1.5
left (.6)	1.0
both (1.4)	2.3
429–460 engs—one (.7)	1.0
both (1.1)	1.7

Lincoln Continental, Mark IV, Mark V

(G) Muffler, Renew

1974–80—one (.6)	.9
both (.9)	1.4
Welded type add	.3

(G) Resonator, Renew
Continental

1974–80—one (.4)	.7
both (.5)	1.0
Mark IV, V	
1974–80—one (.5)	.8
both (.7)	1.1

(G) Exhaust Pipe, Renew
Includes: Replace exhaust control valve if required.

1974–76—one (.6)	1.0
both (.7)	1.2
1977–80—one (.4)	.7

(G) Exhaust Manifold, Renew
1974–80
Continental

right (1.1)	1.6

	Chilton
(Factory Time)	Time
left (.8)	1.3
both (1.6)	2.7
Mark IV, V	
right (.8)	1.3
left (.9)	1.5
both (1.4)	2.5

Mercury

(G) Muffler, Renew

1974–78—one (.6)	.9
both (.9)	1.4
1979–80—one (.8)	1.4
Welded type add	.3

(G) Tail Pipe, Renew

1974–80—one (.2)	.5
both (.3)	.8
Welded type add	.3

(G) Exhaust Pipe, Renew

Includes: Replace exhaust control valve if required.

1974–76—one (.6)	.9
both (.7)	1.1
1977–78—each (.4)	.7
1979–80 (.6)	.9

(G) Exhaust Manifold, Renew

1974–80

302 eng—right (.7)	1.1
left (.9)	1.3
both (1.3)	2.0
351W eng—right (.7)	1.1
left (.6)	1.0
both (1.0)	1.9
351 C/M—400 engs—right (1.1) ...	1.5
left (.6)	1.0
both (1.4)	2.3
429–460 engs—one (.7)	1.0
both (1.1)	1.7

Mustang II, Bobcat, Pinto, Fairmont, Zephyr

(G) Muffler, Renew

1974–80—single inlet (.5)	.8
dual inlet (.6)	1.0
Welded type add	.3

(G) Tail Pipe, Renew

1974–80 (.2)	.5
Welded type add	.3

(G) Exhaust Pipe, Renew

Includes: Replace exhaust control valve if required.

1974–80—single (.6)	.9
dual (.9)	1.2

(G) Resonator, Renew

1974–80—one (.4)	.8

(G) Exhaust Manifold, Renew

1974–80

Four (1.1)	1.7
Six (1.2)	1.9
V-6—right (1.4)	2.0
left (1.2)	1.8
V-8—Mustang II right (1.3)	2.0
left (1.0)	1.7
Fairmont & Zephyr	
right (.7)	1.3

	Chilton
(Factory Time)	Time
left (.6)	1.1
w/A.C. add	.3

Oldsmobile

(G) Muffler, Renew

1974–75 (.6)	.7
1976–77 (.5)	.7
1978–80 (.4)	.7

(G) Tail Pipe, Renew

1974–80 (.4)	.5

(G) Resonator, Renew

1974–80 (.5)	.7

(G) Exhaust Pipe, Renew

1974–80 (.5)	.7

(G) Intermediate Exhaust Pipe, Renew

1974–80 (.4)	.6

(G) Exhaust Crossover Pipe, Renew

1974–80 (.4)	.7

(G) Exhaust Manifold, Renew

1974–76 (.8)	1.2
1977–80—V-6—each (.6)	1.0
V-8—each—exc below (.8)	1.2
350 eng, Code G or L	
right side (1.3)	1.7
Diesel—right side (.9)	1.3
left side (.7)	1.1
w/A.C. add (.5)	.5
w/A.I.R. add (.2)	.2

Olds Cutlass, Omega (1974–79)

(G) Muffler, Renew

1974–77 (.5)	.7
1978–80 (.4)	.7

(G) Tail Pipe, Renew

1974–80—Cutlass (.4)	.5
Omega (.3)	.5

(G) Exhaust Pipe, Renew

1974–75 (.4)	.5
1976–80 (.5)	.6

(G) Intermediate Exhaust Pipe, Renew

1974–80 (.4)	.7

(G) Exhaust Crossover Pipe, Renew

1974–80 (.4)	.6

(G) Exhaust Manifold, Renew

Six—1974–76 (.8)	1.1
V-6—1977–80—right side (.7)	1.0
left side (.6)	.9
V-8—1974–76—right side (.6)	.9
left side (.7)	1.0
1977–80—exc below	
right side (.8)	1.1
left side (.8)	1.1
305–350 engs, Code G, H, L or U	
right side (1.4)	1.7
left side (.8)	1.1
1979–80—Diesel—right side (.9) ..	1.3
left side (.7)	1.1
w/A.C. add (.5)	.5
w/A.I.R. add (.2)	.2

Olds Toronado

(G) Muffler, Renew

1974–80—one (.4)	.7
both (.6)	1.1

(Factory Time)	Chilton Time
(G) Resonator, Renew	
1974–78—one (.4)	.7
both (.6)	1.1
(G) Tail Pipe and Resonator Assy., Renew	
1979–80 (.3)	.6
(G) Front Exhaust Pipe, Renew	
1974–80—one (.4)	.6
both (.6)	.9
(G) Intermediate Exhaust Pipe, Renew	
1974–80 (.4)	.7
(G) Exhaust Manifold, Renew	
1974–76—right side (.6)	1.0
left side (.5)	.9
w/A.C. add (.1)	.1
1977–78—right side (.9)	1.3
left side (.6)	1.0
1979–80—each (.6)	1.0

Olds Starfire

(G) Muffler, Renew	
1975–80 (.4)	.7
(G) Tailpipe, Renew	
1975–80 (.3)	.4
(G) Exhaust Pipe, Renew	
1975–80 (.5)	.7
(G) Intermediate Exhaust Pipe, Renew	
1975–80 (.4)	.7
(G) Exhaust Manifold, Renew	
Four—1976–77 (1.7)	2.1

Plymouth

(G) Muffler, Renew	
1974–76—each (.7)	.9
1977–78—each (.6)	.9
(G) Tail Pipe, Renew	
1974–78—one (.4)	.6
(G) Exhaust Pipe, Renew	
Six—1974–76 (.7)	.9
1977–78 (.5)	.7
V-8—1974–76—single (.8)	1.0
dual one (.5)	.8
1977–78—single (.6)	1.0
dual one (.5)	.8
Cut at muffler add (.2)	.2
(G) Exhaust Manifold or Gaskets, Renew	
Six—1974–76 (2.0)	3.0
1977–78 (1.7)	3.0
V-8—1974	
318 eng—right (.7)	1.0
left (.6)	1.0
360 eng—right (.8)	1.3
left (.9)	1.4
1975–76	
318 eng—right (.6)	.9
left (.7)	1.0
360 eng—right (1.0)	1.4
left (1.3)	1.6
400, 440 engs—right (.8)	1.1
left (1.0)	1.4
1977–78	
318 eng—right (.7)	1.0
left (.6)	.9
360 eng—right (.7)	1.0
left (1.3)	1.6

(Factory Time)	Chilton Time
400, 440 engs—right (.8)	1.1
left (1.3)	1.7
w/Air inj add (.4)	.4
w/A.C. add (.4)	.4
(G) Intake and Exhaust Manifold Gaskets, Renew	
Six—1974–78 (1.7)	2.3
w/A.C. add (.4)	.4

Pontiac & Grand Prix

(G) Muffler, Renew	
1974–80—each (.5)	.7
If welded add	.2
(G) Tail Pipe, Renew	
1974–80—each (.5)	.7
If welded add	.2
(G) Resonator, Renew	
1974–80—each (.3)	.6
(G) Front Exhaust Pipe, Renew	
1974–76 (.7)	1.0
1977–80 (.4)	.7
(G) Exhaust Crossover Pipe, Renew	
1974–76 (.8)	1.1
1977–80 (.5)	.8
(G) Rear Exhaust Pipe, Renew	
1977–80 (.4)	.7
(G) Exhaust Manifold or Gasket, Renew	
Pontiac	
V-6—1977–80—right side (.7)	1.1
left side (.6)	1.0
V-8—1974–76—each (.6)	1.0

Pontiac Astre & Sunbird

(G) Muffler, Renew	
1975–80 (.5)	.7
(G) Tail Pipe, Renew	
1975–80 (.3)	.5
(G) Resonator, Renew	
1975–80 (.3)	.6
(G) Front Exhaust Pipe, Renew	
1975–76 (.6)	.9
1977–80 (.5)	.8
(G) Exhaust Crossover Pipe, Renew	
1976–80 (.5)	.8
(G) Rear Exhaust Pipe, Renew	
1975–80 (.4)	.7
(G) Exhaust Manifold or Gasket, Renew	
1975–80	
Four—140 eng (1.7)	2.1
151 eng code 1 (1.6)	2.0
151 eng code V (.7)	1.3
V-6—right side (.7)	1.1
left side (.9)	1.3
V-8—right side (1.4)	1.8
left side (1.3)	1.7
w/A.C. add (.3)	.3
w/P.S. add (.3)	.3

Firebird, Phoenix (1978–79), LeMans, Ventura (1974–77)

(G) Muffler, Renew	
1974–80—each (.5)	.7
If welded add	.2
(G) Tail Pipe, Renew	
1974—each (.6)	.8

(Factory Time)	Chilton Time		(Factory Time)	Chilton Time
1975–80—each (.5)	.7		**(G) Exhaust Manifold or Gaskets, Renew**	
If welded add	.2		Six—1974–76 (2.0)	3.0
(G) Front Exhaust Pipe, Renew			1977–80 (1.7)	3.0
1974–76 (.7)	1.0		**V-8**—1974	
1977–80 (.4)	.7		318 eng—right (.7)	1.0
(G) Exhaust Crossover Pipe, Renew			left (.6)	1.0
1974–76 (.6)	.9		360 eng—right (.8)	1.3
1977–80 (.5)	.8		left (.9)	1.4
(G) Rear Exhaust Pipe, Renew			1975–76	
1975–80 (.4)	.7		318 eng—right (.6)	.9
(G) Exhaust Manifold or Gasket, Renew			left (.7)	1.0
Four—1977–80—eng Code 1 (1.6)	2.0		360 eng—right (1.0)	1.4
eng Code V (.7)	1.3		left (1.3)	1.6
Six—1974–76 (1.2)	1.6		1977–80	
V—1977–80—right side (.7)	1.1		318 eng—right (.7)	1.0
loft oido			left (.6)	.9
V-8—1974–76—each (.8)	1.2		360 eng—right (.7)	1.0
1977–80			left (1.3)	1.6
305–350 engs, Code G-H-U-L			w/Air inj add (.4)	.4
right side (1.4)	1.8		w/A.C. add (.4)	.4
left side (.8)	1.2			
350–403 engs, Code R-K				
each (.8)	1.2			
301–350–400 engs, Code W-Y-P-Z			**Vega & Monza**	
Firebird—Phoenix—Ventura			**(G) Muffler, Renew**	
right side (.6)	1.0		1974–80 (.5)	.7
left side (.7)	1.1		V-8 add (.1)	.1
LeMans			**(G) Tail Pipe, Renew**	
right side (1.0)	1.4		1974–80—Vega (.3)	.5
left side (1.3)	1.7		Monza (.4)	.6
w/A.C. add (.5)	.5		**(G) Resonator Assy., Renew**	
w/P.S. add (.3)	.3		1975–76 (.5)	.7
			(G) Exhaust Pipe (Rear), Renew	
Valiant, Dart, Barracuda, Challenger, Aspen, Volare, LeBaron, Diplomat			1974–80 (.5)	.7
			(G) Exhaust Pipe (Front), Renew	
			Four—1974–77 (.6)	.9
			1978–80 (.5)	.8
(G) Muffler, Renew			**V-6**—1978–80 (1.0)	1.4
1974–76—each (.7)	.9		**V-8**—1975–80 (1.0)	1.4
1977–80—each (.6)	.9		**(G) Exhaust Manifold, Renew**	
(G) Tail Pipe, Renew			**Four**—1974–77 (1.7)	2.2
1974–80—one (.4)	.6		1978–80—eng Code I (.6)	2.2
(G) Exhaust Pipe, Renew			eng Code V (.7)	1.5
Six—1974–76 (.7)	.9		**V-6**—1978–80—right (.7)	1.1
1977–80 (.5)	.7		left (.9)	1.3
V-8—1974–76—single (.8)	1.0		**V-8**—1975–80—right (1.4)	1.9
dual one (.5)	.8		left (1.3)	1.8
1977–80—single (.6)	1.0		w/A.C. add (.4)	.4
dual one (.5)	.8		w/P.S. add (.2)	.2
Cut at muffler add (.2)	.2		w/A.I.R. add (.3)	.3

FRONT SUSPENSION

Note: On all front suspension operations alignment charges must be added if performed. Time given does not include alignment.

(Factory Time)	Chilton Time
American Motors	
(G) Check Alignment of Front End	
All models (.5)	.5
Note: Deduct if alignment is performed.	

(Factory Time)	Chilton Time
(G) Caster, Camber and Toe-In, Adjust	
Includes: Adjust front wheel bearings.	
All models (1.2)	1.4
w/A.C. interference add	.5
(G) Toe-In, Adjust	
All models (.4)	.6
(G) Front Wheel Bearings, Clean and Repack (Both Wheels)	
w/Drum brakes (.5)	.7
w/Disc brakes (.9)	1.2

(Factory Time)	Chilton Time
(G) Upper Ball Joint, Renew	
Add alignment charges.	
Except Pacer	
1974–80—one (.8)	1.2
both (1.3)	2.1
Pacer	
1975–80—one (.6)	1.0
both (.9)	1.7
(G) Upper Control Arm, Renew (One)	
Add alignment charges.	
Except Pacer	
1974–76 (.7)	1.2
1977–80 (1.2)	1.6
Pacer	
1975–80 (.5)	1.0
(G) Lower Control Arm Bushing, Renew (One)	
Add alignment charges.	
Except Pacer	
1977–80 (.7)	1.1
Pacer	
w/Drum brakes—1975–76 (.9)	1.3
w/Disc brakes—1975–80 (1.1)	1.5
(G) Upper Control Arm Bushing, Renew (One)	
Add alignment charges.	
Except Pacer	
1974–76 (.9)	1.4
1977–80 (1.4)	1.9
Pacer	
1975–80 (.6)	1.1
(G) Strut Rod, Renew	
Add alignment charges.	
1974–80—one (.5)	.7
both (.8)	1.1
(G) Front Coil Spring, Renew (One)	
Except Pacer	
w/Drum brakes—1974–76 (.7)	1.2
w/Disc brakes—1974–80 (.7)	1.2
Pacer	
w/Drum brakes—1975–76 (.9)	1.4
w/Disc brakes—1975–80 (1.1)	1.6
(G) Front Shock Absorbers, Renew	
1974–80—one (.3)	.5
both (.4)	.8
(G) Lower Ball Joint, Renew	
Add alignment charges.	
Except Pacer	
w/Drum brakes	
1974–76—one (.8)	1.2
both (1.3)	2.1
w/Disc brakes	
1974–80—one (1.0)	1.4
both (1.7)	2.5
Pacer—1975–80	
w/Drum brakes	
one (.6)	1.0
both (1.1)	1.9
w/Disc brakes	
one (.8)	1.2
both (1.5)	2.3

AMC/Jeep

(Factory Time)	Chilton Time
(G) Check Alignment of Front End	
All models (.4)	.5
Note: Deduct if alignment is performed.	

(Factory Time)	Chilton Time
(G) Toe In, Adjust	
All models (.3)	.4
(G) Caster & Toe In, Adjust	
Includes: Adjust front wheel bearings.	
All models (1.0)	1.4
(G) Front Wheel Bearings, Clean and Repack	
Includes: Clean, inspect, replace. Install new seals and adjust.	
All models—one (.7)	.9
both (1.3)	1.6
(G) Front Shock Absorber or Bushings, Renew	
1974–80—one (.3)	.5
(G) Front Spring, Renew	
1974–80—exc below (.5)	.8
CJ series (.6)	.9

Buick LeSabre, Electra, Riviera (1974–78)

(Factory Time)	Chilton Time
(G) Check Alignment of Front End	
All models	.5
Note: Deduct if alignment is performed.	
(G) Toe-In, Adjust	
All models (.4)	.6
(G) Caster, Camber and Toe-In, Adjust	
Includes: Adjust front wheel bearings.	
All models (.7)	1.4
w/A.C. interference add	.5
(G) Front Wheel Bearings, Clean and Repack (Both Wheels)	
1974–80 (1.1)	1.4
(G) Front Shock Absorber, Renew	
1974–80—one (.3)	.5
both (.5)	.8
(G) Upper Ball Joint, Renew	
Add alignment charges.	
1974–76—one (.7)	.9
both (1.3)	1.7
1977–80—one (.6)	.9
both (1.1)	1.7
(G) Lower Ball Joint, Renew	
Add alignment charges.	
1974–80—one (.6)	.9
both (1.1)	1.7
(G) Front Spring, Renew (One)	
Includes: Adjust toe-in.	
1974–80 (.9)	1.5

Buick Riviera (1979–80)

(Factory Time)	Chilton Time
(G) Check Alignment of Front End	
All models	.5
Note: Deduct if alignment is performed.	
(G) Caster, Camber and Toe-In, Adjust	
Includes: Adjust front wheel bearings.	
All models (1.0)	1.7
w/A.C. interference add	.5
(G) Toe-In Adjust	
All models (.4)	.6
(G) Front Wheel Bearing or Hub, Renew	
1979–80—one side (.9)	1.1
both sides (1.6)	2.0

	Chilton			Chilton
(Factory Time)	Time		(Factory Time)	Time

(G) Upper Ball Joint, Renew
Add alignment charges.
1979–80—one (.6)	.9
both (1.1)	1.7

(G) Lower Ball Joint, Renew
Add alignment charges.
1979–80—one (1.0)	1.4
both (1.8)	2.7

(G) Front Shock Absorbers, Renew
1979–80—one (.4)	.6
both (.5)	.9

Buick Apollo, Century, Gran Sport, Regal, Skylark (1974–79)

(G) Check Alignment of Front End
All models	.5

Note: Deduct if alignment is performed.

(G) Caster, Camber and Toe-In, Adjust
Includes: Adjust front wheel bearings.
All models (.7)	1.4
w/A.C. interference add	.5

(G) Toe-In, Adjust
All models (.4)	.6

(G) Front Wheel Bearings, Clean and Repack (Both Wheels)
1974–80	1.4

(G) Front Shock Absorber, Renew
1974–80—one (.3)	.5
both (.5)	.8

(G) Upper Ball Joint, Renew
Add alignment charges.
1974–76—one (.7)	.9
both (1.3)	1.7
1977–80—one (.6)	.9
both (1.1)	1.7

(G) Lower Ball Joint, Renew
Add alignment charges.
1974–80—one (.6)	.9
both (1.1)	1.7

(G) Front Coil Spring, Renew (One)
Includes: Adjust toe-in.
1974–76—Century (1.0)	1.5
Apollo—Skylark (1.6)	2.1
1977–80 (.8)	1.5

Buick Skyhawk

(G) Check Alignment of Front End
All models	.5

Note: Deduct if alignment is performed.

(G) Toe-In, Adjust
All models (.4)	.6

(G) Caster, Camber and Toe-In, Adjust
Includes: Adjust front wheel bearings.
All models (.7)	1.4
w/A.C. interference add	.5

(G) Front Wheel Bearings, Clean and Repack (Both Wheels)
1975–80	1.4

(G) Front Shock Absorber, Renew
1975–80—one (.3)	.5
both (.5)	.8

(G) Upper and Lower Ball Joints, Renew
Add alignment charges.
1975–80—one side (1.0)	1.6
both sides (1.9)	3.0

(G) Upper Ball Joint, Renew
Add alignment charges.
1975–80—one (.6)	.9
both (1.1)	1.7

(G) Lower Ball Joint, Renew
Add alignment charges
1975–80—one (.6)	.9
both (1.1)	1.7

Cadillac

(G) Check Alignment of Front End
All models	.5

Note: Deduct if alignment is performed.

(G) Toe In, Adjust
All models (.4)	.6

(G) Caster, Camber and Toe-In, Adjust
Includes: Adjust front wheel bearings.
All models (.7)	1.4
w/A.C. interference add	.5

(G) Front Wheel Bearings, Clean and Repack (Both Wheels)
1974–80	1.6

(G) Front Shock Absorber, Renew
1974–80—one (.3)	.5
both (.5)	.8

(G) Lower Ball Joint, Renew
Add alignment charges.
1974–76—one (1.6)	2.0
both (2.9)	3.6
1977–80—one (.6)	1.0
both (1.0)	1.7

(G) Upper Ball Joint, Renew
Includes: Align front end.
1974–76—one (1.8)	2.2
both (2.5)	3.2
1977–80—one (1.4)	1.8
both (1.9)	2.6

(G) Front Spring, Renew
Includes: Align front end.
1974–76—one (2.2)	3.0
both (3.2)	4.6
1977–80—one (1.5)	2.3
both (2.2)	3.6

Cadillac Seville

(G) Check Alignment of Front End
All models	.5

Note: Deduct if alignment is performed.

(G) Toe-In, Adjust
All models (.4)	.6

(G) Caster, Camber and Toe-In, Adjust
Includes: Adjust front wheel bearings.
All models (1.2)	1.7
w/A.C. interference add	.5

(G) Front Wheel Bearings, Clean and Repack (Both Wheels)
1976–80	1.4

(Factory Time)	Chilton Time
(G) Front Shock Absorbers, Renew	
1976–80—one (.3)	.5
both (.5)	.8
(G) Lower Ball Joint, Renew	
Add alignment charges.	
1976—one (1.6)	2.0
both (2.9)	3.6
1977–80—one (.6)	1.0
both (1.0)	1.7
(G) Upper Ball Joint, Renew	
Add alignment charges.	
1976–80—one (1.6)	2.0
both (2.3)	3.0
(G) Front Spring, Renew	
Includes: Align front end.	
1976–80—one (2.5)	3.4
both (3.5)	5.2

Cadillac Eldorado

(G) Check Alignment of Front End	
All models	.5
Note: Deduct if alignment is performed.	
(G) Toe-In, Adjust	
All models (.4)	.6
(G) Torsion Bar, Adjust	
All models (.3)	.5
(G) Caster, Camber and Toe-In, Adjust	
Includes: Adjust front wheel bearings.	
All models (1.0)	1.7
w/A.C. interference add	.5
(G) Front Hub Bearings, Renew	
1974–80—one whl (1.8)	2.1
both whls (2.4)	3.0
(G) Front Shock Absorber, Renew	
1974–78—one (.3)	.5
both (.5)	.8
1979–80—one (.4)	.6
both (.5)	.9
(G) Lower Ball Joint, Renew	
Add alignment charges.	
1974–78—one (1.3)	1.7
both (2.4)	3.2
1979–80—one (2.0)	2.4
both (2.8)	3.6
(G) Upper Ball Joint, Renew	
Includes: Align front end.	
1974–78—one (1.5)	2.0

Camaro, Chevelle, Malibu, Monte Carlo, Nova

(G) Check Alignment of Front End	
All models	.5
Note: Deduct if alignment is performed.	
(G) Toe-In, Adjust	
All models (.4)	.6
(G) Caster, Camber and Toe-In, Adjust	
Includes: Adjust front wheel bearings.	
All models (.7)	1.4
w/A.C. interference add	.5
(G) Front Wheel Bearings, Clean and Repack (Both Wheels)	
Conventional brakes (.7)	1.2
Disc brakes (1.1)	1.6

(Factory Time)	Chilton Time
(G) Front Shock Absorber, Renew	
1974–80—one (.3)	.5
both (.5)	.8
(G) Upper Ball Joint, Renew	
Add alignment charges.	
1974–80—one (.6)	1.0
both (1.1)	1.6
(G) Lower Ball Joint, Renew	
Add alignment charges.	
1974–76—one (.6)	1.0
both (1.1)	1.6
1977–80—one (.6)	1.0
both (1.0)	1.6
(G) Front Spring, Renew	
Add alignment charges.	
1974–76—one (.9)	1.3
both (1.6)	2.3
1977—one (.8)	1.3
both (1.4)	2.3
1978–80—one (.7)	1.3
both (1.2)	2.3

Chevrolet & Corvette

(G) Check Alignment of Front End	
All models	.5
Note: Deduct if alignment is performed.	
(G) Toe In, Adjust	
All models (.4)	.6
(G) Caster, Camber and Toe In, Adjust	
Includes: Adjust front wheel bearings.	
All models (.7)	1.4
w/A.C. interference add	.5
(G) Front Wheel Bearings, Clean and Repack (Both Wheels)	
1974–80 (1.1)	1.6
(G) Front Shock Absorber, Renew	
1974–80—one (.3)	.5
both (.5)	.8
(G) Upper and Lower Ball Joints, Renew (One Side)	
Add alignment charges.	
1974–80 (1.1)	2.0
(G) Upper Ball Joint, Renew (One)	
Add alignment charges.	
1974–80 (.6)	1.0
(G) Lower Ball Joint, Renew (One)	
Add alignment charges.	
1974–80—Chev. (.6)	1.0
Corv. (.8)	1.3
(G) Front Spring, Renew (One)	
Add alignment charges.	
Chevrolet	
1974–76 (.9)	1.6
1977–80 (.7)	1.6
Corvette	
1974–80 (.8)	1.5

Chevette

(G) Check Alignment of Front End	
1976–80	.5
Note: Deduct if alignment is performed.	

	Chilton			Chilton
(Factory Time)	Time		(Factory Time)	Time

(G) Toe In, Adjust
1976–80 (.4) 5

(G) Caster, Camber and Toe In, Adjust
Includes: Adjust front wheel bearings.
1976–80 (.7) 1.1
w/A.C. interference add 5

(G) Front Wheel Bearings, Clean and Repack (Both Wheels)
1976–80 (1.0) 1.6

(G) Front Shock Absorber, Renew
1976–80—one (.3) 5
both (.4) 7

(G) Upper and Lower Ball Joints, Renew (One Side)
Add alignment charges.
1976–80 (1.1) 2.0

(G) Upper Ball Joint, Renew
Add alignment charges.
1976–80—one (.5) 9
both (.7) 1.3

(G) Lower Ball Joint, Renew (One)
Add alignment charges
1976–80—one (.6) 9
both (1.0) 1.6

(G) Front Spring, Renew
Add alignment charges.
1976–80—one (.7) 1.0
both (1.2) 1.8

Citation, Omega, Phoenix, Skylark—All 1980

(G) Check Alignment of Front End
All models 5
Note: Deduct if alignment is performed.

(G) Toe-In, Adjust
All models (.5) 7

(G) Camber and Toe-In, Adjust
All models (.9) 1.4
w/A.C. interference add 5

(G) Lower Ball Joint, Renew
Add alignment charges.
1980—one (.5) 9
both (.8) 1.6

(G) Front Shock Absorbers, Renew
Add alignment charges if necessary.
1980—one (.7) 9
both (1.3) 1.7

(G) Front Spring Seat or Insulator, Renew
Add alignment charges if necessary.
1980—one (.8) 1.1
both (1.4) 2.0

Chrysler, Cordoba, Imperial

(G) Check Alignment of Front End
All models 5
Note: Deduct if alignment is performed.

(G) Toe-In, Adjust
All models 6

(G) Caster, Camber and Toe-In, Adjust
Includes: Adjust caster, camber, toe, car height and center steering wheel.
All models (1.1) 1.4

Adjust headlamps add 4
w/A.C. interference add 5

(G) Car Height, Adjust
1974–80 (.3) 6
Adjust headlamps add 4

(G) Front Wheel Bearings, Clean and Repack (Both Wheels)
1974–75 (1.5) 1.8
1976–80 (1.1) 1.4

(G) Front Shock Absorber or Bushings, Renew
1974–76—one (.4) 6
both (.6) 1.0
1977–80—one (.3) 6
both (.5) 1.0

(G) Upper and Lower Ball Joints, Renew (One Side)
Add alignment charges.
1974–80 .... 2.5

(G) Upper Ball Joint, Renew
Add alignment charges.
1973–76—one (.7) 1.0
both (1.3) 2.0
1977–78—one (.6) 1.0
both (1.1) 2.0
1979–80—one (.8) 1.2
both (1.5) 2.4

Dodge

(G) Toe-In, Adjust
All models 6

(G) Check Alignment of Front End
All models 5
Note: Deduct if alignment is performed.

(G) Caster, Camber and Toe-In, Adjust
Includes: Adjust caster, camber, toe, car height and center steering wheel.
All models (1.1) 1.4
Adjust headlamps add 3
w/A.C. interference add 5

(G) Car Height, Adjust
1974–80 (.3) 6
Adjust headlamps add 3

(G) Front Wheel Bearings, Clean and Repack (Both Wheels)
Includes: R&R dust seal.
1974–75 (1.5) 1.8
1976–80 (1.1) 1.4

(G) Front Shock Absorber or Bushings, Renew
1974–76—one (.4) 6
both (.6) 1.0
1977–80—one (.3) 6
both (.5) 1.0

(G) Upper and Lower Ball Joints, Renew (One Side)
Add alignment charges.
1974–80
w/Disc brks 2.2

(G) Upper Ball Joint, Renew
Add alignment charges.
1974–76—one (.7) 1.0
both (1.3) 2.0
1977–80—one (.6) 1.0
both (1.1) 2.0

(Factory Time)	Chilton Time

(G) Lower Ball Joint, Renew
Add alignment charges.

1974–76—exc below	
one (.7)	1.2
both (1.2)	2.3
Polara, Monaco	
one (1.2)	1.8
both (2.3)	3.0
1977–80—one (.9)	1.4
both (.17)	3.0

Horizon & Omni

(G) Check Alignment of Front End

All models	.5

Note: Deduct if alignment is performed.

(G) Toe Out, Adjust

All models	.4

(G) Camber and Toe Out, Adjust
Includes: Adjust camber, toe out and center steering wheel.

All models (1.0)	1.5

(G) Lower Ball Joint, Renew (One)
Add alignment charges.

1978–80 (.4)	.8

(G) Front Spring, Renew (One)

1978–80 (.8)	1.4

Capri & Mustang (1979–80)

(G) Toe-In, Adjust

All models (.4)	.5

(G) Check Alignment of Front End

All models (.4)	.5

Note: Deduct if alignment is performed.

(G) Camber and Toe-In, Adjust
Includes: Adjust front wheel bearings.

All models (1.0)	1.4
w/A.C. interference add	.5

(G) Front Wheel Bearings, Clean and Repack (Both Wheels)

All models	1.7

(G) Front Shock Absorbers or Bushings, Renew

1979–80—one (.4)	.6
both (.6)	.8

(G) Front Spring, Renew

1979–80—one (1.2)	1.8
both (2.2)	3.0

Comet, Cougar, Monarch, Montego, Lincoln Versailles

(G) Check Alignment of Front End

All models (.4)	.5

Note: Deduct if alignment is performed.

(G) Toe-In, Adjust

All models (.4)	.5

(G) Caster, Camber and Toe-In, Adjust
Includes: Adjust front wheel bearings.

All models (1.3)	1.6
w/A.C. interference add	.5

(Factory Time)	Chilton Time

(G) Front Wheel Bearings, Clean and Repack

Conventional brakes	
both wheels (.9)	1.4
Disc brakes	
both wheels (1.3)	1.7

(G) Front Shock Absorber or Bushings, Renew

1974–80—one (.4)	.6
both (.6)	.8

(G) Front Spring, Renew

1974–80—exc below—one (.6)	1.2
both (1.0)	2.1
Versailles—one (1.0)	1.5
both (1.6)	2.6

Elite, Granada, Maverick, Torino, LTD II, Thunderbird (1977–79)

(G) Check Alignment of Front End

All models (.4)	.5

Note: Deduct if alignment is performed.

(G) Toe-In, Adjust

All models (.4)	.5

(G) Caster, Camber and Toe-In, Adjust
Includes: Adjust front wheel bearings.

All models (1.3)	1.6
w/A.C. interference add	.5

(G) Front Wheel Bearings, Clean and Repack

Conventional brakes	
both wheels (.9)	1.4
Disc brakes	
both wheels (1.3)	1.7

(G) Front Shock Absorber or Bushings, Renew

1974–80—exc below—one (.4)	.6
both (.6)	.8
Maverick—one (.5)	.7
both (.7)	.9

(G) Front Spring, Renew

1974–80—one (.6)	1.2
both (1.0)	2.1

Ford

(G) Check Alignment of Front End

All models (.4)	.5

Note: Deduct if alignment is performed.

(G) Toe In, Adjust

All models (.4)	.5

(G) Caster, Camber and Toe In, Adjust
Includes: Adjust front wheel bearings.

All models (.9)	1.6
w/A.C. interference add	.5

(G) Front Wheel Bearings, Clean and Repack

1974–80	
both wheels (1.3)	1.7

(G) Front Shock Absorber or Bushings, Renew

1974–80—one (.4)	.6
both (.6)	.8

	Chilton Time
(Factory Time)	

(G) Front Spring, Renew
1974–78—one (.6)	**1.0**
both (1.1)	**1.6**
1979–80—one (.7)	**1.1**
both (1.2)	**2.0**

Lincoln Continental, Mark IV, Mark V

(G) Check Alignment of Front End
| All models (.4) . . . . | **.5** |

Note: Deduct if alignment is performed.

(G) Toe In, Adjust
| All models (.4) . . . . | **.5** |

(G) Caster, Camber and Toe In, Adjust
Includes: Adjust front wheel bearings.
| All models (1.3) . . . . | **1.6** |
| w/A.C. interference add . . . . | **.5** |

(G) Front Wheel Bearings, Clean and Repack
| both wheels (1.3) . . . . | **1.7** |

(G) Front Shock Absorber or Bushings, Renew
| 1974–80—one (.4) . . . . | **.6** |
| both (.6) . . . . | **.8** |

Mercury

(G) Check Alignment of Front End
| All models (.4) . . . . | **.5** |

Note: Deduct if alignment is performed.

(G) Toe In, Adjust
| All models (.4) . . . . | **.5** |

(G) Caster, Camber and Toe In, Adjust
Includes: Adjust front wheel bearings.
| All models (.9) . . . . | **1.6** |
| w/A.C. interference add . . . . | **.5** |

(G) Front Wheel Bearings, Clean and Repack
1974–80
| both wheels (1.3) . . . . | **1.7** |

(G) Front Spring, Renew
1974–78—one (.6)	**1.0**
both (1.1)	**1.6**
1979–80—one (.7)	**1.1**
both (1.2)	**2.0**

Mustang II, Bobcat, Pinto, Fairmont, Zephyr

(G) Check Alignment of Front End
| All models (.4) . . . . | **.5** |

Note: Deduct if alignment is performed.

(G) Toe In, Adjust
| All models (.4) . . . . | **.5** |

(G) Caster, Camber and Toe In, Adjust
Includes: Adjust front wheel bearings.
| All models (1.2) . . . . | **1.4** |
| w/A.C. interference add . . . . | **.5** |

	Chilton Time
(Factory Time)	

(G) Front Wheel Bearings, Clean and Repack
Conventional brakes
| both wheels (.9) . . . . | **1.4** |
Disc brakes
| both wheels (1.3) . . . . | **1.7** |

(G) Front Shock Absorber or Bushings, Renew
| 1974–80—exc below—one (.4) . . . | **.6** |
| both (.6) . . . . | **.8** |
Fairmont & Zephyr
| one (.7) . . . . | **1.0** |
| both (1.1) . . . . | **1.5** |

(G) Front Spring, Renew
Pinto & Bobcat
1074–76—one (.7)	**1.3**
both (1.1)	**1.9**
1977–80—one (.6)	**1.3**
both (.9)	**1.9**
Mustang II
1974–79—one (.7)	**1.3**
both (1.2)	**2.0**
Fairmont & Zephyr
1978–80—one (1.2)	**1.8**
both (2.2)	**3.0**

Oldsmobile

(G) Check Alignment of Front End
| All models . . . . | **.5** |

Note: deduct if alignment is performed.

(G) Toe In, Adjust
| All models (.4) . . . . | **.6** |

(G) Caster, Camber and Toe In, Adjust
Includes: Adjust front wheel bearings.
| All models (.7) . . . . | **1.3** |
| w/A.C. interference add . . . . | **.5** |

(G) Front Wheel Bearings, Clean and Repack (Both Wheels)
| 1974–75 (1.2) . . . . | **1.4** |
| 1976–80 (1.1) . . . . | **1.4** |

(G) Front Shock Absorber, Renew
| 1974–78—one (.3) . . . . | **.4** |

(G) Upper and Lower Ball Joints, Renew (One Side)
| 1974–80 (1.1) . . . . | **1.5** |

(G) Upper Ball Joint, Renew (One)
Add alignment charges.
| 1974–80 (.6) . . . . | **.9** |

(G) Lower Ball Joint, Renew (One)
Add alignment charges.
| 1974–80 (.6) . . . . | **.9** |

(G) Front Spring, Renew (One)
Includes: R&R wheel and shock. Disconnect stabilizer link and control arm pivot bolts. Add alignment charges.
| 1974–75 (1.2) . . . . | **1.4** |
| 1976–80 (1.0) . . . . | **1.4** |

Olds Cutlass, Omega (1974–79)

(G) Check Alignment of Front End
| All models . . . . | **.5** |

Note: deduct if alignment is performed.

	Chilton Time
(G) Toe In, Adjust	
All models (.4)	.6
(G) Caster, Camber and Toe In, Adjust	
Includes: Adjust front wheel bearings.	
All models (.7)	1.3
w/A.C. interference add	.5
(G) Front Wheel Bearings, Clean and Repack	
Conventional brakes	
both wheels (.7)	.8
Disc brakes	
both wheels (1.1)	1.3
(G) Front Shock Absorber, Renew	
1974–78—one (.3)	.5
both (.5)	.8
1979–80—one (.4)	.5
both (.5)	.8
(G) Upper and Lower Ball Joints, Renew (One Side)	
1974–80 (1.1)	1.5
(G) Upper Ball Joint, Renew (One)	
Add alignment charges.	
1974–80—one (.6)	.9
both (1.1)	1.6
(G) Lower Ball Joint, Renew	
Add alignment charges.	
1974–80—one (.6)	.9
both (1.0)	1.5
(G) Front Spring, Renew	
Includes: R&R wheel and shock. Disconnect stabilizer link and control arm pivot bolts.	
Add alignment charges.	
1974–75—one (1.3)	1.7
both (2.3)	2.8
1976–80—one (1.0)	1.7
both (1.9)	2.8

Olds Toronado

	Chilton Time
(G) Check Alignment of Front End	
All models	.5
Note: deduct if alignment is performed.	
(G) Toe In, Adjust	
All models (.4)	.6
(G) Caster, Camber and Toe In, Adjust	
Includes: Check carrying height.	
All models (1.0)	1.4
w/A.C. interference add	.5
(G) Front Hub Bearings, Clean and Repack (Both Wheels)	
1974–80 (1.7)	2.0
(G) Front Shock Absorber, Renew	
1974–78—one (.3)	.4
both (.5)	.7
1979–80—one (.4)	.5
both (.5)	.7
(G) Lower Ball Joint, Renew	
1974–80—one (1.0)	1.4
both (1.9)	2.7
(G) Upper Ball Joint, Renew	
Add alignment charges.	
1974–75—one (.7)	.9
both (1.3)	1.7
1976–80—one (.6)	.9
both (1.1)	1.7

Olds Starfire

	Chilton Time
(G) Check Alignment of Front End	
All models	.5
Note: deduct if alignment is performed.	
(G) Toe In, Adjust	
All models (.4)	.6
(G) Caster, Camber and Toe In, Adjust	
Includes: Adjust front wheel bearings.	
All models (.7)	1.3
w/A.C. interference add	.5
(G) Front Wheel Bearings, Clean and Repack (Both Wheels)	
1975–80 (1.1)	1.4
(G) Front Shock Absorber, Renew	
1975–78—one (.3)	.4
both (.5)	.7
1979–80—one (.4)	.5
both (.5)	.7
(G) Upper and Lower Ball Joints, Renew	
Add alignment charges.	
1975–80—one side (1.1)	1.5
both sides (2.0)	2.9
(G) Upper Ball Joint, Renew	
Add alignment charges.	
1975–80—one (.6)	.9
both (1.1)	1.7
(G) Lower Ball Joint, Renew	
Add alignment charges.	
1975–80—one (.6)	.9
both (1.0)	1.6
(G) Front Spring, Renew	
1975–80—one (.7)	1.0
both (1.2)	1.8

Plymouth

	Chilton Time
(G) Check Alignment of Front End	
All models	.5
Note: deduct if alignment is performed.	
(G) Toe In, Adjust	
All models	.6
(M) Caster, Camber and Toe In, Adjust	
Includes: Adjust caster, camber, toe, car height and center steering wheel.	
All models (1.1)	1.4
Adjust headlamps add	.3
w/A.C. interference add	.5
(G) Front Wheel Bearings, Clean and Repack (Both Wheels)	
Includes: R&R dust seal.	
1974–75 (1.5)	1.8
1976–78 (1.1)	1.4
(G) Car Height, Adjust	
1974–78 (.3)	.6
Adjust headlamps add	.3
(G) Upper and Lower Ball Joints, Renew (One Side)	
Add alignment charges.	
1974–78	2.2
(G) Upper Ball Joint, Renew	
Add alignment charges.	
1974–76—one (.7)	1.0
both (1.3)	2.0

(Factory Time)	Chilton Time
1977–78—one (.6)	1.0
both (1.1)	2.0

(G) Lower Ball Joint, Renew
Add alignment charges.

1974–76—one (.7)	1.2
both (1.2)	2.3
1977–78—one (.9)	1.4
both (1.7)	3.0

(G) Front Shock Absorber or Bushings, Renew

1974–76—one (.4)	.6
both (.6)	1.0
1977–78—one (.3)	.6
both (.5)	1.0

Pontiac & Grand Prix

(G) Check Alignment of Front End

All models	.5

Note: deduct if alignment is performed.

(G) Toe-In, Adjust

All models (.4)	.6

(G) Caster, Camber and Toe-In, Adjust
Includes: Adjust front wheel bearings.

All models (.7)	1.4
w/A.C. interference add	.5

(G) Front Wheel Bearings, Clean and Repack (Both Wheels)

1974–80 (1.2)	1.5

(G) Upper and Lower Ball Joints, Renew (One Side)
Add alignment charges.

1974–80 (1.0)	1.7

G Upper Ball Joint, Renew (One)
Add alignment charges.

1974–80 (.6)	.9

(G) Lower Ball Joint, Renew (One)
Add alignment charges.

1974–80 (.6)	1.0

(G) Front Spring, Renew (One)
Includes: Align front end.

1974–80 (1.5)	2.1

Pontiac Astre & Sunbird

(G) Check Alignment of Front End

All models	.5

Note: Deduct deduct if alignment is performed.

(G) Toe-In, Adjust

All models (.4)	.6

(G) Caster, Camber and Toe-In, Adjust
Includes: Adjust front wheel bearings.

All models (.7)	1.4
w/A.C. interference add	.5

(G) Front Wheel Bearings, Clean and Repack (Both Wheels)

1975–80 (1.1)	1.4

(G) Front Shock Absorbers, Renew

1975–80—one (.3)	.5
both (.5)	.8

(G) Upper and Lower Ball Joints, Renew (One Side)
Add alignment charges.

1975–80 (1.0)	1.7

(Factory Time)	Chilton Time

(G) Upper Ball Joint, Renew (One)
Add alignment charges.

1975–80 (.6)	.9

(G) Lower Ball Joint, Renew (One)
Add alignment charges.

1975–80 (.6)	1.0

(G) Front Spring, Renew (One)
Includes: Align front end.

1975–77 (1.4)	2.0
1978–80 (1.0)	1.6

Firebird, Phoenix (1978–79), LeMans, Ventura (1974–77)

(G) Check Alignment of Front End

All models	.5

Note: deduct if alignment is performed.

(G) Toe-In, Adjust

All models (.4)	.6

(G) Caster, Camber and Toe-In, Adjust
Includes: Adjust front wheel bearings.

All models (.7)	1.4
w/A.C. interference add	.5

(G) Front Wheel Bearings, Clean and Repack (Both Wheels)

1974–80 (1.1)	1.4

(G) Front Shock Absorbers, Renew

1974–80—one (.3)	.5
both (.5)	.8

(G) Upper and Lower Ball Joints, Renew (One Side)
Add alignment charges.

1974–80 (1.0)	1.7

(G) Upper Ball Joint, Renew (One)
Add alignment charges.

1974–80 (.6)	.9

(G) Lower Ball Joint, Renew (One)
Add alignment charges.

1974–80 (.6)	1.0

(G) Front Spring, Renew (One)
Includes: Align front end.

1974–80 (1.5)	2.1

Thunderbird (1974–76)

(G) Check Alignment of Front End

All models (.4)	.5

Note: deduct if alignment is performed.

(G) Toe In, Adjust

All models (.5)	.6

(G) Caster, Camber and Toe In, Adjust
Includes: Adjust front wheel bearings.

All models (1.4)	1.4
w/A.C. interference add	.5

(G) Front Wheel Bearings, Clean and Repack

both wheels (1.3)	1.7

(G) Front Shock Absorber or Bushings, Renew

1974–76—one (.4)	.6
both (.6)	.8

(G) Front Coil Spring, Renew
Add alignment charges.

1974–76 (1.2)	1.7

(Factory Time)	Chilton Time		(Factory Time)	Chilton Time

Valiant, Dart, Barracuda, Challenger, Aspen, Volare, LeBaron, Diplomat

(G) Check Alignment of Front End
All models 5
Note: deduct if alignment is performed.
(G) Toe-In, Adjust
All models 6
(G) Caster, Camber and Toe-In, Adjust
Includes: Adjust caster, camber, toe, car height and center steering wheel.
All models (1.1) 1.4
Adjust headlamps add 3
w/A.C. interference add 5
(G) Car Height, Adjust
1974–80 (.3) .6
Adjust headlamps add 3
(G) Front Wheel Bearings, Clean and Repack (Both Wheels)
wo/Disc brks
All models (.9) 9
w/Disc brks
1974–75 (1.5) 1.8
1976–80 (1.1) 1.4
(G) Front Shock Absorbers or Bushings, Renew
1974–76—one (.3) 6
both (.6) 1.0
1977–80—one (.3) 6
both (.5) 1.0
(G) Upper and Lower Ball Joints, Renew (One Side)
Add alignment charges.
1974–80
w/Disc brks 2.1
(G) Upper Ball Joint, Renew
Add alignment charges.
1974–76—one (.7) 1.0
both (1.3) 2.0
1977–80—one (.6) 1.0
both (1.1) 2.0

(G) Lower Ball Joint, Renew
Add alignment charges.
1974–80—one (1.0) 1.4
both (1.9) 2.4

Vega & Monza

(G) Check Alignment of Front End
All models 5
Note: deduct if alignment is performed.
(G) Toe In, Adjust
All models (.4) 6
(G) Caster, Camber and Toe In, Adjust
Includes: Adjust front wheel bearings.
All models (.7) 1.4
w/A.C. interference add 5
(G) Front Wheel Bearings, Clean and Repack (Both Wheels)
1974–80 (1.0) 1.6
(G) Front Shock Absorber, Renew
1974–80—one (.3) 5
both (.5) 8
(G) Front Spring, Renew
Add alignment charges.
1974–76—one (.7) 1.0
both (1.2) 1.8
1977–80—one (1.0) 1.3
both (1.7) 2.3
(G) Upper and Lower Ball Joints, Renew
1974–80—one side (1.1) 2.0
both sides (2.1) 3.0
(G) Upper Ball Joint, Renew
Add alignment charges.
1974–80—one (.6) 8
both (1.1) 1.4
(G) Lower Ball Joint, Renew
Add alignment charges.
1974–80—one (.6) 8
both (1.0) 1.4

CYLINDER HEAD AND VALVE SYSTEM

Note: Does not include machine shop operations.

(Factory Time)	Chilton Time

American Motors

(G) Cylinder Head Gasket, Renew
Includes: Clean carbon.
Four—1977–80 (2.6) 3.9
Six—except Pacer
1974–76 (2.1) 3.9
1977–80 (1.8) 3.9
Pacer
1975–80 (2.8) 4.6

(Factory Time)	Chilton Time

V-8—1974–76
one side (3.0) 4.4
both sides (4.4) 6.3
1977–80
one side (2.7) 4.4
both sides (4.1) 6.3
All engines
w/P.S. add (.3) 3
w/A.C. add (.6) 6
w/Air guard add (1.0) 1.0
(G) Cylinder Head, Renew
Includes: Transfer parts not supplied with replacement head. Clean carbon from cylinder block.

	Chilton Time
(Factory Time)	
Four—1977–80 (4.3)	**6.5**
Six—except Pacer	
1974–76 (2.4)	**4.4**
1977–80 (2.1)	**4.4**
Pacer	
1975–80 (3.1)	**5.1**
V-8—1974–76	
one side (3.3)	**4.9**
both sides (4.8)	**7.3**
1977–80	
one side (3.0)	**4.9**
both sides (4.5)	**7.3**
All engines	
w/P.S. add (.3)	**.3**
w/A.C. add (.6)	**.6**
w/Air guard add (1.0)	**1.0**

(P) Clean Carbon and Grind Valves
Includes: R&R cylinder head(s), recondition seats, reface valves, replace valve stem oil seals. Minor engine tune-up.

Four—1977–80 (4.5)	**7.4**
Six—except Pacer	
1974–76 (4.9)	**8.8**
1977–80 (3.9)	**8.8**
Pacer	
1975–80 (4.9)	**8.8**
V-8—1974–76 (8.0)	**12.0**
1977–80 (6.7)	**12.0**
All engines	
w/P.S. add (.3)	**.3**
w/A.C. add (.6)	**.6**
w/Air guard add (1.0)	**1.0**

(G) Valve Springs or Valve Stem Oil Seals, Renew (Head on Car)

Four—1977–80	
one cyl (1.5)	**2.6**
all cyls (1.8)	**3.2**
Six—except Pacer	
1974–76—one cyl (.8)	**1.3**
all cyls (1.2)	**2.5**
1977–80—one cyl (.7)	**1.3**
all cyls (1.1)	**2.5**
Pacer	
1975–80—one cyl (.9)	**1.4**
all cyls (1.3)	**2.6**
V-8—1974–76	
one cyl (.7)	**1.3**
all cyls (2.4)	**3.8**
1977–80	
one cyl (.7)	**1.3**
all cyls (2.1)	**3.8**

(G) Valve Tappets, Renew (All)
Includes: R&R cylinder head on 6 cylinder models.

Four—1977–80 (1.5)	**2.6**
Six—except Pacer	
1974–76 (2.5)	**4.4**
1977–80 (2.0)	**4.4**
Pacer	
1975–80 (3.0)	**4.9**
V-8—1974–76 (2.5)	**4.6**
1977–80 (2.7)	**4.6**
All engines	
w/A.C. add (.3)	**.3**
w/P.S. add (.4)	**.4**
w/Air guard add (.2)	**.2**

(G) Rocker Arm, Push Rod and/or Pivot, Renew

Six—except Pacer	
1974–76—one cyl (.6)	**1.0**

	Chilton Time
(Factory Time)	
1977–80—one cyl (.5)	**1.0**
Pacer	
1975–80—one cyl (.7)	**1.4**
each adtnl cyl-all models (.1)	**.2**
V-8—1974–80	
one cyl (.5)	**1.1**
all cyls (1.2)	**1.9**

(G) Rocker Arm Shaft, Renew

Six—1974 (.8)	**1.4**

(G) Valves, Adjust

Four—1977–80 (.7)	**1.2**

AMC/Jeep

(G) Cylinder Head Gasket, Renew
Includes: Clean carbon.

1974–80—Six (2.1)	**3.5**
V-8—one (3.4)	**4.7**
both (5.1)	**6.0**
w/P.S. add (.3)	**.3**
w/A.C. add (.6)	**.6**
w/Air Guard add (.3)	**.3**

(G) Cylinder Head, Renew
Includes: Clean carbon.

1974–80—Six (2.4)	**3.9**
V-8—one (3.7)	**5.1**
both (5.4)	**6.4**
w/P.S. add (.3)	**.3**
w/A.C. add (.6)	**.6**
w/Air Guard add (.3)	**.3**

(P) Clean Carbon & Grind Valves
Includes: R&R cylinder head(s), recondition seats, replace valve stem oil seals. Minor tune up.

1974–80—Six (4.9)	**6.3**
V-8 (8.8)	**11.2**
w/P.S. add (.3)	**.3**
w/A.C. add (.6)	**.6**
w/Air Guard add (.3)	**.3**

(G) Valve Tappets, Renew (All)
Includes: R&R 6 cyl head.

1974–80—Six or V-8 (2.5)	**3.9**
w/A.C. add (.3)	**.3**
w/Air Guard add (.2)	**.2**

(G) Valve Springs or Valve Stem Oil Seals, Renew (Head On Car)

1974–80—Six (1.3)	**2.2**
V-8 (2.1)	**3.7**

(G) Rocker Arm, Push Rod and/or Pivot, Renew (One)

1974–80—Six (.5)	**.7**
V-8 (.5)	**.8**

(G) Rocker Arm Shaft, Renew

1974—Six (.8)	**1.0**

Buick LeSabre, Electra, Riviera (1974–78)

(G) Cylinder Head Gasket, Renew
Includes: Clean gasket surfaces, clean carbon, make all necessary adjustments.

V-6—1976–80—one (2.1)	**3.0**
both (3.1)	**4.6**
w/Turbocharger add (1.4)	**1.4**
V-8—1974–76—one (2.7)	**3.6**
both (4.0)	**5.5**

(Factory Time)	Chilton Time
1977–80	
350 eng, Code J	
one (2.4)	3.3
both (3.6)	5.1
350–403 engs, Code R or K	
one (3.4)	4.3
both (4.9)	6.4
305–350 engs, Code U or L	
one (4.3)	5.2
both (6.1)	7.6
350 eng, Code X	
one (2.4)	3.3
both (3.6)	5.1
301 eng, Code Y	
one (3.0)	3.9
both (3.9)	5.4
w/A.C. add (.5)	.5
w/P.S. add (.3)	.3
w/A.I.R. add (.2)	.2

(G) Cylinder Head, Renew
Includes: Transfer all parts, reface valves, make all necessary adjustments.

V-6—1976–80—one (2.7)	4.0
both (4.3)	6.1
w/Turbocharger add (1.4)	1.4
V-8—1974–76—one (3.7)	4.8
both (6.0)	7.8
1977–80	
350 eng, Code J	
one (3.1)	4.2
both (5.0)	6.8
350–403 engs, Code R or K	
one (4.2)	5.3
both (6.5)	8.3
305–350 engs, Code U or L	
one (5.2)	6.3

Buick
Serial Number
4B37 C 7H100001
1977 Engine Codes

C	Buick	231	2bbl	—	V-6
Y	Pont.	301	2bbl	—	V-8
U	Chev.	305	2bbl	—	V-8
R	Olds	350	4bbl	—	V-8
L	Chev.	350	4bbl	—	V-8
J	Pont.	350	4bbl	—	V-8
H	Pont.	350	2bbl	—	V-8
K	Olds	403	4bbl	—	V-8

1978–79 Engine Codes

C	Chev.	196	2bbl	—	V-6
C	Buick	231	2bbl	—	V-6
A	Buick	231	2bbl	—	V-6
G	Buick	231	2bbl	(Turbo)	V-6
2	Buick	231	2bbl	—	V-6
3	Buick	231	4bbl	(Turbo)	V-6
Z	Buick	231	2bbl	(Calif.)	V-6
F	Olds	260	2bbl	—	V-8
Y	Pont.	301	2bbl	—	V-8
H	Chev.	305	4bbl	—	V-8
U	Chev.	305	2bbl	—	V-8
U	Olds	350	2bbl	—	V-8
L	Chev.	350	4bbl	—	V-8
X	Buick	350	4bbl	—	V-8
R	Olds	350	4bbl	—	V-8
Z	Pont.	400	4bbl	—	V-8
K	Olds	403	4bbl	—	V-8

(Factory Time)	Chilton Time
both (7.6)	9.4
350 eng, Code X	
one (3.1)	4.2
both (5.0)	6.8
301 eng, Code Y	
one (4.0)	5.1
both (5.9)	7.7
w/A.C. add (.5)	.5
w/P.S. add (.3)	.3
w/A.I.R. add (.2)	.2

(P) Clean Carbon and Grind Valves
Includes: R&R cylinder heads, clean gasket surfaces, clean carbon, reface valves and seats. Minor tune up.

V-6—1976–80 (4.2)	7.1
w/Turbocharger add (1.4)	1.4
V-8—1974–76 (5.0)	8.8
1977–80	
350 eng, Code J (5.3)	7.8
350–403 engs, Code R or K (7.2)	9.3
305–350 engs, Code U or L (8.8)	10.4
305 eng, Code X (4.9)	7.8
301 eng, Code Y (5.4)	8.7
w/A.C. add (.5)	.5
w/P.S. add (.3)	.3
w/A.I.R. add (.2)	.2

(G) Valve Tappets, Renew
Includes: Drain and refill cooling system. R&R intake manifold. Make all necessary adjustments.

V-6—1976–80—one bank (1.4)	2.3
both banks (1.8)	2.9
w/Turbocharger add (1.3)	1.4
V-8—1974–76—one bank (1.7)	2.3
both banks (2.2)	3.3
1977–80	
350 eng, Code J	
one bank (1.5)	2.1
both banks (2.0)	3.1
350–403 engs, Code R or K	
one bank (2.2)	2.8
both banks (3.1)	3.8
305–350 engs, Code U or L	
one bank (2.6)	3.1
both banks (3.3)	4.1
305 eng, Code X	
one bank (1.5)	2.1
both banks (2.0)	3.1
301 eng, Code Y	
one bank (2.5)	3.1
both banks (3.4)	4.1
w/A.C. add (.3)	.3
w/A.I.R. add (.3)	.3

(G) Valve Spring or Valve Stem Oil Seals, Renew (Head on Car)

V-6—1976–80—one cyl (.6)	.8
one cyl-each bank (1.2)	1.4
w/Turbocharger add (1.3)	1.4
V-8—1974–76—one cyl (.8)	1.1
one cyl-each bank (1.4)	1.9
1977–80	
350 eng, Code J	
one cyl (.7)	1.0
one cyl-each bank (1.4)	1.9
350–403 engs, Code R or K	
one cyl (.6)	.9
one cyl-each bank (1.1)	1.6
305–350 engs, Code U or L	
one cyl (.9)	1.2

(Factory Time)	Chilton Time
one cyl-each bank (1.6)	2.1
305 eng, Code X	
one cyl (.7)	1.0
one cyl-each bank (1.4)	1.9
301 eng, Code Y	
one cyl (.6)	.9
one cyl-each bank (1.1)	1.6
Each adtnl cyl-all engines (.3)	.4
w/A.C. add (.3)	.3
w/A.I.R. add (.3)	.3

(G) Rocker Arm Shafts and/or Assys., Renew

V-6—1976–80—one side (.4)	.6
both sides (.7)	.9
w/Turbocharger add (1.3)	1.4
V-8—1974–76—one side (.6)	.8
both sides (1.0)	1.2
1977	
350 eng, Code J	
one side (.5)	.7
both sides (.8)	1.0
350–403 engs, Code R or K	
one side (.6)	.8
both sides (1.1)	1.3
1978–80	
350 eng, Code X	
one side (.5)	.7
both sides (.8)	1.0
w/A.C. add (.3)	.3
w/A.I.R. add (.3)	.3
Recond each side add (.2)	.3

(G) Rocker Arms, Renew

V-8—1977–80	
350–403 engs, Code R or K	
one side (.6)	.9
both sides (1.1)	1.5
305–350 engs, Code U or L	
one side (1.0)	1.3
both sides (1.5)	1.9
301 eng, Code Y	
one side (.6)	.9
both sides (1.0)	1.4
w/A.C. add (.3)	.3
w/A.I.R. add (.3)	.3

(G) Push Rods, Renew

V-6—1976–80—one side (.4)	.6
both sides (.7)	.9
w/Turbocharger add (1.3)	1.4
V-8—1974–76—one side (.6)	.8
both sides (1.0)	1.2
1977–80	
350 eng, Code J	
one side (.5)	.7
both sides (.8)	1.0
350–403 engs, Code R or K	
one side (.6)	.8
both sides (1.1)	1.3
305–350 engs, Code U or L	
one side (1.0)	1.2
both sides (1.5)	1.7
350 eng, Code X	
one side (.5)	.7
both sides (.8)	1.0
301 eng, Code Y	
one side (.6)	.8
both sides (1.0)	1.2
w/A.C. add (.3)	.3
w/A.I.R. add (.3)	.3

(Factory Time)	Chilton Time

Buick Riviera (1979–80)

(G) Cylinder Head Gasket, Renew
Includes: Clean gasket surfaces, clean carbon, make all necessary adjustments.

V-6—1979–80—right side (2.9) ...	3.8
left side (3.2)	4.1
both sides (4.5)	6.0
V-8—1979–80—Eng Code R	
one side (2.7)	3.6
both sides (4.9)	6.4
w/A.I.R. add (.3)	.3
w/A.C. add (.3)	.3
w/P.S. add (.2)	.2

(G) Cylinder Head, Renew
Includes: Transfer all parts, reface valves, make all necessary adjustments.

V-6—1979–80—right side (3.5) ...	4.8
left side (3.8)	5.1
both sides (5.7)	7.5
V-8—1979–80—Eng Code R	
one side (3.5)	4.6
both sides (6.5)	8.3
w/A.I.R. add (.3)	.3
w/A.C. add (.3)	.3
w/P.S. add (.2)	.2

(P) Clean Carbon and Grind Valves
Includes: R&R cylinder heads, clean gasket surfaces, clean carbon, reface valves and seats. Minor tune up.

V-6—1979–80 (5.6)	8.5
V-8—1979–80—Eng Code R (6.5) .	9.3
w/A.I.R. add (.3)	.3
w/A.C. add (.3)	.3
w/P.S. add (.2)	.2

(G) Valve Tappets, Renew
Includes: Drain and refill cooling system. R&R intake manifold. Make all necessary adjustments.

V-6—1979–80—one bank (2.2) ...	3.1
both banks (2.6)	3.7
V-8—1979–80—Eng Code R	
one bank (2.2)	2.8
both banks (3.1)	3.8
w/A.C. add (.2)	.2
w/A.I.R. add (.4)	.4

(G) Valve Spring or Valve Stem Oil Seals, Renew (Head on Car)

V-6—1979–80—one cyl (.6)	.8
one cyl—each bank (1.2)	1.4
w/Turbocharger add (1.3)	1.4
V-8—1979–80—Eng Code R	
one cyl (.6)	.9
one cyl—each bank (1.1)	1.6
each adtnl cyl—all engines (.3) ...	.4
w/A.C. add (.3)	.3
w/A.I.R. add (.3)	.3

(G) Rocker Arm Shafts and/or Assy., Renew

V-6—1979–80	
one side (.4)	.6
both sides (.7)	.9
w/Turbocharger add (1.3)	1.4
V-8—1979–80—Eng Code R	
one side (.6)	.8
both sides (1.1)	1.3
w/A.C. add (.3)	.3
w/A.I.R. add (.3)	.3
Recond each side add (.2)	.3

	Chilton Time
(G) Rocker Arms and/or Pivots, Renew	
V-8—1979–80—Eng Code R	
one side (.6)	.9
both sides (1.1)	1.5
w/A.C. add (.3)	.3
(G) Push Rods, Renew	
V-6—1979–80	
one side (.4)	.6
both sides (.7)	.9
w/Turbocharger add (1.3)	1.4
V-8—1979–80—Eng Code R	
one side (.6)	.8
both sides (1.1)	1.3
w/A.C. add (.3)	.3
w/A.I.R. add (.3)	.3

Buick Apollo, Century, Gran Sport, Regal, Skylark (1974–79)

(G) Cylinder Head Gasket, Renew
Includes: Clean gasket surfaces, clean carbon, make all necessary adjustments.

	Chilton Time
Six—1974–75 (2.4)	3.5
V-6—1975–80—one (2.1)	3.0
both (3.1)	4.6
w/Turbocharger add (1.4)	1.4
V-8—1974–76—one (2.7)	3.6
both (4.0)	5.5
1977–80	
350 eng, Code J	
one (2.4)	3.3
both (3.6)	5.1

**Buick
Serial Number
4B37 C 7H100001
1977 Engine Codes**

C	Buick	231	2bbl	—	V-6
Y	Pont.	301	2bbl	—	V-8
U	Chev.	305	2bbl	—	V-8
R	Olds	350	4bbl	—	V-8
L	Chev.	350	4bbl	—	V-8
J	Pont.	350	4bbl	—	V-8
H	Pont.	350	2bbl	—	V-8
K	Olds	403	4bbl	—	V-8

1978–79 Engine Codes

C	Chev.	196	2bbl	—	V-6
C	Buick	231	2bbl	—	V-6
A	Buick	231	2bbl	—	V-6
G	Buick	231	2bbl	(Turbo)	V-6
2	Buick	231	2bbl	—	V-6
3	Buick	231	4bbl	(Turbo)	V-6
Z	Buick	231	2bbl	(Calif.)	V-6
F	Olds	260	2bbl	—	V-8
Y	Pont.	301	2bbl	—	V-8
H	Chev.	305	4bbl	—	V-8
U	Chev.	305	2bbl	—	V-8
U	Olds	350	2bbl	—	V-8
L	Chev.	350	4bbl	—	V-8
X	Buick	350	4bbl	—	V-8
R	Olds	350	4bbl	—	V-8
Z	Pont.	400	4bbl	—	V-8
K	Olds	403	4bbl	—	V-8

	Chilton Time
350–403 engs, Code R or K	
one (3.4)	4.3
both (4.9)	6.4
305–350 engs, Code U, H or L	
one (4.5)	5.4
both (6.2)	7.7
w/A.C. add (.5)	.5
w/P.S. add (.5)	.3
w/A.I.R. add (.2)	.2
(G) Cylinder Head, Renew	
Includes: Transfer all parts, reface valves, make all necessary adjustments.	
Six—1974–75 (3.4)	4.5
V-6—1975–80—one (2.7)	4.0
both (4.3)	6.1
w/Turbocharger add (1.4)	1.4
V-8—1974–76—one (3.7)	4.8
both (6.0)	7.8
1977–80	
350 eng, Code J	
one (3.1)	4.2
both (5.0)	6.8
350–403 engs, Code R or K	
one (4.2)	5.3
both (6.5)	8.3
305–350 engs, Code U, H or L	
one (5.4)	6.3
both (7.7)	9.5
w/A.C. add (.5)	.5
w/P.S. add (.3)	.3
w/A.I.R. add (.2)	.2
(P) Clean Carbon and Grind Valves	
Includes: R&R cylinder heads, clean gasket surfaces, clean carbon, reface valves and seats. Minor tune up.	
Six—1974–75 (4.8)	6.0
V-6—1975–80 (4.2)	7.1
w/Turbocharger add (1.4)	1.4
V-8—1974–76 (5.0)	8.8
1977–80	
350 eng, Code J (5.3)	7.8
350–403 engs, Code R or K (7.2)	9.3
305–350 engs, Code U, H or L (7.7)	9.8
w/A.C. add (.5)	.5
w/P.S. add (.3)	.3
w/A.I.R. add (.2)	.2
(G) Valve Tappets, Renew	
Includes: Drain and refill cooling system. R&R intake manifold. Make all necessary adjustments.	
Six—1974–75 (1.3)	2.0
V-6—1975–80—one bank (1.4)	2.3
both banks (1.8)	2.9
w/Turbocharger add (1.3)	1.4
V-8—1974–76—one bank (1.7)	2.3
both banks (2.2)	3.3
1977–80	
350 eng, Code J	
one bank (1.5)	2.1
both banks (2.0)	3.1
350–403 engs, Code R or K	
one bank (2.2)	2.8
both banks (3.1)	3.8
305–350 engs, Code U, H or L	
one bank (2.6)	3.1
both banks (3.3)	4.1
w/A.C. add (.3)	.3
w/A.I.R. add (.3)	.3

(Factory Time)	Chilton Time

(G) Valve Spring or Valve Stem Oil Seals, Renew (Head on Car)

Six—1974–75—one cyl (.6)	.9
each adtnl cyl (.1)	.2
V-6—1975–80—one cyl (.6)	.8
one cyl-each bank (1.2)	1.4
w/Turbocharger add (1.3)	1.4
V-8—1974–76—one cyl (.8)	1.1
one cyl-each bank (1.4)	1.9
1977–80	
350 eng, Code J	
one cyl (.7)	1.0
one cyl-each bank (1.4)	1.9
350–403 engs, Code R or K	
one cyl (.6)	.9
one cyl-each bank (1.1)	1.6
305–350 engs, Code U, H or L	
one cyl (.9)	1.2
one cyl-each bank (1.6)	2.1
each adtnl cyl-all engines (.3)	.4
w/A.C. add (.3)	.3
w/A.I.R. add (.3)	.3

(G) Rocker Arm Shafts and/or Assy., Renew

Six—1974–75 (.7)	.9
V-6—1975–80—one side (.4)	.6
both sides (.7)	.9
w/Turbocharger add (1.3)	1.4
V-8—1974–76—one side (.6)	.8
both sides (1.0)	1.2
1977	
350 eng, Code J	
one side (.5)	.7
both sides (.8)	1.0
350–403 engs, Code R or K	
one side (.6)	.8
both sides (1.1)	1.3
w/A.C. add (.3)	.3
w/A.I.R. add (.3)	.3
Recond each side add (.2)	.3

(G) Rocker Arms, Renew

V-8—1977–80	
350–403 engs, Code R or K	
one side (.6)	.9
both sides (1.1)	1.5
305–350 engs, Code U, H or L	
one side (1.0)	1.3
both sides (1.5)	1.9
w/A.C. add (.3)	.3
w/A.I.R. add (.3)	.3

(G) Push Rods, Renew

Six—1974–75—all (.7)	1.0
V-6—1975–80—one side (.4)	.6
both sides (.7)	.9
w/Turbocharger add (1.3)	1.4
V-8—1974–76—one side (.6)	.8
both sides (1.0)	1.2
1977–80	
350 eng, Code J	
one side (.5)	.7
both sides (.8)	1.0
350–403 engs, Code R or K	
one side (.6)	.8
both sides (1.1)	1.3
305–350 engs, Code U, H or L	
one side (1.0)	1.2
both sides (1.5)	1.7
w/A.C. add (.3)	.3
w/A.I.R. add (.3)	.3

(Factory Time)	Chilton Time

Buick Skyhawk

(G) Cylinder Head Gasket, Renew
Includes: Clean gasket surfaces, clean carbon, make all necessary adjustments.

1975–80—right side (2.1)	3.0
left side (2.3)	3.2
both sides (3.4)	4.9
w/A.C. add (.4)	.4
w/P.S. add (.3)	.3
w/A.I.R. add (.3)	.3

(G) Cylinder Head, Renew
Includes: Transfer all parts, reface valves, make all necessary adjustments.

1975–80—right side (2.7)	4.0
left side (2.9)	4.2
both sides (4.6)	6.4
w/A.C. add (.4)	.4
w/P.S. add (.3)	.3
w/A.I.R. add (.3)	.3

(P) Clean Carbon and Grind Valves
Includes: R&R cylinder heads, clean gasket surfaces, clean carbon, reface valves and seats. Minor tune up.

1975–80 (4.5)	7.4
w/A.C. add (.4)	.4
w/P.S. add (.3)	.3
w/A.I.R. add (.3)	.3

(G) Valve Tappets, Renew
Includes: Drain and refill cooling system. R&R intake manifold. Make all necessary adjustments.

1975–80—one bank (1.4)	2.3
both banks (1.8)	2.9
w/A.C. add (.2)	.3
w/A.I.R. add (.3)	.3

(G) Valve Spring or Valve Stem Oil Seals, Renew (Head on Car)

1975–80—one cyl (.6)	.8
one cyl-each bank (1.2)	1.4
each adtnl cyl (.3)	.4
w/A.C. add (.2)	.3
w/A.I.R. add (.3)	.3

(G) Rocker Arm Shafts and/or Assy., Renew

1975–80—one side (.4)	.6
both sides (.7)	.9
Recond each side add (.2)	.3
w/A.C. add (.2)	.3
w/A.I.R. add (.3)	.3

(G) Push Rods, Renew

1975–80—one side (.4)	.6
both sides (.7)	.9
w/A.C. add (.2)	.3
w/A.I.R. add (.3)	.3

Cadillac

GASOLINE ENGINES

(G) Cylinder Head Gasket, Renew
Includes: Clean carbon and make all necessary adjustments.

1974—right (2.1)	3.5
left (1.9)	3.3
both (3.4)	5.4
1975–77—right (2.4)	3.8
left (2.2)	3.6

(Factory Time)	Chilton Time
both (3.7)	5.7
1978–80—right (2.8)	4.2
left (2.6)	4.0
both (4.3)	5.7
w/A.C. add	.5
w/A.I.R. add	.2

(G) Cylinder Head, Renew
Includes: Transfer all components, reface valves, clean carbon.

1974—right (2.8)	4.2
left (2.6)	4.0
both (4.5)	7.4
1975–77—right (3.1)	4.5
left (2.9)	4.3
both (4.8)	7.7
1978–80—right (4.3)	5.7
left (4.0)	5.4
both (7.1)	7.7
w/A.C. add	.5
w/A.I.R. add	.2

(P) Clean Carbon and Grind Valves
Includes: R&R cylinder heads, grind valves and seats. Minor tune up.

1974 (6.8)	9.7
1975–77 (6.0)	9.7
1978–80 (6.6)	9.7
w/A.C. add	.5
w/A.I.R. add	.2

(G) Valve Tappets, Renew
Includes: Test and bleed lifter, make all necessary adjustments.

1974—one (1.9)	2.5
one each bank (2.2)	2.8
all both banks (2.8)	3.4
1975–80—one (2.4)	3.1
one each bank (2.6)	3.2
all both banks (3.1)	4.0
w/A.C. add	.5

(G) Valve Springs or Valve Stem Oil Seals, Renew (Head on Car)

1974–77—right bank—one (.7) . . .	1.0
left bank—one (1.0)	1.3
each adtnl (.1)	.2
1978–80—each bank—one (.7) . . .	1.0
each adtnl (.2)	.2

(G) Rocker Arm T-Bar Assy., and/or Push Rod, Renew

1974–80—one (.6)	1.0
all—one bank (1.0)	1.5

DIESEL ENGINE

(G) Cylinder Head Gasket, Renew
Includes: Clean carbon and make all necessary adjustments.

1979–80—right (4.7)	5.6
left (4.1)	5.6
both (6.2)	7.7

(G) Cylinder Head, Renew
Includes: Transfer all components, reface valves, clean carbon.

1979–80—right (5.7)	7.1
left (5.1)	6.5
both (8.3)	9.7

(P) Clean Carbon and Grind Valves
Includes: R&R cylinder heads, grind valves and seats. Make all necessary adjustments.

1979–80 (8.5)	10.5

(Factory Time)	Chilton Time

(G) Valve tappets, Renew
Includes: Test and bleed lifters, make all necessary adjustments.

1979–80—one (3.1)	4.0
one—each bank (3.3)	4.2
all—both banks (5.3)	6.8

(G) Valve Springs or Valve Stem Oil Seals, Renew (Head on Car)

1979–80—one (1.7)	2.1
one—each bank (2.2)	2.7
each adtnl (.2)	.3

(G) Rocker Arm T-Bar Assy., and/or Push Rod, Renew

1979–80—each bank—one (1.4) . .	1.9
each adtnl (.1)	.2

Cadillac Seville

GASOLINE ENGINE

(G) Cylinder Head Gasket, Renew
Includes: Clean carbon and make all necessary adjustments.

1976–77—right (2.8)	3.7
left (2.4)	3.3
both (4.3)	5.8
1978–80—right (3.2)	4.1
left (2.9)	3.7
both (4.9)	6.4
w/A.I.R. add (.2)	.2

(G) Cylinder Head, Renew
Includes: Transfer all components, reface valves, clean carbon.

1976–77—right (3.6)	4.7
left (3.2)	4.3
both (5.9)	7.8
1978–80—right (4.6)	5.7
left (4.3)	5.4
both (7.7)	9.8
w/A.I.R. add (.2)	.2

(P) Clean Carbon and Grind Valves
Includes: R&R cylinder heads, grind valves and seats. Minor tune up.

1976–77 (6.6)	8.8
1978–80 (7.2)	9.4
w/A.I.R. add (.2)	.2

(G) Valve Tappets, Renew
Includes: Test and bleed lifter, make all necessary adjustments.

1976–77—one (2.4)	3.1
one each bank (2.6)	3.3
all both banks (2.7)	4.0
1978–80—one side (2.6)	3.3
all—both sides (3.1)	4.4

(G) Valve Springs or Valve Stem Oil Seals, Renew (Head on Car)

1976–77—right bank—one (1.0) . .	1.3
left bank—one (.5)	.9
one—each bank (1.6)	2.1
each adtnl (.2)	.2
1978–80—right bank—one (1.0) . .	1.3
left bank—one (.9)	1.3
one—each bank (1.6)	2.1
each adtnl (.2)	.2

(G) Rocker Arm T-Bar Assy., and/or Push Rod, Renew

1976–77—right bank—one (.9) . . .	1.2
left bank—one (.5)	.8
each adtnl (.1)	.2

(Factory Time)	Chilton Time
1978–80—one bank (.9)	1.2
all—both banks (1.0)	2.0

DIESEL ENGINE

(G) Cylinder Head Gasket, Renew
Includes: Clean carbon and make all necessary adjustments.

1978–80—right (4.7)	5.6
left (4.1)	5.0
both (6.2)	7.7

(G) Cylinder Head, Renew
Includes: Transfer all components, reface valves, clean carbon.

1978–80—right (5.7)	7.1
left (5.1)	6.5
both (8.3)	9.7

(P) Clean Carbon and Grind Valves
Includes: R&R cylinder heads, grind valves and seats. Make all necessary adjustments.

1978–80 (8.5)	10.5

(G) Rocker Arm Cover or Gaskets, Renew

1978–80—each (1.4)	1.7

(G) Valve Tappets, Renew
Includes: Test and bleed lifters, make all necessary adjustments.

1978–80—one (3.1)	4.0
one each bank (3.3)	4.2
all—both banks (5.3)	6.8

(G) Valve Springs or Valve Stem Oil Seals, Renew (Head on Car)

1978–80—one (1.7)	2.1
one each bank (2.2)	2.7
each adtnl (.2)	.3

(G) Rocker Arm T-Bar Assy., and/or Push Rod, Renew

1978–80—each bank—one (1.4)	1.9
each adtnl (.1)	.2

Cadillac Eldorado

GASOLINE ENGINES

(G) Cylinder Head Gasket, Renew
Includes: Clean carbon and make all necessary adjustments.

1974—right (2.1)	3.5
left (1.9)	3.3
both (3.4)	5.4
1975–77—right (2.4)	3.8
left (2.2)	3.6
both (3.7)	5.7
1978–80—right (3.2)	4.1
left (2.9)	3.7
both (4.9)	6.4
w/A.C. add	.5
w/A.I.R. add	.2

(G) Cylinder Head, Renew
Includes: Transfer all components, reface valves, clean carbon.

1974—right (2.8)	4.1
left (2.6)	3.9
both (4.5)	7.4
1975–77—right (3.1)	4.7
left (2.9)	4.3

(Factory Time)	Chilton Time
both (4.8)	7.7
1978–80—right (4.6)	5.7
left (4.3)	5.4
both (7.7)	9.8
w/A.C. add	.5
w/A.I.R. add	.2

(P) Clean Carbon and Grind Valves
Includes: R&R cylinder heads, grind valves, and seats. Minor tune up.

1974 (6.8)	9.7
1975–77 (6.0)	9.7
1978–80 (7.2)	9.4
w/A.C. add	.5
w/A.I.R. add	.2

(G) Valve Tappets, Renew
Includes: Test and bleed lifters, make all necessary adjustments.

1974—one (1.9)	2.5
one each bank (2.2)	2.8
all both banks (2.8)	3.4
1975–77—one (2.4)	3.1
one each bank (2.6)	3.3
all both banks (3.3)	4.0
1978–80—one bank (2.4)	3.3
all—both banks (3.1)	4.4
w/A.C. add	.5

(G) Valve Springs or Valve Stem Oil Seals, Renew (Head on Car)

1974–77—right bank—one (.7)	1.0
left bank—one (1.0)	1.3
each adtnl (.1)	.2
1978–80—right bank—one (1.0)	1.3
left bank—one (.9)	1.3
one—each bank (1.6)	2.1
each adtnl (.2)	.2

G) Rocker Arm T-Bar Assy., and/or Push Rod, Renew

1974–77—one (.6)	1.0
all one bank (1.0)	1.5
1978–80—one bank (.9)	1.2
all both banks (1.0)	2.0

DIESEL ENGINE

(G) Compression Test

1979–80	1.3

(G) Cylinder Head Gasket, Renew
Includes: Clean carbon and make all necessary adjustments.

1979–80—right (4.7)	5.6
left (4.1)	5.0
both (6.2)	7.7

(G) Cylinder Head, Renew
Includes: Transfer all components, reface valves, clean carbon.

1979–80—right (5.7)	7.1
left (5.1)	6.5
both (8.3)	9.7

(P) Clean Carbon and Grind Valves
Includes: R&R cylinder heads, grind valves and seats. Make all necessary adjustments.

1979–80 (8.5)	10.5

(G) Valve Tappets, Renew
Includes: Test and bleed lifters, make all necessary adjustments.

1979–80—one (3.1)	4.0
one each bank (3.3)	4.2
all—both banks (5.3)	6.8

	Chilton Time		Chilton Time
(Factory Time)		(Factory Time)	

(G) Valve Springs or Valve Stem Oil Seals, Renew (Head on Car)

1979–80—one (1.7)	2.1
one each bank (2.2)	2.7
each adtnl (.2)	.3

(G) Rocker Arm T-Bar Assy., and/or Push Rod, Renew

1979–80—each bank—one (1.4) ..	1.9
each adtnl (.1)	.2

Camaro, Chevelle, Malibu, Monte Carlo, Nova

(G) Cylinder Head Gasket, Renew
Includes: Clean carbon and make all necessary adjustments.

Six—1974 (1.9)	3.2
1975–80 (2.9)	4.2
V-6—1978–80	
200 eng—one side (3.2)	4.4
both sides (4.5)	6.7
231 eng—one side (2.1)	3.3
both sides (3.1)	5.3
V-8—1974—one side (4.0)	5.2
both sides (5.8)	8.1
1975–80—right side (4.5)	5.7
left side (3.9)	5.1
both sides (6.2)	8.5
w/P.S. add (.3)	.3
w/A.C. add (.5)	.5
w/A.I.R. add (.2)	.2

(G) Cylinder Head, Renew
Includes: Transfer all components, reface valves, clean carbon.

Six—1974 (2.9)	5.1
1975–80 (4.8)	6.1
V-6—1978–80	
200 eng—one side (3.2)	4.5
both sides (4.5)	7.0
231 eng—one side (2.7)	4.3
both sides (4.3)	6.3
V-8—1974—one side (4.8)	6.1
both sides (7.4)	9.9
1975–80—right side (5.4)	6.7
left side (4.8)	6.1
both sides (7.7)	10.2
w/P.S. add (.3)	.3
w/A.C. add (.5)	.5
w/A.I.R. add (.2)	.2

(P) Clean Carbon and Grind Valves
Includes: R&R cylinder head, grind valves and seats. Minor tune up.

Six—1974 (3.5)	6.1
1975–80 (4.8)	7.1
V-6—1978–80	
200 eng—one side (4.2)	6.0
both sides (6.3)	9.1
231 eng—one side (2.9)	5.2
both sides (4.5)	7.0
V-8—1974—one side (5.4)	6.9
both sides (8.7)	11.5
1975–80—right side (5.8)	7.3
left side (5.2)	6.7
both sides (9.0)	11.8
w/P.S. add (.3)	.3
w/A.C. add (.5)	.5
w/A.I.R. add (.2)	.2

(G) Valve Tappets, Adjust

Six—1974–80 (.5)	.8
V-6—1978–80 (.6)	1.1
V-8—1974–80 (.7)	1.2

(G) Valve Tappets, Renew
Includes: R&R intake manifold on V-6 & V-8 engines. Make all necessary adjustments.

Six—1974—one (.8)	1.4
all (1.3)	2.1
1975–80—one (.7)	1.3
all (1.2)	2.0
V-6—1978–80	
200 eng—one (1.9)	2.9
all (2.6)	3.6
231 eng—one (1.4)	2.4
all (1.8)	2.8
V-8—1974—one (2.0)	3.0
all (2.8)	3.8
1975–80—one (2.5)	3.5
all (3.3)	4.3
w/A.C. add (.2)	.2
w/A.I.R. add (.1)	.1

(G) Valve Springs or Valve Stem Oil Seals, Renew (Head on Car)

Six—1974—one (.7)	1.0
all (2.0)	3.0
1975–80—one (.8)	1.0
all (2.0)	3.0
V-6—1978–80	
200 eng—one (.8)	1.2
all (2.8)	3.8
231 eng—one (.6)	1.1
all (2.6)	3.7
V-8—1974—one (.8)	1.2
all (3.0)	4.0
1975–80—one (.9)	1.3
all (3.1)	4.1
w/A.C. add (.2)	.2
w/A.I.R. add (.1)	.1

(G) Valve Rocker Arms or Push Rods, Renew

Six—1974—one (.5)	.9
all (.7)	1.3

Chevrolet & Corvette

(G) Cylinder Head Gasket, Renew
Includes: Clean carbon and make all necessary adjustments.

Six—1977–80 (2.9)	5.0
w/A.C. (.5)	.5
w/P.S. or A.I.R. add (.6)	.6
V-8—1974–76	
350, 400 engs—one (4.2)	5.5
both (6.0)	8.2
454 eng—one (4.3)	5.6
both (6.3)	8.5
1977–80—305, 350 engs	
right (4.3)	5.6
left (4.0)	5.3
both (6.0)	8.2
w/P.S. add (.3)	.3
w/A.C. add (.6)	.6
w/A.I.R. add (.3)	.3

(G) Cylinder Head, Renew
Includes: Transfer all components, reface valves, clean carbon.

(Factory Time)	Chilton Time
Six—1977–80 (4.8)	7.0
w/A.C. add (.5)	.5
w/P.S. or A.I.R. add (.6)	.6
V-8—1974–76	
350, 400 engs—one (5.0)	6.3
both (7.6).......................	9.5
454 eng—one (5.0)	6.3
both (7.9).......................	9.8
1977–80—305, 350 engs	
right (5.2)	6.5
left (4.9)	6.2
both (7.7)	10.2
w/P.S. add (.3)	.3
w/A.C. add (.6)	.6
w/A.I.R. add (.3)	.3

(P) Clean Carbon and Grind Valves
Includes: R&R cylinder head, grind valves and seats. Minor tune up.

Six—1977–80 (4.8)	7.7
w/A.C. add (.5)	.5
w/P.S. or A.I.R. add (.6)	.6
V-8—1974–76	
350, 400 engs—one side (5.6)	8.3
both sides (8.9)	12.0
454 eng—one side (5.7)	8.4
both sides (9.0)	12.2
1977–80—305, 350 engs	
right (5.8)	8.5
left (5.3)	8.0
both (8.7)	12.0
w/P.S. add (.3)	.3
w/A.C. add (.6)	.6
w/A.I.R. add (.3)	.3

(G) Valve Tappets, Adjust

Six—1977–80 (.5)	.7
V-8—1974–80	
305, 350 engs (.7)	1.2
400, 454 engs (1.0)	1.5

(G) Valve Tappets, Renew
Includes: R&R intake manifold on V-8. Make all necessary adjustments.

Six—1977–80—one (.7)	1.4
all (1.2).........................	2.6
V-8—1974–76—one (2.4)	3.4
all (3.2).........................	4.2
1977–80—one (2.5)	3.5
all (3.3).........................	4.3
w/A.C. add (.2)	.2
w/A.I.R. add (.3)	.3

(G) Valve Springs or Valve Stem Oil Seals, Renew (Head on Car)

Six—1977–80—one (.8)	1.1
all (2.0).........................	3.0
V-8—1974–75—one (.8)	1.2
all (3.0).........................	4.0
1976–80—one (1.4)...............	1.7
all (3.8).........................	5.0
w/A.C. add (.2)	.2
w/A.I.R. add (.1)	.1

(G) Valve Rocker Arms or Push Rods, Renew

Six—1977–80—one (.6)	.9
each adtnl (.3)	.3
V-8—1974—one (.6)	.9
all (1.9)	2.5
1975–80—one (.7)	1.0
all (1.5)	2.5
w/A.C. add (.2)	.2
w/A.I.R. add (.1)	.1

(Factory Time)	Chilton Time
(G) Rocker Arm Stud, Renew	
Six—1977–80—one (.9)	1.2
V-8—1974–75—one (.7)	1.0
1976–80—one (.9)	1.2
each adtnl (.3)	.3
w/A.C. add (.2)	.2
w/A.I.R. add (.1)	.1

Chevette

(G) Cylinder Head Gasket, Renew
Includes: Clean carbon and make all necessary adjustments.

1976–80 (3.3)	4.5
w/A.C. add (.3)	.3
w/A.I.R. add (.2)	.2

(G) Cylinder Head, Renew
Includes: Transfer all components, reface valves, clean carbon.

1976–80 (4.8)	6.7
w/A.C. add (.3)	.3
w/A.I.R. add (.2)	.2

(P) Clean Carbon and Grind Valves
Includes: R&R cylinder head, grind valves and seats. Minor tune up.

1976–80 (4.7)	7.0
w/A.C. add (.3)	.3
w/A.I.R. add (.2)	.2

(G) Valve Rocker Arms, Renew

1976–80—one (.6)	1.0
all (.9)	1.5

(G) Valve Rocker Arm Adjusters, Renew

1976–80—one (.6)	1.0
all (.9)	1.5

(G) Valve Tappets, Renew

1976–80—one (.6)	1.1
all (.9)	1.7

(G) Valve Spring or Valve Stem Oil Seals, Renew (Head On Car)

1976–80—one (.7)	1.2
all (1.2)	2.0

Citation, Omega, Phoenix, Skylark—All 1980

(G) Cylinder Head Gasket, Renew
Includes: Clean carbon and make all necessary adjustments.

Four—1980 (2.7)	3.9
w/Cruise control add (.2)	.2
w/A.C. add (.5)	.5
V-6—1980—right (3.7)	5.0
left (3.9)	5.2
both (4.6)	6.4
w/Cruise control add (.2)	.2
w/A.C. add (.4)	.4
w/P.S. add (.3)	.3

(G) Cylinder Head, Renew
Includes: Transfer all components, reface valves, clean carbon.

Four—1980 (3.5)	5.0
w/Cruise control add (.2)	.2
w/A.C. add (.5)	.5
V-6—right (4.3)	6.1
left (4.6)	6.4

(Factory Time)	Chilton Time		(Factory Time)	Chilton Time
both (5.9)	7.7		both (6.9)	9.4
w/Cruise control add (.2)	.2		400–440 engs—one (5.1)	6.0
w/A.C. add (.4)	.4		both (6.6)	9.6
w/P.S. add (.3)	.3		w/A.C. add (.4)	.5

(P) Clean Carbon and Grind Valves
Includes: R&R cylinder heads, grind valves and seats. Minor engine tune up.

Four—1980 (4.3)	6.0
w/Cruise control add (.2)	.2
w/A.C. add (.5)	.5
V-6—1980 (6.4)	8.7
w/Cruise control add (.2)	.2
w/A.C. add (.4)	.4
w/P.S. add (.3)	.3

(G) Valve Rocker Arms or Push Rods, Renew

Four—1980	
one or two (.6)	.9
three or more (.8)	1.1
V-6—1980	
one or two (.8)	1.1
three or six (1.0)	1.3
all (1.9)	2.2
w/Cruise control add (.2)	.2

(G) Valve Rocker Arm Stud, Renew (One)
Includes: Drain and refill cooling system on V-6 engine.

Four—1980 (.5)	.8
each adtnl (.1)	.1
V-6—1980 (.9)	1.2
each adtnl (.2)	.2
w/Cruise control add (.2)	.2

(G) Valve Spring and/or Valve Stem Oil Seals, Renew (Head on Car)

Four—1980—one cyl (.7)	1.0
all cyls (1.4)	1.9
V-6—1980	
one cyl (1.1)	1.4
one cyl—each bank (2.2)	2.8
all cyls—both banks (2.9)	3.6
w/Cruise control add (.2)	.2

(G) Valve Tappets, Renew
Includes: R&R intake manifold and make all necessary adjustments.

Four—1980—one (2.2)	2.8
all (2.7)	3.4
V-6—1980—one (2.8)	3.7
all (3.3)	4.3
w/Cruise control add (.2)	.2

Chrysler, Cordoba, Imperial

(G) Cylinder Head Gasket, Renew
Includes: Clean carbon.

Six—1979–80 (2.6)	3.5
V-8—1974–80	
318–360 engs—one (3.1)	3.8
both (4.3)	5.4
400–440 engs—one (3.4)	4.2
both (4.3)	6.1
w/A.C. add (.4)	.5

(G) Cylinder Head, Renew
Includes: Reface and adjust valves, clean carbon.

Six—1979–80 (5.4)	6.5
V-8—1974–80	
318–360 engs—one (4.4)	5.4

(P) Clean Carbon and Grind Valves
Includes: R&R cylinder heads, adjust valve clearance when required, minor engine tune up.

Six—1979–80 (4.9)	8.1
V-8—1974–80	
318–360 engs (8.8)	11.0
400–440 engs (7.2)	12.0
w/A.C. add (.4)	.5
w/100 amp alter add (.4)	.4

(G) Valve Tappets, Renew
Note: Factory time based on using magnetic tool thru push rod opening to remove lifters. Chilton experience finds it better and safer to R&R intake manifold, since the lifters have a tendency to stick in the block and sometimes come apart. Includes: R&R cylinder head on 6 cyl engine.

Six—1979–80	
mechanical—one or all (3.3)	4.4
hydraulic—one or all (2.5)	4.4
V-8—1974–80	
318–360 engs	
one (2.0)	3.0
one—each bank (2.1)	3.4
all—both banks (2.2)	3.9
400–440 engs	
one (.9)	2.2
one—each bank (1.6)	3.0
all—both banks (3.0)	4.4
w/A.C. add (.4)	.5
w/100 amp alter add (.4)	.4

(G) Valve Spring or Valve Stem Oil Seal, Renew (Head on Car)
Includes: Adjust valve clearance when required.

Six—1979–80—one (.9)	1.3
all (2.2)	3.0
V-8—1974–80	
one (.7)	1.1
one—each bank (1.3)	1.7
all—both banks (3.2)	4.0
w/A.C. add (.4)	.5
w/100 amp alter add (.4)	.4

(G) Rocker Arm Assembly, Recondition
Includes: Renew arms as required and shaft if necessary.

Six—1979–80 (.9)	1.4
V-8—1974–80	
one side (.6)	1.3
both sides (1.0)	2.1
w/A.C. add (.4)	.5
w/100 amp alter add (.4)	.4

(G) Valve Push Rods, Renew

Six—1979–80—one (.8)	1.0
all (1.1)	1.4
V-8—1974–80	
318–360 engs	
one (.5)	.7
one—each bank (.8)	1.3
all—both banks (1.3)	2.0
400–440 engs	
one (.8)	1.0
one—each bank (1.3)	1.6

(Factory Time)	Chilton Time
all—both banks (1.9)	2.3
w/A.C. add (.4)	.5
w/Air inj add (.3)	.3
(G) Valves, Adjust	
Six—1979–80 (.7)	1.0
w/A.C. add (.2)	.4

Dodge

(G) Cylinder Head Gasket, Renew
Includes: Clean carbon.

	Chilton Time
Six—1974–75 (2.4)	3.0
1976 (2.9)	3.5
1977–80 (2.6)	3.5
V-8—1974–76	
318, 360 engs	
one (3.1)	3.8
both (4.3)	5.4
400, 440 engs—exc below	
one (3.5)	4.2
both (5.5)	6.1
Coronet & Charger	
one (3.2)	4.2
both (5.6)	6.1
1977–80—318, 360 engs	
one (2.8)	3.8
both (3.7)	5.4
400, 440 engs	
one (3.4)	4.2
both (4.3)	6.1
w/A.C. add (.4)	.5

(G) Cylinder Head, Renew
Includes: Reface and adjust valves, clean carbon.

	Chilton Time
Six—1974–75 (3.9)	4.8
1976 (4.8)	5.9
1977–80 (5.4)	6.5
V-8—1974–80	
318, 360 engs	
one (4.4)	5.4
both (6.9)	9.4
400, 440 engs—exc below	
one (5.1)	6.0
both (6.6)	9.6
Royal Monaco	
one (4.3)	6.0
both (6.2)	9.6
w/A.C. add (.4)	.5

(P) Clean Carbon and Grind Valves
Includes: R&R cylinder heads, adjust valve clearance when required. Minor engine tune up.

	Chilton Time
Six—1974–75 (5.0)	7.2
1976 (5.4)	8.1
1977–80 (4.9)	8.1
V-8—1974–75	
318, 360 engs (8.0)	11.0
400, 440 engs (8.8)	12.0
1976–318, 360 engs (7.7)	11.0
400, 440 engs (8.5)	12.0
1977–80	
318, 360 engs (6.7)	11.0
400, 440 engs (7.2)	12.0
w/A.C. add (.4)	.5
w/100 amp alter add (.4)	.4

(G) Valve Tappets, Adjust

	Chilton Time
Six—1974 (1.0)	1.2
1975–80 (.7)	1.0

(G) Rocker Arm Cover or Gasket, Renew

	Chilton Time
Six—1974–80 (.4)	.5
V-8—1974–80—one (.3)	.6
both (.5)	1.0
w/A.C. add (.1)	.1
w/100 amp alter add (.4)	.4

(G) Valve Tappets, Renew
Includes: R&R head and adjust valve clearance on 6 cyl. R&R intake manifold and clean carbon on V-8's, except 400 and 440 engines.

	Chilton Time
Six—1974–75—one (.9)	*1.2
all (1.3)	*1.8
1976—one or all (3.0)	3.4
1977–80—one or all (3.3)	4.0
V-8—1974–76	
318, 360 engs	
one (.9)	*1.4
all (2.3)	*3.6
1977–80—318, 360 engs	
one (2.1)	3.0
all (2.2)	3.4
1974–80—400, 440 engs	
one (.6)	*2.2
all (1.8)	*3.2
w/A.C. add (.4)	.5
w/100 amp alter add (.4)	.4

* Note: factory time based on using magnetic tool thru push rod opening to remove lifters. Chilton experience finds it better and safer to R&R intake manifold, since the lifters have a tendency to stick in the block and sometimes come apart.

(G) Valve Spring or Valve Stem Oil Seals, Renew (Head on Car)
Includes: Adjust valve clearance when required.

	Chilton Time
Six—1974–76—one (1.0)	1.4
all (2.6)	3.2
1977–80—one or all (2.2)	3.2
V-8—1974–76—one (2.5)	3.4
all (4.4)	5.0
1977–80—one (1.4)	1.8
all (3.2)	4.0
w/A.C. add (.5)	.5
w/100 amp alter add (.4)	.4

(G) Rocker Arm Assembly, Recondition
Includes: Renew arms as required and shaft if necessary.

	Chilton Time
Six—1974–80 (.8)	1.5
V-8—1974–80—318, 360 engs	
one side (.6)	1.3
both sides (1.0)	2.1
400, 440 engs	
one side (.6)	1.1
both sides (1.0)	1.8
w/A.C. add (.5)	.5
w/100 amp alter add (.4)	.4

(G) Valve Push Rods, Renew
Includes: Adjust valve clearance when required.

	Chilton Time
Six—1974–80—one (.8)	1.0
all (1.1)	1.4
V-8—1974–80—one (.5)	1.0
one each bnk (.8)	1.6
all both bnks (1.3)	2.0
w/A.C. add (.5)	.5

	(Factory Time)	Chilton Time

Horizon & Omni

(G) Cylinder Head Gasket, Renew
Includes: Clean carbon
1978–80 (2.6)	3.8
w/A.C. add (.4)	.4
w/Air inj add (.3)	.3

(G) Cylinder Head, Renew
Includes: Transfer all necessary parts. Clean carbon, make all necessary adjustments.
1978–80 (6.6)	9.2
w/A.C. add (.4)	.4
w/Air inj add (.3)	.3

(P) Clean Carbon and Grind Valves
Includes: R&R cylinder head, adjust valve clearance when required. Minor engine tune up.
1978–80 (7.1)	9.9
w/A.C. add (.4)	.4
w/Air inj add (.1)	.1

(G) Valve Springs, Renew
Includes: Adjust valve clearance when required.
1978–80—one (2.7)	4.0
all (4.0)	5.3
w/A.C. add (.4)	.4
w/Air inj add (.1)	.1

(G) Valve Stem Oil Seals, Renew (Head on Car)
1978–80—all (4.6)	5.9
w/A.C. add (.4)	.4
w/Air inj add (.1)	.1

Capri & Mustang (1979–80)

(G) Cylinder Head Gasket, Renew
Includes: Check cylinder head and block flatness: Clean carbon and make all necessary adjustments.
Four—1979–80 (3.7)	5.1
V-6—1979–80—one (3.5)	4.6
both (4.4)	5.7
V-8—1979–80—one (3.4)	4.9
both (4.8)	6.1

(G) Cylinder Head, Renew
Includes: Transfer all components, clean carbon. Reface valves, check valve spring tension, assembled height and valve head runout.
Four—1979–80 (5.8)	7.5
V-6—1979–80—one (4.5)	5.6
both (6.4)	8.2
V-8—1979–80—one (4.8)	6.5
both (7.6)	9.4

(P) Clean Carbon and Grind Valves
Includes: R&R cylinder heads, check valve spring tension, valve seat and head runout, stem to guide clearance and spring assembled height. Minor tune up.
Four—1979–80 (6.3)	8.0
V-6—1979–80 (7.4)	10.0
V-8—1979–80 (8.3)	11.0

(G) Rocker Arm Shaft Assy., Recondition
V-6—1979–80—one (1.2)	1.9
both (2.0)	2.8

	(Factory Time)	Chilton Time

(G) Valve Push Rod, Renew
V-6—1979–80—one (.8)	1.3
all—one side (1.0)	1.5
all—both sides (1.4)	2.0
V-8—1979–80—one (.5)	.7
all—one side (.6)	1.0
all—both sides (1.0)	1.7

(G) Rocker Arm Stud, Renew
V-8—1979–80—one (.6)	1.1
each adtnl (.1)	.1

(G) Rocker Arm, Renew
V-8—1979–80—one (.5)	.8
all—one side (.6)	1.0
all—both sides (1.0)	1.5

Comet, Cougar, Monarch, Montego, Lincoln Versailles

(G) Cylinder Head Gasket, Renew
Includes: Check cylinder head and block flatness. Clean carbon and make all necessary adjustments.
Six—1974–80 (2.2)	3.5
V-8—1974–80	
302, 351W engs	
one (3.2)	4.3
both (4.5)	5.8
351C/M, 400 engs	
one (3.5)	4.6
both (4.7)	6.0
460 eng	
one (4.5)	5.6
both (5.6)	7.5
w/P.S. add (.2)	.2
w/A.C. add (.3)	.3

(G) Cylinder Head, Renew
Includes: Transfer all components, clean carbon. Reface valves, check valve spring tension, assembled height and valve head runout.
Six—1974–80 (4.6)	6.2
V-8—1974–80	
302, 351W engs	
one (4.4)	5.9
both (7.0)	9.4
351C/M, 400 engs	
one (4.9)	6.4
both (7.5)	9.5
460 eng	
one (6.1)	7.5
both (8.8)	10.2
w/P.S. add (.2)	.2
w/A.C. add (.3)	.3

(P) Clean Carbon and Grind Valves
Includes: R&R cylinder heads, reface valves and seats. Check valve spring tension, valve seat and head runout, stem to guide clearance and spring assembled height. Minor tune up.
Six—1974–80 (4.9)	7.6
V-8—1974–80	
302, 351W engs (8.0)	11.0
351C/M, 400 engs (8.2)	11.0
460 eng (9.1)	12.0
w/P.S. add (.2)	.2
w/A.C. add (.3)	.3

(Factory Time)	Chilton Time
V-8—1974–80	
302, 351W engs	
one (.4)	.7
both (.7)	1.0
351C/M, 400 engs	
one (.5)	.7
both (.8)	1.1
460 eng	
one (.5)	.7
both (.8)	1.1

(G) Rocker Arm Shaft Assy., Recondition

Six—1974–80 (1.1)	1.6

(G) Valve Push Rod, Renew

Six—1974–80—one (.8)	1.1
all (.8)	1.4
V-8—1974–80	
302, 351W engs	
all—one side (.6)	1.0
all—both sides (1.0)	1.8
351C/M, 400 engs	
all—one side (.7)	1.1
all—both sides (1.2)	2.0
460 eng	
all—one side (.7)	1.1
all—both sides (1.2)	2.0

(G) Rocker Arm Stud, Renew (One)

Six—1974–80 (.8)	1.2
V-8—1974–80 (.6)	1.1

(G) Rocker Arm, Renew

V-8—1974–80	
351C/M, 400 engs	
one (.6)	1.0
all—one side (.7)	1.2
all—both sides (1.2)	1.7
460 eng	
one (.6)	1.0
all—one side (.7)	1.5
all—both sides (1.2)	1.9

(G) Valve Tappets, Renew
Includes: R&R intake manifold on V-8. Adjust carburetor and ignition timing.

Six—1974–80	
one or all (2.4)	*3.1
V-8—1974–80	
302, 351W engs	
one (2.1)	3.0
all (2.8)	3.7
460 eng	
one or all (3.3)	4.6
*If necessary to R&R head add	
(2.4)	3.7

(G) Valve Tappets, Renew (Without Removing Intake Manifold)

V-8—1974–80	
351C/M, 400 engs	
one (.6)	.9
one—each side (.9)	1.3
all—both sides (1.5)	2.6

(G) Valve Spring or Valve Stem Oil Seals, Renew (Head on Car)

Six—1974–80—one (.8)	1.0
all (1.6)	2.1
V-8—1974–80	
302, 351W engs	
one (.7)	1.2
all (2.6)	3.4
351C/M, 400 engs	
one (.7)	1.2

(Factory Time)	Chilton Time
all (2.6)	3.4
460 eng	
one (.6)	1.1
all (2.4)	3.2

Elite, Granada, Maverick, Torino, LTD II, Thunderbird (1977–79)

(G) Cylinder Head Gasket, Renew
Includes: Check cylinder head and block flatness. Clean carbon and make all necessary adjustments.

Six—1974–80 (2.2)	3.5
V-8—1974–80	
302, 351W engs	
one (3.2)	4.3
both (4.5)	5.8
351C/M, 400 engs	
one (3.5)	4.6
both (4.7)	6.0
460 eng	
one (4.5)	5.6
both (5.6)	7.5
w/P.S. add (.2)	.2
w/A.C. add (.3)	.3

(G) Cylinder Head, Renew
Includes: Transfer all components, clean carbon. Reface valves, check valve spring tension, assembled height and valve head runout.

Six—1974–80 (4.6)	6.2
V-8—1974–80	
302, 351W engs	
one (4.4)	5.9
both (7.0)	9.4
351C/M, 400 engs	
one (4.9)	6.4
both (7.5)	9.5
460 eng	
one (6.1)	7.5
both (8.8)	10.2
w/P.S. add (.2)	.2
w/A.C. add (.3)	.3

(P) Clean Carbon and Grind Valves
Includes: R&R cylinder heads, replace valves and seats. Check valve spring tension, valve seat and head runout, stem to guide clearance and spring assembled height. Minor tune up.

Six—1974–80 (4.9)	7.6
V-8—1974–80	
302, 351W engs (8.0)	11.0
351C/M, 400 engs (8.2)	11.0
460 eng (9.1)	12.0
w/P.S. add (.2)	.2
w/A.C. add (.3)	.3

(G) Rocker Arm Cover or Gasket, Renew

Six—1974–80 (.6)	.9
V-8—1974–80	
302, 351W engs	
one (.4)	.7
both (.7)	1.0

	Chilton Time
(Factory Time)	
351C/M, 400 engs	
one (.5)	.7
both (.8)	1.1
460 eng	
one (.5)	.7
both (.8)	1.1
(G) Rocker Arm Shaft Assy., Recondition	
Six—1974-80 (1.1)	1.6
(G) Valve Push Rod, Renew	
Six—1974-80—one (.8)	1.1
all (.8)	1.4
V-8—1974-80	
302, 351W engs	
all—one side (.6)	1.0
all—both sides (1.0)	1.8
351C/M, 400 engs	
all—one side (.7)	1.1
all—both sides (1.2)	2.0
460 eng	
all—one side (.7)	1.1
all—both sides (1.2)	2.0
(G) Rocker Arm Stud, Renew (One)	
Six—1974-80 (.8)	1.2
V-8—1974-80 (.6)	1.1
(G) Rocker Arm, Renew	
V-8—1974-80	
351C/M, 400 engs	
one (.6)	1.0
all—one side (.7)	1.2
all—both sides (1.2)	1.7
460 eng	
one (.6)	1.0
all—one side (.7)	1.5
all—both sides (1.2)	1.9
(G) Valve Tappets, Renew	
Includes: R&R intake manifold on V-8. Adjust carburetor and ignition timing.	
Six—1974-80	
one or all (2.4)	*3.1
V-8—1974-80	
302, 351W engs	
one (2.1)	3.0
all (2.8)	3.7
460 eng	
one or all (3.3)	4.6
*If necessary to R&R head add	
(2.4)	3.7
(G) Valve Tappets, Renew (Without Removing Intake Manifold)	
V-8—1974-80	
351C/M, 400 engs	
one (.6)	.9
one—each side (.9)	1.3
all—both sides (1.5)	2.6
(G) Valve Spring or Valve Stem Oil Seals, Renew (Head on Car)	
Six—1974-80—one (.8)	1.0
all (1.6)	2.1
V-8—974-80	
302, 351W engs	
one (.7)	1.2
all (2.6)	3.4
351C/M, 400 engs	
one (.7)	1.2
all (2.6)	3.4
460 eng	
one (.6)	1.1
all (2.4)	3.2

Ford

	Chilton Time
(Factory Time)	
(G) Cylinder Head Gasket, Renew	
Includes: Check cylinder head and block flatness. Clean carbon and make all necessary adjustments.	
1974-78	
351, 400 engs—one (3.5)	4.6
both (4.7)	6.0
429, 460 engs—one (4.6)	5.7
both (6.4)	7.7
1979-80	
302, 351 engs—one (3.7)	4.8
both (4.8)	6.2
w/A.C. add (.4)	.4
2/P.S. add (.3)	.3
(G) Cylinder Head, Renew	
Includes: Transfer all components, clean carbon. Reface valves, check valve spring tension, assembled height and valve head runout.	
1974-78	
351, 400 engs—one (4.9)	6.4
both (7.5)	9.5
429, 460 engs—one (6.5)	8.0
both (9.8)	12.1
1979-80	
302, 351 engs—one (4.9)	6.4
both (7.3)	9.5
w/A.C. add (.4)	.4
w/P.S. add (.3)	.3
(P) Clean Carbon and Grind Valves	
Includes: R&R cylinder heads, check valve spring tension, valve seat and head runout stem to guide clearance and spring assembled height. Minor tune up.	
1974-78	
351, 400 engs (8.5)	11.4
429, 460 engs (9.9)	12.9
1979-80—302, 351 engs (8.3)	11.4
w/A.C. add (.4)	.4
w/P.S. add (.3)	.3
(G) Valve Tappets, Renew	
Includes: R&R intake manifold, adjust carburetor and ignition timing.	
1974-78	
351, 400 engs (2.6)	3.7
429, 460 engs (3.5)	4.6
1979-80—302, 351 engs (3.2)	4.3
(G) Valve Spring or Valve Stem Oil Seals, Renew (Head on Car)	
1974-78	
351, 400 engs—one (.7)	1.2
all (2.5)	3.2
429, 460 engs—one (.6)	1.1
all (2.5)	3.2
1979-80	
302, 351 engs—one (1.0)	1.4
one—each side (1.5)	1.9
all—both sides (2.5)	3.2
(G) Rocker Arm, Renew	
1974-78	
one (.6)	1.0
all—one side (.7)	1.5
all—both sides (1.2)	1.9
1979-80	
right side—one (1.0)	1.3
left side—one (.8)	1.1
all—both sides (1.5)	2.0

	Chilton Time
(Factory Time)	

(G) Rocker Arm Stud, Renew

1974–78—one (.6)	**1.0**
Each addtl add (.1)	**.1**
1979–80	
right side—one (1.0)	**1.4**
left side—one (.8)	**1.2**
each adtnl (.1)	**.1**

(G) Valve Push Rods, Renew

1974–78	
one (.6)	**1.1**
all—one side (.7)	**1.6**
all—both sides (1.2)	**2.0**
1979–80	
right side—one (1.0)	**1.4**
left side—one (.8)	**1.2**
all—both sides (1.5)	**2.2**

Lincoln Continental, Mark IV, Mark V

(G) Cylinder Head Gasket, Renew
Includes: Check cylinder head and block flatness. Clean carbon and make all necessary adjustments.

1974—460 eng—right (4.2)	**5.4**
left (4.7)	**5.8**
both (6.4)	**7.9**
1975–78—460 eng—right (4.5) . . .	**5.6**
left (4.7)	**5.7**
both (6.7)	**8.2**
1977–80—400 eng—right (3.5) . . .	**4.5**
left (3.4)	**4.5**
both (4.7)	**6.2**

(G) Cylinder Head, Renew
Includes: Transfer all components, clean carbon. Reface valves, check valve spring tension, assembled height and valve head runout.

1974—460 eng—right (5.8)	**6.9**
left (6.3)	**7.3**
both (9.6)	**11.1**
1975–78—460 eng—right (6.1) . . .	**7.1**
left (6.3)	**7.3**
both (9.9)	**11.4**
1977–80—400 eng—right (4.9) . . .	**5.9**
left (4.8)	**5.8**
both (7.5)	**9.0**

(P) Clean Carbon and Grind Valves
Includes: R&R cylinder heads, check valve spring tension, valve seat and head runout, stem to guide clearance and spring assembled height. Minor tune up.

1974—460 eng (9.8)	**13.3**
1975–78—460 eng (10.2)	**13.7**
1977–80—400 eng (8.2)	**11.9**

(G) Valve Tappets, Renew
Includes: R&R intake manifold, adjust carburetor and ignition timing.

Continental

1974–80—one or all (3.2)	**4.0**

Mark IV, V

1974–80—one or all (3.4)	**4.2**

(G) Valve Spring or Valve Stem Oil Seals, Renew (Head On Car)

Continental

1974–78—460 eng—one (.6)	**1.1**
one—each side (1.0)	**1.4**
all—both sides (2.4)	**3.1**

	Chilton Time
(Factory Time)	

Mark IV, V

1974–78—460 eng—one (.7)	**1.0**
one—each side (1.1)	**1.4**
all—both sides (2.5)	**3.1**
1977–80—400 eng—one (.7)	**1.0**
one—each side (1.1)	**1.4**
all—both sides (2.6)	**3.2**

(G) Rocker Arm, Renew

1974–80—one (.6)	**1.1**
all—one side (.7)	**1.6**
all—both sides (1.2)	**2.0**

(G) Rocker Arm Stud, Renew (One)

1974–80 (.6)	**1.1**
each adtnl add (.1)	**.1**

(G) Valve Push Rods, Renew

1974–80—one (.6)	**1.1**
all—one side (.7)	**1.6**
all—both sides (1.2)	**2.0**

Mercury

(G) Cylinder Head Gasket, Renew
Includes: Check cylinder head and block flatness. Clean carbon and make all necessary adjustments.

1974–78	
351, 400 engs—one (3.5)	**4.6**
both (4.7)	**6.0**
429, 460 engs—one (4.6)	**5.7**
1979–80—302, 351 engs—one	
(3.7)	**4.8**
both (4.8)	**6.2**
both (6.4)	**7.7**
w/A.C. add (.4)	**.4**
w/P.S. add (.3)	**.3**

(G) Cylinder Head, Renew
Includes: Transfer all components, clean carbon. Reface valves, check valve spring tension, assembled height and valve head runout.

1974–78	
351, 400 engs—one (4.9)	**6.4**
both (7.5)	**9.5**
429, 460 engs—one (6.5)	**8.0**
both (11.1)	**12.1**
1979–80—302, 351 engs—one	
(4.9)	**6.4**
both (7.3)	**9.5**
w/A.C. add (.4)	**.4**
w/P.S. add (.3)	**.3**

(P) Clean Carbon and Grind Valves
Includes: R&R cylinder heads, check valve spring tension, valve seat and head runout, stem to guide clearance and spring assembled height. Minor tune up.

1974–78	
351, 400 engs (8.5)	**11.4**
429, 460 engs (9.9)	**12.9**
1979–80—302, 351 engs (8.3)	**11.4**
w/A.C. add (.4)	**.4**
w/P.S. add (.3)	**.3**

(G) Rocker Arm Cover or Gasket, Renew

1974–78	
351, 400 engs—one (.5)	**.7**
both (.8)	**1.1**
429, 460 engs—one (.5)	**.6**
both (.7)	**1.0**

(Factory Time)	Chilton Time
1979–80—302, 351 engs—right	
(.9)	1.2
left (.7)	1.0
both (1.2)	1.7

(G) Valve Tappets, Renew
Includes: R&R intake manifold, adjust carburetor and ignition timing.

1974–78	
351, 400 engs (2.6)	3.7
429, 460 engs (3.5)	4.6
1979–80—302, 351 engs (3.2)	4.3

(G) Valve Spring or Valve Stem Oil Seals, Renew (Head on Car)

1974–78	
351, 400 engs—one (.7)	1.2
all (2.5)	3.2
429, 460 engs—one (.6)	1.1
all (2.5)	3.2
1979–80—302, 351 engs—one (1.0)	1.4
one—each side (1.5)	1.9
all—both sides (2.5)	3.2

(G) Rocker Arm, Renew

1974–78	
one (.6)	1.0
all—one side (.7)	1.5
all—both sides (1.2)	1.9
1979–80—right side—one (1.0)	1.4
left side—one (.8)	1.2
all—both sides (1.5)	2.0

(G) Rocker Arm Stud, Renew

1974–78—one (.6)	1.0
Each adtnl add (.1)	.1
1979–80—right side—one (1.0)	1.4
left side—one (.8)	1.2
each adtnl (.1)	.1

(G) Valve Push Rods, Renew

1974–78	
one (.6)	1.1
all—one side (.7)	1.6
all—both sides (1.2)	2.0
1979–80—right side—one (1.0)	1.4
left side—one (.8)	1.2
all—both sides (1.5)	2.2

Mustang II, Bobcat, Pinto, Fairmont, Zephyr

(G) Cylinder Head Gasket, Renew
Includes: Check cylinder head and block flatness. Clean carbon and make all necessary adjustments.

Four—1974–80 (4.0)	5.1
Six—1978–80 (2.5)	3.8
V-6—1974–80—right (3.4)	4.5
left (3.2)	4.3
V-8—1975–80—right (3.8)	4.9
left (3.6)	4.7
w/P.S. add (.3)	.3
w/A.C. add (.2)	.2

(G) Cylinder Head, Renew
Includes: Transfer all components, clean carbon. Reface valves, check valve spring tension, assembled height and valve head runout.

Four—1974–80 (6.1)	7.5
Six—1978–80 (4.9)	5.9

(Factory Time)	Chilton Time
V-6—1974–80—one (4.4)	5.5
both (6.0)	7.5
V-8—1975–80—one (5.0)	6.5
both (7.6)	9.4
w/P.S. add (.3)	.3
w/A.C. add (.2)	.2

(G) Valve Tappets, Adjust

Four—1974–80 (1.0)	1.6
V-6—1974–80 (1.4)	2.0

(P) Clean Carbon and Grind Valves
Includes: R&R cylinder heads, check valve spring tension, valve seat and head runout, stem to guide, clearance and spring assembled height. Minor tune up.

Four—1974–80 (6.6)	7.7
Six—1978–80 (5.2)	7.9
V-6—1974–80 (7.2)	9.8
V-8—1975–80 (8.6)	11.6
w/P.S. add (.3)	.3
w/A.C. add (.2)	.2

(G) Valve Tappets, Renew
Includes: R&R intake manifold where required. Adjust carburetor and ignition timing.

Four—1974–80 (1.3)	2.5
Six—1978–80 (2.3)	*3.4
V-6—1974–80 (4.1)	5.8
V-8—1975–80 (3.5)	4.7
*If necessary to R&R head add	
(2.5)	3.8

(G) Valve Spring or Valve Stem Oil Seals, Renew (Head on Car)

Four—1974–80—one (.9)	1.2
all (1.8)	2.3
Six—1978–80—one (.7)	1.0
all (1.5)	2.0
V-6—1974–80—one (.9)	1.2
all (2.1)	2.4
V-8—1975–80—one (1.1)	1.4
all (3.2)	4.0

(G) Rocker Arm, Renew

V-6—1975–80—one (.9)	1.1
all (1.6)	2.0

(G) Rocker Arm Stud, Renew

V-8—1975–80—one (.8)	1.2

(G) Valve Push Rod, Renew

Four—1974–80—one (.8)	1.0
all (1.1)	1.5
Six—1978–80—one (.7)	.9
all (.7)	1.4
V-6—1974–80—one (.9)	1.3
all (1.6)	2.0
V-8—1975–80—one (.7)	1.1
all (1.2)	1.7

(G) Rocker Arm Shaft Assy., Recondition

Six—1978–80 (1.0)	1.6
V-6—1975–80—one (1.3)	1.9
both (2.2)	2.8

Oldsmobile

GASOLINE ENGINES

(G) Cylinder Head Gasket, Renew
Includes: Drain and refill cooling system. Clean gasket surfaces. Make all necessary

(Factory Time)	Chilton Time

adjustments including carburetor and timing.

1974–76—one (3.0)		3.9
both (4.3)		5.8
1977–80—V-6—one (2.1)		3.0
both (3.1)		4.6
V-8—exc below—one (3.4)		4.3
both (4.9)		6.4
350 eng, Code G or L		
one (3.9)		4.8
both (6.0)		7.5
w/A.C. add (.6)		.6
w/A.I.R. add (.2)		.2

(G) Cylinder Head, Renew
Includes: Drain and refill cooling system. Clean gasket surfaces, transfer parts, reface valves and minor engine tune up.

1974–76—one (3.8)		4.9
both (5.9)		7.7
1977–80—V-6—one (2.7)		3.4
both (4.3)		6.1
V-8—exc below—one (4.2)		5.3
both (6.5)		8.3
350 eng, code G or L		
one (4.7)		5.8
both (7.6)		9.4
w/A.C. add (.6)		.6
w/A.I.R. add (.2)		.2

(P) Clean Carbon and Grind Valves
Includes: Drain and refill cooling system R&R cylinder heads. Recondition valve seats, adjust valve stem length. Minor engine tune up.

1974–76—one blank (4.2)		5.4
both banks (6.7)		8.7
1977–80—V-6—one bank (3.0) ...		4.5
both banks (4.8)		7.1
V-8—exc below—one bank (4.6) .		5.8
both banks (7.2)		9.3
350 eng, Code G or L		
one bank (5.2)		6.3
both banks (8.7)		10.4
w/A.C. add (.6)		.6
w/A.I.R. add (.2)		.2

**Oldsmobile
Serial Number
3 B37 B 7L100001
1977 Engine Codes**

	Chev.	140	2bbl	— L-4
C	Buick	231	2bbl	— V-6
F	Olds	260	2bbl	— V-8
U	Chev.	305	2bbl	— V-8
G	Chev.	350	2bbl	— V-8
R	Olds	350	4bbl	— V-8
L	Chev.	350	4bbl	— V-8
K	Olds	403	4bbl	— V-8

1978–79 Engine Codes

V	Pont.	151	2bbl	— L-4
I	Pont.	151	2bbl	— L-4
A	Buick	231	2bbl	— V-6
F	Olds	260	2bbl	— V-8
H	Chev.	305	2bbl	— V-8
U	Chev.	305	4bbl	— V-8
R	Olds	350	4bbl	— V-8
L	Chev.	350	4bbl	— V-8
N	Olds	350	Diesel	— V-8
K	Olds	403	4bbl	— V-8

(Factory Time)	Chilton Time

(G) Valve Tappets, Renew
Includes: Drain and refill cooling system. R&R intake manifold. Make all necessary adjustments.

1974–76—one bank (2.0)		2.9
both banks (2.4)		3.5
1977–80—V-6—one bank (1.5) ...		2.4
both banks (1.8)		3.0
V-8—exc below—one bank (2.2) .		2.8
both banks (3.1)		3.8
350 eng, Code G or L		
one bank (2.5)		3.4
both banks (3.5)		4.4
w/A.C. add (.3)		.3
w/A.I.R. add (.1)		.1

(G) Valve Spring or Valve Stem Oil Seal, Renew (Head on Car)

1974–80—V-8—one (.6)		.9
one each bank (1.1)		1.7
each adtnl (.2)		.2
1977–80—V-6—one (.6)		.8
one each bank (1.1)		1.7
each adtnl (.3)		.3
w/A.C. add (.3)		.3

(G) Rocker Arm, Pivot and/or Push Rod, Renew

1974–80—V-8—one side (.6)		.8
both sides (1.1)		1.5
1977–80—V-6—one side (.4)		.7
both sides (.7)		1.1
w/A.C. add (.3)		.3

DIESEL ENGINE

(G) Cylinder Head Gasket, Renew
Includes: R&R injector pump and lines. R&R intake manifold and disconnect exhaust manifolds. Clean gasket surfaces, bleed lifters and adjust timing. Drain and refill cooling system.

1978–80—left side (3.6)		4.4
right side (3.8)		4.6
both sides (5.3)		7.9
w/A.C. add (.3)		.3

(G) Cylinder Head, Renew
Includes: R&R injector pump and lines. R&R intake manifold and disconnect exhaust manifolds. Clean gasket surfaces. Transfer parts, reface valves. Bleed lifters and adjust timing. Drain and refill cooling system.

1978–80—left side (4.6)		5.8
right side (5.0)		6.2
both sides (7.3)		9.9
w/A.C. add (.3)		.3

(P) Clean Carbon and Grind Valves
Includes: R&R injector pump and lines. R&R cylinder heads, clean carbon. Recondition valves and valve seats. Check and adjust valve stem length. Bleed lifters, drain and refill cooling system.

1978–80—left side (5.1) .....;....		6.3
right side (5.3)		6.5
both sides (8.3)		10.9
w/A.C. add (.3)		.3

(G) Valve Tappets, Renew
Includes: R&R injector pump and lines, intake manifold and rocker arms. Drain and refill cooling system.

1978–80—one side (2.5)		3.2
both sides (3.2)		4.2

(Factory Time)	Chilton Time

(G) Valve Spring or Valve Stem Oil Seals, Renew (Head on Car)
Includes: R&R injector pump and lines.

1978–80—one (1.5)	1.9
each one bank (2.0)	2.7
each adtnl (.3)	.3

(G) Rocker Arm, Pivot and/or Push Rod, Renew
Includes: R&R injector pump and lines.

1978–80—one (1.5)	1.9
one each bank (2.0)	2.7
each adtnl (.3)	.3

Olds Cutlass, Omega (1974–79)

GASOLINE ENGINES

(G) Cylinder Head Gasket, Renew
Includes: Drain and refill cooling system. Clean gasket surfaces. Make all necessary adjustments including carburetor and timing.

Six—1974–76 (2.5)	3.1
V-6—1977–80—one (2.1)	3.0
both (3.1)	4.6
V-8—1974–76—one (2.9)	3.8
both (4.1)	5.6
1977–80—exc below—one (3.4) . .	4.3
both (4.9)	6.4
305–350 engs, Code G, H, L or U	
one (3.9)	4.8
both (6.0)	7.5
w/A.C. add (.6)	.6
w/A.I.R. add (.2)	.2

(G) Cylinder Head, Renew
Includes: Drain and refill cooling system. Clean gasket surfaces, transfer parts, reface valves. Minor engine tune up.

Six—1974–76 (3.3)	4.2
V-6—1977–80—one (2.7)	4.0
one (4.3)	6.1
V-8—1974–76—one (3.7)	4.8
both (5.5)	7.3
1977–80—exc below (4.2)	5.3
both (6.5)	8.3
305–350 engs, Code G, H, L or U	
one (4.7)	5.8
both (7.6)	9.4
w/A.C. add (.6)	.6
w/A.I.R. add (.2)	.2

(P) Clean Carbon and Grind Valves
Includes: Drain and refill cooling system. R&R cylinder heads. Recondition valve seats, adjust valve stem length. Minor engine tune up.

Six—1974–76 (4.0)	5.7
V-6—1977–80—one bank (3.0) . . .	4.5
both banks (4.8)	7.1
V-8—1974–76—one bank (4.1) . . .	5.3
both banks (6.6)	8.6
1977–80—exc below—one bank (4.6)	5.8
both banks (7.2)	9.3
305–350 engs, Code G, H, L or U	
one bank (5.2)	6.3
both banks (8.7)	10.4
w/A.C. add (.6)	.6
w/A.I.R. add (.2)	.2

(Factory Time)	Chilton Time

(G) Valve Tappets, Renew
Includes: Drain and refill cooling system. R&R intake manifold. Make all necessary adjustments.

Six—1974–76—one (.5)	.9
all (.8)	1.4
V-6—1977–80—one bank (1.5) . . .	2.4
both banks (1.9)	3.0
V-8—1974–76—one bank (2.1) . . .	2.7
both banks (2.7)	3.7
1977–80—exc below—one bank (2.2)	2.8
both banks (3.1)	3.8
305–350 engs, Code G, H, L or U	
one bank (2.5)	3.4
both banks (3.5)	4.4
w/A.C. add (.3)	.3
w/A.I.R. add (.1)	.1

(G) Valve Spring or Valve Stem Oil Seal, Renew (Head on Car)

Six—1974–76—one (.9)	1.1
V-6—1977–80—one (.6)	.8
one each bank (1.1)	1.7
V-8—1974–80—one (.6)	.9
one each bank (1.1)	1.7
each adtnl all engs (.2)	.3
w/A.C. add (.3)	.3

(G) Rocker Arm, Pivot and/or Push Rod, Renew

Six—1974–76—one (.6)	.8
each adtnl (.1)	.1
V-6—1977–80—one side (.4)	.7
both sides (.7)	1.1
V-8—1974–80—one side (.6)	.8
both sides (1.1)	1.5
w/A.C. add (.3)	.3

(G) Valves, Adjust

Six—1974–76 (.8)	1.1

DIESEL ENGINE

(G) Cylinder Head Gasket, Renew
Includes: R&R injector pump and lines. R&R intake manifold and disconnect exhaust manifolds. Clean gasket surfaces, bleed lifters and adjust timing. Drain and refill cooling system.

1979–80—left side (3.6)	4.4
right side (3.8)	4.6
both sides (5.3)	7.9
w/A.C. add (.3)	.3

(G) Cylinder Head, Renew
Includes: R&R injector pump and lines. R&R intake manifold and disconnect exhaust manifolds. Clean gasket surfaces. Transfer parts, reface valves. Bleed lifters and adjust timing. Drain and refill cooling system.

1979–80—left side (4.6)	5.8
right side (5.0)	6.2
both sides (7.3)	9.9
w/A.C. add (.3)	.3

(P) Clean Carbon and Grind Valves
Includes: R&R injector pump and lines. R&R cylinder heads, clean carbon. Recondition valves and valve seats. Check and adjust valve stem length. Bleed lifters, drain and refill cooling system.

1979–80—left side (5.1)	6.3

| | Chilton |
| (Factory Time) | Time |

right side (5.3)	6.5
both sides (8.3)	10.9
w/A.C. add (.3)	.3

(G) Valve Tappets, Renew
Includes: R&R injector pump and lines, intake manifold and rocker arms. Drain and refill cooling system.

| 1979–80—one side (2.5) | 3.2 |
| both sides (3.2) | 4.2 |

(G) Valve Spring or Valve Stem Oil Seals, Renew (Head On Car)
Includes: R&R injector pump and lines.

1979–80—one (1.5)	1.9
one each bank (2.0)	2.7
each adtnl (.3)	.3

(G) Rocker Arm, Pivot and/or Push Rod, Renew
Includes: R&R injector pump and lines.

1979–80—one (1.5)	1.9
one each bank (2.0)	2.7
each adtnl (.3)	.3

Olds Toronado

GASOLINE ENGINES

(G) Cylinder Head Gasket, Renew
Includes: Drain and refill cooling system. Clean gasket surfaces. Make all necessary adjustments including carburetor and timing.

1974–78—one (2.7)	3.5
both (4.0)	5.5
1979–80—one (3.1)	3.9
both (4.8)	6.3
w/A.C. add (.3)	.3
w/A.I.R. add (.2)	.2

(G) Cylinder Head, Renew
Includes: Drain and refill cooling system. Clean gasket surfaces, transfer parts, reface valves. Minor engine tune up.

1974–78—one (3.5)	4.6
both (5.6)	7.4
1979–80—one (3.9)	5.0
both (6.4)	8.2
w/A.C. add (.3)	.3
w/A.I.R. add (.2)	.2

(P) Clean Carbon and Grind Valves
Includes: Drain and refill cooling system. R&R cylinder heads. Recondition valve seats, adjust valve stem length. Minor engine tune up.

1974–78—one bank (3.9)	5.1
both banks (6.4)	8.4
1979–80—one bank (4.1)	5.3
both banks (6.8)	8.8
w/A.C. add (.3)	.3
w/A.I.R. add (.2)	.2

(G) Valve Tappets, Renew
Includes: Drain and refill cooling system. R&R intake manifold. Make all necessary adjustments.

1974–80—one bank (2.2)	2.8
both banks (3.1)	3.8
w/A.C. add (.3)	.3

(G) Valve Spring or Valve Stem Oil Seal, Renew (Head on Car)

| 1974–80—one (.6) | .9 |

one each bank (1.1)	1.7
each adtnl (.2)	.2
w/A.C. add (.2)	.2

(G) Rocker Arm, Pivot and/or Push Rod, Renew

1974–80—one side (.6)	.8
both sides (1.1)	1.5
w/A.C. add (.2)	.2

DIESEL ENGINE

(G) Cylinder Head Gasket, Renew
Includes: R&R injector pump and lines. R&R intake manifold and disconnect exhaust manifolds. Clean gasket surfaces, bleed lifters and adjust timing. Drain and refill cooling system.

1979–80—left side (3.6)	4.4
right side (3.8)	4.6
both sides (5.3)	7.9
w/A.C. add (.3)	.3

(G) Cylinder Head, Renew
Includes: R&R injector pump and lines. R&R intake manifold and disconnect exhaust manifolds. Clean gasket surfaces. Transfer parts, reface valves. Bleed lifters and adjust timing. Drain and refill cooling system.

1979–80—left side (4.6)	5.8
right side (5.0)	6.2
both sides (7.3)	9.9
w/A.C. add (.3)	.3

(P) Clean Carbon and Grind Valves
Includes: R&R injector pump and lines. R&R cylinder heads, clean carbon. Recondition valves and valve seats. Check and adjust valve stem length. Bleed lifters, drain and refill cooling system.

1979–80—left side (5.1)	6.3
right side (5.3)	6.5
both sides (8.3)	10.9
w/A.C. add (.3)	.3

(G) Valve Tappets, Renew
Includes: R&R injector pump and lines, intake manifold and rocker arms. Drain and refill cooling system.

| 1979–80—one side (2.5) | 3.2 |
| both sides (3.2) | 4.2 |

(G) Valve Spring or Valve Stem Oil Seals, Renew (Head on Car)
Includes: R&R injector pump and lines.

1979–80—one (1.5)	1.9
one each bank (2.0)	2.7
each adtnl (.3)	.3

(G) Rocker Arm, Pivot and/or Push Rod, Renew
Includes: R&R injector pump and lines.

1979–80—one (1.5)	1.9
one each bank (2.0)	2.7
each adtnl (.3)	.3

Olds Starfire

(G) Cylinder Head Gasket, Renew
Includes: Drain and refill cooling system. Clean gasket surfaces. Make all necessary adjustments including carburetor and timing.

| Four—1976–77 (2.6) | 3.4 |

(Factory Time)	Chilton Time
1978–80 (2.6)	3.4
V-6—1975–80—left side (2.3)	3.2
right side (2.1)	3.0
both sides (3.4)	4.9
V-8—1977–80—one side (4.3)	5.2
both sides (6.2)	7.7
w/A.C. add (.9)	.9
w/P.S. add (.2)	.2
w/A.I.R. add (.6)	.6

(G) Cylinder Head, Renew
Includes: Drain and refill cooling system. Clean gasket surfaces, transfer parts, reface valves. Minor engine tune up.

Four—1976–77 (5.4)	6.5
1978–80 (3.4)	4.5
V-6—1975–80—left side (2.9)	4.0
right side (2.7)	3.9
both sides (4.6)	6.4
V-8—1977–80—one side (5.1)	6.2
both sides (7.8)	9.6
w/A.C. add (.9)	.9
w/P.S. add (.2)	.2
w/A.I.R. add (.6)	.6

(P) Clean Carbon and Grind Valves
Includes: Drain and refill cooling system. R&R cylinder heads. Recondition valve seats, adjust valve stem length. Minor engine tune up.

Four—1976–77 (5.2)	6.5
1978–80 (3.2)	4.5
V-6—1975–80—one bank (3.0) ...	4.5
both banks (4.8)	7.1
V-8—1977–80—one bank (5.7) ...	6.8
both banks (9.0)	10.7
w/A.C. add (.9)	.9
w/P.S. add (.2)	.2
w/A.I.R. add (.6)	.6

(G) Cam Follower (Lifter), Renew
Includes: R&R camshaft and make all necessary adjustments.

Four—1976–77—one (1.9)	2.7
all (2.1)	3.1

(G) Valve Tappets, Renew
Includes: Drain and refill cooling system. R&R intake manifold on V-6 and V-8 engines. Make all necessary adjustments.

Four—1978–80—one (.8)	1.2
all (1.3)	2.0
V-6—1975–80—one bank (1.5) ...	2.4
both banks (1.9)	2.9
V-8—1977–80—one bank (2.2) ...	2.8
both banks (3.1)	3.8
w/A.C. add (.9)	.9
w/P.S. add (.2)	.2
w/A.I.R. add (.3)	.3

(G) Valve Spring or Valve Stem Oil Seals, Renew (Head on Car)

Four—1976–77—one (1.6)	2.8
all (2.3)	3.5
1978–80—one (.8)	1.2
all (2.0)	3.2
V-6—1975–80—one (.6)	1.0
one each bank (1.1)	1.7
V-8—1977–80—one (.6)	1.0
one each bank (1.1)	1.7
each adtnl (.3)	.3
w/A.C. add (.2)	.2
w/A.I.R. add (.2)	.2

(G) Camshaft Housing or Gasket, Renew

Four—1976–77 (.3)	.5

(G) Rocker Arms, Push Rods and/or Pivots, Renew

Four—1978–80—one cyl (.6)	.8
each adtnl (.1)	.1
V-6—1975–80—one (.6)	.8
one each bank (1.1)	1.5
V-8—1977–80—one (.5)	.7
one each bank (.9)	1.3
each adtnl (.1)	.1
w/A.C. add (.2)	.2
w/A.I.R. add (.2)	.2

(G) Rocker Arm Stud, Renew

V-8—1977–80—one (.7)	1.0
one each bank (1.3)	1.9
each adtnl (.3)	.3
w/A.C. add (.2)	.2
w/A.I.R. add (.2)	.2

(G) Rocker Arm Shaft, Renew

V-6—1975–80—one side (.4)	.8
both sides (.7)	1.2
w/A.C. add (.2)	.2
w/A.I.R. add (.2)	.2

Plymouth

(G) Cylinder Head Gasket, Renew
Includes: Clean carbon.

Six—1974–75 (2.4)	3.0
1976 (2.9)	3.5
1977–78 (2.6)	3.5
V-8—1974–76	
318, 360 engs	
one (3.1)	3.8
both (4.3)	5.4
400, 440 engs—exc below	
one (3.5)	4.2
both (5.5)	6.1
Satellite & Gran Fury	
one (3.2)	4.2
both (5.6)	6.1
1977–78—318, 360 engs	
one (2.8)	3.8
both (3.7)	5.4
400, 440 engs—Fury	
one (3.4)	4.2
both (4.3)	6.1
Gran Fury	
one (3.0)	4.2
both (3.9)	6.1
w/A.C. add (.4)	.5

(G) Cylinder Head, Renew
Includes: Reface and adjust valves, clean carbon.

Six—1974–75 (3.9)	4.8
1976 (4.8)	5.9
1977–78 (5.4)	6.5
V-8—1974–78	
318, 360 engs	
one (4.4)	5.4
both (6.9)	9.4
400, 440 engs—exc below	
one (5.1)	6.0
both (6.6)	9.6

(Factory Time)	Chilton Time
Gran Fury	
one (4.3)	6.0
both (6.2)	9.6
w/A.C. add (.4)	.5

(P) Clean Carbon and Grind Valves
Includes: R&R cylinder head, adjust clearance when required. Minor engine tune up.

Six—1974–75 (5.0)	7.2
1976 (5.4)	8.1
1977–78 (4.9)	8.1
V-8—1974–75	
318, 360 engs (8.0)	11.0
400, 440 engs (8.8)	12.0
1976—318, 360 engs (7.7)	11.0
400, 440 engs (8.5)	12.0
1977–78	
318, 360 engs (6.7)	11.0
400, 440 engs (7.2)	12.0
w/A.C. add (.4)	.5
w/100 amp alter add (.4)	.4

(G) Valve Tappets, Adjust

Six—1974 (1.0)	1.2
1975–78 (.7)	1.0

(G) Valve Tappets, Renew
Includes: R&R head and adjust valve clearance on 6 cyl. R&R intake manifold and clean carbon on V-8's, except 400 and 440 engines.

Six—1974–75—one (.9)	*1.2
all (1.3)	*1.8
1976—one or all (3.0)	3.4
1977–78—one or all (3.3)	4.0
V-8—1974–76	
318, 360 engs	
one (.9)	*1.4
all (2.3)	*3.6
1977–78—318, 360 engs	
one (2.1)	3.0
all (2.2)	3.4
1974–78—400, 440 engs	
one (.6)	*2.2
all (1.8)	*3.2
w/A.C. add (.4)	.5
w/100 amp alter add (.4)	.4

* Note: factory time based on using magnetic tool thru push rod opening to remove lifters. Chilton experience finds it better and safer to R&R intake manifold, since the lifters have a tendency to stick in the block and sometimes come apart.

(G) Valve Spring or Valve Stem Oil Seals, Renew (Head on Car)
Includes: Adjust valve clearance when required.

Six—1974–76—one (1.0)	1.4
all (2.6)	3.2
1977–78—one or all (2.2)	3.2
V-8—1974–76—one (2.5)	3.4
all (4.4)	5.0
1977–78—one (1.4)	1.8
all (3.2)	4.0
w/A.C. add (.5)	.5
w/100 amp alter add (.4)	.4

(G) Rocker Arm Assembly, Recondition
Includes: Renew arms as required and shaft if necessary.

Six—1974–78 (.8)	1.5

(Factory Time)	Chilton Time
V-8—1974–78—318, 360 engs	
one side (.6)	1.3
both sides (1.0)	2.1
400, 440 engs	
one side (.6)	1.1
both sides (1.0)	1.8
w/A.C. add (.5)	.5
w/100 amp alter add (.4)	.4

(G) Valve Push Rods, Renew
Includes: Adjust valve clearance when required.

Six—1974–78—one (.8)	1.0
all (1.1)	1.4
V-8—1974–78—one (.5)	1.0
one each bnk (.8)	1.6
all both bnks (1.3)	2.0
w/A.C. add (.5)	.5

Pontiac & Grand Prix

(G) Cylinder Head Gasket, Renew
Includes: R&R cylinder head, clean carbon, make all necessary adjustments.

Pontiac	
V-6—1977–80—one (2.1)	3.0
both (3.1)	4.6
V-8—1974–76—one (2.6)	3.8
both (4.2)	5.9
1977–80	
350-403 engs, Code R-K	
one (3.4)	4.3
both (4.9)	6.4
350 eng, Code X	
one (2.3)	3.2
both (3.6)	5.1

Pontiac
Serial Number
ZA37 B 7P100001
1977 Engine Codes

B	Chev.	140	2bbl	—	L-4
U	Pont.	151	2bbl	—	L-4
C	Buick	231	2bbl	—	V-6
Y	Pont.	301	2bbl	—	V-8
U	Chev.	305	2bbl	—	V-8
R	Olds	350	4bbl	—	V-8
P	Pont.	350	2bbl	—	V-8
L	Chev.	350	4bbl	—	V-8
Z	Pont.	400	4bbl	—	V-8
K	Olds	403	4bbl	—	V-8
1978–79 Engine Codes					
I	Pont.	151	2bbl	—	L-4
V	Pont.	151	2bbl	—	L-4
C	Buick	231	2bbl	—	V-6
A	Buick	231	2bbl	—	V-6
Y	Pont.	301	2bbl	—	V-8
W	Pont.	301	4bbl	—	V-8
U	Chev.	305	2bbl	—	V-8
H	Chev.	305	4bbl	—	V-8
L	Chev.	350	4bbl	—	V-8
U	Olds	350	4bbl	—	V-8
R	Olds	350	4bbl	—	V-8
X	Buick	350	4bbl	—	V-8
Z	Pont.	400	4bbl	—	V-8
K	Olds	403	4bbl	—	V-8

(Factory Time)	Chilton Time
301-350-400 engs, Code W-Y-P-Z	
one (3.0)	3.9
both (3.9)	5.4
Grand Prix	
V-6—1978–80—one (2.1)	3.0
both (3.1)	4.6
V-8—1974–76—one (2.6)	3.8
both (4.2)	5.9
1977–80	
305 eng, Code U-H	
one (4.3)	5.2
both (6.0)	7.5
301-350-400 engs, Code W-Y-P-Z	
one (3.0)	3.9
both (3.9)	5.4
350-403 engs, Code R-K	
one (3.4)	4.3
both (4.9)	6.4
w/A.C. add (.5)	.5
w/P.S. add (.2)	.2
w/A.I.R. add (.2)	.2

(G) Cylinder Head, Renew
Includes: Clean gasket surfaces, clean carbon. Transfer all parts, reface valves, make all necessary adjustments.

	Chilton Time
Pontiac	
V-6—1977–80—one (2.7)	4.0
both (4.3)	6.1
V-8—1974–76—one (4.2)	5.5
both (6.7)	7.8
1977–80	
350-403 engs, Code R-K	
one (3.8)	4.9
both (5.9)	7.7
350 eng, Code X	
one (3.0)	4.1
both (5.0)	6.8
301-350-400 engs, Code W-Y-P-Z	
one (4.0)	5.1
both (5.9)	7.7
Grand Prix	
V-6—1978–80—one (2.7)	4.0
both (4.3)	6.1
V-8—1974–76—one (4.2)	5.5
both (6.7)	7.8
1977–80	
305 eng, Code U-H	
one (5.2)	6.3
both (7.8)	9.6
301-350-400 engs, Code W-Y-P-Z	
one (4.0)	5.1
both (5.9)	7.7
350-403 engs, Code R-K	
one (3.8)	4.9
both (5.9)	7.7
w/A.C. add (.5)	.5
w/P.S. add (.2)	.2
w/A.I.R. add (.2)	.2

(P) Clean Carbon and Grind Valves
Includes: R&R cylinder heads, reface valves and seats. Minor tune up.

	Chilton Time
Pontiac	
V-6—1977–80 (4.2)	7.1
V-8—1974–76 (7.7)	10.8
1977–80	
350-403 engs	
Code R-K (6.4)	8.7
350 eng, Code X (6.0)	7.8
301-350-400 engs	
Code W-Y-P-Z (5.2)	8.7

(Factory Time)	Chilton Time
Grand Prix	
V-6—1978–80 (4.2)	7.1
V-8—1974–76 (7.7)	10.8
1977–80	
305 eng, Code U-H (8.8)	10.6
301-350-400 engs	
Code W-Y-P-Z (6.9)	8.7
350-403 engs	
Code R-K (6.4)	8.7
w/A.C. add (.5)	.5
w/P.S. add (.2)	.2
w/A.I.R. add (.2)	.2

(G) Valve Tappets, Renew
Includes: Drain and refill cooling system. R&R intake manifold. Make all necessary adjustments.

	Chilton Time
Pontiac	
V-6—1977–80—one bank (1.4)	2.3
both banks (1.8)	2.9
V-8—1974–76—one bank (2.3)	2.9
both banks (2.6)	3.9
1977–80	
350-403 engs, Code R-K	
one bank (2.2)	2.7
both banks (3.1)	3.7
350 eng, Code X	
one bank (1.5)	2.1
both banks (2.0)	3.1
301-350-400 engs, Code W-Y-P-Z	
one bank (2.2)	2.8
both banks (2.5)	3.8
Grand Prix	
V-6—1978–80—one bank (1.4)	2.3
both tanks (1.8)	2.9
V-8—1974–76—one bank (2.3)	2.9
both banks (2.6)	3.9
1977–80	
305 eng, Code U-H	
one bank (2.5)	3.1
both banks (3.3)	4.1
301-350-400 engs, Code W-Y-P-Z	
one bank (2.2)	2.8
both banks (2.5)	3.8
350-403 engs, Code R-K	
one bank (2.2)	2.7
both banks (3.1)	3.7
w/A.C. add (.4)	.4
w/A.I.R. add (.4)	.4

(G) Valve Spring or Valve Stem Oil Seals, Renew (Head on Car)

	Chilton Time
V-6—1977–80—one cyl (.6)	.8
V-8—1974–76—one cyl (.7)	.9
1977–80	
350-403 engs, Code R-K	
one cyl (.6)	.8
350 eng, Code X	
one cyl (.7)	.9
301-350-400 engs, Code W-Y-P-Z	
one cyl (.7)	.9
305 eng, Code U-H	
one cyl (1.1)	1.4
Each adtnl cyl-all engs (.4)	.4
w/A.C. add (.3)	.3
w/A.I.R. add (.3)	.3

(G) Rocker Arm Shafts and/or Assy's., Renew

	Chilton Time
V-6—1977–80—each (.4)	.6
V-8—1978–80	
350 eng, Code X	
each (.5)	.7

(Factory Time)	Chilton Time
w/A.C. add (.3)	.3
w/A.I.R. add (.3)	.3
Recond each side add (.2)	.3

(G) Rocker Arm Ball and/or Push Rod, Renew

V-8—1974–76	
one side (.6)	.9
1977–80	
350-403 engs, Code R-K	
one side (.6)	.9
301-350-400 engs, Code W-Y-P-Z	
one side (.4)	.7
305 eng, Code U-H	
one side (1.2)	1.5

Pontiac Astre & Sunbird

(G) Camshaft Cover and/or Gasket, Renew

1975–77	
Four—140 eng (.3)	.5

(P) Clean Carbon and Grind Valves

Includes: R&R cylinder heads, reface valves and seats. Minor tune up.

1975–80	
Four—140 eng (5.2)	8.3
151 eng code 1 (3.2)	6.8
code V (3.6)	6.3
V-6 (4.2)	7.1
V-8 (8.4)	10.8
w/A.C. add (.3)	.3
w/P.S. add (.2)	.2
w/A.I.R. add (.3)	.3

(G) Valve Tappets, Renew

Includes: Drain and refill cooling system. R&R intake manifold. Make all necessary adjustments.

1976–80	
Four—151 eng—all (1.6)	2.5
V-6—one bank (1.4)	2.3
both banks (1.8)	2.9
V-8—one bank (2.5)	3.1
both banks (3.3)	4.1

(G) Cam Followers, Renew

1975–77	
Four—140 eng—all (2.1)	3.5

(G) Cylinder Head Gasket, Renew

Includes: R&R cylinder head, clean carbon, make all necessary adjustments.

1975–80	
Four—140 eng (2.6)	3.5
151 eng code 1 (2.6)	3.5
code V (3.0)	4.0
V-6—one (2.1)	3.0
both (3.4)	4.9
V-8—one (4.4)	5.3
both (6.2)	7.7
w/A.C. add (.3)	.3
w/P.S. add (.2)	.2
w/A.I.R. add (.3)	.3

(G) Cylinder Head, Renew

Includes: Clean gasket surfaces, clean carbon. Transfer all parts, reface valves, make all necessary adjustments.

1975–80	
Four—140 eng (5.4)	7.3
151 eng code 1 (3.4)	5.3
code V (3.8)	5.3
V-6—one (2.4)	3.7

(Factory Time)	Chilton Time
both (4.0)	5.8
V-8—one (5.3)	6.4
both (8.0)	9.8
w/A.C. add (.3)	.3
w/P.S. add (.2)	.2
w/A.I.R. add (.3)	.3

(G) Valve Spring or Valve Stem Oil Seals, Renew (Head on Car)

1975–80	
Four—140 eng	
one cyl (2.1)	3.3
all cyls (2.8)	4.0
151 eng	
one cyl (.8)	1.1
each adtnl cyl (.4)	.4
V 6	
one cyl (.6)	.8
each adtnl cyl (.3)	.3
V-8—one cyl (.7)	1.2
each adtnl cyl (.4)	.4

(G) Rocker Arm Shafts and/or Assy's., Renew

1976–80	
V-6—each side (.4)	.6
w/A.I.R. add (.2)	.2
Recond each side add (.2)	.3

(G) Rocker Arm Ball and/or Push Rod, Renew

1975–80	
Four—140 eng	
one cyl (1.9)	2.4
all cyls (2.1)	3.0
151 eng	
one cyl (.6)	.8
all cyls (.8)	1.2
V-8—one cyl (.7)	.9
one side (1.0)	1.3

(G) Rocker Arm Stud, Renew

1976–80	
Four—151 eng—one (.6)	.8
each adtnl (.1)	.1
V-8—one (.8)	1.0
each adtnl (.3)	.3

Firebird, Phoenix (1978–79), LeMans, Ventura (1974–77)

(G) Cylinder Head Gasket, Renew

Includes: R&R cylinder head, clean carbon, make all necessary adjustments.

Four—1977–80—eng Code 1 (2.6)	3.6
eng Code V (3.0)	4.0
Six—1974–76 (2.9)	3.9
V-6—1977–80	
one side (2.1)	3.0
both sides (3.1)	4.6
V-8—1974–76	
one side (2.6)	3.5
both sides (4.2)	5.7
1977–80	
305-350 engs, Code G-H-U-L	
right side (4.5)	5.4
left side (3.9)	4.8
both sides (6.2)	7.7
350-403 engs, Code R-K	
one side (3.4)	4.3
both sides (4.9)	6.4

	Chilton Time
(Factory Time)	

(Factory Time)	Chilton Time

301-350-400 engs, Code W-Y-P-Z
one side (3.0) **3.9**
both sides (3.9) **5.4**
w/A.C. add (.5) .... **.5**
w/P.S. add (.6) .... **.6**
w/A.I.R. add (.6) .... **.6**

(G) Cylinder Head, Renew
Includes: Clean gasket surfaces, clean carbon. Transfer all parts, reface valves, make all necessary adjustments.

Four—1977–80—eng Code 1 (3.4) **4.9**
eng Code V (3.8) **5.3**
Six—1974–76 (4.8) **6.3**
V-6—1977–80—one (2.7) **4.0**
both (4.3) **6.1**
V-8—1974–76—one (4.2) **5.5**
both (6.7) **7.8**
1977–80
305-350 engs, Code G-H-U-L
right side (5.4) **6.5**
left side (4.8) **5.9**
both sides (8.0) **9.8**
350-403 engs, Code R-K
one (3.8) **4.9**
both (5.9) **7.7**
301-350-400 engs, Code W-Y-P-Z
one (4.0) **5.1**
both (5.9) **7.7**
w/A.C. add (.5) .... **.5**
w/P.S. add (.6) .... **.6**
w/A.I.R. add (.6) .... **.6**

(P) Clean Carbon and Grind Valves
Includes: R&R cylinder heads, reface valves and seats. Minor tune up.

Four—1977–80—eng Code 1 (3.2) **5.9**
eng Code V (3.6) **6.3**
Six—1974–76 (5.2) **7.3**
V-6—1977–80 (4.2) **7.1**
V-8—1974–76 (7.7) **10.8**
1977–80
305-350 engs
Code G-H-U-L (8.4) **10.8**
350-403 engs
Code R-K (6.4) **8.7**
301-350-400 engs
Code W-Y-P-Z (5.2) **8.7**
w/A.C. add (.5) .... **.5**
w/P.S. add (.6) .... **.6**
w/A.I.R. add (.6) .... **.6**

(G) Valve Tappets, Renew
Includes: Drain and refill cooling system. R&R intake manifold. Make all necessary adjustments.

Four—1977–80
one cyl (.8) **1.4**
all cyls (1.3) **2.0**
Six—1974–76
one cyl (.8) **1.4**
all cyls (1.3) **2.0**
V-6—1977–80
one bank (1.4) **2.3**
both banks (1.8) **2.3**
V-8—1974–76
one bank (2.3) **2.9**
both banks (2.6) **3.9**
1977–80
305-350 engs, Code G-H-U-L
one bank (2.5) **3.1**
both banks (3.3) **4.1**

350-403 engs, Code R-K
one bank (2.2) **2.7**
both banks (3.1) **3.7**
301-350-403 engs, Code W-Y-P-Z
one bank (2.2) **2.8**
both banks (2.5) **3.8**
w/A.C. add (.4) .... **.4**

(G) Valve Spring or Valve Stem Oil Seals, Renew (Head on Car)
Four—1977–80
one cyl (.8) **1.0**
Six—1974–76
one cyl (.9) **1.1**
V-6—1977–80
one cyl (.6) .... **.8**
V-8—1974–76
one cyl (.7) .... **.9**
1977–80
305-350 engs, Code G-H-U-L
one cyl (1.1) **1.3**
350-403 engs, Code R-K
one cyl (.6) .... **.8**
301-350-400 engs, Code W-Y-P-Z
one cyl (.6) .... **.8**
each adtnl cyl all engs (.4) .... **.4**
w/A.C. add (.4) .... **.4**

(G) Rocker Arm Shafts and/or Assy's., Renew
V-6—1977–80—each (.4) .... **.6**
Recond each side add (.2) .... **.3**
w/A.I.R. add (.3) .... **.3**

(G) Rocker Arm Ball and/or Push Rod, Renew
Four—1977–80
one cyl (.6) .... **.9**
all cyls (.8) **1.2**
Six—1974–76
one cyl (.7) **1.0**
all cyls (.9) **1.3**
V-8—1974–76
one side (.6) .... **.9**
1977–80
305-350 engs, Code G-H-U-L
one cyl (.9) **1.2**
one side (1.2) **1.6**
350-403 engs, Code R-K
one side (.6) .... **.9**
301-350-400 engs, Code W-Y-P-Z
one side (.6) .... **.9**
w/A.C. add (.3) .... **.3**

Thunderbird (1974–76)

(G) Cylinder Head Gasket, Renew
Includes: Check cylinder head and block flatness. Clean carbon and make all necessary adjustments.

1974–76—right (4.2) **5.2**
left (4.5) **5.3**
both (6.0) **7.3**
w/A.C.—right (4.2) **5.3**
left (4.7) **5.5**
both (6.4) **7.8**
w/Thermactor add (.3) .... **.3**

(G) Cylinder Head, Renew
Includes: Transfer all components, clean carbon. Reface valves, check valve spring

	Chilton
(Factory Time)	**Time**

tension, assembled height and valve
head runout.

1974–76—right (5.8)	**7.8**
left (6.1)	**7.9**
both (9.6)	**11.5**
w/A.C.—right (5.8)	**7.9**
left (6.3)	**8.1**

(G) Valve Tappets, Renew

1974–76 (3.4)	**4.3**
w/Thermactor add (.2)	**.2**

(P) Clean Carbon and Grind Valves
*Includes: R&R cylinder heads, check valve
spring tension, valve seat and head runout, stem to guide clearance and spring
assembled height. Minor tune up.*

1974–76 (11.1)	**13.7**
w/A.C. (11.5)	**14.2**
w/Thermactor add (.3)	**.3**

**(G) Valve Spring or Valve Stem Oil
Seals, Renew (Head on Car)**

1974–76—one (.7)	**1.0**
each additional same side (.1) ...	**.3**
w/Thermactor add (.2)	**.2**

(G) Rocker Arm, Renew

1974–76 (.6)	**.9**
w/Thermactor add (.2)	**.2**

(G) Rocker Arm Stud, Renew

1974–76 (.6)	**1.0**
Each adtnl add (.1)	**.1**

(G) Valve Push Rods, Renew

1974–76—one (.6)	**.9**
w/Thermactor add (.2)	**.2**

Valiant, Dart, Barracuda, Challenger, Aspen, Volare, Diplomat, LeBaron

(G) Cylinder Head Gasket, Renew
Includes: Clean carbon.

Six—1974–75 (2.4)	**3.0**
1976 (2.9)	**3.5**
1977–80 (2.6)	**3.5**
V-8—1974–76—one (3.1)	**3.9**
both (4.3)	**5.4**
1977–80—one (2.8)	**3.9**
both (3.7)	**5.4**
w/A.C. add (.4)	**.5**

(G) Cylinder Head, Renew
*Includes: Reface and adjust valves, clean
carbon.*

Six—1974–75 (3.9)	**4.8**
1976 (4.8)	**6.2**
1977–80 (5.4)	**6.5**
V-8—1974–80—one (4.4)	**5.7**
both (6.9)	**9.4**
w/A.C. add (.4)	**.5**

(P) Clean Carbon and Grind Valves
*Includes: R&R cylinder heads, adjust valve
clearance when required. Minor engine
tune up.*

Six—1974–75 (5.0)	**7.2**
1976 (5.4)	**8.1**
1977–80 (4.9)	**8.1**
V-8—1974–75 (8.0)	**11.0**
1976 (7.7)	**11.0**
1977–80 (6.7)	**11.0**
w/A.C. add (.4)	**.5**

	Chilton
(Factory Time)	**Time**

(G) Valve Tappets, Adjust

Six—1974 (1.0)	**1.2**
1975–80 (.7)	**1.0**

(G) Valve Tappets, Renew
*Includes: R&R head and adjust valve clear-
ance on 6 cyl. R&R intake manifold and
clean carbon on V-8's.*

Six—1974–75—one (.9)	***1.2**
all (1.3)	***1.8**
1976—one or all (3.0)	**3.4**
1977–80—one or all (3.3)	**4.0**
V-8—1974–76—one (.9)	***1.4**
all (2.3)	***3.6**
1977–80—one (2.1)	**3.0**
all (2.2)	**3.4**
w/A.C. add (.4)	**.5**

** Note: factory time based on using magnetic
tool thru push rod opening to remove lifters.
Chilton experience finds it better and safer to
R&R intake manifold, since the lifters have a
tendency to stick in the block and sometimes
come apart.*

**(G) Valve Spring or Valve Stem Oil
Seals, Renew (Head On Car)**
*Includes: Adjust valve clearance when
required.*

Six—1974–76—one (1.0)	**1.4**
all (2.6)	**3.2**
1977–80—one or all (2.2)	**3.2**
V-8—1974–76—one (2.5)	**3.4**
All (4.4)	**5.4**
1977–80—one (1.4)	**2.0**
all (3.2)	**4.0**
w/A.C. add (.5)	**.5**

(G) Rocker Arm Assembly, Recondition
*Includes: Renew arms as required and
shaft if necessary.*

Six—1974–80 (.8)	**1.5**
V-8—1974–80—one side (.6)	**1.3**
both sides (1.0)	**2.1**
w/A.C. add (.5)	**.5**

(G) Valve Push Rods, Renew
*Includes: Adjust valve clearance when
required.*

Six—1974–80—one (.8)	**1.0**
all (1.1)	**1.4**
V-8—1974–80—one (.5)	**1.0**
one each bnk (.8)	**1.6**
all both bnks (1.3)	**2.0**
w/A.C. add (.5)	**.5**

Vega & Monza

(G) Cylinder Head Gasket, Renew
*Includes: Clean carbon and make all nec-
essary adjustments.*

Four—1974–77—exc below (2.6) .	**3.8**
Vega Cosworth (5.2)	**7.1**
1977–80—eng code 1 (2.6)	**3.8**
eng Code V (3.0)	**4.2**
V-6—1978–80—right (2.1)	**4.0**
left (2.3)	**4.2**
both (3.4)	**5.7**
V-8—1975–80—right (4.4)	**6.3**
left (4.3)	**6.2**

(Factory Time)	Chilton Time
both (6.2)	8.5
w/P.S. add (.4)	.4
w/A.C. add (.9)	.9
w/A.I.R. add (.6)	.6

(G) Cylinder Head, Renew
Includes: Transfer all components, reface valves, clean carbon.

Four—1974–77—exc below (5.4) .	7.3
Vega Cosworth (8.4)	10.3
1978–80—eng Code 1 (3.4)	5.3
eng Code V (3.8)	5.7
V-6—1978–80—right (2.7)	4.6
left (2.9)	4.8
both (4.6)	6.9
V-8—1975–80—right (5.4)	7.3
left (5.1)	7.0
both (7.7)	10.4
w/P.S. add (.4)	.4
w/A.C. add (.9)	.9
w/A.I.R. add (.6)	.6

(P) Clean Carbon and Grind Valves
Includes: R&R cylinder heads, grind valves and seats. Minor engine tune up.

Four—1974–77—exc below (5.2) .	8.3
Vega Cosworth (8.9)	11.3
1978–80—eng Code 1 (3.4)	6.8
eng Code V (3.6)	7.2
V-6—1978–80—right (2.9)	5.3
left (3.1)	5.5
both (4.8)	7.3
V-8—1975–80—right (5.7)	8.0
left (5.7)	8.0
both (9.0)	11.9
w/P.S. add (.4)	.4
w/A.C. add (.9)	.9
w/A.I.R. add (.6)	.6

(G) Valve Tappets, Adjust

Four—1974–77 (.5)	.7
1978–80 (.5)	.7
V-6—1978–80 (.6)	1.1
V-8—1975–80 (.7)	1.2

(G) Cam Followers, Renew

Four—1974–77—exc below	
—one (1.9)	3.1
all (2.1)	3.5
Vega Cosworth—one (2.7)	3.9
all (3.8)	5.2

(G) Valve Tappets, Renew
Includes: R&R intake manifold on V-6 and

(Factory Time)	Chilton Time
V-8 engines. Make all necessary adjustments.	
Four—1978–80—eng Code 1	
one (.8)	1.3
all (1.3)	2.0
eng Code V—one (1.7)	2.3
all (2.2)	3.0
V-6—1978–80—one (1.4)	2.4
all (1.8)	2.8
V-8—1975–80—one (2.5)	3.5
all (3.3)	4.3
w/A.C. add (.9)	.9
w/A.I.R. add (.5)	.5

(G) Valve Spring or Valve Stem Oil Seals, Renew (Head on Car)

Four—1974–77—one (2.1)	3.3
all (2.8)	4.0
1978–80—one (.8)	1.2
all (2.0)	3.2
V-6—1978–80—one (.6)	1.0
all (2.9)	4.1
V-8—1975–80—one (1.2)	1.6
all (4.3)	5.5
w/A.C. add (.5)	.5
w/A.I.R. add (.2)	.2

(G) Camshaft Housing Cover or Gasket, Renew

Four—1974–77—exc below (.3) ..	.6
Vega Cosworth (.4)	.7

(G) Valve Rocker Arms or Push Rods, Renew

V-6—1978–80—one side (.4)	.9
both sides (.7)	1.3
V-8—1975–80—one (.7)	1.0
all (1.5)	2.2
w/A.C. add (.5)	.5
w/A.I.R. add (.2)	.2

(G) Rocker Arm Stud, Renew

Four—1978–80—one (.6)	.9
each adtnl (.1)	.3
V-8—1975–80—one (.9)	1.2
each adtnl (.3)	.3
w/A.C. add (.5)	.5
w/A.I.R. add (.2)	.2

(G) Rocker Arm Shaft Assy., Renew

V-6—1978–80—one side (.4)	.8
both sides (.7)	1.2
w/A.C. add (.5)	.5
w/A.I.R. add (.3)	.3

CLUTCH

(Factory Time)	Chilton Time
American Motors	

(G) Clutch Assembly, Renew
Includes: R&R transmission, R&R clutch housing, adjust clutch pedal free play, and R&R exhaust pipes on V-8.

1974–76—Six (1.6)	3.0
V-8 (1.9)	3.3
1977–80	
Four (1.9)	3.3

(Factory Time)	Chilton Time
Six (1.6)	3.0
V-8 (1.6)	3.0

(G Clutch Release Bearing, Renew
Includes: R&R transmission and adjust clutch pedal free play.

1974–76 (.8)	1.8
1977–80	
Four (1.6)	1.8
Six (.8)	1.8
V-8 (.8)	1.8

| | Chilton | | | Chilton |
| (Factory Time) | Time | | (Factory Time) | Time |

AMC/Jeep

(G) Clutch Assembly, Renew
Includes: R&R transmission and transfer case as a unit, clutch housing R&R and adjust pedal free play and height.

1974–80—3 spd—exc below (3.2)	**4.3**
CJ series (2.6)	**3.6**
4 spd—exc below (2.6)	**3.6**
CJ series (2.4)	**3.3**

(G) Clutch Release Bearing, Renew
Includes: R&R transmission and adjust pedal free play.

1974–80—3 spd—exc below (2.5)	**3.4**
CJ series (2.0)	**2.7**
4 spd—exc below (2.0)	**2.7**
CJ series (1.8)	**2.5**

Buick Apollo, Century, Gran Sport, Regal, Skylark (1974–79)

(G) Clutch Assembly, Renew
Includes: R&R trans and adjust free play.

1974–76 (2.6)	**3.4**
1977–80 (1.6)	**2.4**

(G) Clutch Release Bearing, Renew
Includes: R&R trans.

Century—Regal

1974–76 (1.7)	**2.5**
1977–80 (1.2)	**2.0**

Apollo—Skylark

1974–80 (1.2)	**2.0**

Buick Skyhawk

(G) Clutch Assembly, Renew
Includes: R&R trans and adjust free play.

1975–76 (2.4)	**3.2**
1977–80 (1.8)	**2.6**
w/5 speed add (.4)	**.5**

(G) Clutch Release Bearing, Renew
Includes: R&R trans.

1975–76 (1.9)	**2.7**
1977–80 (1.4)	**2.2**
w/5 speed add (.4)	**.5**

Camaro, Chevelle, Malibu, Monte Carlo, Nova

(G) Clutch Assembly, Renew
Includes: R&R trans, and adjust free play.

3 Speed—Monte Carlo, Malibu, Chevelle

1974 (1.7)	**2.9**
1975–77 (2.0)	**3.2**
1978–80 (1.6)	**2.9**

Camaro, Nova

1974 (1.7)	**2.9**
1975–80 (2.0)	**3.2**

4 Speed—Chevelle, Nova

1974–80 (2.0)	**3.2**

Camaro

1974 (1.7)	**2.9**
1975–80 (2.0)	**3.2**

Monte Carlo, Malibu

1978–80 (1.8)	**3.0**

(G) Clutch Release Bearing or Fork, Renew
Includes: R&R trans and adjust free play.

3 Speed—Monte Carlo, Malibu, Chevelle

1974 (1.4)	**2.6**
1975–77 (1.7)	**2.9**
1978–80 (1.1)	**2.5**

Camaro

1974 (1.5)	**2.7**
1975–77 (1.8)	**3.0**
1978–80 (1.7)	**3.0**

Nova

1974 (.9)	**3.0**
1975–77 (1.8)	**3.0**
1978–79 (1.7)	**3.0**

4 Speed—Chevelle, Nova

1974 (1.3)	**2.5**
1975–80 (1.8)	**3.0**

Camaro

1974 (1.1)	**2.4**
1975–80 (1.8)	**3.0**

Monte Carlo, Malibu

1978–80 (1.2)	**2.5**

Chevrolet & Corvette

(G) Clutch Assembly, Renew
Includes: R&R trans and adjust free play.

Corvette

1974 (3.8)	**4.9**
1975–80 (2.8)	**4.6**

(G) Clutch Release Bearing or Fork, Renew
Includes: R&R trans and adjust free play.

Corvette

1974 (3.0)	**3.9**
1975–80 (2.5)	**3.9**

Chevette

(G) Clutch Assembly, Renew
Includes: R&R trans and adjust free play.

1976–80 (1.7)	**3.5**

(G) Clutch Release Bearing or Fork, Renew
Includes: R&R trans and adjust free play.

1976–80 (1.7)	**3.5**

(G) Clutch Control Cable, Renew

1976–80 (.5)	**.8**

Citation, Omega, Phoenix, Skylark—All 1980

(G) Clutch Release Bearing, Renew
Includes: R&R trans and make all necessary adjustments.

1980 (2.2)	**3.8**

(G) Clutch Assembly, Renew
Includes: R&R trans and make all necessary adjustments.

1980 (2.4)	**4.2**

	Chilton Time
(Factory Time)	

Dodge

(G) Clutch Assembly, Renew
3 Speed
  1974–76 (1.3) 2.5
  1977–78 (1.7) 2.7
4 Speed
  1974 (2.2) 3.1
(G) Clutch Release Bearing, Renew
3 Speed
  1974–78 (1.4) 2.0
4 Speed
  1974 (1.8) 2.6

Horizon & Omni

(G) Clutch Assembly, Renew
  1978–80 (2.8) 3.6
(G) Clutch Release Bearing, Renew
Note: Not necessary to R&R trans/axle assy.
  1978–80 (.5) 8
(G) Clutch Release Cable, Renew
  1978–80 (.3) 5

Capri & Mustang (1979–80)

(G) Clutch Assembly, Renew
Includes: R&R flywheel housing and adjust free play.
  Four—1979–80 (1.9) 2.5
  V-8—1979–80 (1.7) 2.3
(G) Clutch Release Bearing, Renew
Includes: R&R trans and adjust free play.
  Four—1979–80 (1.6) 2.2
  V-8—1979–80 (1.1) 1.7
(G) Clutch Cable, Renew
  1979–80 (.4) 8

Comet, Cougar, Monarch, Montego, Lincoln Versailles

(G) Clutch Assembly, Renew
Includes: R&R flywheel housing and adjust free play.
  1974–80
  3 speed (1.7) 2.4
  4 speed (2.0) 2.9
(G) Clutch Release Bearing, Renew
Includes: R&R trans and adjust free play.
  1974–80
  3 speed (1.2) 2.0
  4 speed (1.4) 2.2

Elite, Granada, Maverick, Torino, LTD II, Thunderbird (1977–79)

(G) Clutch Assembly, Renew
Includes: R&R flywheel housing and adjust free play.
  1974–80
  3 speed (1.7) 2.4
  4 speed (2.0) 2.9

	Chilton Time
(Factory Time)	

(G) Clutch Release Bearing, Renew
Includes: R&R trans and adjust free play.
  1974–80
  3 speed (1.2) 2.0
  4 speed (1.4) 2.2

Mustang II, Bobcat, Pinto, Fairmont, Zephyr

(G) Clutch Assembly, Renew
Includes: R&R flywheel housing and adjust free play.
  1974–80
  3 speed (2.1) 3.0
  4 speed (2.7) 3.6
(G) Clutch Release Bearing, Renew
Includes: R&R trans and adjust free play.
  1974–80
  3 speed (1.3) 2.1
  4 speed (1.8) 2.6
(G) Clutch Cable, Renew
  1974–80—exc below (.5) 8
  Mustang II (.7) 1.0

Olds Cutlass, Omega (1974–79)

(G) Clutch Assembly, Renew
3 speed
  1974–75—column shift (1.6) 2.4
  floor shift (1.8) 2.6
  1976–80 (1.6) 2.4
4 Speed
  1978–80 (1.6) 2.4
5 Speed
  1976–80 (2.0) 2.8
(G) Clutch Release Bearing, Renew
3 Speed
  1974–75—column shift (1.2) 2.0
  floor shift (1.4) 2.2
  1976–80 (1.2) 2.0
4 Speed
  1978–80 (1.2) 2.0
5 Speed
  1976–80 (1.6) 2.4

Olds Starfire

(G) Clutch Assembly, Renew
Includes: R&R trans and adjust free play.
  4 Speed
  1975–80 (1.8) 2.6
  5 Speed
  1976–80 (2.2) 3.0
(G) Clutch Release Bearing, Renew
Includes: R&R trans and adjust free play.
  4 Speed
  1975–80 (1.7) 2.5
  5 Speed
  1976–80 (2.1) 2.9
(G) Clutch Control Cable, Renew
  1975–80 (.6) 8

Plymouth

(G) Clutch Assembly, Renew
3 Speed
  1974–76 (1.3) 2.5

(Factory Time)	Chilton Time
1977–78 (1.7)	2.7
4 Speed	
1974 (2.2)	3.1
(G) Clutch Release Bearing, Renew	
3 Speed	
1974–78 (1.4)	2.0
4 Speed	
1974 (1.8)	2.6

Pontiac & Grand Prix

(G) Clutch Assembly, Renew
Includes: R&R trans and flywheel housing. Make all necessary adjustments.

1978–80 (1.7)	2.5

(G) Clutch Release Bearing, Renew
Includes: R&R trans and make all necessary adjustments.

1978–80 (1.2)	2.0

Pontiac Astre & Sunbird

(G) Clutch Assembly, Renew
Includes: R&R trans and flywheel housing. Make all necessary adjustments.

1975–80	
3 spd (1.8)	2.6
4 spd—exc below (2.5)	3.3
Brazil—4 spd (1.7)	2.5
5 spd (2.2)	3.0

(G) Clutch Release Bearing, Renew
Includes: R&R trans and make all necessary adjustments.

1975–80	
3 spd (1.5)	2.3
4 spd (1.4)	2.2
5 spd (2.0)	3.0

Firebird, Phoenix (1978–79), LeMans, Ventura (1974–77)

(G) Clutch Assembly, Renew
Includes: R&R trans and flywheel housing. Make all necessary adjustments.

1974—Firebird—LeMans	
3 spd (2.2)	*3.0
4 spd (2.4)	3.2
Ventura	
3 spd (1.7)	*2.5
4 spd (1.9)	2.7
1975–80—3 spd (1.7)	*2.5
4 spd (1.9)	2.7
5 spd (2.2)	3.0
* w/Floor shift add (.2)	.2

(Factory Time)	Chilton Time
(G) Clutch Release Bearing, Renew	

Includes: R&R trans and make all necessary adjustments.

1974—Firebird—LeMans	
3 spd (1.5)	*2.3
4 spd (1.7)	2.5
Ventura	
3 spd (1.0)	*1.8
4 spd (1.2)	2.0
1975–80—3 spd (1.2)	*2.0
4 spd (1.4)	2.2
5 spd (2.0)	2.8
* w/Floor shift add (.2)	.2

Valiant, Dart, Barracuda, Challenger, Aspen, Volare, LeBaron, Diplomat

(G) Clutch Assembly, Renew

3 Speed	
1974–76 (1.3)	2.5
1977–80 (1.5)	2.7
4 Speed	
1974–76 (2.6)	3.3
1977–80 (1.9)	2.7

(G) Clutch Release Bearing, Renew

3 Speed	
1974–80 (1.1)	2.0
4 Speed	
1974 (1.8)	2.6
1975–76 (2.1)	2.7
1977–80 (1.5)	2.1

Vega & Monza

(G) Clutch Assembly, Renew
Includes: R&R trans and adjust free play.

3 Speed	
1974–76 (2.3)	3.5
4 Speed	
1974–80 (2.5)	3.7
5 Speed	
1975–80 (2.2)	3.5

(G) Clutch Release Bearing or Fork, Renew
Includes: R&R trans and adjust free play.

3 Speed	
1974–76 (1.8)	3.0
4 Speed	
1974–80 (2.0)	3.2
5 Speed	
1975–80 (2.0)	3.2

(G) Clutch Control Cable, Renew

1974–77 (.4)	.7
1978–80 (.5)	.8

DATSUN LABOR (Chilton Time)

SECTION I

	F-10	200SX	510	610-710	B110 B210
Tune Up					
Engine Tune-Up (Minor)	2.2	2.3	2.1	2.3	2.2

	F-10	200SX	510	610-710	B110 B210
Fuel System					
Carburetor, Adjust (on Car)	.3	.3	.3	.3	.3
Carburetor, Renew					
One	1.1	1.2	1.1	1.2	1.1
Both	—	—	—	—	—
Carburetor, R&R and Recondition					
One	2.2	2.3	2.1	2.3	2.2
Both	—	—	—	—	—
Fuel Pump, Renew					
Mech.	.6	.5	.6	.5	.5
Elec.	—	.6	—	.6	—
Intake Manifold or Gasket, Renew	5.4■	2.2	1.9	2.2	1.7
Alternator					
Alternator, Renew	.7	.7	.7	.7	.7
Alternator, R&R and Recondition	1.7	1.7	1.7	1.7	1.7
Alternator, R&R and Renew Bearings	1.2	1.2	1.2	1.2	1.2
Alternator Regulator, Renew	.5	.5	.5	.5	.5
Starting System					
Starter, Renew	.9	.8	.9	.8	.8
Starter, R&R and Recondition	1.9	1.8	1.9	1.8	1.8
Starter Drive, Renew	1.2	1.2	1.5	1.2	1.2
Starter Solenoid, Renew	1.1	1.1	1.3	1.1	1.1
Brake System					
Brakes, Adjust (Minor)	.4	.3	.4	.3	.3
Brake Shoes or Disc Pads, Renew					
Front	.8	.8	1.0	.8	.8
Rear	2.2	2.2	2.2	2.2	2.2
Brake Drum, Renew					
Front (one)	—	—	—	—	—
Rear (one)	.5	.5	.5	.5	.5
Reface Drum (one)	.4	.4	.4	.4	.4
Wheel Cylinder, Renew—One	.9	.9	.9	.9	.9
Wheel Cylinder, R&R and Recondition—One	1.1	1.1	1.1	1.1	1.1
Master Cylinder, Renew	.8	.8	.8	.8	.8
Master Cylinder, R&R and Recondition	1.2	1.2	1.2	1.2	1.2
Bleed Brakes	.5	.5	.5	.5	.5
Disc Brake Rotor, Renew (one)	1.0	1.0	1.0	1.0	1.0
Disc Brake Rotor, Reface (one)	.6	.6	.6	.6	.6
Disc Brake Caliper, Renew (one)	.7	.7	.7	.7	.7
Disc Brake Caliper, R&R and Recondition (one)	1.1	1.1	1.1	1.1	1.1
Cooling System					
Fan Belt, Renew	.3	.3	.3	.3	.3
Thermostat, Renew	.5	.5	.5	.5	.5
Radiator Assembly, Renew					
Std. Trans.	.8	.9	.9	.9	.7
Auto. Trans.	.9	1.1	1.1	1.1	.9
Water Pump, Renew	1.1	1.5	1.5	1.4	1.1
Exhaust System					
Muffler, Renew	1.2	1.2	1.2	1.2	1.2
Exhaust Pipe, Renew					
Front	1.0	1.1	1.1	1.1	1.1

■ Includes: R&R Engine Assy.

	F-10	200SX	510	610-710	B110 B210
Center	—	.9	.9	.9	.9
Rear	.8	.8	.6	.8	.8
Exhaust Manifold or Gasket, Renew	5.6■	2.7	2.8	2.3	2.0

Front Suspension

	F-10	200SX	510	610-710	B110 B210
Toe In, Adjust	1.0	1.0	1.0	1.0	1.0
Caster, Camber, Toe In, Adjust	—	—	—	—	—
Front Wheel Bearings, Repack	1.3†	2.0	2.0	2.0	2.0
*Lower Ball Joint, Renew (one)	1.3	1.3	1.3	1.3	1.3
Front Wheel Bearing, Renew—One Side	1.6	1.3	1.0	1.3	1.3
*Control Arm, Renew					
Upper	—	—	—	—	—
Lower	.9	.9	.9	.9	.9
Both	—	—	—	—	—
*Front Strut Shock Assembly, R&R and Recondition	2.7	2.7	2.7	2.7	2.7
Shock Absorber, Renew					
Front	—	—	—	—	—
Rear	.6	.6	.6	.6	.6
Shock Absorber, R&R and Recondition	—	—	—	—	—
Front Strut Assembly, Renew—One	1.9	2.0	1.9	2.0	2.0

Cylinder Head & Valves

	F-10	200SX	510	610-710	B110 B210
Compression Test	.6	.5	.5	.5	.5
Cylinder Head Gasket, Renew	4.0	4.0	4.0	4.0	3.0
Cylinder Head, Renew	6.0	6.0	6.0	6.0	4.8
Valve Spring and/or Valve Stem Oil Seal, Renew Head on Engine					
(one)	1.2	1.2	1.2	1.2	1.2
(all)	2.5	2.5	2.5	2.5	2.5
Rocker Arm and/or Shaft, Renew					
(one)	1.2	.7	.7	.7	1.1
(all)	1.5	1.0	1.0	1.0	1.3
Push Rod, Renew					
(one)	1.1	—	—	—	.9
(all)	1.6	—	—	—	1.2
■ Valve Lifters, Renew (all)	7.5	—	—	—	6.9
Adjust Valves	1.0	1.0	1.0	1.0	1.0
Clean Carbon and Grind Valves	8.5	8.5	8.5	8.5	6.8

Clutch

	F-10	200SX	510	610-710	B110 B210
Clutch Assembly, Renew	3.0	3.9	3.9	3.9	3.6
Clutch Release Bearing, Renew	2.4	3.6	3.6	3.6	3.4
Clutch Master Cylinder, Renew	.8	.8	.8	.8	.8
Clutch Master Cylinder, R&R and Recondition	1.3	1.3	1.3	1.3	1.3
Clutch Slave Cylinder, Renew	.7	.7	.7	.7	.7
Clutch Slave Cylinder, R&R and Recondition	1.0	1.0	1.0	1.0	1.0

DATSUN LABOR (Chilton Time)

SECTION II	810	240Z	260Z	280Z	Trucks
Tune Up					
Engine Tune-Up (Minor)	2.3	2.4	2.5	2.3	2.3
Fuel System					
Carburetor, Adjust (on Car)	—	.4	.4	—	4

*Alignment Not Included ■Includes R&R Engine Assy. †F-10 One Side Only

	810	240Z	260Z	280Z	Trucks
Carburetor, Renew					
One	—	1.5	1.6	—	1.1
Both	—	2.0	2.4	—	—
Carburetor, R&R and Recondition					
One	—	2.3	2.2	—	2.3
Both	—	3.8	3.8	—	—
Fuel Pump, Renew					
Mech.	—	—	—	—	.6
Elec.	.7	.7	.7	.7	—
Intake Manifold or Gasket, Renew	2.9	2.9	2.9	2.9	2.2

Alternator

	810	240Z	260Z	280Z	Trucks
Alternator, Renew	.7	.7	.7	.7	.7
Alternator, R&R and Recondition	1.7	1.7	1.7	1.7	1.7
Alternator, R&R and Renew Bearings	1.2	1.2	1.2	1.2	1.2
Alternator Regulator, Renew	.5	.5	.5	.5	.5

Starting System

	810	240Z	260Z	280Z	Trucks
Starter, Renew	.8	.9	.8	.8	.8
Starter, R&R and Recondition	1.8	1.9	1.8	1.8	1.8
Starter Drive, Renew	1.2	1.5	1.2	1.2	1.2
Starter Solenoid, Renew	1.1	1.3	1.1	1.1	1.1

Brake System

	810	240Z	260Z	280Z	Trucks
Brakes, Adjust (Minor)	.4	.3	.3	.3	.4
Brake Shoes or Disc Pads, Renew					
Front	1.0	.8	.8	.8	1.0
Rear	2.2	2.2	2.2	2.2	2.2
Brake Drum, Renew					
Front (one)	—	—	—	—	.6
Rear (one)	.5	.5	.5	.5	.5
Reface Drum (one)	.4	.4	.4	.4	.4
Wheel Cylinder, Renew—One	.9	.9	.9	.9	.9
Wheel Cylinder, R&R and Recondition—One	1.1	1.1	1.1	1.1	1.1
Master Cylinder, Renew	.8	1.0	.8	.8	.8
Master Cylinder, R&R and Recondition	1.2	1.4	1.2	1.2	1.2
Brake Hose, Renew					
Front (one)	.6	.6	.6	.6	.6
Front (both)	1.0	1.0	1.0	1.0	1.0
Rear	.6	.6	.6	.6	.6
Bleed Brakes	.5	.5	.5	.5	.5
Disc Brake Rotor, Renew (one)	1.0	1.0	1.0	1.0	—
Disc Brake Rotor, Reface (one)	.6	.6	.6	.6	—
Disc Brake Caliper, Renew (one)	.7	.7	.7	.7	—
Disc Brake Caliper, R&R and Recondition (one)	1.1	1.1	1.1	1.1	—

Cooling System

	810	240Z	260Z	280Z	Trucks
Fan Belt, Renew	.3	.3	.3	.3	.3
Thermostat, Renew	.5	.5	.5	.5	.5
Radiator Assembly, Renew					
Std. Trans.	.8	.8	.8	.8	.9
Auto Trans.	1.0	1.0	1.0	1.0	1.1
Water Pump, Renew	1.5	1.5	1.5	1.5	1.4

Exhaust System

	810	240Z	260Z	280Z	Trucks
Muffler, Renew	1.2	1.2	1.2	1.2	1.2
Exhaust Pipe, Renew					
Front	1.0	1.0	1.0	1.0	1.1
Rear	.9	.9	.9	.9	.9

	810	240Z	260Z	280Z	Trucks
Center	.6	.6	.6	.6	.6
Exhaust Manifold or Gasket, Renew	3.0	3.0	3.1	3.0	2.3

Front Suspension

	810	240Z	260Z	280Z	Trucks
Toe In, Adjust	1.0	1.0	1.0	1.0	1.0
Caster, Camber, Toe In, Adjust	—	—	—	—	2.0
Front Wheel Bearings, Repack	2.0	2.0	2.0	2.0	1.7
*Upper Ball Joint, Renew (one)	—	—	—	—	1.7
*Lower Ball Joint, Renew (one)	1.3	1.3	1.3	1.3	—
Front Wheel Bearing, Renew—One Side	1.3	1.3	1.3	1.3	1.1
*Control Arm, Renew					
Upper	—	—	—	—	1.4
Lower	.9	.9	.9	.9	1.4
Both	—	—	—	—	2.5
*Front Strut Shock Assembly, R&R and Recondition	2.1	2.1	2.1	2.1	
Shock Absorber, Renew					
Front	—	—	—	—	.5
Rear	—	—	—	—	.6
Shock Absorber, R&R and Recondition	2.5	2.5	2.5	2.5	—
Front Strut Assembly, Renew—One	2.0	1.9	2.0	2.0	—

Cylinder Heads & Valves

	810	240Z	260Z	280Z	Trucks
Compression Test	.6	.6	.6	.6	.5
Cylinder Head Gasket, Renew	4.5	4.5	4.5	4.5	4.0
Cylinder Head, Renew	7.4	7.4	7.4	7.4	6.0
Valve Spring and/or Valve Stem Oil Seal,					
Renew Head on Engine					
(one)	1.2	1.2	1.2	1.2	1.2
(all)	3.1	3.1	3.1	3.1	2.5
Rocker Arm and/or Shaft, Renew					
(one)	1.0	1.0	1.0	1.0	.7
(all)	1.5	1.5	1.5	1.5	1.0
Push Rod, Renew					
(one)	—	—	—	—	—
(all)	—	—	—	—	—
■Valve Lifters, Renew (all)	—	—	—	—	—
Adjust Valves	1.2	1.2	1.2	1.2	1.0
Clean Carbon and Grind Valves	10.0	10.0	10.0	10.0	8.5

Clutch

	810	240Z	260Z	280Z	Trucks
Clutch Assembly, Renew	4.4	4.4	4.4	4.4	3.9
Clutch Release Bearing, Renew	4.1	4.1	4.1	4.1	3.6
Clutch Master Cylinder, Renew	.8	.8	.8	.8	.8
Clutch Master Cylinder, R&R and Recondition	1.3	1.3	1.3	1.3	1.3
Clutch Slave Cylinder, Renew	.7	.7	.7	.7	.7
Clutch Slave Cylinder, R&R and Recondition	1.0	1.0	1.0	1.0	1.0

HONDA LABOR (Chilton Time)

	CIVIC	CIVIC A.I.R.	CIVIC CVCC	CIVIC WAGON	ACCORD
Tune Up					
Engine Tune Up (Minor)	1.4	1.4	1.4	1.4	1.4
Fuel System					
Carburetor, Adjust (on car)	.3	.3	.3	.3	.3
Carburetor, Renew	1.2	1.2	1.4	1.4	1.9
Carburetor, R&R and Recondition	2.5	2.5	3.0	3.0	3.6

*Alignment Not Included   ■Includes: R&R Engine

	CIVIC	CIVIC A.I.R.	CIVIC CVCC	CIVIC WAGON	ACCORD
Fuel Pump, Renew	.5	.5	.7	.5	.9
Intake Manifold and/or Gasket, Renew	.9	.9	2.4	2.4	2.4

Alternator

Alternator, Renew	.6	.6	.6	.6	.6
Alternator, R&R and Recondition	1.4	1.4	1.4	1.4	1.4
Alternator, R&R and Renew Bearings	.9	.9	.9	.9	.9
Voltage Regulator, Renew	.3	.3	.4	.4	.4

Starting System

Starter, Renew	.7	.7	.7	.7	.7
Starter, R&R and Renew Drive	1.0	1.0	1.0	1.0	1.0
Starter, R&R and Recondition	1.5	1.5	1.5	1.5	1.5
Starter, R&R and Renew Solenoid	.9	.9	.9	.9	.9

Brake System

Brake Shoes or Disc Pads, Renew					
Front whls.	.9	.9	.9	.9	.9
Rear whls.	1.3	1.3*	1.3	1.3	1.3
Four whls.	2.0	2.0	2.0	2.0	2.0
Wheel Cylinders, Renew—Rear					
(one)	1.1	1.1	1.1	1.1	1.1
(both)	1.6	1.6	1.6	1.6	1.6
Wheel Cylinders, R&R and Recondition					
(one)	1.4	1.4	1.4	1.4	1.4
(both)	1.9	1.9	1.9	1.9	1.9
Master Cylinder, Renew	.9	.9	.9	.9	1.3
Master Cylinder, R&R and Recondition	1.8	1.8	1.8	1.8	1.8
Bleed Brakes	.4	.4	.4	.4	.4
Disc Brake Rotors, Renew—Front					
(one)	1.6	1.6	1.6	1.6	1.8
(both)	2.6	2.6	2.6	2.6	2.6
Disc Brake Caliper, Renew—Front					
(one)	.9	.9	.9	.9	.9
(both)	1.3	1.3	1.3	1.3	1.3
Brake Caliper, R&R and Recondition—Front					
(one)	1.4	1.4	1.4	1.4	1.4
(both)	1.9	1.9	1.9	1.9	1.9
Reface Disc Rotor, Add	.5	.5	.5	.5	.5
Brake, Drum, Renew—Rear					
(one)	.9	.9	.9	.9	.9
(both)	1.5	1.5	1.5	1.5	1.5
Reface Rear Drum, Add	.5	.5	.5	.5	.5

Cooling System

Fan Belt, Renew	.4	.4	.4	.4	.4
Thermostat, Renew	.6	.6	.6	.6	.6
Radiator, Renew	1.5	1.5	1.3	1.3	1.4
Water Pump, Renew	.8	.8	.8	.8	1.0

Exhaust System

Exhaust Pipe, Renew	.9	.9	1.0	1.0	.9
Exhaust Pipe (Front), Renew	—	—	.9	.9	.8
Muffler, Renew	.8	.8	.8	.8	.7
Exhaust Manifold, Renew					
1973–75	.8	.8	2.4	2.4	2.4
1976–80	—	—	*4.3	*4.3	*4.3

*Includes R&R Cylinder Head.

	CIVIC	CIVIC A.I.R.	CIVIC CVCC	CIVIC WAGON	ACCORD

Front Suspension

Toe In, Adjust	.6	.6	.6	.6	.6
Front Wheel Bearing, Renew (one whl.)	2.0	2.0	2.0	2.0	2.1
Front Spring, Renew					
(one)	1.5	1.5	1.5	1.5	1.5
(both)	2.2	2.2	2.2	2.2	2.2
†Lower Control Arm, Renew (one)	1.1	1.1	1.1	1.1	1.1
Ball Joint, Renew (one)	1.3	1.3	1.3	1.3	1.3
Front Strut Shock Absorber, R&R and Recondition (one)	1.7	1.7	1.7	1.7	1.7
Front Strut Assembly, Renew (one)	1.5	1.5	1.5	1.5	1.5

Cylinder Head & Valves

Compression Test	.5	.5	.5	.5	.5
Cylinder Head, Renew	5.9	6.3	5.6	5.6	6.3
Cylinder Head Gasket, Renew	3.0	3.4	4.8	4.8	5.4
Valve Spring and/or Valve Stem Oil Seal, Renew (Head on Engine)					
One	1.2	1.2	1.2	1.2	1.2
All	1.9	1.9	1.9	1.9	1.9
Rocker Arms and/or Shaft, Renew					
(one)	1.7	1.7	1.8	1.8	1.7
(all)	2.0	2.0	2.1	2.1	2.0
Adjust Valves	.5	.5	.7	.7	.7
Pre Chamber, R&R and Recondition (Head on Engine)					
One	—	—	2.0	2.0	3.1
All	—	—	2.4	2.4	3.4
Clean Carbon and Grind Valves	7.0	7.4	6.7	6.7	7.4

Clutch

Clutch Assembly, Renew	3.2	3.2	3.2	3.2	3.2
Clutch Release Bearing, Renew	2.9	2.9	2.9	2.9	2.9
Clutch Cable, Renew	.6	.6	.5	.5	—
Clutch Master Cylinder, Renew	—	—	—	—	1.2
Clutch Master Cylinder, R&R and Recondition .	—	—	—	—	1.9
Clutch Slave Cylinder, Renew	—	—	—	—	1.0
Clutch Slave Cylinder, R&R and Recondition ..	—	—	—	—	1.7

TOYOTA LABOR (Chilton Time)

SECTION I

	Crown	Mark II	Corona 4 cyl	Celica ST	Mark II/6

Tune Up

Engine Tune Up (Minor)	2.3	1.6	1.6	1.6	2.3

Fuel System

Carburetor, Adjust (on car)	.4	.4	.4	.4	.4
Carburetor, Renew	1.0	1.3	1.3	1.3	.9
Carburetor, R&R and Recondition	2.3	3.0	3.0	3.0	2.5
Fuel Pump, Renew	.7	.6	.6	.6	.6
Intake Manifold Gasket, Renew	1.8	1.8	1.8	1.8	1.8

Alternator

Alternator, Renew	1.0	.8	.8	.8	1.4
Alternator, R&R and Recondition	2.2	2.0	2.0	2.0	2.7

†Includes: Alignment

	Crown	Mark II	Corona 4 cyl	Celica ST	Mark II/6
Alternator, R&R and Renew Bearings	1.3	1.1	1.1	1.1	1.8
Voltage Regulator, Renew	.7	.6	.6	.6	.7

Starting System

Starter, Renew	.9	.9	.9	.9	.9
Starter Drive, Renew	1.8	1.8	1.8	1.8	1.5
Starter, R&R and Recondition	2.0	2.0	2.0	2.0	1.8
Starter Solenoid, Renew	1.0	1.0	1.0	1.0	1.0

Brake System

Brakes, Adjust (Minor)	.9	.9	.9	.9	.7
Brake Shoes, Renew					
Front whls	—	1.7	—	—	1.7
Rear whls	1.7	1.7	1.7	1.7	1.7
Wheel Cylinder, Renew					
Front (one)	—	1.2	—	—	1.2
Rear (one)	1.4	1.4	1.4	1.4	1.4
Wheel Cylinder, Recondition					
Front (one)	—	1.3	—	—	1.3
Rear (one)	1.5	1.5	1.5	1.5	1.5
Master Cylinder, Renew	2.2	1.6	1.6	1.7	1.8
Master Cylinder, R&R and Recondition ...	2.3	2.0	2.0	2.2	2.2
Brake Drum, Renew					
Front	—	1.2	—	—	1.2
Rear	.9	1.1	1.1	1.2	.9
Brake Drum, Reface (add)	.3	.3	.3	.3	.3
Bleed Brakes	1.0	.8	.8	.8	1.3
Disc Brake Rotor, Renew (one)	1.5	1.5	1.5	1.3	1.3
Disc Brake Pads, Renew—Front whls	.9	.9	.9	.9	.9
Disc Caliper, Renew (one)	1.2	1.2	1.2	1.2	1.2
Resurface Disc, Add	.6	.6	.6	.6	.6
Brake Caliper, R&R and Recondition					
(one)	1.7	1.7	1.7	1.7	1.7
(both)	2.2	2.2	2.2	2.2	2.2

Cooling System

Fan Belt, Renew	.6	.5	.5	.5	.5
Thermostat, Renew	.6	.6	.6	.6	.6
Radiator, R&R or Renew	1.2	1.2	1.2	1.2	1.2
Water Pump, Renew	1.6	1.3	1.3	1.1	1.3

Exhaust System

Muffler, Renew	1.2	.8	1.0	1.1	.8
Exhaust Pipe, Renew					
Front	1.2	1.1	1.1	1.1	1.0
Center	—	—	1.0	—	.8
Tail Pipe, Renew	1.0	.9	.9	1.0	.7
Exhaust Manifold or Gasket, Renew	1.4	1.4	1.4	1.5	1.3

Front Suspension

Caster, Camber and Toe In, Adjust	1.2	1.2	1.2	—	1.2
Toe In, Adjust	.5	.5	.5	.5	.5
Front Wheel Bearings, Repack					
(disc)	1.4	1.4	1.4	1.4	1.4
(drum)	—	.9	—	—	.9
Front Wheel Bearings, Renew (one whl) ..	1.0	1.0	1.0	1.0	1.0
†Control Arm, Renew					
(upper)	2.4	2.1	2.1	—	2.1

†Includes: Alignment

	Crown	Mark II	Corona 4 cyl	Celica ST	Mark II/6
(lower)	3.2	3.1	3.1	1.4	2.5
(both)	4.7	4.5	4.5	—	3.9
†Ball Joint, Renew					
(upper)	2.1	2.1	2.1	—	2.1
(lower)	2.7	2.4	2.4	1.4	2.5
(both)	4.0	3.7	3.7	—	3.8
†Front Strut Shock Absorber, R&R and					
Recondition (one)	—	—	—	1.9	—
Front Shock Absorber, Renew					
(one)	.6	.6	.6	—	.6
(both)	.8	.8	.8	—	.8
†Front Strut Assembly, Renew (one)	—	—	—	1.7	—

Cylinder Head & Valves

	Crown	Mark II	Corona 4 cyl	Celica ST	Mark II/6
Compression Test	.6	.6	.6	.6	.6
Cylinder Head Gasket, Renew	5.0	4.0	4.0	4.0	5.0
Cylinder Head, Renew	10.3	8.4	8.4	8.4	10.3
Valve Spring and/or Valve Stem Oil Seal,					
Renew (Head on Engine)					
One	1.5	1.2	1.2	1.2	1.5
All	2.6	1.9	1.9	1.9	2.6
*Push Rods and/or Rocker Arms, Renew					
(one)	2.4	3.0	3.0	3.0	2.4
(all)	2.8	3.5	3.5	3.5	2.8
*Valve Lifters, Renew					
(one)	—	—	—	—	—
(all)	—	—	—	—	—
Adjust Valves	.9	.9	.9	.9	.9
Clean Carbon and Grind Valves	11.5	9.7	9.7	9.7	11.5

Clutch

	Crown	Mark II	Corona 4 cyl	Celica ST	Mark II/6
Clutch Assembly, Renew	3.5	3.2	3.2	3.3	3.5
Clutch Release Bearing, Renew	3.1	2.8	2.8	2.8	3.1
Clutch Master Cylinder, Renew	1.0	1.0	1.0	1.0	1.0
Clutch Master Cylinder, Recondition	1.5	1.5	1.5	1.5	1.5
Clutch Slave Cylinder, Renew	.7	.7	.7	.7	.7
Clutch Slave Cylinder, Recondition	1.2	1.2	1.2	1.2	1.2
Clutch Cable, Renew	—	—	—	—	—

TOYOTA LABOR (Chilton Time)

SECTION II

	Carina	Corolla 1600cc	Corolla 1200cc	Hi Lux	Land Cruiser
Tune Up					
Engine Tune Up (Minor)	1.6	1.6	1.4	1.6	2.0
Fuel System					
Carburetor, Adjust (on car)	.4	.4	.4	.4	.4
Carburetor, Renew	1.3	1.3	1.3	1.5	1.5
Carburetor, R&R and Recondition	2.5	2.5	2.5	2.7	3.0
Fuel Pump, Renew	1.0	1.0	1.0	.8	.8
Intake Manifold Gasket, Renew	1.3	1.3	1.3	1.5	3.6
Alternator					
Alternator, Renew	.8	.8	.8	.8	.8
Alternator, R&R and Recondition	2.0	2.0	2.0	2.0	2.0

†To check alignment add—.8　　　　　*For OHV engine refer to Section II

	Carina	Corolla 1600cc	Corolla 1200cc	Hi Lux	Land Cruiser
Alternator, R&R and Renew Bearings	1.2	1.2	1.2	1.2	1.2
Voltage Regulator, Renew	.6	.6	.6	.6	.6

Starting System

Starter, Renew	.9	1.5†	1.5†	.9	.9
Starter Drive, Renew	1.8	2.5†	2.5†	1.8	1.8
Starter, R&R and Recondition	2.0	2.7†	2.7†	2.0	2.0
Starter Solenoid, Renew	1.0	1.8†	1.8†	1.0	1.0

Brake System

Brakes, Adjust (Minor)	.9	.9	.9	.9	1.3
Brake Shoes, Renew					
Front whls	—	—	—	1.7	1.7
Rear whls	1.7	1.7	1.7	1.7	1.7
Wheel Cylinder, Renew					
Front (one)	—	—	—	1.5	1.5
Rear (one)	1.4	1.4	1.4	1.4	1.4
Wheel Cylinder, Recondition					
Front (one)	—	—	—	1.7	1.7
Rear (one)	1.6	1.6	1.6	1.6	1.6
Master Cylinder, Renew	1.0	1.4	1.4	1.6	1.5
Master Cylinder, R&R and Recondition	1.4	2.0	2.0	2.1	2.0
Brake Drum, Renew					
Front	—	—	—	1.3	1.3
Rear	1.2	1.2	1.2	.9	1.2
Brake Drum, Reface (add)	.3	.3	.3	.3	.3
Bleed Brakes	.8	.8	.8	.8	.8
Disc Brake Rotor, Renew (one)	1.2	1.2	1.2	1.5	1.5
Disc Brake Pads, Renew—Front whls	.9	.9	.9	.9	.9
Disc Caliper, Renew (one)	1.0	1.0	1.0	1.2	1.2
Resurface Disc, Add	.6	.6	.6	.6	.6
Brake Caliper, R&R and Recondition					
(one)	1.3	1.3	1.3	1.4	1.4
(both)	1.8	1.8	1.8	1.9	1.9

Cooling System

Fan Belt, Renew	.5	.5	.5	.5	.5
Thermostat, Renew	.6	.6	.6	.6	.6
Radiator, R&R or Renew	1.0	.8	.8	1.0	1.0
Water Pump, Renew	1.1	1.1	1.1	1.1	1.7

Exhaust System

Muffler, Renew	1.1	1.0	1.0	.8	.7
Exhaust Pipe, Renew					
Front	1.1	1.1	1.1	1.2	1.0
Center	—	.9	.9	1.0	.8
Tail Pipe, Renew	1.0	1.0	1.0	.9	.7
Exhaust Manifold or Gasket, Renew	1.2	1.2	1.2	1.4	3.6

Front Suspension

Caster, Camber and Toe In, Adjust	—	—	—	1.6	2.0
Toe In, Adjust	.5	.5	.5	.6	.6
Front Wheel Bearings, Repack					
(disc)	1.4	1.4	1.4	2.2	2.2
(drum)	—	—	—	1.5	1.5
Front Wheel Bearings, Renew (one whl)	1.0	1.0	1.0	1.3	1.5
Front Spring, Renew—Leaf (one)	—	—	—	—	1.1

†W/A.I.R. add—1.0

	Carina	Corolla 1600cc	Corolla 1200cc	Hi Lux	Land Cruiser
Front Spring Shackle, Renew (one)	—	—	—	—	.8
†Control Arm, Renew					
(upper).................................	—	—	—	1.5	—
(lower).................................	1.4	1.4	1.4	1.9	—
(both)	—	—	—	3.0	—
†Ball Joint, Renew					
(upper).................................	—	—	—	1.4	—
(lower).................................	1.4	1.4	1.4	1.7	—
(both)	—	—	—	2.8	—
†Front Strut Shock Absorber, R&R and Recondition (one)	1.9	1.9	1.9	—	—
Front Shock Absorber, Renew					
(one)	—	—	—	.6	.8
(both)	—	—	—	1.0	1.4
†Front Strut Assembly, Renew (one)	1.7	1.7	1.7	—	—

Cylinder Head & Valves

	Carina	Corolla 1600cc	Corolla 1200cc	Hi Lux	Land Cruiser
Compression Test	.6	.6	.6	.6	.6
Cylinder Head Gasket, Renew	4.0	4.0	4.0	4.2	6.9
w/Air Pump, Add......................	—	—	.4	—	—
Cylinder Head, Renew	7.9	7.9	7.9	8.3	12.4
Valve Spring and/or Valve Stem Oil Seal, Renew Head on Engine					
(one)	1.2	1.2	1.2	1.3	1.5
(all)	1.9	1.9	1.9	2.0	2.6
*Push Rods and/or Rocker Arms, Renew					
(one)	1.5	1.5	1.5	2.5	1.5
(all)	1.8	1.8	1.8	3.0	1.8
*Valve Lifters, Renew					
(one)	2.2	2.2	2.2	—	2.2
(all)	2.9	2.9	2.9	—	2.9
Adjust Valves	.8	.8	.8	.9	.9
Clean Carbon and Grind Valves	9.2	9.2	9.2	9.5	13.6

Clutch

	Carina	Corolla 1600cc	Corolla 1200cc	Hi Lux	Land Cruiser
Clutch Assembly, Renew	3.3	3.3	3.3	3.4	4.6
Clutch Release Bearing, Renew	2.9	2.9	3.0	3.0	4.2
Clutch Master Cylinder, Renew	1.0	1.0	1.0	1.0	1.0
Clutch Master Cylinder, Recondition	1.5	1.5	1.5	1.5	1.5
Clutch Slave Cylinder, Renew	.7	.7	.7	.7	.7
Clutch Slave Cylinder, Recondition	1.2	1.2	1.2	1.2	1.2
Clutch Cable, Renew.......................	—	—	.6	—	—

VOLKSWAGEN LABOR (Chilton Time)
SECTION I

		Type 1			
	Beetle	Super Beetle	K. Ghia	Thing	Type 2
### Tune Up					
Engine Tune Up (Minor)	1.8	1.8	1.8	2.0	2.0
### Fuel System					
Carburetor, Adjust (on car)	.2	.2	.2	.2	.2
Carburetor, Renew					
One	1.0	1.0	1.0	1.0	1.0
Both	—	—	—	—	1.5

†To check alignment add—.8   *For OHC engines refer to Section I

	Type 1				
	Beetle	Super Beetle	K. Ghia	Thing	Type 2
Carburetor, R&R and Recondition					
One	2.0	2.0	2.0	2.0	2.0
Both	—	—	—	—	3.5
Fuel Pump, Renew	.8	.8	.8	.8	.8
w/1700 cc add	—	—	—	—	.2
Intake Manifold, Renew	2.5	2.5	2.5	2.5	1.5
w/A.C. add	.4	.4	.4	—	.4

Alternator & Generator

Generator, Renew	2.8	2.8	2.8	—	2.8
Generator, R&R and Recondition	3.9	3.9	3.9	—	4.4
Generator, R&R and Renew Bearings	3.4	3.4	3.4	—	3.6
Voltage Regulator, Renew	.5	.5	.5	—	.5
Alternator, Renew	2.6	2.6	2.6	2.6	1.9
w/A.C. add	.5	.5	.5	—	.6
Alternator, R&R and Recondition	4.3	4.3	4.3	4.3	3.6
w/A.C. add	.5	.5	.5	—	.6
Alternator Regulator, Renew	.5	.5	.5	.5	.5

Starting System

Starter, Renew	1.2	1.2	1.2	1.2	1.2
w/A.C. add	.4	.4	.4	—	—
Starter, R&R and Recondition	3.5	3.5	3.5	3.5	3.5
w/A.C. add	.4	.4	.4	—	—
Starter Solenoid, Renew	1.3	1.3	1.3	1.3	1.1
w/A.C. add	.4	.4	.4	—	—
Starter Drive, Renew	1.7	1.7	1.7	1.7	1.5

Brake System

Brakes, Adjust (Minor)	.8	.8	.8	.8	.8
Bleed Brakes	.8	.8	.8	.8	.8
Brake Shoes, Renew					
Front..................................	1.5	1.5	1.5	1.5	1.5
Rear	1.5	1.5	1.5	1.5	1.5
All	2.2	2.2	2.2	2.2	2.2
Brake Drum, Renew					
Front..................................	.9	.9	.9	.9	.9
Rear	.5	.5	.5	.5	.5
Brake Drum, Reface					
Front (add)	.5	.5	.5	.5	.5
Rear (add)	.3	.3	.3	.3	.3
Disc Brake Pads, Renew	.7	.7	.7	.7	.7
Wheel Cylinder, Renew					
Front (one)	1.5	1.5	1.5	1.5	1.5
Rear (one)	1.5	1.5	1.5	1.5	1.5
Wheel Cylinder, R&R and Recondition					
Front (one)	1.8	1.8	1.8	1.8	1.8
Rear (one)	1.8	1.8	1.8	1.8	1.8
Master Cylinder, Renew	2.0	2.0	2.0	2.0	1.7
Master Cylinder, R&R and Recondition	2.6	2.6	2.6	2.6	2.1
Brake Hose, Renew					
Front (one)	.5	.5	.5	.5	.5
Front (both)	.9	.9	.9	.9	.9
Rear	.6	.6	.6	.6	.6
Brake Caliper, Renew (one)	.9	.9	.9	.9	.9
Brake Caliper, Recondition (one)	1.9	1.9	1.9	1.9	1.9
Disc Brake Rotor, Renew (one)	1.4	1.4	1.4	1.4	.9
Resurface Rotor add	.9	.9	.9	.9	.9

	Type 1				
	Beetle	Super Beetle	K. Ghia	Thing	Type 2

Cooling System

Thermostat, Renew	.6	.6	.6	.6	.6
Cooling Fan, Renew	3.0	3.0	3.0	3.0	2.0
Fan Housing, R&R or Renew	2.3	2.3	2.3	2.3	6.0
w/A.C. add	.4	.4	.4	—	1.0
Fan Belt, Renew	.3	.3	.3	.3	.3
w/A.C. add	.3	.3	.3	—	.3

Exhaust System

Muffler, Renew					
One	1.5	1.5	1.5	1.0	1.3
Both	—	—	—	1.6	—
w/A.C. add	.4	.4	.4	—	—
Tail Pipe, Renew	.5	.5	.5	.5	.5
Connecting Pipe, Renew					
One	—	—	—	.8	—
Both	—	—	—	1.0	—

Front Suspension

Toe In, Adjust	.6	.6	.6	.6	.6
Front Wheel Bearings, Repack					
Drum	1.2	1.2	1.2	1.2	1.2
Disc	1.5	1.5	1.5	1.5	1.5
Front Wheel Bearing and Cup, Renew (one side)	.8	.8	1.0	.8	.8
Control Arm, Renew					
Upper	1.0	—	1.0	—	1.0
Lower	1.0	.9	1.0	.9	1.0
Both	1.8	—	1.8	—	1.8
Ball Joint, Renew					
Upper	1.6	—	1.6	—	1.6
Lower	1.6	1.2	1.6	1.2	1.6
Both	2.4	—	2.4	—	2.4
Strut Assembly, Renew					
One	—	1.1	—	1.1	—
Both	—	2.0	—	2.0	—
Strut Assembly Shock Absorber, Overhaul					
One	—	1.4	—	1.4	—
Both	—	2.5	—	2.5	—
Front Shock Absorber, Renew					
One	.6	—	.6	—	.6
Both	1.0	—	1.0	—	1.0

Cylinder Head and Valve System

Compression Test	.8	.8	.8	.8	.8
w/A.C. add	.3	.3	.3	.3	.3
*Cylinder Head, Renew—Std. Trans.					
One	6.0	6.0	6.0	6.0	6.0
Both	7.4	7.4	7.4	7.4	7.4
*Cylinder Head, Renew—Auto. Trans.					
One	6.4	6.4	6.4	6.4	6.7
Both	7.8	7.8	7.8	7.8	7.8
Cylinder Head Gasket, Renew—Std. Trans.					
One	5.7	5.7	5.7	5.7	8.1
Both	7.0	7.0	7.0	7.0	9.2
Cylinder Head Gasket, Renew—Auto. Trans.					
One	6.2	6.2	6.2	—	—
Both	7.5	7.5	7.5	—	—
w/A.C. add	.9	.9	.9	—	1.0

*Includes R&R Engine

	Type 1				
	Beetle	Super Beetle	K. Ghia	Thing	Type 2
Valve Spring and/or Valve Stem Oil Seal, Renew (Head on Engine)					
One	1.2	1.2	1.2	1.2	1.2
All	2.3	2.3	2.3	2.3	2.3
Push Rod and/or Rocker Arms, Renew					
One	1.0	1.0	1.0	1.0	1.0
All	1.6	1.6	1.6	1.6	1.6
Adjust Valves, Cold	.8	.8	.8	.8	.8
Clean Carbon and Grind Valves					
Std. Trans.	8.5	8.5	8.5	8.5	—
Auto. Trans.	9.0	9.0	9.0	—	10.5
w/A.C. add	.9	.9	.9	—	1.0
Valve Push Rod Tubes or Seals, Renew (both sides)					
Std. Trans.	7.0	7.0	7.0	7.0	7.0
Auto. Trans.	7.4	7.4	7.4	—	—
w/A.C. add	.9	.9	.9	—	1.0

Clutch

	Beetle	Super Beetle	K. Ghia	Thing	Type 2
Clutch Pedal, Adjust	.5	.5	.5	.5	.5
Clutch Cable, Renew	1.5	1.5	1.5	1.5	1.3
Clutch Assembly, Renew	3.9	3.9	3.9	3.9	3.9
w/A.C. add	.5	.5	.5	—	.9
Clutch Release Bearings, Renew	2.7	2.7	2.7	2.7	4.9
w/A.C. add	.5	.5	.5	—	.9

VOLKSWAGEN LABOR (Chilton Time)
SECTION II

	Type 3			Type 4
	w/Carb	w/F.I.	Type 4	Sq. Back

Tune Up

	w/Carb	w/F.I.	Type 4	Type 4 Sq. Back
Engine Tune Up (Minor)	2.0	2.3	2.3	2.3

Fuel System

	w/Carb	w/F.I.	Type 4	Type 4 Sq. Back
Carburetor, Adjust (On Car)	.2	—	—	—
Carburetor, Renew				
One	1.0	—	—	—
Both	1.4	—	—	—
Carburetor, R&R and Recondition				
One	2.0	—	—	—
Both	3.4	—	—	—
Fuel Pump, Renew	.7	.7	.7	.7
Intake Manifold, Renew	.6	1.3	1.3	1.3
Test Fuel Injection System	—	.3	.3	.3
Electronic Control Unit, Renew	—	.4	.4	.4

Alternator & Generator

	w/Carb	w/F.I.	Type 4	Type 4 Sq. Back
Generator, Renew	1.4	1.4	—	—
Generator, R&R and Recondition	2.4	2.4	—	—
Generator, R&R and Renew Bearings	1.9	1.9	—	—
Voltage Regulator, Renew	.5	.5	—	—
Alternator, Renew	—	—	2.0	2.0
Alternator, R&R and Recondition	—	—	4.3	4.3
Alternator, R&R and Renew Bearings	—	—	2.6	2.6
Alternator Regulator, Renew	—	—	.5	.5

	Type 3			Type 4
	w/Carb	w/F.I.	Type 4	Sq. Back

Starting System

Starter, Renew	1.2	1.2	1.2	1.2
Starter, R&R and Recondition	3.5	3.5	3.5	3.5
Starter Solenoid, Renew	1.2	1.2	1.2	1.2
Starter Drive, Renew	1.8	1.8	1.8	1.8

Brake System

Brakes, Adjust	.8	.8	.6	.8
Bleed Brakes	.8	.8	.8	.8
Brake Shoes, Renew				
Front	1.5	1.5	—	—
Rear	1.5	1.5	1.5	1.5
Brake Drum, Renew				
Front	.9	.9	.9	.9
Rear	.5	.5	.5	.5
Brake Drum, Reface				
Front (add)	.5	.5	.5	.5
Rear (add)	.3	.3	.3	.3
Disc Brake Pads, Renew	.7	.7	.7	.7
Wheel Cylinder, Renew				
Front one	1.0	1.0	—	—
Rear	1.5	1.5	1.5	1.5
Wheel Cylinder, R&R and Recondition				
Front one	1.8	1.8	—	—
Back one	1.8	1.8	1.8	1.8
Master Cylinder, Renew	1.5	1.5	1.5	1.5
Master Cylinder, R&R and Recondition	2.6	2.6	2.3	2.3
Brake Caliper, Renew—One	1.2	1.2	1.2	1.2
Brake Caliper, R&R and Recondition—One	1.9	1.9	1.9	1.9
Disc Brake Rotor, Renew—One	1.4	1.4	1.4	1.4
Resurface rotor add	.9	.9	.9	.9

Cooling System

Thermostat, Renew	.5	.5	.6	.6
Cooling Fan, Renew	4.4	4.4	1.5	1.5
w/A.C. add	.9	.9	—	—
Fan Housing, Renew	3.5	3.5	5.3	5.3
w/A.C. add	.9	.9	.5	.5
Fan Belt, Renew	.3	.3	.3	.3
w/A.C. add	.3	.3	.3	.3

Exhaust System

Muffler, Renew	1.8	1.8	1.4	1.4
Tail Pipe, Renew—One	.5	.5	.5	.5

Front Suspension

Toe In, Adjust	.6	.6	.6	.6
Front Wheel Bearings, Repack				
Drum	1.2	1.2	1.2	1.2
Disc	1.5	1.5	1.5	1.5
Front Wheel Bearing and Cup, Renew—One side	1.0	1.0	.9	.9
Control Arm, Renew				
Upper	1.0	1.0	—	—
Lower	1.0	1.0	.9	.9
Both	1.8	1.8	—	—

	Type 3			Type 4
	w/Carb	w/F.I.	Type 4	Sq. Back
Ball Joint, Renew				
Upper	1.6	1.6	—	—
Lower	1.6	1.6	1.2	1.2
Both	2.4	2.4	—	—
Front Strut Assembly, Renew				
One	—	—	1.2	1.2
Both	—	—	2.1	2.1
Front Strut Shock Absorber, R&R and Recondition				
One	—	—	1.5	1.5
Both	—	—	2.7	2.7
Front Shock Absorber, Renew				
One	.6	.6	—	—
Both	1.0	1.0	—	—

Cylinder Head & Valve System

	w/Carb	w/F.I.	Type 4	Sq. Back
Compression Test	.8	.8	.8	.8
w/A.C. add	.2	.2	.2	.2
Cylinder Head Gasket, Renew—Std. Trans.				
One	6.0	6.0	7.4	7.4
Both	7.3	7.3	8.6	8.6
Cylinder Head Gasket, Renew—Auto. Trans.				
One	6.5	6.5	8.1	8.1
Both	7.3	7.3	9.2	9.2
w/A.C. add	1.3	1.3	—	—
Cylinder Head, Renew—Std. Trans.				
One	6.5	6.5	7.9	7.9
Both	7.3	7.3	9.6	9.6
Cylinder Head, Renew—Auto. Trans.				
One	7.1	7.1	8.6	8.6
Both	8.1	8.1	10.0	10.0
Valve Spring and/or Valve Stem Oil Seal, Renew (Head on Engine)				
One	1.2	1.2	1.2	1.2
All	1.9	1.9	1.9	1.9
Push Rod and/or Rocker Arms, Renew				
(one)	1.0	1.0	1.0	1.0
(all)	1.5	1.5	1.5	1.5
Push Rod Tubes and/or Seals, Renew				
One side	5.6	5.6	1.2	1.2
Both sides	6.4	6.4	2.0	2.0
Clean Carbon and Grind Valves				
Std. Trans.	8.8	8.8	10.9	10.9
Auto. Trans.	9.3	9.3	11.3	11.3
w/A.C. add	1.3	1.3	—	—
Adjust Valves, Cold	.8	.8	.8	.8

Clutch

	w/Carb	w/F.I.	Type 4	Sq. Back
Clutch Pedal, Adjust	.5	.5	.5	.5
Clutch Cable, Renew	1.0	1.0	—	—
Clutch Master Cylinder, Renew	—	—	1.0	1.0
Clutch Master Cylinder, Recondition	—	—	1.5	1.5
Clutch Slave Cylinder, Renew	—	—	.9	.9
Clutch Slave Cylinder, Recondition	—	—	1.2	1.2
Clutch Hydraulic System, Bleed	—	—	.4	.4
Clutch Assembly, Renew	4.8	4.8	5.6	5.6
w/A.C. add	.9	.9	.5	.5
Clutch Release Bearing, Renew	3.6	3.6	5.1	5.1
w/A.C. add	.9	.9	.5	.5

VOLKSWAGEN LABOR (Chilton Time)

	Rabbit & Scirocco Gasoline Engine	Diesel Engine	Dasher

Tune Up

Engine Tune Up (Minor)	1.5	—	1.5

Fuel System

Carburetor, Adjust (On Car)	.2	—	.2
Carburetor, Renew	.7	—	.7
Carburetor R&R and Recondition	1.7	—	1.7
Fuel Pump, Renew	.4	—	.4
Intake Manifold Gasket, Renew	1.8	—	1.2

Continuous Injection System

Intake Manifold Gasket, Renew	1.4	—	1.4

Diesel Fuel Injection

Intake Manifold Gasket, Renew	—	1.3	—

Alternator

Alternator, Renew	.6	.6	1.0
Alternator, Recondition	2.3	2.3	2.7
Alternator, R&R and Renew Bearings	1.0	1.0	1.4
Voltage Regulator, Test and Renew	.3	.3	.5

Starting System

Starter, Renew	.6	.6	1.2
Starter Drive, Renew	1.6	1.6	2.2
Starter, R&R and Recondition	2.5	2.5	3.5
Starter Solenoid, Renew	.9	.9	1.5

Brake System

Brakes, Adjust (Minor)	.8	.8	.8
Bleed Brakes	.8	.8	.8
Rear Brake Shoes, Renew	1.5	1.5	1.5
Rear Wheel Cylinder, Renew (each)	1.1	1.1	1.1
Rear Wheel Cylinder, R&R and Recondition	1.8	1.8	1.8
Master Cylinder, Renew	1.5	1.5	1.5
Master Cylinder, R&R and Recondition	2.1	2.1	2.1
Disc Brake Pads, Renew	.7	.7	.7
Disc Brake Caliper, Renew (one)	1.2	1.2	1.2
Disc Brake Caliper, R&R and Recondition (one)	1.9	1.9	1.9
Disc Brake Rotor, Renew (one)	.9	.9	.9
Disc Brake Rotor, Reface (one)	.4	.4	.4
Brake Drum, Renew—Rear	.8	.8	.8
Brake Drum, Reface (add)	.4	.4	.4

Cooling System

Fan Belt, Renew	.3	.3	.3
Thermostat, Renew	.6	.6	.6

	Rabbit & Scirocco Gasoline Engine	Diesel Engine	Dasher
Radiator Hoses, Renew			
Upper	.2	.2	.2
Lower	.2	.2	.2
Water Pump, Renew	1.3	1.3	1.3
Radiator, R&R or Renew	.8	.8	.8

Exhaust System

	Rabbit & Scirocco Gasoline Engine	Diesel Engine	Dasher
Muffler, Renew			
Front	1.0	1.0	1.0
Rear	.6	.6	.6
Exhaust Pipes, Renew			
Front	1.4	1.4	.6
Rear	.4	.4	.5
Tail Pipe, Renew	—	—	.6

Front Suspension

	Rabbit & Scirocco Gasoline Engine	Diesel Engine	Dasher
Toe In, Adjust	.6	.6	.6
Wheel Bearings, Renew (One Side)	1.6	1.6	1.6
Lower Control Arm, Renew			
(one)	.9	.9	.9
(both)	1.3	1.3	1.3
Lower Ball Joint, Renew			
(one)	.8	.8	.8
(both)	1.2	1.2	1.2
Front Strut Shock Absorber, R&R and Recondition (one)	2.0	2.0	2.4
Front Strut Assembly, Renew			
(One Side)	1.5	1.5	2.0
(Both Sides)	2.4	2.4	3.5

Cylinder Head & Valve System

	Rabbit & Scirocco Gasoline Engine	Diesel Engine	Dasher
Compression Test	.8	1.1	.8
Cylinder Head Gasket, Renew	4.0	4.0	3.5
Cylinder Head, Renew	5.5*	5.5*	5.0*
Valve Spring and/or Valve Stem Oil Seal, Renew (Head on Engine)			
One	2.4	2.4	2.4
All	3.0	3.0	3.0
Adjust Valves	.9	.9	.9
Clean Carbon and Grind Valves	7.5	7.5	6.5
Valve Cover Gasket, Renew	.3	.3	.3
Valve Lifters, Renew	2.5	2.5	2.4

Clutch

	Rabbit & Scirocco Gasoline Engine	Diesel Engine	Dasher
Clutch Assembly, Renew	4.6	4.6	4.7
Clutch Release Bearing, Renew	4.1	4.1	4.2
Clutch Cable, Renew	.7	.7	.7
Adjust Clutch Pedal Free Play	.5	.5	.5

*Includes transfer parts

Parts Prices

Like all manufactured products, the cost of parts for cars and trucks varies in response to economic and automotive market conditions, the cost of raw materials, and the overhead expenses of the individual merchandiser. The prices quoted in this book are those in effect at the time of publication and are representative of two distinct pricing structures.

The cost of *professionally installed* parts reflects the manufacturer's suggested retail price for the item and includes a reasonable profit on the resale of the part to recover the cost of transportation, overhead, and other shop expenses. The prices quoted are excerpted from the 1980 *Chilton's Professional Labor Guide and Parts Manual,* and the range includes the cost of parts for various years, models, and equipment of each car line or group of cars, installed by a professional mechanic.

The cost of *do-it-yourself* parts are estimates of the lowest and highest prices for the same or equivalent parts. The price for do-it-yourself parts will vary considerably depending on the manufacturer (brand name) of the part, the retail establishment from which it is purchased (discount auto store, automotive chain store, automotive jobber, etc.), and whether the part is new or remanufactured. See Chapter 3 for a discussion of sources for automotive parts, and be sure to check the price for the part applicable to your individual year, make, and model of vehicle.

American Motors

	Prof. Installed*	Do-It-Yourself*
Contact point set**	4.00–5.20	3.50–4.50
Condenser**	1.75–2.75	1.50–2.25
Rotor (distributor)**	1.35–2.75	1.00–2.25
Distributor cap		
Point-type ignition	4.25–7.50	4.00–6.75
Electronic ignition	4.25–6.25	3.50–5.00
Ignition (spark plug) wire set		
Point-type ignition	9.75–18.00	8.25–15.50
Electronic ignition	11.75–18.00	10.00–15.50
Alternator (new)		
Standard	106.75–145.75	49.00–120.00
Starter		
4-cyl.	79.50	49.00–65.00
6-cyl.	101.75	49.00–80.00
V8	101.75	49.00–80.00
Carburetor (new)		
1-barrel	80.00–118.50	65.00–95.00
2-barrel	118.00–155.25	95.00–125.00
4-barrel	155.25–202.00	125.00–160.00
Carburetor repair kit (minor)	11.00–16.25	9.00–13.00
Carburetor overhaul kit (major)	23.00–32.50	18.50–26.00
Fuel pump (new)	21.00–25.00	15.00–20.00
Drum brake shoe set, 2 whls. (new)	24.00–27.00	11.00–22.00
Disc brake pad set, 2 whls. (new)	24.00	11.00–20.00
Brake caliper (disc brakes)	56.00–75.00	45.00–60.00
Master cylinder (new)	50.00–70.00	29.00–56.00
Repair kit	14.50–19.00	11.50–15.00
Water pump (new)		
4-cyl.	42.25	20.00–34.00
6-cyl.	39.50–40.50	22.00–32.00
V8	37.50–40.50	30.00–32.00
Radiator core (new)	124.00–172.00	110.00–155.00
Muffler	28.00–35.00	15.00–28.00
Ball joint, upper	13.25–16.25	10.50–13.00
Shock absorber	14.00–26.00	10.00–20.00
Clutch disc	33.00–68.00	25.00–55.00
Clutch pressure plate	54.00–108.00	42.00–87.00
Clutch throwout bearing	15.00–18.00	12.00–15.00

*See note at beginning of section
**Can be purchased in kit form more economically

AMC/Jeep

	Prof. Installed*	Do-It-Yourself*
Contact point set**	4.00–5.20	3.50–4.50
Condenser**	1.75	1.50
Rotor (distributor)**	1.35–2.50	1.00–2.25
Distributor cap		
Point-type ignition	5.00–7.50	4.25–6.50
Electronic ignition	4.75–6.25	4.00–5.25
Ignition (spark plug) wire set		
Point-type ignition	12.75–18.00	10.75–15.00

	Prof. Installed*	Do-It-Yourself*
Electronic ignition	11.75–18.00	10.00–15.00
Alternator (new)		
Standard	106.75–145.75	49.00–120.00
Starter		
6-cyl.	101.75	49.00–80.00
V8	101.75	49.00–80.00
Carburetor (new)		
6-cyl.	80.00–136.00	65.00–110.00
V8	153.50–227.25	120.00–185.00
Carburetor overhaul kit (major)	9.50–25.50	7.50–20.00
Fuel pump (new)	21.00–25.00	16.50–20.00
Drum brake shoe set, 2 whls. (new)	23.50–32.75	11.00–25.50
Disc brake pad set, 2 whls. (new)	21.75–23.50	11.00–18.50
Brake caliper (disc brakes)	91.25–100.00	72.00–80.00
Master cylinder (new)	45.75–70.00	29.00–56.00
Repair kit	12.50–15.50	10.50–12.00
Water pump (new)		
6-cyl.	38.25–39.50	30.00–32.00
V8	37.50–38.25	30.00–31.50
Radiator (new)	191.75–221.75	170.00–200.00
Muffler	28.25–43.50	22.50–35.00
Ball joint, lower	23.00	18.50
Ball joint, upper	23.00	18.50
Shock absorber	14.75–17.75	12.00–15.00
Clutch disc	48.75–65.00	34.00–52.00
Clutch pressure plate	66.50–86.50	52.00–65.00
Clutch throwout bearing	16.25–17.75	13.00–15.00

*See note at beginning of section
**Can be purchased in kit form more economically

Buick LeSabre, Electra, Riviera (1974–78)

	Prof. Installed*	Do-It-Yourself*
Contact point set**	6.00–11.35	5.00–9.50
Condenser**	2.00	1.75
Rotor (distributor)**	3.00–6.75	2.50–5.75
Distributor cap		
Point-type ignition	8.35	7.00
Electronic ignition	12.25–18.00	10.50–15.50
Ignition (spark plug) wire set		
Point-type ignition	23.45	20.00
Electronic ignition	40.75–48.00	34.00–41.00
Alternator (new)		
Standard	127.50–133.00	49.00–110.00
Heavy-duty	266.00	150.00–210.00
Starter		
6-cyl.	136.25–140.25	49.00–115.00
V8	112.50–142.00	49.00–115.00
Carburetor (new)		
6-cyl.	145.00–239.00	92.00–191.00

	Prof. Installed*	Do-It-Yourself*
V8	91.00–218.00	72.00–175.00
Carburetor overhaul kit (major)	10.00–25.00	8.00–20.00
Fuel pump (new)	21.00–27.00	17.00–22.00
Drum brake shoe set, 2 whls. (new)	11.50–39.50	11.00–32.00
Disc brake pad set, 2 whls. (new)	33.50–39.50	11.00–32.00
Brake caliper (disc brakes)		
Front housing	89.00–112.75	70.00–90.00
Rear	161.50–180.00	125.00–145.00
Master cylinder (new)	45.00–60.00	29.00–48.00
Repair kit	15.00–34.00	12.00–27.25
Water pump (new)		
6-cyl.	40.00–42.00	32.00–34.00
V8	34.75–60.00	30.00–50.00
Radiator (new)	132.00–288.00	110.00–234.00
Muffler	40.00–139.00	15.00–110.00
Ball joint, lower	20.00–22.00	16.00–17.50
Ball joint, upper	19.00–20.00	15.00–16.00
Shock absorber	16.35	12.50

*See note at beginning of section
**Can be purchased in kit form more economically

Buick Riviera (1979–80)

	Prof. Installed*	Do-It-Yourself*
Contact point set	N/A	N/A
Condenser	N/A	N/A
Rotor (distributor)	7.00	5.00–6.00
Distributor cap		
Point-type ignition	N/A	N/A
Electronic ignition	13.50–18.50	12.00–16.00
Ignition (spark plug) wire set		
Point-type ignition	N/A	N/A
Electronic ignition	Sold separately—N/A as a set	—
Alternator (new)		
Standard	127.50–133.00	49.00–110.00
Heavy-duty	266.00	150.00–210.00
Starter		
6-cyl.	148.75	48.00–120.00
V8	148.75	48.00–120.00
Diesel	328.50	250.00–270.00
Carburetor (new)		
6-cyl.	239.00	165.00–190.00
V8	199.00–218.00	130.00–185.00
Carburetor overhaul kit (major)	25.00–25.75	15.00–20.00

	Prof. Installed*	Do-It-Yourself*
Fuel pump (new)		
Carbureted engine ...	24.50–24.75	15.00–20.00
Diesel	29.25–75.00	22.00–60.00
Drum brake shoe set, 2 whls. (new)	31.00	11.00–25.00
Disc brake pad set, 2 whls. (new)	43.75	11.00–35.00
Brake caliper (disc brakes)		
Front	116.00	90.00–95.00
Rear	158.00	110.00–125.00
Master cylinder (new)	67.75–69.00	40.00–55.00
Repair kit	12.25–13.25	7.00–10.50
Water pump (new)		
6-cyl.	40.25	30.00–32.00
V8	48.75–60.00	30.00–48.00
Radiator (new)	171.00–234.00	150.00–190.00
Muffler	41.25–41.75	15.00–30.00
Shock absorber	16.25	10.00–15.00

*See note at beginning of section
N/A—Not Applicable

Buick Apollo, Century, Gran Sport, Regal, Skylark (1974–79)

	Prof. Installed*	Do-It-Yourself*
Contact point set**	5.00–8.75	3.00–7.50
Condenser**	1.75	1.50
Rotor (distributor)**	4.00–7.00	3.50–6.00
Distributor cap		
Point-type ignition	5.00–8.25	4.00–7.00
Electronic ignition	12.00–18.00	7.50–15.50
Ignition (spark plug) wire set		
Point-type ignition	11.00–19.00	8.00–12.00
Electronic ignition	48.00–49.75 (some models priced separately)	40.00
Alternator (new)		
Standard	127.50–133.00	49.00–110.00
Heavy-duty	266.00	150.00–210.00
Starter		
6-cyl.	112.50–136.25	48.00–112.00
V8	112.50–142.00	48.00–115.00
Carburetor (new)		
6-cyl.	69.00–219.00	45.00–175.00
V8	162.00–239.00	125.00–190.00
Carburetor overhaul kit (major)	19.75–27.75	12.00–21.50
Fuel pump (new)	15.75–28.50	12.00–23.00
Drum brake shoe set, 2 whls. (new)	21.50–35.25	11.00–28.00
Disc brake pad set, 2 whls. (new)	34.25–51.50	11.00–42.00

	Prof. Installed*	Do-It- Yourself*
Brake caliper (disc brakes)		
housing	73.75– 104.25	58.00–85.00
Master cylinder (new)	30.25–67.75	30.00–54.00
Repair kit	13.25–26.00	8.00–20.00
Water pump (new)		
6-cyl.	28.75–42.00	20.00–34.00
V8	34.00–60.00	20.00–50.00
Radiator (new)	129.00– 268.00	115.00– 215.00
Muffler	35.00–64.25	19.00–54.00
Ball joint, lower	20.00–28.50	15.00–20.00
Ball joint, upper	19.50–20.25	15.00–18.00
Shock absorber	16.50	10.00–15.00
Clutch disc	46.00–60.25	30.00–48.00
Clutch pressure plate	88.00– 106.50	50.00–85.00
Clutch throwout bearing . .	18.50–22.00	12.00–17.50

*See note at beginning of section
**Can be purchased in kit form more economically

Buick Skyhawk

	Prof. Installed*	Do-It- Yourself*
Contact point set	N/A	N/A
Condenser	N/A	N/A
Rotor (distributor)	7.00	5.00–6.00
Distributor cap		
Point-type ignition	N/A	N/A
Electronic ignition	13.50–17.50	12.00–16.00
Ignition (spark plug) wire set		
Point-type ignition	N/A	N/A
Electronic ignition	Sold sepa- rately— N/A as a set	—
Alternator (new)		
Standard	127.50	49.00– 110.00
Heavy-duty	133.00	75.00– 110.00
Starter		
4-cyl.	112.50– 136.25	48.00– 112.00
6-cyl.	112.50– 136.25	48.00– 112.00
Carburetor (new)		
4-cyl.	124.00– 156.00	75.00– 125.00
6-cyl.	158.00– 163.00	95.00– 130.00
Carburetor overhaul kit		
(major)	23.75–25.75	15.00–20.00
Fuel pump (new)	31.00	20.00–25.00
Drum brake shoe set, 2 whls. (new)	25.75–31.75	11.00–25.00
Disc brake pad set, 2 whls. (new)	42.50–54.50	11.00–44.00
Brake caliper (disc brakes)	93.50	60.00–75.00
Master cylinder (new)	61.25–68.75	35.00–55.00
Repair kit	13.00–16.75	8.00–13.00

	Prof. Installed*	Do-It- Yourself*
Water pump (new)		
4-cyl.	42.00	20.00–34.00
6-cyl.	42.00	20.00–34.00
Radiator (new)	114.00– 148.00	100.00– 134.00
Muffler	29.50–44.00	15.00–35.00
Ball joint, lower	20.00	14.00–16.00
Ball joint, upper	19.50	14.00–16.00
Shock absorber	16.50	12.00–15.00
Clutch disc	50.75–52.75	30.00–42.00
Clutch pressure plate	82.25–98.00	50.00–80.00
Clutch throwout bearing . .	18.50	12.00–16.50

*See note at beginning of section
N/A—Not Applicable

Cadillac

	Prof. Installed*	Do-It- Yourself*
Contact point set**	5.50–6.25	1.00–5.50
Condenser**	2.00	1.75
Rotor (distributor)**	3.25–7.50	2.50–6.00
Distributor cap		
Point-type ignition	9.00	6.50–7.50
Electronic ignition	12.25–18.00	7.50–15.00
Ignition (spark plug) wire set		
Point-type ignition	20.50	12.50–16.00
Electronic ignition	35.75–37.50	14.00–30.00
Alternator (new)		
Standard	133.00	49.00– 110.00
Heavy-duty	266.00	150.00– 210.00
Starter		
V8	136.25– 142.00	48.00– 115.00
Diesel	328.50	250.00– 270.00
Carburetor (new)	158.00– 244.00	100.00– 195.00
Carburetor repair kit (minor)	10.50–15.50	6.50–12.00
Carburetor overhaul kit (major)	24.00–25.00	15.00–20.00
Fuel pump (new)		
Carbureted engine . . .	28.75–36.50	17.00–30.00
Fuel-injected engine . .	131.00	95.00– 110.00
Diesel	29.25–75.00	20.00–60.00
Drum brake shoe set, 2 whls. (new)	32.00–44.00	11.00–35.00
Disc brake pad set, 2 whls. (new)	33.75–43.75	11.00–35.00
Brake caliper (disc brakes)		
Front (housing)	93.50– 112.75	75.00–90.00
Rear (assembly)	180.00	125.00– 145.00
Master cylinder (new)	50.50–67.75	30.00–54.00
Repair kit	14.25–16.50	9.00–13.00
Water pump (new)		
V8	60.00–78.00	40.00–65.00
Radiator (new)	121.50	85.00– 100.00

	Prof. Installed*	Do-It-Yourself*
Muffler	43.75–60.00	15.00–48.00
Ball joint, lower	20.00–22.00	15.00–17.00
Ball joint, upper	19.50–20.25	15.00–17.00
Shock absorber	16.50	12.00–15.00

*See note at beginning of section
**Can be purchased more economically in kit form

Cadillac Seville

	Prof. Installed*	Do-It-Yourself*
Contact point set	N/A	N/A
Condenser	N/A	N/A
Rotor (distributor)	5.75–7.00	4.75–6.00
Distributor cap		
Point-type ignition	N/A	N/A
Electronic ignition	12.25–18.00	10.50–15.50
Ignition (spark plug) wire set		
Point-type ignition	N/A	N/A
Electronic ignition	20.50–37.50	16.00–32.00
Alternator (new)		
Standard	266.00	175.00–210.00
Heavy-duty	298.50	175.00–240.00
Starter		
Gasoline engine	129.00–132.50	49.00–105.00
Diesel	328.50	250.00–270.00
Fuel pump (new)		
Fuel-injected engine	51.50–72.00	30.00–57.50
Diesel	29.25–75.00	20.00–60.00
Drum brake shoe set, 2 whls. (new)	32.75	20.00–25.00
Disc brake pad set, 2 whls. (new)	33.75–35.25	20.00–28.00
Brake caliper (disc brakes)		
Front	89.25–110.25	55.00–90.00
Rear	161.50–180.00	100.00–145.00
Master cylinder (new)	58.00–66.00	35.00–55.00
Repair kit	15.00–16.50	10.00–13.50
Water pump (new)		
4-cyl.	60.00	35.00–48.00
Radiator (new)	219.00–236.00	180.00–190.00
Muffler	47.00	20.00–37.00
Ball joint, lower	20.00	15.00–18.00
Shock absorber	16.50	12.00–15.00

*See note at beginning of section
N/A—Not Applicable

Cadillac Eldorado

	Prof. Installed*	Do-It-Yourself*
Contact point set**	6.00	4.00
Condenser**	2.00	1.50
Rotor (distributor)**	3.00–7.00	2.25–6.00

	Prof. Installed*	Do-It-Yourself*
Distributor cap		
Point-type ignition	9.00	7.25
Electronic ignition	12.25–18.00	9.75–14.50
Ignition (spark plug) wire set		
Point-type ignition	20.50	16.50
Electronic ignition	37.50–38.50 (some models priced separately)	30.00–31.00
Alternator (new)		
Standard	108.50–133.00	87.00–107.00
Heavy-duty	266.00–298.50	160.00–240.00
Starter		
V8	147.00–148.75	115.00–120.00
Diesel	328.50	265.00
Carburetor (new)	158.00–244.00	125.00–200.00
Carburetor repair kit (minor)	10.50–14.50	8.00–12.00
Carburetor overhaul kit (major)	24.00–25.00	20.00
Fuel pump (new)		
Carbureted engine	28.75–56.25	22.50–45.00
Fuel-injected engine	56.25–131.00	45.00–105.00
Diesel	29.25	25.00
Drum brake shoe set, 2 whls. (new)	29.25–43.75	24.00–35.00
Disc brake pad set, 2 whls. (new)	32.25–43.75	25.00–35.00
Brake caliper (disc brakes)		
Front	94.00–116.00	75.00–95.00
Rear	158.00–175.00	125.00–140.00
Master cylinder (new)	50.50–88.00	40.00–70.00
Repair kit	12.25–16.50	9.75–13.25
Water pump (new)	60.00–68.00	48.00–55.00
Radiator (new)	171.00–256.00	155.00–230.00
Muffler	41.50–60.00	32.00–48.00
Ball joint, lower	41.50	33.50
Ball joint, upper	20.75	16.50
Shock absorber	16.50	13.25

*See note at beginning of section
**Can be purchased in kit form more economically

Camaro, Chevelle, Malibu, Monte Carlo, Nova

	Prof. Installed*	Do-It-Yourself*
Contact point set**	4.00–6.25	3.50–5.25
Condenser**	2.50	1.00–1.50
Rotor (distributor)	2.25–5.75	1.25–4.00
Distributor cap		
Point-type ignition	4.50–7.50	4.00–6.75
Electronic ignition	8.75–14.50	7.50–12.50

	Prof. Installed*	Do-It-Yourself*
Ignition (spark plug) wire set		
Point-type ignition	11.00–19.00	8.00–14.00
Electronic ignition	Sold separately— N/A as a set	—
Alternator (new)		
Standard	127.50	49.00– 110.00
Heavy-duty	133.00	100.00– 110.00
Starter		
6-cyl.	129.00– 136.25	48.00– 110.00
V8	126.00– 152.00	48.00– 125.00
Carburetor (new)		
6-cyl.	86.00– 219.00	50.00– 175.00
V8	98.00– 211.00	75.00– 168.00
Carburetor repair kit (minor)	5.50–20.25	5.00–16.00
Carburetor overhaul kit (major)	18.50–25.75	14.00–20.00
Fuel pump (new)	15.75–31.00	12.50–25.00
Drum brake shoe set, 2 whls. (new)	21.50–30.00	11.00–24.00
Disc brake pad set, 2 whls. (new)	33.75–51.50	11.00–42.00
Brake caliper (disc brakes)	74.50– 104.25	55.00–85.00
Master cylinder (new)	44.75–74.75	30.00–60.00
Repair kit	12.00–16.75	9.00–15.00
Water pump (new)		
6-cyl.	28.75–40.00	20.00–32.00
V8	34.00–48.00	20.00–40.00
Radiator core (new)	127.00– 132.00	115.00– 105.00
Muffler	38.50–58.50	15.00–45.00
Ball joint, lower	20.00–22.50	15.00–17.50
Ball joint, upper	19.50–24.25	15.00–20.00
Shock absorber	16.50	12.00–15.00
Clutch disc	42.00–61.00	30.00–50.00
Clutch pressure plate	70.00–89.00	45.00–72.00
Clutch throwout bearing ..	16.50–18.00	12.00–16.00

*See note at beginning of section
** Can be purchased more economically in kit form

Chevrolet & Corvette

	Prof. Installed*	Do-It-Yourself*
Contact point set**	6.25–8.30	5.25–6.75
Condenser**	2.50	1.00–1.50
Rotor (distributor)**	3.00–5.50	1.25–4.00
Distributor cap		
Point-type ignition	6.25–7.50	5.25–6.75
Electronic ignition	8.75–14.50	7.50–12.50
Ignition (spark plug) wire set		
Point-type ignition	19.00–23.60	12.00–18.00
Electronic ignition	Sold separately— N/A as a set	—

	Prof. Installed*	Do-It-Yourself*
Alternator (new)		
Standard	127.50	49.00– 110.00
Heavy-duty	133.00	100.00– 110.00
Starter		
6-cyl.	129.50	49.00– 110.00
V8	129.00– 159.50	49.00– 125.00
Carburetor (new)		
6-cyl.	126.00– 143.00	85.00– 115.00
V8	100.00– 234.00	75.00– 190.00
Carburetor repair kit (minor)	8.60–19.00	7.00–16.00
Carburetor overhaul kit (major)	18.50–25.75	12.50–20.00
Fuel pump (new)	18.00–29.00	15.00–24.00
Drum brake shoe set, 2 whls. (new)	29.00–35.25	11.00–28.00
Disc brake pad set, 2 whls. (new)	34.00–39.00	11.00–32.00
Brake caliper (disc brakes)		
Front	84.25– 106.30	65.00–85.00
Rear	69.25–80.50	45.00–65.00
Master cylinder (new)	44.75–81.50	30.00–65.00
Repair kit	15.00–20.00	12.50–16.00
Water pump (new)		
6-cyl.	28.75	22.00–24.00
V8	34.00–51.75	22.00–40.00
Radiator (new)	170.00– 263.00	150.00– 235.00
Muffler	41.00–85.00	19.00–68.00
Ball joint, lower	20.75–24.00	15.00–20.00
Ball joint, upper	20.25–25.00	15.00–20.00
Shock absorber	16.50	12.00–15.00
Clutch disc	55.25	38.00–45.00
Clutch pressure plate	89.00	60.00–75.00
Clutch throwout bearing ..	16.50–18.00	12.00–16.00

*See note at beginning of section
** Can be purchased more economically in kit form

Chevette

	Prof. Installed*	Do-It-Yourself*
Contact point set	N/A	N/A
Condenser	N/A	N/A
Rotor (distributor)	4.00–5.50	3.50–4.50
Distributor cap		
Point-type ignition	N/A	N/A
Electronic ignition	10.00	8.00–9.00
Ignition (spark plug) wire set		
Point-type ignition	N/A	N/A
Electronic ignition	25.00	8.00–22.00
Alternator (new)		
Standard	141.25	50.00– 115.00
Starter	128.75– 136.25	49.00– 110.00
Carburetor (new)	100.00– 158.00	65.00– 125.00

	Prof. Installed*	Do-It-Yourself*
Carburetor overhaul kit (major)	18.50–50.50	13.50–45.00
Fuel pump (new)	20.25–25.50	15.00–20.00
Drum brake shoe set, 2 whls. (new)	30.50	11.00–24.00
Disc brake pad set, 2 whls. (new)	31.25	11.00–25.00
Brake caliper (disc brakes) Front	67.50–73.50	45.00–60.00
Master cylinder (new)	66.00–71.50	30.00–60.00
Repair kit	13.50–15.00	9.00–12.00
Water pump (new)	31.75–35.25	22.00–28.00
Radiator core (new)	97.25–115.00	85.00–105.00
Muffler	37.25–41.75	19.00–32.50
Ball joint, lower	19.00	14.00–17.00
Ball joint, upper	19.00–19.50	14.00–17.50
Shock absorber	16.50	12.00–15.00
Clutch disc	40.00	25.00–32.00
Clutch pressure plate	55.00	35.00–44.00
Clutch throwout bearing ..	17.50	12.00–15.00

*See note at beginning of section
N/A—Not Applicable

Citation, Omega, Phoenix, Skylark—All 1980

	Prof. Installed*	Do-It-Yourself*
Contact point set	N/A	N/A
Condenser	N/A	N/A
Rotor (distributor)	5.75	4.00–5.00
Distributor cap		
Point-type ignition	N/A	N/A
Electronic ignition	13.50	9.50–11.00
Alternator (new)		
Standard	130.00–135.00	49.00–110.00
Heavy-duty	183.50	110.00–150.00
Starter		
4-cyl.	138.50	85.00–110.00
6-cyl.	138.50	85.00–110.00
Carburetor (new)	220.00	150.00–175.00
Carburetor repair kit (minor)	7.75–13.75	6.00–11.00
Carburetor overhaul kit (major)	16.50–20.00	12.00–17.50
Fuel pump (new)	22.50–45.75	15.00–36.00
Disc brake pad set, 2 whls. (new)	38.25	25.00–30.00
Water pump (new)		
4-cyl.	53.25	40.00–42.00
6-cyl.	40.00	30.00–32.00
Radiator core (new)	135.00–185.00	120.00–170.00
Muffler	34.50–39.75	19.00–32.50
Ball joint, lower	28.75	18.00–22.00
Shock absorber	27.50	18.00–22.00
Clutch disc	49.75–53.50	30.00–42.00

	Prof. Installed*	Do-It-Yourself*
Clutch pressure plate	78.25–86.25	55.00–70.00
Clutch throwout bearing ..	18.50	12.00–16.00

*See note at beginning of section
N/A—Not Applicable

Chrysler, Cordoba, Imperial

	Prof. Installed*	Do-It-Yourself*
Contact point set	N/A	N/A
Condenser	N/A	N/A
Rotor (distributor)	1.75	1.50
Distributor cap		
Point-type ignition	N/A	N/A
Electronic ignition	5.00–5.75	4.50–5.00
Ignition (spark plug) wire set		
Point-type ignition	N/A	N/A
Electronic ignition	20.00–42.75	12.00–35.00
Alternator (new)		
Standard	114.00–128.00	49.00–105.00
Heavy-duty	246.75	170.00–200.00
Starter	130.00–135.00	50.00–110.00
Carburetor (new)	88.00–221.00	60.00–175.00
Carburetor overhaul kit (major)	10.00–24.25	7.50–20.00
Fuel pump (new)	22.50–26.25	15.00–21.00
Drum brake shoe set, 2 whls. (new)	27.50–30.50	11.00–24.00
Disc brake pad set, 2 whls. (new)	27.50–38.00	11.00–32.00
Brake caliper (disc brakes) housing	81.50–90.75	60.00–72.00
Master cylinder (new)	45.00–52.00	32.00–42.00
Repair kit	26.00–28.75	18.00–22.50
Water pump (new)	37.50–39.50	20.00–32.00
Radiator (new)	180.50–301.00	160.00–240.00
Muffler	33.25–45.75	19.00–35.00
Ball joint, lower	18.75–23.75	15.00–18.00
Ball joint, upper	18.25–19.75	15.00–17.00
Shock absorber	15.25–21.00	15.00–17.00

*See note at beginning of section
N/A—Not Applicable

Dodge

	Prof. Installed*	Do-It-Yourself*
Contact point set	N/A	N/A
Condenser	N/A	N/A
Rotor (distributor)	1.75–2.50	1.50–2.00
Distributor cap		
Point-type ignition	N/A	N/A
Electronic ignition	5.00–5.75	4.50–5.00
Ignition (spark plug) wire set		
Point-type ignition	N/A	N/A
Electronic ignition	15.00–42.75	10.00–35.00

	Prof. Installed*	Do-It-Yourself*
Alternator (new)		
Standard	114.00–128.00	49.00–105.00
Heavy-duty	246.75	170.00–200.00
Starter		
6-cyl.	130.00–135.00	50.00–110.00
V8	130.00–135.00	50.00–110.00
Carburetor (new)		
6-cyl.	79.50–188.50	55.00–150.00
V8	96.00–188.25	70.00–150.00
Carburetor repair kit (minor)	8.25–23.50	5.50–18.50
Carburetor overhaul kit (major)	10.75–23.00	7.50–18.50
Fuel pump (new)	20.50–26.50	15.00–22.00
Drum brake shoe set, 2 whls. (new)	27.50–30.50	12.00–24.00
Disc brake pad set, 2 whls. (new)	27.50–38.00	12.00–32.00
Brake caliper (disc brakes)	81.50–89.00	55.00–72.00
Master cylinder (new)	45.00–52.00	30.00–42.00
Repair kit	26.00–28.75	18.00–24.00
Water pump (new)		
6-cyl.	37.50	20.00–22.00
V8	37.50–39.50	20.00–32.00
Radiator (new)	165.00–301.00	150.00–240.00
Muffler	35.75–45.75	19.00–35.00
Ball joint, lower	23.75	16.00–19.00
Ball joint, upper	18.25–19.75	15.00–18.00
Shock absorber	15.25–21.00	15.00–17.00
Clutch disc	36.00–65.00	25.00–52.00
Clutch pressure plate	49.00–113.00	35.00–90.00
Clutch throwout bearing ..	10.25–20.75	8.00–16.00

*See note at beginning of section
N/A—Not Applicable

Horizon and Omni

	Prof. Installed*	Do-It-Yourself*
Contact point set	N/A	N/A
Condenser	N/A	N/A
Rotor (distributor)	1.75	1.50
Distributor cap		
Point-type ignition	N/A	N/A
Electronic ignition	5.00	3.75–4.00
Ignition (spark plug) wire set		
Point-type ignition	N/A	N/A
Electronic ignition	14.50	10.00–12.00
Alternator (new)		
Standard	65.00–118.50	45.00–95.00
Starter	58.00	35.00–45.00
Carburetor (new)	117.00–121.00	80.00–100.00
Carburetor repair kit (minor)	6.00–18.50	5.00–15.00
Fuel pump (new)	25.00	15.00–20.00

	Prof. Installed*	Do-It-Yourself*
Drum brake shoe set, 2 whls. (new)	25.00	11.00–20.00
Disc brake pad set, 2 whls. (new)	26.00	11.00–20.00
Master cylinder (new)	50.00–52.00	30.00–42.00
Repair kit	45.00	32.00–36.00
Water pump (new)	30.00	20.00–24.00
Radiator (new)	141.50	110.00–130.00
Muffler	31.00	19.00–24.00
Shock absorber	51.00	35.00–40.00
Clutch disc	34.00	22.00–27.00
Clutch pressure plate	47.00–51.00	30.00–40.00

*See note at beginning of section
N/A—Not Applicable

Capri and Mustang (1979–80)

	Prof. Installed*	Do-It-Yourself*
Contact point set	N/A	N/A
Condenser	N/A	N/A
Rotor (distributor)	2.00	1.50
Distributor cap		
Point-type ignition	N/A	N/A
Electronic ignition	10.50–13.00	6.00–10.50
Ignition (spark plug) wire set		
Point-type ignition	N/A	N/A
Electronic ignition	28.25–39.00	16.00–31.00
Alternator (new)		
Standard	120.50–124.50	40.00–100.00
Heavy-duty	207.50–221.00	80.00–175.00
Starter		
4-cyl.	75.25	45.00–60.00
6-cyl.	121.75	45.00–100.00
V8	101.50	45.00–80.00
Carburetor (new)		
4-cyl.	170.25	100.00–135.00
6-cyl.	148.50–307.00	85.00–245.00
V8	158.75–307.00	90.00–245.00
Fuel pump (new)	25.50–31.50	15.00–25.00
Drum brake shoe set, 2 whls. (new)	28.00	11.00–22.50
Disc brake pad set, 2 whls. (new)	22.25–28.25	11.00–23.00
Brake caliper (disc brakes) Front	59.50	35.00–48.00
Master cylinder (new)	53.25	30.00–45.00
Repair kit	20.00	12.00–16.00
Water pump (new)		
4-cyl.	37.75–39.75	20.00–32.00
6-cyl.	45.50	20.00–36.00
V8	61.50–63.50	20.00–50.00
Radiator (new)	113.25–180.75	100.00–165.00
Muffler	60.50–94.00	25.00–75.00
Ball joint, lower	40.50①	25.00–35.00

	Prof. Installed*	Do-It- Yourself*
Shock absorber	82.00	55.00–65.00
Clutch disc	32.00–34.25	24.00–30.00
Clutch pressure plate	42.50–44.00	28.00–35.00
Clutch throwout bearing ..	17.75–18.25	12.00–14.00

*See note at beginning of section
N/A—Not Applicable
① Serviced by replacement of lower control arm

	Prof. Installed*	Do-It- Yourself*
Ball joint, upper	37.95– 51.25①	25.00–42.00
Shock absorber	17.00	15.00–17.00
Clutch disc	31.75–34.00	20.00–27.00
Clutch pressure plate	36.75	21.00–29.00
Clutch throwout bearing ..	17.25–18.25	12.00–15.00

*See note at beginning of section
** Can be purchased more economically in kit form
① Serviced by replacement of upper or lower control arm

Comet, Cougar, Monarch, Montego, Lincoln Versailles

	Prof. Installed*	Do-It- Yourself*
Contact point set**	5.50	3.00–4.50
Condenser**	2.00	1.00–1.50
Rotor (distributor)**	1.75–6.00	1.50–4.50
Distributor cap		
Point-type ignition	6.50–7.50	4.50–6.50
Electronic ignition	7.00–14.25	4.50–11.50
Ignition (spark plug) wire set		
Point-type ignition	17.25–22.00	12.00–17.50
Electronic ignition	17.25–52.50	16.00–42.00
Alternator (new)		
Standard	120.50– 124.50	48.00– 100.00
Heavy-duty	207.50– 363.25	100.00– 290.00
Starter		
6-cyl.	121.75– 127.25	49.00– 105.00
V8	121.75– 125.00	49.00– 105.00
Carburetor (new)		
6-cyl.	73.00– 158.75	40.00– 125.00
V8	128.00– 307.00	75.00– 250.00
Carburetor repair kit (minor)	3.25–14.00	3.00–12.00
Carburetor overhaul kit (major)	9.75–27.00	6.00–21.50
Fuel pump (new)	23.75–27.75	15.00–21.50
Drum brake shoe set, 2 whls. (new)	19.50–23.65	11.00–18.50
Disc brake pad set, 2 whls. (new)	20.00–30.50	11.00–24.00
Brake caliper (disc brakes)		
Front	55.75–65.75	35.00–52.00
Rear	126.50	85.00– 100.00
Master cylinder (new)	50.25–57.00	29.00–45.00
Repair kit	18.25–25.25	11.00–20.00
Water pump (new)		
6-cyl.	36.50–43.75	20.00–35.00
V8	61.50–69.75	20.00–56.00
Radiator (new)	121.00– 170.75	100.00– 155.00
Muffler	37.00– 114.00	19.00–90.00
Ball joint, lower	37.00– 59.25①	25.00–48.00

Elite, Granada, Maverick, Torino, LTD II, Thunderbird (1977–79)

	Prof. Installed*	Do-It- Yourself*
Contact point set**	5.50–6.50	3.00–4.50
Condenser**	2.00	1.00–1.50
Rotor (distributor)**	1.75–2.00	1.50–4.50
Distributor cap		
Point-type ignition	6.50–7.50	4.50–6.50
Electronic ignition	7.00–13.00	4.50–10.50
Ignition (spark plug) wire set		
Point-type ignition	21.50	12.00–17.00
Electronic ignition	17.25–52.50	12.00–42.00
Alternator (new)		
Standard	120.50– 124.50	48.00– 100.00
Heavy-duty	221.00– 363.25	100.00– 290.00
Starter		
6-cyl.	121.75– 127.25	49.00– 105.00
V8	121.75– 127.25	49.00– 105.00
Carburetor (new		
6-cyl.	80.00– 134.75	48.00– 110.00
V8	113.25– 307.00	70.00– 245.00
Carburetor repair kit (minor)	3.25–11.00	3.00–9.00
Carburetor overhaul kit (major)	11.00–27.00	6.00–21.50
Fuel pump (new)	23.75–25.75	15.00–21.50
Drum brake shoe set, 2 whls. (new)	19.50–24.00	11.00–18.50
Disc brake pad set, 2 whls. (new)	20.00	11.00–16.00
Brake caliper (disc brakes)		
Front	59.50–65.75	35.00–52.00
Rear	126.50	85.00– 100.00
Master cylinder (new)	50.25–57.00	29.00–45.00
Repair kit	18.25–25.25	11.00–20.00
Water pump (new)		
6-cyl.	36.50–43.75	20.00–35.00
V8	61.50–69.75	20.00–56.00
Radiator (new)	121.00– 170.00	100.00– 155.00
Muffler	37.00– 114.00	19.00–90.00
Ball joint, lower	24.75– 59.25①	15.00–48.00
Ball joint, upper	39.75①	24.00–32.00

	Prof. Installed*	Do-It-Yourself*
Shock absorber	17.00	15.00–17.00
Clutch disc	31.75–34.00	20.00–27.00
Clutch pressure plate	33.75–36.75	20.00–30.00
Clutch throwout bearing ..	17.25–18.25	12.00–15.00

*See note at beginning of section.
**Can be purchased more economically in kit form.
① Serviced by replacement of upper or lower control arm.

Ford

	Prof. Installed*	Do-It-Yourself*
Contact point set**	5.35	3.00–4.25
Condenser**	2.00	1.25–1.50
Rotor (distributor)**	1.75–2.00	1.25–1.50
Distributor cap		
Point-type ignition	7.75	4.00–6.50
Electronic ignition	7.75–13.00	4.50–10.50
Ignition (spark plug) wire set		
Point-type ignition	21.50	16.00–17.00
Electronic ignition	21.50–52.50	16.00–41.50
Alternator (new)		
Standard	120.50–124.50	48.00–100.00
Heavy-duty	221.50–363.50	100.00–290.00
Starter	125.00–127.25	49.00–105.00
Carburetor (new)	129.00–307.00	75.00–245.00
Carburetor repair kit (minor)	4.00–11.00	3.00–9.00
Carburetor overhaul kit (major)	11.00–22.50	6.50–17.50
Fuel pump (new)	23.75–27.75	15.00–22.00
Drum brake shoe set, 2 whls. (new)	16.00–35.50	11.00–28.00
Disc brake pad set, 2 whls. (new)	20.00–35.50	11.00–28.00
Brake caliper (disc brakes)		
Front	65.75–70.00	40.00–56.00
Rear	127.00	80.00–100.00
Master cylinder (new)	50.25–67.50	29.00–55.00
Repair kit	23.00	15.00–18.50
Water pump (new)	60.25–69.75	20.00–55.00
Radiator (new)	139.75–176.25	125.00–150.00
Muffler	50.50–121.50	19.00–100.00
Ball joint, lower	59.25①	35.00–48.00
Ball joint, upper	41.75①	25.00–35.00
Shock absorber	17.00	15.00–17.50

*See note at beginning of section.
**Can be purchased more economically in kit form.
① Serviced by replacement of upper or lower control arm.

Lincoln Continental, Mark IV, Mark V

	Prof. Installed*	Do-It-Yourself*
Contact point set	N/A	N/A
Condenser	N/A	N/A
Rotor (distributor)	1.00–2.00	1.00–1.50
Distributor cap		
Point-type ignition	N/A	N/A
Electronic ignition	7.50–13.25	4.00–10.50
Ignition (spark plug) wire set		
Point-type ignition	N/A	N/A
Electronic ignition	21.75–52.50	16.00–41.50
Alternator (new)		
Standard	124.50–161.00	48.00–100.00
Heavy-duty	221.00–363.25	100.00–290.00
Starter	125.00	49.00–105.00
Carburetor (new)	158.75–263.00	95.00–210.00
Carburetor repair kit (minor)	4.00–11.00	3.00–9.00
Carburetor overhaul kit (major)	12.75–27.00	8.50–21.50
Fuel pump (new)	23.00–27.75	15.00–22.00
Drum brake shoe set, 2 whls. (new)	24.00–37.50	11.00–30.00
Disc brake pad set, 2 whls. (new)	20.00	11.00–16.00
Brake caliper (disc brakes)		
Front	65.75	40.00–52.00
Rear	127.00	80.00–100.00
Master cylinder (new)	44.50–67.00	29.00–55.00
Water pump (new)	61.50–69.75	20.00–55.00
Radiator (new)	170.00–177.50	153.00–160.00
Muffler	70.25–196.50	30.00–156.00
Ball joint, lower	59.25①	35.00–48.00
Ball joint, upper	41.75①	25.00–35.00
Shock absorber	17.00	15.00–17.00

*See note at beginning of section.
N/A Not Applicable
① Serviced by replacement of upper or lower control arm.

Mercury

	Prof. Installed*	Do-It-Yourself*
Contact point set	N/A	N/A
Condenser	N/A	N/A
Rotor (distributor)	1.75–6.00	1.25–5.00
Distributor cap		
Point-type ignition	N/A	N/A
Electronic ignition	7.75–14.75	4.00–12.00
Ignition (spark plug) wire set		
Point-type ignition	N/A	N/A
Electronic ignition	21.50–52.50	16.00–41.50
Alternator (new)		
Standard	120.50–207.50	48.00–165.00
Heavy-duty	221.00–363.25	100.00–290.00
Starter	125.00–127.25	49.00–105.00

	Prof. Installed*	Do-It-Yourself*
Carburetor (new)	130.00–307.00	75.00–250.00
Carburetor repair kit (minor)	4.25–11.00	3.00–9.00
Carburetor overhaul kit (major)	22.50–27.00	13.00–21.50
Fuel pump (new)	23.50–27.50	15.00–22.00
Drum brake shoe set, 2 whls. (new)	23.00–35.50	11.00–30.00
Disc brake pad set, 2 whls. (new)	20.00–22.25	11.00–17.50
Brake caliper (disc brakes)		
Front	65.75–70.00	40.00–55.00
Rear	127.00	80.00–100.00
Master cylinder (new)	45.00–67.00	20.00–55.00
Repair kit	23.00	13.50–18.50
Water pump (new)	60.25–70.00	20.00–50.00
Radiator (new)	140.00–177.50	115.00–160.00
Muffler	50.50–121.50	19.00–95.00
Ball joint, lower	59.25①	35.00–58.00
Ball joint, upper	41.75①	25.00–35.00
Shock absorber	17.00	15.00–17.00

*See note at beginning of section.
N/A Not Applicable.
① Serviced by replacement of upper or lower control arm.

Mustang II, Bobcat, Pinto, Fairmont, Zephyr

	Prof. Installed*	Do-It-Yourself*
Contact point set**	5.00–6.75	3.00–5.50
Condenser**	4.25	1.00–1.50
Rotor (distributor)**	1.50–2.00	1.00–1.50
Distributor cap		
Point-type ignition	5.50–10.50	4.00–8.00
Electronic ignition	10.50–13.50	4.50–10.50
Ignition (spark plug) wire set		
Point-type ignition	15.50–21.75	9.00–16.50
Electronic ignition	28.25–50.25	9.00–40.00
Alternator (new)		
Standard	120.50–124.50	48.00–100.00
Heavy-duty	207.50–363.25	110.00–290.00
Starter		
4-cyl.	75.25	49.00–60.00
6-cyl.	101.50–125.00	49.00–100.00
V8	101.50	45.00–80.00
Carburetor (new)		
4-cyl.	129.00–177.25	100.00–140.00
6-cyl.	78.25–307.00	48.00–250.00
V8	158.75–307.00	95.00–250.00
Fuel pump (new)	24.50–37.00	15.00–20.00
Drum brake shoe set, 2 whls. (new)	19.50–28.00	11.00–22.50
Disc brake pad set, 2 whls. (new)	19.50–22.25	11.00–18.00

	Prof. Installed*	Do-It-Yourself*
Brake caliper (disc brakes)		
Front	55.75	35.00–45.00
Rear	55.75	35.00–45.00
Master cylinder (new)	53.00–61.50	30.00–45.00
Repair kit	18.75–24.50	12.00–20.00
Water pump (new)		
4-cyl.	34.75–38.50	20.00–30.00
6-cyl.	43.75–45.50	20.00–36.00
V8	58.75–61.50	20.00–50.00
Radiator (new)	115.75–311.75	100.00–250.00
Muffler	40.50–121.00	19.00–95.00
Ball joint, lower	40.50①	30.00–32.00
Ball joint, upper	39.75①	25.00–32.00
Shock absorber	17.00–82.00	15.00–65.00
Clutch disc	29.75–37.25	20.00–30.00
Clutch pressure plate	24.75–43.50	20.00–35.00
Clutch throwout bearing ..	17.75–18.25	12.00–14.00

*See note at beginning of section.
** Can be purchased more economically in kit form.
① Serviced by replacement of upper or lower control arm.

Oldsmobile

	Prof. Installed*	Do-It-Yourself*
Contact point set**	6.25	3.00–3.50
Condenser**	1.75	1.00–1.50
Rotor (distributor)**	2.75–5.75	1.50–2.50
Distributor cap		
Point-type ignition	7.50	4.00–6.00
Electronic ignition	12.25–17.50	9.00–13.50
Ignition (spark plug) wire set		
Point-type ignition ..	21.50	16.00–17.50
Electronic ignition	32.75–47.95 (some models priced separately)	16.00–38.50
Alternator (new)		
Standard	127.50–133.00	49.00–110.00
Heavy-duty	266.00	125.00–212.00
Starter		
6-cyl.	135.00–136.25	48.00–110.00
V8	129.00–142.00	48.00–115.00
Diesel	328.50	250.00–270.00
Carburetor (new)		
6-cyl.	156.00–206.00	95.00–165.00
V8	133.00–218.00	80.00–175.00
Carburetor overhaul kit (major)	12.50–20.25	11.00–16.00
Fuel pump (new)		
Carbureted engine ...	18.00–25.00	15.00–20.00
Diesel	29.95	20.00–24.00
Drum brake shoe set, 2 whls. (new)	29.25–35.75	11.00–28.00

	Prof. Installed*	Do-It-Yourself*
Disc brake pad set, 2 whls. (new)	33.75–35.25	11.00–28.00
Brake caliper (disc brakes)	89.25–112.75	55.00–90.00
Master cylinder (new)	44.75–60.00	27.00–48.00
Repair kit	15.00–22.75	12.00–20.00
Water pump (new)		
6-cyl.	40.25	19.00–32.00
V8	48.75–50.00	19.00–40.00
Radiator (new)	170.00–240.00	150.00–215.00
Muffler	41.25–58.75	19.00–48.00
Ball joint, lower	20.00–22.00	15.00–17.50
Ball joint, upper	19.50–20.25	12.00–16.00
Shock absorber	16.50	12.00–15.00

*See note at beginning of section.
** Can be purchased more economically in kit form.

	Prof. Installed*	Do-It-Yourself*
Master cylinder (new)	33.00–68.00	29.00–55.00
Repair kit	15.00–22.75	12.00–17.50
Water pump (new)		
6-cyl.	25.50–34.25	19.00–28.00
V8	34.25–50.00	19.00–40.00
Radiator (new)	140.00–300.00	125.00–240.00
Muffler	35.00–64.25	19.00–52.00
Ball joint, lower	20.00–24.00	14.00–20.00
Ball joint, upper	19.50–24.50	14.00–20.00
Shock absorber	16.50	12.00–15.00
Clutch disc	41.75–53.75	25.00–45.00
Clutch pressure plate	69.50–84.00	42.00–67.50
Clutch throwout bearing	18.75–22.00	12.00–17.50

*See note at beginning of section.
** Can be purchased more economically in kit form.

Olds Cutlass, Omega (1974–79)

	Prof. Installed*	Do-It-Yourself*
Contact point set**	5.00–6.25	3.00–3.50
Condenser**	2.00	1.00–1.50
Rotor (distributor)**	1.50–5.75	1.00–3.50
Distributor cap		
Point-type ignition	5.75–7.50	4.00–6.00
Electronic ignition	10.50–17.50	9.00–13.50
Ignition (spark plug) wire set		
Point-type ignition	11.00–20.50	8.00–16.00
Electronic ignition	47.95 (some models priced separately)	12.00–38.50
Alternator (new)		
Standard	127.50–133.00	49.00–110.00
Heavy-duty	183.50–266.00	90.00–212.00
Starter		
6-cyl.	126.00–136.25	48.00–110.00
V8	112.50–152.00	48.00–120.00
Diesel	328.50	250.00–270.00
Carburetor (new)		
1-barrel	69.00–105.00	35.00–85.00
2-barrel	126.00–219.00	75.00–175.00
4-barrel	170.00–212.00	90.00–170.00
Carburetor overhaul kit (major)	5.50–20.50	5.00–16.00
Fuel pump (new)		
Carbureted engine	18.00–24.75	15.00–20.00
Diesel	29.25	20.00–24.00
Drum brake shoe set, 2 whls. (new)	21.50–30.50	11.00–24.00
Disc brake pad set, 2 whls. (new)	33.75–51.50	11.00–40.00
Brake caliper (disc brakes)	74.50–104.25	45.00–85.00

Olds Toronado

	Prof. Installed*	Do-It-Yourself*
Contact point set	N/A	N/A
Condenser	N/A	N/A
Rotor (distributor)	5.75	3.00–3.50
Distributor cap		
Point-type ignition	N/A	N/A
Electronic ignition	12.25–15.00	10.00–12.00
Ignition (spark plug) wires		
Point-type ignition	N/A	N/A
Electronic ignition	6.00–8.20 each	16.00–20.00 (set)
Alternator (new)		
Standard	127.50–133.00	49.00–110.00
Heavy-duty	266.00	125.00–212.00
Starter		
V8	116.00–150.00	48.00–125.00
Diesel	330.00	250.00–270.00
Carburetor (new)	153.00–199.00	90.00–160.00
Carburetor overhaul kit (major)	12.00–15.50	9.00–12.00
Fuel pump (new)		
Carbureted engine	19.00–28.25	15.00–20.00
Diesel	29.25	20.00–24.00
Drum brake shoe set, 2 whls. (new)	30.00–38.25	11.00–30.00
Disc brake pad set, 2 whls. (new)	43.75–63.00	11.00–50.00
Brake caliper (disc brakes)		
Front	93.00–116.00	55.00–95.00
Rear	158.00	95.00–125.00
Master cylinder (new)	53.90–88.50	29.00–70.00
Repair kit	12.25–18.25	9.00–15.00
Water pump (new)	48.75–50.00	19.00–40.00
Radiator (new)	235.00–265.00	200.00–235.00
Muffler	41.75	19.00–32.00
Ball joint, lower	39.75	24.00–32.00

	Prof. Installed*	Do-It-Yourself*
Ball joint, upper	21.20	12.00–16.00
Shock absorber	16.25–16.95	12.00–15.00

*See note at beginning of section.
N/A Not Applicable.

	Prof. Installed*	Do-It-Yourself*
Clutch pressure plate	66.00–82.25	40.00–65.00
Clutch throwout bearing ..	18.50	12.00–15.00

*See note at beginning of section.
N/A Not applicable.

Olds Starfire

	Prof. Installed*	Do-It-Yourself*
Contact point set	N/A	N/A
Condenser	N/A	N/A
Rotor (distributor)	4.00–5.50	2.50–4.50
Distributor cap		
Point-type ignition	N/A	N/A
Electronic ignition	10.00–18.25	7.50–14.50
Ignition (spark plug) wire set		
Point-type ignition	N/A	N/A
Electronic ignition	41.00	9.00–32.50
		(priced separately on some models)
Alternator (new)		
Standard	127.50	49.00–105.00
Heavy-duty	133.00	49.00–110.00
Starter		
4-cyl.	133.50–142.00	48.00–120.00
6-cyl.	112.50–135.00	48.00–115.00
V8	136.25	48.00–105.00
Carburetor (new)		
4-cyl.	142.00–220.00	85.00–175.00
6-cyl.	124.00–219.00	75.00–175.00
V8	124.00–206.00	75.00–175.00
Carburetor overhaul kit (major)	16.75–50.50	12.00–40.00
Fuel pump (new)	31.00	15.00–24.00
Drum brake shoe set, 2 whls. (new)	25.75–31.25	11.00–25.00
Disc brake pad set, 2 whls. (new)	42.50	11.00–34.00
Brake caliper (disc brakes)	93.25–94.50	54.00–75.00
Master cylinder (new)	61.25–68.75	30.00–55.00
Repair kit	13.00–16.75	8.00–14.00
Water pump (new)		
4-cyl.	28.75–36.25	19.00–30.00
6-cyl.	43.00	19.00–35.00
V8	45.25	19.00–36.00
Radiator Core (new)	94.75–148.00	80.00–120.00
Muffler	29.50–49.25	19.00–40.00
Ball joint, lower	20.00	12.00–16.00
Ball joint, upper	19.50	12.00–16.00
Shock absorber	16.50	12.00–15.00
Clutch disc	43.50–52.75	25.00–42.00

Plymouth

	Prof. Installed*	Do-It-Yourself*
Contact point set	N/A	N/A
Condenser	N/A	N/A
Rotor (distributor)	1.75	1.00–1.50
Distributor cap		
Point-type ignition	N/A	N/A
Electronic ignition	5.00–5.75	4.00–4.50
Ignition (spark plug) wire set		
Point-type ignition	N/A	N/A
Electronic ignition	15.00–42.75	12.00–33.50
		(priced separately on some models)
Alternator (new)		
Standard	114.00–128.00	48.00–105.00
Heavy-duty	246.75	150.00–200.00
Starter		
6-cyl.	130.00	49.00–105.00
V8	130.00	49.00–105.00
Carburetor (new)		
6-cyl.	79.50–99.00	48.00–80.00
V8	96.00–226.25	60.00–180.00
Carburetor repair kit (minor)	4.00–23.00	3.50–17.00
Fuel pump (new)	20.50–25.00	15.00–20.00
Drum brake shoe set, 2 whls. (new)	27.50–30.50	11.00–24.00
Disc brake pad set, 2 whls. (new)	27.75–38.00	11.00–32.00
Brake caliper (disc brakes) housing only	81.50–89.00	48.00–72.00
Master cylinder (new)	45.00–52.00	29.00–40.00
Repair kit	26.00–30.00	18.00–24.00
Water pump (new)		
6-cyl.	37.50	19.00–30.00
V8	37.75	19.00–30.00
Radiator (new)	159.50–301.00	140.00–240.00
Muffler	35.75–45.50	19.00–40.00
Ball joint, lower	18.75	12.00–16.00
Ball joint, upper	18.25	12.00–16.00
Shock absorber	15.25	12.00–14.00
Clutch disc	35.25–65.00	20.00–55.00
Clutch pressure plate	49.00–113.00	30.00–90.00
Clutch throwout bearing ..	13.75–21.50	12.00–16.00

*See note at beginning of section.
N/A Not Applicable.

Pontiac & Grand Prix

	Prof. Installed*	Do-It-Yourself*
Contact point set**	5.00–5.75	3.00–4.50
Condenser**	1.50	1.00–1.50
Rotor (distributor)**	2.75–5.75	1.50–2.50
Distributor cap		
Point-type ignition	7.50	4.00–6.00
Electronic ignition	12.25–17.50	9.00–13.50
Ignition (spark plug) wire set		
Point-type ignition	23.50	8.00–18.00
Electronic ignition	38.95 (some models priced separately)	12.00–31.50
Alternator (new)		
Standard	127.50–133.00	49.00–110.00
Heavy-duty	266.00	125.00–212.00
Starter		
6-cyl.	129.00–136.25	48.00–110.00
V8	132.50–142.00	48.00–115.00
Carburetor (new)		
6-cyl.	156.00–219.00	85.00–175.00
V8	136.00–221.00	75.00–175.00
Carburetor repair kit (minor)	8.75–20.25	6.00–16.00
Fuel pump (new)	17.00–29.50	15.00–22.00
Drum brake shoe set, 2 whls. (new)	21.50–35.25	11.00–28.00
Disc brake pad set, 2 whls. (new)	32.25–43.75	11.00–38.00
Brake caliper (disc brakes)		
Front	74.50–112.70	45.00–85.00
Master cylinder (new)	33.00–103.00	29.00–81.00
Repair kit	13.25–22.00	10.00–17.00
Water pump (new)		
6-cyl.	33.75–48.00	19.00–42.00
V8	37.25–50.00	19.00–42.00
Radiator (new)	166.00–263.00	125.00–215.00
Muffler	37.50–58.50	19.00–45.00
Ball joint, lower	20.00–22.00	14.00–18.00
Ball joint, upper	18.50–19.50	14.00–18.00
Shock absorber	16.50	12.00–15.00
Clutch disc	50.50	30.00–40.00
Clutch pressure plate	88.00–88.75	55.00–72.00
Clutch throwout bearing	13.25–14.50	11.00–12.00

*See note at beginning of section.
** Can be purchased more economically in kit form.

Pontiac Astre & Sunbird

	Prof. Installed*	Do-It-Yourself*
Contact point set	N/A	N/A
Condenser	N/A	N/A
Rotor (distributor)	4.00–5.75	2.50–4.50

	Prof. Installed*	Do-It-Yourself*
Distributor cap		
Point-type ignition	N/A	N/A
Electronic ignition	10.00–18.00	7.50–14.50
Ignition (spark plug) wire set		
Point-type ignition	N/A	N/A
Electronic ignition	48.00 (some models priced separately)	9.00–32.50
Alternator (new)		
Standard	127.50	49.00–105.00
Heavy-duty	133.00	49.00–110.00
Starter		
4-cyl.	134.75–160.75	48.00–130.00
6-cyl.	112.50–136.25	48.00–115.00
V8	136.25	48.00–105.00
Carburetor (new)		
1-barrel	84.00–105.00	48.00–81.00
2-barrel	132.00–219.00	80.00–175.00
Carburetor overhaul kit (major)	9.00–50.50	7.00–40.00
Fuel pump (new)	22.50–31.00	15.00–20.00
Drum brake shoe set, 2 whls. (new)	25.75–31.25	11.00–25.00
Disc brake pad set, 2 whls. (new)	42.50	11.00–34.00
Brake caliper (disc brakes)		
Front	93.25–93.75	54.00–75.00
Master cylinder (new)	61.25–67.75	30.00–55.00
Repair kit	13.50–17.25	8.00–15.00
Water pump (new)		
4-cyl.	28.75–36.25	19.00–30.00
6-cyl.	33.75–35.00	20.00–32.00
V8	45.25	19.00–36.00
Radiator Core (new)	87.75–148.00	75.00–120.00
Muffler	29.50–49.25	19.00–40.00
Ball joint, lower	20.00	12.00–16.00
Ball joint, upper	19.50	12.00–16.00
Shock absorber	16.50	12.00–15.00
Clutch disc	43.50–52.75	25.00–42.00
Clutch pressure plate	61.25–82.25	35.00–65.00
Clutch throwout bearing	15.25	11.00–14.00

*See note at beginning of section.
N/A Not Applicable.

Firebird, LeMans, Phoenix (1978–79), Ventura (1974–77)

	Prof. Installed*	Do-It-Yourself*
Contact point set	4.25–5.75	3.00–4.50
Condenser**	1.50	1.00–1.50
Rotor (distributor)**	1.75–5.75	1.50–2.50
Distributor cap		
Point-type ignition	4.75–7.50	4.00–6.00
Electronic ignition	10.25–18.00	7.50–15.00

	Prof. Installed*	Do-It-Yourself*
Ignition (spark plug) wire set		
Point-type ignition	11.00–14.25 (some models priced separately)	8.00–12.00
Electronic ignition	39.00–48.00 (some models priced separately)	12.00–38.50
Alternator (new)		
Standard	127.50–133.00	49.00–110.00
Heavy-duty	266.00	125.00–212.00
Starter		
4-cyl.	134.75–160.75	48.00–128.00
6-cyl.	126.00–136.25	48.00–110.00
V8	110.25–142.00	48.00–115.00
Carburetor (new)		
4-cyl.	69.00–220.00	45.00–175.00
6-cyl.	109.00–219.00	65.00–175.00
V8	153.00–230.00	90.00–185.00
Carburetor overhaul kit (major)	18.50–28.00	12.00–24.00
Fuel pump (new)	15.75–28.50	12.00–24.00
Drum brake shoe set, 2 whls. (new)	10.75–31.80	11.00–24.00
Disc brake pad set, 2 whls. (new)	34.25–51.50	11.00–40.00
Brake caliper (disc brakes)	74.50–104.25	45.00–80.00
Master cylinder (new)	33.00–70.75	29.00–56.00
Repair kit	12.00–22.00	9.00–18.00
Water pump (new)		
4-cyl.	28.75	19.00–24.00
6-cyl.	25.50–33.75	19.00–26.00
V8	33.50–50.00	19.00–40.00
Radiator (new)	129.00–278.00	110.00–250.00
Muffler	35.00–93.75	19.00–80.00
Ball joint, lower	20.00	14.00–18.00
Ball joint, upper	18.50–19.50	14.00–18.00
Shock absorber	16.50	12.00–15.00
Clutch disc	43.00–87.50	25.00–70.00
Clutch pressure plate	48.25–109.00	30.00–88.00
Clutch throwout bearing ..	13.25–21.25	11.00–12.00

*See note at beginning of section.
**Can be purchased more economically in kit form.

Thunderbird (1974–76)

	Prof. Installed*	Do-It-Yourself*
Contact point set	N/A	N/A
Condenser	N/A	N/A
Rotor (distributor)	1.75	1.25–1.50

	Prof. Installed*	Do-It-Yourself*
Distributor cap		
Point-type ignition	N/A	N/A
Electronic ignition	13.00	4.50–10.50
Ignition (spark plug) wire set		
Point-type ignition	N/A	N/A
Electronic ignition	21.75–47.25	16.00–37.50
Alternator (new)		
Standard	124.50	48.00–100.00
Heavy-duty	221.00–286.00	125.00–230.00
Starter	125.00	49.00–100.00
Carburetor (new)	181.25–254.75	105.00–203.00
Carburetor repair kit (minor)	4.00–10.80	3.00–8.00
Carburetor overhaul kit (major)	12.50–27.00	10.00–22.00
Fuel pump (new)	23.00–27.75	15.00–22.50
Drum brake shoe set, 2 whls. (new)	23.80	11.00–19.00
Disc brake pad set, 2 whls. (new)	20.00–30.50	11.00–24.00
Brake caliper (disc brakes)		
Front	65.75	40.00–52.00
Rear	127.00	75.00–100.00
Master cylinder (new)	44.50–67.00	29.00–55.00
Repair kit	22.75–23.00	14.00–18.00
Water pump (new)	69.75	19.00–56.00
Radiator (new)	170.75	130.00–150.00
Muffler	61.75–122.75	29.00–95.00
Ball joint, upper	41.75①	30.00–35.00
Shock absorber	17.00	12.00–15.00

*See note at beginning of section.
N/A Not Applicable.
① Served by replacement of upper control arm.

Valiant, Dart, Barracuda, Challenger, Aspen, Volare, LeBaron, Diplomat

	Prof. Installed*	Do-It-Yourself*
Contact point set	N/A	N/A
Condenser	N/A	N/A
Rotor (distributor)	1.75–2.75	1.00–2.00
Distributor cap		
Point-type ignition	N/A	N/A
Electronic ignition	5.00–5.75	3.50–4.50
Ignition (spark plug) wire set		
Point-type ignition	N/A	N/A
Electronic ignition	15.00–28.50 (some models priced separately)	12.00–22.50
Alternator (new)		
Standard	114.00–133.00	48.00–110.00

	Prof. Installed*	Do-It-Yourself*
Heavy-duty	246.75	150.00–200.00
Starter		
6-cyl.	130.00	49.00–105.00
V8	130.00–135.00	49.00–110.00
Carburetor (new)		
6-cyl.	79.50–158.75	48.00–125.00
V8	81.50–188.25	60.00–150.00
Carburetor repair kit (minor)	10.75–23.00	6.00–19.00
Fuel pump (new)	20.50–23.50	15.00–20.00
Drum brake shoe set, 2 whls. (new)	24.50–30.50	11.00–24.00
Disc brake pad set, 2 whls. (new)	27.75–28.75	11.00–24.00
Brake caliper (disc brakes) housing		
Front	77.50–89.00	48.00–72.00
Master cylinder (new)	45.25–52.00	29.00–40.00
Repair kit	26.50–30.25	18.00–24.00
Water pump (new)		
6-cyl.	37.50	19.00–30.00
V8	37.75–39.50	19.00–35.00
Radiator (new)	149.25–229.75	125.00–210.00
Muffler	28.00–45.00	18.00–40.00
Ball joint, lower	18.75–28.50	12.00–24.00
Ball joint, upper	18.25	12.00–16.00
Shock absorber	15.25	12.00–14.00
Clutch disc	36.00–65.00	20.00–55.00
Clutch pressure plate	49.00–82.75	30.00–65.00
Clutch throwout bearing ..	21.50–26.45	12.00–16.00

*See note at beginning of section.
N/A Not Applicable.

Vega & Monza

	Prof. Installed*	Do-It-Yourself*
Contact point set**	4.50	2.50–3.00
Condenser**	2.25	1.00–1.50
Rotor (distributor)**	2.00–8.20	1.00–6.50
Distributor cap		
Point-type ignition	5.50	4.00–5.00
Electronic ignition	6.25–18.15	6.00–14.50

	Prof. Installed*	Do-It-Yourself*
Ignition (spark plug) wire set		
Point-type ignition	11.00	8.00–9.00
Electronic ignition	45.00 (some models priced sepa-rately)	9.00–36.00
Alternator (new)		
Standard	127.50	49.00–105.00
Heavy-duty	133.00–141.50	49.00–120.00
Starter		
4-cyl.	134.75–207.50	48.00–170.00
6-cyl.	136.25	48.00–105.00
V8	126.00–140.00	48.00–120.00
Carburetor (new)		
1-barrel	65.00–97.00	40.00–80.00
2-barrel	93.25–219.00	50.00–175.00
Carburetor repair kit (minor)	5.75–20.25	4.00–15.00
Carburetor overhaul kit (major)	15.00–50.50	12.00–40.00
Fuel pump (new)		
Carbureted engine ...	22.50–31.00	15.00–20.00
Fuel-injected engine ..	131.00	75.00–105.00
Drum brake shoe set, 2 whls. (new)	30.00–31.25	11.00–25.00
Disc brake pad set, 2 whls. (new)	37.50–54.50	11.00–42.00
Brake caliper (disc brakes)	93.25–94.50	54.00–75.00
Master cylinder (new)	61.00–67.75	30.00–55.00
Repair kit	14.00–17.00	11.00–15.00
Water pump (new)		
4-cyl.	28.25–45.00	19.00–36.00
6-cyl.	38.75	19.00–30.00
V8	45.25	19.00–36.00
Radiator Core (new)	87.75–152.00	75.00–125.00
Muffler	29.50–60.00	19.00–48.00
Ball joint, lower	19.85	12.00–16.00
Ball joint, upper	19.45	12.00–16.00
Shock absorber	16.35	12.00–15.00
Clutch disc	43.50–57.75	25.00–45.00
Clutch pressure plate	55.00–82.25	32.00–65.00
Clutch throwout bearing ..	16.00	11.00–14.00

*See note at beginning of section.
** Can be purchased more economically in kit form.

State Auto-Repair Laws

Your rights in the auto-repair process depend greatly on where you live. Why? Because less than half of the states have any laws governing auto-repair practices. What is a matter of law in California depends on company policy and your own assertiveness in Virginia. Prior to 1973 only three states provided any protection for consumers with auto-repair problems. As of 1979, 21 states, the District of Columbia, and at least three localities (Dallas, Texas, and Prince Georges and Montgomery counties in Maryland) provide some consumer rights and protection.

◆ Disclosures

A central element of auto-repair protection is the requirement of *disclosure*. The idea is to give the consumer better information about what repairs are needed, how much the repairs will cost, when the repairs will be finished, and what guarantees accompany the work. In some states, auto-repair regulations include definitions of deceptive practices and call for correction of shoddy repair work. Some typical provisions of disclosures are described below.

WRITTEN ESTIMATES

Written estimates are required for any work that costs above a certain amount, $25 or $50, for example. The estimate must include a description of the car's problem as described by the customer, a description of repair work to be performed, an estimate of all charges for this work, and an approximate time and date the car can be picked up. If the repair is going to exceed the initial estimate by more than 10%, the customer must be informed and asked to OK the total charges.

The need for written estimates can create a problem for "early bird" customers—people who drop off their cars on the way to work, before the shop opens. California makes its disclosure law flexible enough to accommodate them. The shop still has to fill out a written estimate but then can go over it by phone with the car owner, get an oral authorization to go ahead, and note the time and circumstances on the estimate.

Laws requiring written estimates generally permit the shop to charge a reasonable fee for making the estimate, but require that this fee be disclosed to the customer in advance. The shop also must disclose the nature, extent, and duration of any warranty on the work.

RETURN OF REPLACED PARTS

The shop has to return replaced parts to the car owner unless a warranty agreement requires that they be returned to the manufacturer or distributor, or unless the parts are so big as to make return impractical. Even then, the customer is entitled to see the replaced parts.

INVOICES

At the time the bill is paid, the shop must give the customer an invoice noting all repair work, stating whether new, rebuilt, or reconditioned parts were used, and identifying the mechanic who did the work. Shops must keep copies of these invoices for a specified period of time.

MECHANIC'S LIEN

Most states have what is known as a "mechanic's lien law," which means that if you refuse to pay a bill, no matter how outrageous, the shop can keep your car, no matter how valuable. In some states that require written estimates and authorization for repairs, the mechanic's lien law doesn't apply if the shop hasn't complied with the requirements.

The use of the mechanic's lien law in the auto business is rare. Usually it is only invoked in cases when the owner has agreed to extensive repairs and, after the work is done, decides that the car really isn't worth that much after all. The owner abandons the car and the shop is stuck with the repair bill. The only recourse is for the shop to obtain a mechanic's lien and recover as much of the cost as possible.

POSTED NOTICES

Shops must post signs prominently notifying customers of their rights to a written estimate, a written copy of any guarantee, return of replaced parts, and a detailed invoice. Some states require shops to post a notice stating where complaints can be filed.

DECEPTIVE PRACTICES AND PROHIBITED ACTS

Typical regulations prohibit shops from making false promises to get a car owner to authorize repairs, from allowing customers to sign blank documents relating to any repairs, from charging for any work not performed, from performing unnecessary repairs, or from misrepresenting the cost of authorized repairs.

Critics argue that requirements for written estimates mean that the shop estimates high rather than get caught short, thus driving up the costs of repairs. But proponents argue that the customer can use estimates to look for a shop that will offer a fair price for the repair.

Some states have complemented and strengthened their disclosure laws by requiring repair facilities to register with the state government. Repair facilities generally do not have to meet any specific requirement to register with the state, but they have to obey the law in order to stay in business. Michigan, Hawaii, and the District of Columbia carry auto-repair legislation one step further by requiring mechanics to pass a certification test for the type of repair work they usually perform.

◆ Regulatory Agencies

Following is a list of regulatory bodies in those states that have enacted auto repair legislation.

State	Agency
Alaska	Department of Law
California	California Department of Consumer Affairs, Bureau of Automotive Repair
Colorado	Denver District Attorney's Office
Connecticut	Connecticut Department of Motor Vehicles
District of Columbia	District of Columbia Office of Consumer Protection
Florida	Office of the Attorney General
Hawaii	Motor Vehicle Repair Industry Board of the Department of Regulatory Agencies and Office of Consumer Protection
Idaho	Office of the Attorney General, Division of Consumer Protection
Maryland	Office of the Attorney General, Consumer Protection Division
Massachusetts	Office of the Attorney General
Michigan	Bureau of Automotive Regulation
Minnesota	Commerce Department, Office of Consumer Services
Montana	Department of Business Regulation
Nevada	Office of the Attorney General, Consumer Affairs Office

State	Agency
New Hampshire	Office of the Attorney General, Consumer Protection Division
New Jersey	Office of the Attorney General, Consumer Office for Auto Repair
New York	New York Department of Motor Vehicles
Ohio	Office of the Attorney General, Consumer Frauds Division
Oregon	Department of Commerce, Consumer Services Division
Pennsylvania	Department of Justice, Bureau of Consumer Protection
Rhode Island	Office of the Attorney General
Texas	Office of the Attorney General, Consumer Protection Division
Utah	Division of Consumer Affairs, Trade Commission, Business Regulation
Virginia	Department of Agriculture and Commerce, Office of Consumer Affairs
Washington	Office of the Attorney General, Consumer Protection and Antitrust Division
Wisconsin	Department of Agriculture, Consumer Protection Division

Summary of Repair Laws in Selected Areas of Auto Repair

State	No Law	Motor Vehicle Repair Bureau	Disclosures	Certified Mechanics	Licensed Dealers	Regulatory Body (see p. 281)
Alabama	X					X
Alaska			R2			
Arizona	X					
Arkansas	X					
California		E1	E1, E7		E1	X
Colorado			R3			X
Connecticut		E1	E4		E1	X
Delaware	X		P			
Florida			E3			X
Georgia	X					
Hawaii		E4	E5	E4	E4	X
Idaho			R4			X
Illinois	X		P	P	P	
Indiana	X					
Iowa	X					
Kansas	X					
Kentucky	X					
Louisiana	X					
Maine	X					
Maryland*			E3			X
Massachusetts		P	E1		P	X

Summary of Repair Laws in Selected Areas of Auto Repair

State	No Law	Motor Vehicle Repair Bureau	Disclosures	Certified Mechanics	Licensed Dealers	Regulatory Body (see p. 281)
Michigan		E3	E3	E3	E3	X
Minnesota			E7			X
Mississippi	X					
Missouri	X		P			
Montana			R2			X
Nebraska	X					
Nevada			E4			X
New Hampshire			E4			X
New Jersey			E2		P	X
New Mexico	X					
New York		E4	E4		E3	X
North Carolina	X					
North Dakota	X					
Ohio			E1, E7			X
Oklahoma	X					
Oregon			E6		P	X
Pennsylvania			R4			X
Rhode Island					E3	X
South Carolina	X					
South Dakota	X					
Tennessee	X					
Texas		E1	R3			X
Utah			E5			X
Vermont	X					
Virginia			E7			X
Washington			E6			X
Washington, D.C.		E3	E3	E3	E3	X
West Virginia	X					X
Wisconsin			E5			
Wyoming	X					

E—Enacted by legislation
  1—prior to or in '72
  2—in '73
  3—in '74
  4—in '75
  5—in '76
  6—in '77
  7—in '78 or '79

R—Regulation issued by department
  1—in '75
  2—in '76
  3—in '77
  4—in '78 or '79
P—Pending bill in '79

*Repair facilities must be licensed in Montgomery and Prince Georges counties.

Glossary

Understanding your mechanic is as important as understanding your car. Just about everyone drives a car, but many drivers have difficulty understanding automotive terminology. Talking the language of cars makes it easier to communicate effectively with professional mechanics. It isn't necessary (or recommended) that you diagnose the problem for him, but it will save him time, and you money, if you can accurately describe what is happening. It will also help you to know why your car does what it is doing and what repairs were made.

Accelerator pump—A small pump located in the carburetor that feeds fuel into the air/fuel mixture during acceleration.

Advance—Setting the ignition timing so that spark occurs earlier, before the piston reaches top dead center (TDC).

Air bags—Devices on the inside of the car designed to inflate on impact of crash, protecting the occupants of the car.

Air pump—An emission control device that supplies fresh air to the exhaust manifold to aid in more completely burning exhaust gases.

Alternating current (AC)—Electric current that flows first in one direction, then in the opposite direction, continually reversing flow.

Alternator—A device which produces AC (alternating current) which is converted to DC (direct current) to charge the car battery.

Ammeter—A gauge which measures current flow (amps). Ammeters show whether the battery is charging or discharging.

Ampere (amp)—Unit to measure the rate of flow of electrical current.

Amp/hr. rating (battery)—Measurement of the ability of a battery to deliver a stated amount of current for a stated period of time. The higher the amp/hr. rating, the better the battery.

Antifreeze—A substance (ethylene glycol) added to the coolant to prevent freezing in cold weather.

ATDC—After Top Dead Center. Spark occurs after the piston has reached top dead center and is on the downward stroke.

ATF—Automatic transmission fluid.

Ball joint—A ball and matching socket connecting suspension components (steering knuckle-to-lower control arms). It permits rotating movement in any direction between the components that are joined.

Bead—The portion of a tire that holds it on the rim.

Book value—The average value of a car, widely used to determine trade-in and resale value.

Brake proportioning valve—A valve on the master cylinder which restricts hydraulic brake pressure to the rear wheels to a specified amount, preventing wheel lock-up.

Breaker points—A set of points inside the distributor, operated by a cam, which make and break the ignition circuit.

BTDC—Before Top Dead Center. Spark occurs on the compression stroke, before the piston reaches top dead center.

Belted tire—Tire construction similar to bias-ply tires, but using two or more layers of reinforced belts between body plies and the tread.

Bezel—Piece of metal surrounding radio, headlights, gauges, or similar components; sometimes used to hold the glass face of a gauge in the dash.

Bias ply tire—Tire construction using body ply reinforcing cords that run at alternating angles to the center line of the tread.

Brake caliper—The housing that fits over the brake disc. The caliper holds the brake pads that are pressed against the discs by the caliper pistons, when the brake pedal is depressed.

Brake horsepower—Usable horsepower of an engine measured at the crankshaft.

Brake fade—Loss of braking power, usually caused by excessive heat after repeated brake applications.

Brake pad—The friction pad on a disc brake system.

Brake shoe—The friction lining on a drum brake system.

Block—The basic engine casting containing the cylinders.

Bore—Diameter of a cylinder.

Bushing—A plain, replaceable bearing of soft metal or rubber.

California engine—An engine certified by the EPA for use in California only; conforms to more stringent emission regulations than Federal engine.

Camshaft—A shaft that rotates at one half engine speed, used to operate the intake and exhaust valves. In most engines, the cam bears upon a hydraulic lifter which opens the valve.

Camber—One of the factors of wheel alignment. Viewed from the front of the car, it is the inward or outward tilt of the wheel. The top of the tire will lean outward (positive camber) or inward (negative camber).

Caster—The forward or rearward tilt of an imaginary line drawn through the upper ball joint and the center of the wheel. Viewed from the sides, positive caster (forward tilt) lends directional stability, while negative caster (rearward tilt) produces instability.

Cancer—Rust on a car body.

Carbon monoxide (CO)—One of the by-products of the combustion process. Carbon monoxide is odorless and deadly.

Catalytic converter—A muffler-like device installed in the exhaust system to help control automotive emissions, specifically nitrous oxide.

Cetane rating—A measure of the ignition valve of diesel fuel. The higher the cetane rating, the better the fuel. Diesel fuel cetane rating is roughly comparable to gasoline octane rating.

Choke—The plate near the top of the carburetor that is closed to restrict the amount of air taken into the carburetor, making the fuel mixture richer.

Clutch—Part of the power train used to connect/disconnect power to the rear wheels.

Combustion chamber—The part of the engine in the cylinder head where combustion takes place.

Compression check—A test involving removing each spark plug and inserting a gauge. When the engine is cranked, the gauge will record a pressure reading in the individual cylinder. General operating condition can be determined from a compression check.

Compression ratio—The ratio of the volume between the piston and cylinder head when the piston is at the bottom of its stroke (bottom dead center) and when the piston is at the top of its stroke (top dead center).

Condenser—A small device in the ignition system which absorbs the momentary surge of current produced when the breaker points open. It protects the points from burning.

Control arms—The upper or lower A-shaped suspension components that are mounted on the frame and support the ball joints and steering knuckles.

Coil—Part of the ignition system that boosts the relatively low voltage supplied by the car's electrical system to the high voltage required to fire the spark plugs.

Connecting rod—The connecting link between the crankshaft and piston.

Conventional ignition—Ignition system which uses breaker points.

Coolant—Mixture of water and antifreeze circulated through the engine to carry off heat produced by the engine.

Crankshaft—Engine component (connected to pistons by connecting rods) which converts the reciprocating (up and down) motion of pistons to rotary motion used to turn the driveshaft.

Crankcase—The part of the engine that houses the crankshaft.

Curb weight—The weight of a vehicle without passengers or payload, but including all fluids (oil, gas, coolant, etc.) and other equipment specified as standard.

Detergent—An additive in engine oil to improve its operating characteristics.

Detonation—Instantaneous combustion of fuel, resulting in excessive heat and pressure which can damage engine components. Fuel should burn in the cylinders in a controlled manner, rather than exploding immediately.

Dexron®—A brand of automatic transmission fluid.

Dieseling—The engine continues to run after the car is shut off; caused by fuel continuing to be burned in the combustion chamber.

Differential—The part of the rear suspension that turns both axle shafts at the same time, but allows them to turn at different speeds when the car turns a corner.

Diode—A part of the alternator which converts alternating current to direct current.

Direct current (DC)—Electrical current that flows in one direction only.

Distributor—Device containing the breaker points which distributes high voltage to the proper spark plug at the proper time.

DOHC—Double overhead camshaft engine. Two overhead camshafts are used; one operates exhaust valves, and the other operates intake valves.

Dry charged battery—Battery to which electrolyte is added when the battery is placed in service.

Dwell angle—The number of degrees on the breaker cam that the points are closed.

Electrode—Conductor (positve or negative) of electric current.

Electrolyte—A solution of water and sulphuric acid used to activate the battery. Electrolyte is extremely corrosive.

Electronic ignition—Type of ignition system which uses no breaker points.

Enamel—Type of paint that dries to a smooth, glossy finish.

Ethyl—A substance added to gasoline to improve its resistance to knock, by slowing down the rate of combustion.

EP lubricant—EP (extreme pressure) lubricants are specially formulated for use with gears involving heavy loads (transmissions, differentials, etc.).

Ethylene glycol—The base substance of antifreeze.

Fast idle—The speed of the engine when the choke is on. Fast idle speeds engine warm-up.

Federal engine—An engine certified by the EPA for use in any of the forty-nine states (except California).

Filament—The part of a bulb that glows; the filament creates high resistance to current flow and actually glows from the resulting heat.

Firing order—The numerical sequence in which an engine's cylinders fire.

Flame front—The term used to describe certain aspects of the fuel explosion in the cylinders. The flame front should move in a controlled pattern across the cylinder, rather than simply exploding immediately.

Flat engine—Engine design in which the pistons are horizontally opposed. Porsche and VW are common examples of flat engines.

Flat spot—A point during acceleration when the engine seems to lose power for an instant.

Flooding—A condition created when too much fuel reaches the cylinders; starting will be difficult or impossible.

Flywheel—A heavy disc of metal attached to the rear of the crankshaft. It smooths the firing impulses of the engine and keeps the crankshaft turning during periods when no firing takes place. The starter also engages the flywheel to start the engine.

Foot pound—A measurement of torque (turning force).

Freeze plug—A plug in the engine block which will be pushed out if the coolant freezes. Sometimes called an expansion plug, it protects the block from cracking should the coolant freeze.

Frontal area—The total frontal area of a vehicle exposed to air flow.

Front-end alignment—A service to set caster, camber, and toe-in to the correct specifications. This will ensure that the car steers and handles properly and that the tires wear properly.

Fuel injection—A system replacing the carburetor that sprays fuel into the cylinder through nozzles. The amount of fuel can be more precisely controlled with fuel injection.

Fuse—A device containing a piece of metal rated to pass a given number of amps. If more current than the rated amperage passes through the fuse, the metal will melt and interrupt the circuit.

Fusible link—A piece of wire in a wiring harness that performs the same job as a fuse. If overloaded, the fusible link will melt and interrupt the circuit.

FWD—Front wheel drive.

GAWR—Gross axle weight rating: the total maximum weight an axle is designed to carry.

GCW—Gross combined weight: total combined weight of a tow vehicle and trailer.

Gearbox—Transmission.

Gear ratio—A ratio expressing the number of turns a smaller gear will make to turn a larger gear through one revolution. The ratio is found by dividing the number of teeth in the smaller gear into the number of teeth on the larger gear.

Gel coat—A thin coat of plastic resin covering fiberglass body panels.

Generator—A device which produces direct current (DC) necessary to charge the battery.

GVW—Gross vehicle weight: total weight of fully equipped and loaded vehicle, including passengers, equipment, fuel, oil, etc.

GVWR—Gross vehicle weight rating: total maximum weight a vehicle is designed to carry, including the weight of the vehicle, passengers, equipment, gas, oil, etc.

Header tank—An expansion tank for the radiator coolant. It can be located remotely or built into the radiator.

Heat range—A term used to describe the ability of a spark plug to carry away heat. Plugs with longer nosed insulators take longer to carry heat off effectively.

Heat riser—A flapper in the exhaust manifold that is closed when the engine is cold, causing hot exhaust gases to heat the intake manifold and provide better cold engine operation. A thermostatic spring opens the flapper when the engine warms up.

Hemi—A name given an engine using hemispherical combustion chambers.

Hydrocarbon (HC)—A combination of hydrogen and carbon atoms found in all petroleum-based fuels. Unburned hydrocarbons (those not burned during normal combustion) are about .1 percent of exhaust emissions.

Hydroplaning—A phenomenon of driving when water builds up under the tire tread, causing it to lose contact with the road. Slowing down will usually restore normal tire contact with the road.

Idle mixture—The mixture of air and fuel (usually about 14:1) being fed to the cylinders. The idle mixture screw(s) are sometimes adjusted as part of a tune-up.

Idler arm—Component of the steering linkage which is a geometric duplicate of the steering gear arm. It supports the right side of the center steering link.

Lacquer—A quick drying automotive paint.

Limited slip—A type of differential which transfers driving force to the wheel with the best traction.

Lithium-base grease—Chassis and wheel bearing grease using lithium as a base. Not compatible with sodium-base grease.

Load range—Indicates the number of plies at which a tire is rated. Load range B equals 4-ply rating, C equals 6-ply rating, and D equals an 8-ply rating.

Manifold—A casting connecting a series of outlets to a common opening.

Master cylinder—Reservoir containing hydraulic brake fluid which forces brake fluid to the wheel cylinders or caliper pistons as the brake pedal is depressed.

McPherson strut—A suspension component combining a shock absorber and spring in one unit.

Misfire—Condition occurring when the fuel mixture in a cylinder fails to ignite, causing the engine to run roughly.

Multiweight—Type of oil that provides adequate lubrication at both high and low temperatures.

Nitrous oxide (NOx)—One of the three basic pollutants found in the exhaust emission of an internal combustion engine. The amount of NOx usually varies in an inverse proportion to the amount of HC and CO.

Octane rating—A number indicating the quality of gasoline based on its ability to resist knock. The higher the number, the better the quality. Higher compression engines require higher octane gas.

OEM—Original Equipment Manufactured. OEM equipment is that furnished as a standard by the manufacturer.

Offset—The distance between the vertical center of the wheel and the mounting surface at the lugs. Offset is positive if the center is outside the lug circle; negative offset puts the center line inside the lug circle.

Ohm—Unit used to measure the resistance to flow of electricity.

Oscilloscope—A piece of test equipment that shows electric impulses as a pattern on a screen. Engine performance can be analyzed by interpreting these patterns.

Overhead camshaft—Camshaft mounted above the cylinder head. Overhead camshafts usually operate the valves directly, rather than through hydraulic valve lifters.

Oversteer—The tendency of a car to steer itself increasingly into a corner, forcing the driver to reduce steering pressure. Opposite of understeer.

Oxides of nitrogen—See nitrous oxide (NOx).

PCV valve—A valve usually located in the rocker cover that vents crankcase vapors back into the engine to be reburned.

Percolation—A condition in which the fuel actually "boils," due to excess heat. Percolation prevents proper atomization of the fuel, causing rough running.

Pick-up coil—The coil in which voltage is induced in an electronic ignition.

Ping—A metallic rattling sound produced by the engine under acceleration. It is usually due to incorrect ignition timing or a poor grade of gasoline.

Pinion—The smaller of two gears. The rear axle pinion drives the ring gear which transmits motion to the axle shafts.

Piston ring—Metal rings (usually three) installed in grooves in the piston. Piston rings seal the small space between the piston and wall of the cylinder.

Pitman arm—A lever which transmits steering force from the steering gear to the steering linkage.

Ply rating—A rating given a tire which indicates strength (but not necessarily actual plies). A 2-ply/4-ply rating has only two plies, but the strength of a 4-ply tire.

Polarity—Indication (positive or negative) of the two poles of a battery.

Power-to-weight ratio—Ratio of horsepower to weight of car.

Ppm—Parts per million; unit used to measure exhaust emissions.

Preignition—Early ignition of fuel in the cylinder, sometimes due to glowing carbon deposits in the combustion chamber. Preignition can be damaging, as combustion takes place prematurely.

Pressure plate—A spring loaded plate (part of the clutch) that transmits power to the driven (friction) plate when the clutch is engaged.

Psi—Pounds per square inch; a measurement of pressure.

Pushrod—A steel rod between the hydraulic valve lifter and the valve rocker arm in overhead valve-type (OHV) engines.

Quarter panel—Body shop term for a fender. Quarter panel is the area from the rear door opening to the taillight area and from rear wheelwell to the base of the trunk and roofline.

Rack and pinion—A type of automotive steering system using a pinion gear attached to the end of the steering shaft. The pinion meshes with a long rock attached to the steering linkage.

Radial tire—Tire design which uses body cords running at right angles to the center line of the tire. Two or more belts are used to give tread strength. Radials can be identified by their characteristic sidewall bulge.

Rear main oil seal—A synthetic or rope-type seal that prevents oil from leaking out of the engine past the rear main crankshaft bearing.

Rectifier—A device (used primarily in alternators) that permits electrical current to flow in one direction only.

Reluctor—An iron wheel that rotates inside the distributor and triggers the release of voltage in an electronic ignition.

Refrigerant 12 (R-12)—The generic name of the refrigerant used in automotive air-conditioning systems.

Resin—A liquid plastic used in body work.

Resistor spark plug—A spark plug using a resistor to shorten the spark duration. This suppresses radio interference and lengthens plug life.

Retard—Set the ignition timing so that spark occurs later (fewer degrees before TDC).

Rocker arm—A lever which rotates around a shaft, pushing down (opening) the valve with an end when the other end is pushed up by the pushrod. Spring pressure will later close the valve.

Rocker panel—The body panel below the doors between the wheel opening.

Rotor (distributor)—Rotating piece attached to the distributor shaft that triggers the release of voltage to the spark plug.

RPM—Revolutions per minute (usually indicates engine speed).

Run-on—Condition when the engine continues to run, even when the key is turned off. See dieseling.

Seated beam—A modern automotive headlight. The lens, reflector, and filament form a single unit.

Seat belt interlock—A system whereby the car cannot be started unless the seat belt is buckled.

Shimmy—Vibration (sometimes violent) in the front end caused by misaligned front end, out of balance tires, or worn suspension components.

Short circuit—An electrical malfunction where current takes the path of least resistance to ground (usually through damaged insulation). Current flow is excessive from low resistance resulting in a blown fuse.

Sludge—Thick, black deposits in engine formed from dirt, oil, water, etc. It is usually formed in engines with neglected oil changes.

SOHC—Single overhead camshaft.

Solenoid—An electrically operated, magnetic switching device.

Specific gravity (battery)—The relative weight of liquid (battery electrolyte) as compared to the weight of an equal volume of water.

Spongy pedal—A soft or spongy feeling when the brake pedal is depressed. It is usually due to air in the brake lines.

Sprung weight—The weight of a car supported by the springs.

Stabilizer (sway) bar—A bar linking both sides of the suspension. It resists sway on turns by taking some of an added load from one wheel and putting it on the other.

Steering geometry—Combination of various angles of suspension components (caster, camber, toe-in); roughly equivalent to front-end alignment.

Straight weight—Term designating motor oil as suitable for use within a narrow range of temperatures. Outside the narrow temperature range its flow characteristics will not lubricate adequately.

Stroke—The distance the piston travels from bottom dead center to top dead center.

Synthetic oil—Nonpetroleum-based oil.

Tachometer—Instrument which measures engine speed in rpm.

TDC—Top dead center. The exact top of the piston's stroke.

Thermostat—A temperature-sensitive device in the cooling system that regulates the flow of coolant.

Throwout bearing—As the clutch pedal is depressed, the throwout bearing moves against the spring fingers of the pressure plate, forcing the pressure plate to disengage from the driven disc.

Tie-rod—A rod connecting the steering arms. Tie-rods have threaded ends that are used to adjust toe-in.

Timing chain (belt)—A chain or belt that is driven by the crankshaft and operates the camshaft.

Tire rotation—Moving the tires from one position to another to make them wear evenly.

Tire series—A number expressing the ratio between the height and width of a tire. The height of a 78 series tire is 78 percent of its width.

Toe-in (-out)—A term comparing the extreme front and rear of the front tires. Closer together at the front is toe-in; farther apart at the front is toe-out.

Torque—Measurement of turning or twisting force, expressed as foot-pounds or inch-pounds.

Torsion bar suspension—Long rods of spring steel that take the place of springs. One end of the bar is anchored, and the other arm (attached to the suspension) is free to twist. The bars' resistance to twisting causes springing action.

Transaxle—A single housing containing the transmission and differential. Transaxles are usually found on front-engine/front-wheel-drive or rear-engine/rear-wheel-drive cars.

Tread wear indicators—Bars molded into the tire at right angles to the tread that appear as horizontal bars when 1/16th in. of tread remains.

Tread wear pattern—The pattern of wear on tires which can be "read" to diagnose problems in the front suspension.

Turbocharged—A system to increase engine power by using exhaust gas to drive a compressor. As engine speed and load increase, the compressor forces a greater air/fuel mixture into the cylinder. Under light-load or cruising conditions, the turbocharger "idles," and a normal air/fuel mixture reaches the cylinders.

Understeer—The tendency of a car to continue straight ahead while negotiating a turn.

Unit body—Design in which the car body acts as the frame.

Unleaded fuel—Fuel which contains no lead (a common gasoline additive). The presence of lead in fuel will destroy the functioning elements of a catalytic converter, making it useless.

Unsprung weight—The weight of car components not supported by the springs (wheels, tires, brakes, rear axle, control arms, etc.).

Vacuum advance—A method of advancing the ignition timing by applying engine vacuum to a diaphragm mounted on the distributor.

Valve guides—The guide through which the stem of the valve passes. The guide is designed to keep the valve in proper alignment.

Valve lash (clearance)—The operating clearance in the valve train.

Valve train—The system that operates intake and exhaust valves, consisting of camshaft, valves and springs, lifters, pushrods, and rocker arms.

Vapor lock—Boiling of the fuel in the fuel lines due to excess heat. This will interfere with the flow of fuel in the lines and can completely stop the flow. Vapor lock normally occurs only in hot weather.

Varnish—Term applied to the residue formed when gasoline gets old and stale.

Viscosity—The ability of a fluid to flow. The lower the viscosity rating, the easier the fluid will flow. Thus, 10-weight motor oil will flow much more easily than 40-weight motor oil.

Volt—Unit used to measure the force or pressure of electricity. It is defined as the pressure needed to move 1 amp through a resistance of 1 ohm.

Voltage regulator—A device that controls the current output of the alternator or generator.

Wankel engine—An engine which uses no pistons. In place of pistons triangular-shaped rotors revolve in specially shaped housings.

Wheel alignment—Inclusive term to describe the front-end geometry (caster, camber, toe-in/out).

Wheelbase—Distance between the center of front wheels and the center of rear wheels.

Wheel cylinder—A small cylinder in a drum brake system that receives pressure from the master cylinder and forces the brake shoes into contact with the brake drum.

Wheel weights—Small weights attached to the wheel to balance the wheel and tire assembly. Out-of-balance tires quickly wear out and also give erratic handling when installed on the front.

Index